# SCIENCE, TIME AND SPACE IN THE LATE NINETEENTH-CENTURY PERIODICAL PRESS

T0386209

# Science, Time and Space in the Late Nineteenth-Century Periodical Press

## Movable Types

JAMES MUSSELL
*Birkbeck College, UK*

Routledge
Taylor & Francis Group

LONDON AND NEW YORK

First published 2007 by Ashgate Publishing

2 Park Square, Milton Park, Abingdon, Oxfordshire OX14 4RN
52 Vanderbilt Avenue, New York, NY 10017

*Routledge is an imprint of the Taylor & Francis Group, an informa business*

First issued in paperback 2019

**British Library Cataloguing in Publication Data**
Mussell, James
Science, time, and space in the late nineteenth-century periodical press: movable types. – (The nineteenth century)
    1. Scientific literature – Great Britain – History – 19th century 2. Scientific literature – Great Britain – Periodicals – History – 19th century
    I. Title
    828.8'080936


**Library of Congress Cataloging-in-Publication Data**
Mussell, James.
  Science, time, and space in the late nineteenth-century periodical press / by James Mussell.
    p. cm.
  Includes bibliographical references and index.
  ISBN-13: 978-0-7546-5747-7 (alk. paper)
  ISBN-10: 0-7546-5747-7 (alk. paper)
  1. Science news—History—19th century. 2. Science—Periodicals—History—19th century. 3. Scientific literature—Digital publishing. 4. Communication in science—Methodology.
I. Title.

  Q225.5.M87 2007
  070.4'49509034—dc22

                                      2006033512

ISBN 978-0-7546-5747-7 (hbk)
ISBN 978-0-367-88795-7 (pbk)

# Contents

# The Nineteenth Century Series
## General Editors' Preface

The aim of the series is to reflect, develop and extend the great burgeoning of interest in the nineteenth century that has been an inevitable feature of recent years, as that former epoch has come more sharply into focus as a locus for our understanding not only of the past but of the contours of our modernity. It centres primarily upon major authors and subjects within Romantic and Victorian literature. It also includes studies of other British writers and issues, where these are matters of current debate: for example, biography and autobiography, journalism, periodical literature, travel writing, book production, gender, non-canonical writing. We are dedicated principally to publishing original monographs and symposia; our policy is to embrace a broad scope in chronology, approach and range of concern, and both to recognize and cut innovatively across such parameters as those suggested by the designations 'Romantic' and 'Victorian'. We welcome new ideas and theories, while valuing traditional scholarship. It is hoped that the world which predates yet so forcibly predicts and engages our own will emerge in parts, in the wider sweep, and in the lively streams of disputation and change that are so manifest an aspect of its intellectual, artistic and social landscape.

Vincent Newey
Joanne Shattock
University of Leicester

# List of Figures

# Preface

> He who first shortened the labour of Copyists by device of *Movable Types* was disbanding hired Armies, and cashiering most Kings and Senates, and creating a whole new Democratic world; he had invented the Art of Printing.[1]

In *Sartor Resartus* Thomas Carlyle recognizes that the proliferation of the printed word, made possible by 'movable type', is intertwined with the spread of democracy, capitalism and the consolidation of the modern nation state.[2] Carlyle's 'old-world Grazier, – sick of lugging his slow Ox about the country till he got it bartered for corn or oil', took 'a piece of leather' and by marking it with 'the mere figure of an Ox (or *Pecus*); put it in his pocket and call it *Pecunia*, Money.' This transformation, in which the slow, lumbering ox becomes a more portable representation, allows the Grazier to overcome the spatial-temporal limitations of the beast by separating its value from its material form. However, his pun obscures a vital distinction: whereas money signifies value arbitrarily, the Grazier's piece of leather still refers to a real ox, within which value is located. *Sartor Resartus* was conceived against the resumption of the Gold Standard in England, and was published in *Fraser's Magazine* the same year that the Bank of England Act enforced the tender of banknotes in gold and silver. This shift to gold as an underlying source of value substitutes the Grazier's reference to a specific object with a reference to a perpetually absent object; value thus becomes abstract, and not reliant on the (perhaps disputed) material state of the cow.

Carlyle goes on to elaborate this latter stage:

> Yet hereby did Barter grow Sale, the Leather Money is now Golden and Paper, and all miracles have been out-miracled: for there are Rothschilds and English National Debts; and whoso has sixpence is Sovereign (to the length of sixpence) over all men; commands Cooks to feed him, Philosophers to teach him, Kings to mount guard over him, – to the length of sixpence.[3]

For Carlyle, what began as a simple act of representation, in which the marked leather refers to a specific animal, located in space and time, gained momentum until it structured much of bourgeois culture. Isobel Armstrong, in the introduction to her *Victorian Poetry: Poetry, Politics and Poetics*, demonstrates how Carlyle connects the currencies of money, print and politics:

The move which makes the produce of exploited and alienated labour in a free market structurally similar to alienated political representation, to the uncontrolled representations of language circulating through mechanical printing and to the arbitrary signification of money, brings work, politics, economics and language strikingly together under the problem of representation and the alienated sign.[4]

As Armstrong recognizes, Carlyle sees in the invention of printing the deferral of agency through symbolic representation. Such movements are achieved through a transformation that signals continuity while eliding ontological change. The Grazier's mark of an ox gestures to the value of that ox, presenting it in a more convenient material form; wider signifying systems such as money or movable type seem to offer the means to transcend spatial and temporal limits, but without positing any originary source. Carlyle here is figuring a widespread anxiety that extends into the postmodern; however, as Armstrong shows, it also manifests itself in historically contingent moments. For instance the nineteenth century established various institutions that could judge the material status of the things circulating through culture: the development and extension of copyright law was a response both to the anonymous words reproduced in type as well as the proliferation of printed objects; and the Bank of England Act guaranteed the status of the material objects that it circulated, just as the laboratories of the government chemist scrutinized other aspects of commodity culture.

This book examines the interaction between the material and social realms through the examination of a particular publishing genre at a specific historical moment. The mix of the general (time, space, science) with the delimited (late nineteenth-century periodical press) in my title results from the methodological principles that structure the book. Print culture is predicated on the stability of language across material form, yet as important poststructural works consistently demonstrate, such stability is itself a property of materiality rather than textual meaning. It was the resulting incommensurability of meaning and the material forms that enabled it to move through culture that drew me towards science studies. As Bruno Latour, amongst others, argues, it is in scientific practice – including scientific writing – that we can see the how the manipulation of material form confuses the distinction between the material and the social.[5] The existence of these as exclusive domains that somehow co-exist is thus seen as a result of culture rather than an a condition prior to it: as Barthes's distinction between work and text demonstrates, one cannot exist without the other; rather than insist on the difference between them, I explore the manner in which it is established.[6]

The chapters that follow offer a series of examinations into the status of science in the late nineteenth-century periodical press. Both scientific practice and publishing exploit the malleability of material form while simultaneously eliding the changes that have taken place. I have used configurations of time and space to delimit moments before and after a transformation, and so reveal the social processes that both contest what an object is, and establish its relationships to its predecessors. At the time of writing this material is undergoing a further ontological transformation. Whereas their material bulk has prevented the republication of runs of nineteenth-century serials in paper, digital technologies can republish them by disposing of their troublesome materiality. I suggest that we place this most recent manipulation of material form within the histories of these diverse things, and consider carefully the politics of this new material form. Digital editions provide the opportunity to recognize the complexities of materiality: representing periodical pages preserves the integrity of an object whose purpose was to move other objects; just like their nineteenth-century contemporaries, we must decide what these objects are, and where they came from, in designing their twenty-first century models.

James Mussell

## Notes

1   Thomas Carlyle, *Sartor Resartus*, ed. Kerry McSweeney and Peter Sabor (1833; Oxford, 1987), p. 31.
2   Benedict Anderson, *Imagined Communities: Reflections on the Origin and Spread of Nationalism* (1983; London, 1991), p.14.
3   Carlyle, *Sartor Resartus*, p. 31.
4   Isobel Armstrong, *Victorian Poetry: Poetry, Politics and Poetics* (London, 1993), pp. 5–6.
5   Bruno Latour, *Pandora's Hope* (Cambridge MA, 1999).
6   Roland Barthes, 'From Work to Text', *Image, Music, Text*, ed. and trans. Stephen Heath (1961; London, 1977), pp. 155–64.

# Acknowledgements

This book was written while working on the *Nineteenth-Century Serials Edition* (www.ncse.kcl.ac.uk). The project has substantially developed my understanding of nineteenth-century periodical literature, and has introduced me to many other fruitful areas of research. The members of the Project Team – Isobel Armstrong, Laurel Brake, Gerhard Brey, Arianna Ciula, Marilyn Deegan, Ed King, Paul Spence, Suzanne Paylor, Harold Short, Simon Tanner and Mark Turner – all contributed to stimulating discussions about periodicals and their place in the digital age that have in some way informed this book.

Much of this material draws on research undertaken for my PhD thesis, 'Science and the Periodical in Nineteenth-Century London.' I am grateful to the AHRC for their support throughout this earlier project. I appreciate the guidance of Laurel Brake, and the criticisms of my examiners, Mark Turner and Geoffrey Cantor. The postgraduate community in the School of English and Humanities at Birkbeck College provided a vibrant and enriching environment within which to study.

Parts of Chapter Three and the Conclusion were presented at conferences in Edinburgh and Minneapolis. I am grateful for the useful comments made from the floor, and the Faculty of Continuing Education, Birkbeck College, the British Academy, and the History of Science Society for financial support to attend these events. Catherine Jackson provided useful comments on Chapter Four, particularly regarding nineteenth-century chemistry. I would like to thank the staff at the British Library, Senate House Library, the Royal Society for Chemistry and the Royal Astronomical Society for their help in locating useful material. I am especially grateful to the Royal Astronomical Society and the Royal Society for Chemistry for permission to quote from their archives. Thanks also to the staff at Ashgate, whose encouragement and guidance have seen this book to fruition.

Lastly, I remain indebted to my family and friends. Without their support, encouragement, and willingness to distract me from this project, I doubt it would ever have been published. This book is dedicated to my parents, Daphne and Dick.

Introduction

# 'Movable Types'

> Periodicals are by their nature the most evanescent productions of the press. The world of periodicals is perpetually changing. Old periodicals are passing away; new periodicals are being born. Some continue to live under the old name but with an entirely different table of contents. In other cases the old contents reappear under a new title. Changes of price, of address, of circulation are constantly taking place. In short, all the phenomena of growth are conspicuous everywhere in the world of periodical literature.[1]

> Space considered in isolation is an empty abstraction; likewise energy and time.[2]

Drawing upon a well-established contrast between biological mutation and theological fixity, the renowned editor and proprietor W.T. Stead identifies the instability of serial literature in both time and space. Despite the existence of continuities such as titles, periodical content not only varies from number to number, but can also undergo a complete reorientation as personnel changes and readers are reimagined. As commodities, individual numbers are circulated through society, taking advantage of differing periodicities and distribution mechanisms to target different configurations of readers. While each number is directed towards its own moment, however conceived, serial articles look both forwards and backwards beyond its confines. Each number is also fragmented: not only do internal subdivisions between articles and departments signal shifts in address and subject matter, but as multi-authored texts they gesture towards diverse origins. As Stead recognizes, the only constant is change in periodical literature.

Through incorporating type mobilized from a range of different sources and circulating it as part of a unified object, the periodical can use its diversity to seek out and construct unique configurations of readers, thus identifying and creating niches in the competitive and crowded periodical marketplace. Periodicals are explicitly commercial, with advertising incorporated within paginated letterpress as well as enclosing individual numbers and volumes. The close relationship between writing within periodicals and the wider book trade ensured that the contents too participate within the wider market for print. It is the capacity of print and paper to be reproduced, and remain relatively stable while it is distributed, that enables their circulation. In this book I argue that it is the combination of immutability across space, enabling periodical numbers to be distributed to readers, combined with mutability across time, enacted by the serial appearance of successive numbers, that defines the periodical as genre.

It is for this reason that I have chosen to consider the periodical in terms of time and space. Although different spatial-temporal configurations will produce different versions of a periodical title – for instance at the level of a number per date, or a volume per year, or those published from a certain place, or even a run of volumes gathered on a shelf – they also provide the conditions that structure periodical form. Stephen Kern notes in *The Culture of Time and Space, 1880–1918* that 'time and space are particularly suitable as a framework for a general cultural history, because they are comprehensive, universal and essential.'[3] My study is not a 'general cultural history' – I do consider the cultural manifestations of time and space in the late nineteenth century so ably surveyed by Kern and others – but a consideration of the periodical as cultural object, and so my use of space and time is directed to understanding how it is that this object moves through culture, and what happens to it during its passage. Kern suggests that '[a]ll people, everywhere, in all ages, have a distinctive experience of time and space and, however unconscious, some conception of it.'[4] I deliberately leave this claim unconsidered as it is beyond the scope of my research: instead, I use spatial and temporal configurations to trace movements from (often arbitrarily assigned) origins to (equally arbitrarily assigned) endings. As the above comments from Stead indicate, periodicals resist such demarcations, and indeed much profitable work has been produced that demonstrates how historical actors considered periodicals as ephemeral products within which work could be published before appearing in a more stable booklike form later.[5] Kern argues that the categories of time and space 'provide a comprehensive theoretical framework that allows not only many areas across the cultural spectrum but also integration along a theoretical vertical axis from "high culture" to popular culture and the material aspects of everyday life.'[6] My emphasis is on the necessary discontinuities in print culture, and how they coexist, often in the same object, with its continuities. Rather than interpret late nineteenth-century culture, I use these powerful theoretical tools to demarcate quite specific material cultures.

In *The Production of Space*, Henri Lefebvre warns:

> When codes worked up from literary texts are applied to spaces – to urban spaces say – we remain, as may easily be shown, on the purely descriptive level. Any attempt to use such codes as a means of deciphering social space must surely reduce that space itself to the status of a *message*, and the inhabiting of it to the status of a *reading*.[7]

Perhaps overdetermining the distinction between the two, Lefebvre is keen to establish his analysis on the level of practice rather than interpretation. However, reading is productive, even if its immediate ends are restricted to the reading subject, and it interacts directly with spatial practice. Written works are produced in specific times and spaces, and their interpretation is likewise influenced by the times and spaces of reading. Equally, written works must move through space, helping to transform it into circulation routes, spaces of commercial exchange, library space, educational space etc. ... Not only this, written works also signify space and time, representing in ways that are imagined as meaningful not only to readers, but also to their perceived moments of reading. It is this dynamic, complicated of course by the plurality of spaces through which periodicals move and their repeated movements over time, that I consider here. These composite objects, drawn from a range of times and spaces, are circulated, at set periods, across a space that itself changes over time. To ignore these spatial-temporal dimensions of periodical production and reception – including the various reciprocal connections between them – is to reduce culture to a signifying field and, in doing so, limit its potential to manage material form.

## Periodicals in the Digital Age

The size and complexity of the nineteenth-century periodical archive demands that its current readers engage with it in sophisticated and reflexive ways. The considerable number of individual periodical titles published between 1800 and 1900 alone – estimated at 125,000 by John North in his *Waterloo Directory* – represents a volume of print that can overwhelm current readers.[8] When we recall that these titles often change radically over their run, and are the products of a large number of editors, publishers, printers, advertisers, contributors and illustrators, many of whose interventions are not indicated in the letterpress, the excess of print is further complicated by an excess of historical actors. These figures are as diverse as are the genres to which they contribute: as J.W. Robertson-Smith expains for editors in 1888:

> A considerable distinction exists between the gentlemen who are responsible for the editorial opinions of the fashion periodicals or of the organs of undertakers, Oddfellows, hairdressers, electrical engineers, or gardeners, and the conductors of the scientific papers, the society prints, the 'fad' journals, the 'blood and thunder' publications, or the trade weeklies. The accomplished writers who edit the more imposing magazines, reviews, and quarterlies, are another community by themselves.[9]

While some editors were specialists, either within a genre or even running a single title for a long period, many other 'professional' editors would move around Grub Street, associating themselves with a title for a time before moving on. Consequently, their indvidual performances are often discrete, and scattered across often unexpected domains. Of course, the above list further underrepresents this diversity by describing editors as gentlemen, thereby restricting this description substantially by class and gender.

Since the nineteenth century there have been continued attempts to map what W.T. Stead repeatedly calls the 'mighty maze' of periodical literature.[10] *Poole's Index to Periodical Literature* was first published in two volumes in 1882, and then supplemented in 1888, 1893, 1897, 1903, and 1980. A date and volume key was provided in 1957 and a cumulative author index in 1971.[11] At the moment of writing, *Poole's* is available in an electronic form as part of *Nineteenth-Century Masterfile*, its integration with other nineteenth-century resources – including Stead's indices – providing a much more varied and functional index. The incorporation of indices into larger archives both resolves their individual biases and eccentricities while possibly suppressing their historical interpretive value. As is often recognized, the *Wellesley Index* was so successful at making both the titles and the contributors to the 43 periodicals it indexes visible to the existing interpretive codes of scholarship that it has reflexively dictated the canon of periodical literature.[12]  The current trend in the acquisition of such resources by firms such as Thomson-Gale and Proquest means that such emphases will be recontextualized in a much broader electronic context; however, the *Wellesley*'s bias inscribes its derivation and moment within itself, and it requires sensitive use of search technologies and information structures to prevent the loss of important contextual information in the further abundance of print it is designed to map.

The application of digital technologies to bibliography simultaneously offers the means to recover some of the traces obfuscated by the excess of nineteenth-century print, while also risking to further overdetermine research. As Patrick Leary has argued, the 'extraordinary power, speed, and ubiquity of online searching has brought with it a serendipity of unexpected connections to both information and people that is becoming increasingly central to the progress of Victorian research, and to our working lives as students of the nineteenth century.'[13]  The utility of such techniques requires the construction of large corpuses of nineteenth-century print, which can provide the initial hit that would lead to more detailed and nuanced research. As Leary recognizes, the problem of excess remains: not only is there a tendency to assume the exhaustiveness of such archives; but electronic searches can return an overwhelming number of irrelevant hits. Information that is relevant is present in a fragmented, dislocated form. Although this allows the reader to supply the contextual links, it does violence to the integrity of the source material. Leary suggests that 'the ideal subjects for electronic searching are texts that were assemblages of short, relatively self-contained units to begin with, such as newspapers and some periodicals.'[14]  This material has always been used as a resource for historical data: the position of *The Times* as authoritative source of historical context can be attributed to the existence of *Palmers's Index to the* Times *Newspaper* as well its historical reputation; and the success of *The Times Digital Archive, 1785–1985* will further its use to this end.

It is precisely this use of the periodical archive that most scholarship into the press has tried to counter, and the potential that such a methodology will render all nineteenth-century print into a resource for decontextualized information retrieval is cause for a renewed plea for attention to material context. Laurel Brake and Margaret Beetham have described the cultural discourses that have shaped the current state of the material archive as well as those implicit in our interpretive strategies.[15]  Both authors insist on the fundamental importance of 'coloured wrappers, customised advertisers, title pages, indices, illustrations, and juxtaposed and sequential editorial matter' for an understanding of the dialogic relations both within and between periodical texts.[16] The 'normative process which has resulted in the omnipresence of the volume in our libraries, and in our scholarship' has ensured that large numbers of periodicals have survived but at the expense of constitutive parts of the text.[17] Beetham also highlights that the act of binding is necessarily selective: not only were 'end-papers and advertisements' not considered part of the periodical but the 'cheapest serials and periodicals were not usually considered worth binding at all.'[18] The differing economies that drive online as opposed to paper-based publication offer to both publish material that is currently overlooked by publishers, and also to reconnect material fragmented in hard copy and distributed across libraries, museums and repositories, often in states of decay. However, such optimism remains tempered by the dialectic of excess and scarcity: we now have material in new models of completeness, but risk overlooking other material either as a direct result of the ways in which we access it, or because it remains undigitized.

With a vast print archive becoming increasingly accessible, the methodological problem of excess becomes more visible. Much recent scholarship resides in collections of essays, neatly side-stepping such issues for necessary reasons of brevity. In offering delimited studies of individual titles, actors or incidents, such publications enact the sampling methodology described by Joanne Shattock and Michael Wolff.[19] These are especially effective when organized thematically, where the formal breaks between essays contribute to the overarching continuities of subject.[20] Other studies consider one title or figure at length, using them to consider wider questions of genre, market, and culture.[21] As Cantor and Shuttleworth note, the study of periodicals requires attention to the constitutive role of context: periodicals neither function like conduits, varied media for passing knowledge between author and reader; nor are they passive terrains for the free circulation of texts.[22] Rather, the study of periodicals requires the simultaneous acknowledgement that the individual number is the manifest interaction of its producers – including contributors, editors, readers and the interactions of the market – and that it is part of a series. Any discussion of the periodical press must include form, and this ranges from paper and ink, to the multilayered structure of volume, number, department, and article.

This methodological sensitivity is vital if we are to understand the fragments of the periodical press that survive today. Whether through marginal notes, library stamps, or simply in the selection of pages that remain, these objects bear the marks of their passage through time. These remains are being radically transformed at an increasing rate. Jerome McGann notes that the library, 'the very foundation of modern humanities', is 'undergoing a complete digital transformation.' 'In the coming decades,' he writes, 'the entirety of our cultural inheritance will be transformed and re-edited in digital forms.'[23] Although at present what is being digitized are choice selections from the wider archive this process is well underway. The nineteenth-century periodical archive alone is currently subject to corporate wranglings that will determine not only who will publish these materials electronically, but also the way in which it is done.[24]   When set against vast projects such as Google Print – an ambitious scheme to scan the holdings in the university libraries of Harvard, Stanford, Oxford, Michigan, and the New York Public Library, in order to provide free access to out-of-copyright material – it seems that very soon many of the significant collections of nineteenth-century print will be available online.[25]

The celebration of the serendipitous encounters provided by search engines is not enough. The potential gains in having an expanding number of nineteenth-century resources available online, able to accessed around the world at all times, is a huge advance on the restricted access to spatially and temporally delimited, fragile hard copy. However, this value comes at a cost. Not only are there inequalities of digital literacy and access, but there are also questions of preservation and long-term conservation. McGann's call to action – to engage with the digital transformations going on around us – is sensible and timely. In *Radiant Textuality* he draws attention to the reliance of existing archival and editorial models for digital editions. He suggests that projects conceived along these lines excel at their task, but do not help us to 'imagine what we don't know in a disciplined and deliberated fashion':

> These kinds of issues won't be usefully engaged without reconsidering certain fundamental problems of texts and texuality. The critical possibilities of digital environments require that we revisit what we know, or what we think we know, about the formal and material properties of the codex. We shall see that the advent of digital tools promotes this kind of critical reflection and leads to a view of books and of language itself that breaks with many common and widely held ideas.[26]

McGann's thesis is that it is by creating digital projects that we begin to imagine their application in the humanities: '[t]ranslating paper-based texts into electronic forms', he writes, 'entirely alters one's view of the original materials.'[27]   However, there is also a place for conceiving of the practice of digital publication. McGann suggests that '[u]sing books to study books constrains the analysis to the same conceptual level as the materials to be studied'; it seems that using digital resources conceived along similar lines would also add little. All editions establish a relationship to their source material, and – as McGann persuasively argues – embody this in their form.[28]   I suggest that it is precisely this relationship that remains underdeveloped in many digital editions of nineteenth-century periodicals.

This book is conceived as being part of that project, but restricted to an intervention at the theoretical level. The digitial age is transforming how we communicate, and this applies to the historical objects of scholarly research. However, there are important continuities that the language of 'revolution' obfuscates: we are still writing, reading, editing and publishing; and these activities occur in times and spaces connected to those that precede them. In the chapters that follow I work through a series of studies on the nineteenth-century periodical that explore its material form through the references its constituent parts, and the combined object that they constitute, make to space and time. Publishing exploits the malleability of form, allowing things to remain recognizably the same even while adopting different states. Each transformation therefore both retains some parts of its previous form, establishing a link to another time-space, while masking others. By treating all text the same in digital editions, we transform our texts once more, but without considering either the practice of transformation inherent in publishing, or the histories that it elides.

## Science and the Poetics of Periodical Form

The demands of a large but fragmented material archive has led some critics towards a interdisciplinary methodology rooted in poststructuralist theories that locate the referent of the media in a signifying culture rather than a distinct reality. Lyn Pykett and Mark Turner both rehearse Tony Bennett's criticism of the media as mirror.[29]   Bennett disputes that 'the media are secondary and derivative, somehow less real than the "real" they reflect, existing above society and passively mirroring it rather than forming an active and integral part of it.'   Reflection models introduce a binary opposition between true and false representations which evacuate the agency of the media:

> For the formulation 'media as definers of social reality' admits of only one politics: one in which the power of allegedly distorting systems of signification is opposed by the truth, by a system of signification which effaces itself in allowing the real to speak through it without hindrance or modifications. The objection to this is not merely that it is impossible. It also misconceives the political task which is not to oppose truth to falsehood, but to *take up a position* in relation to dominant systems of signification – a matter that can only be broached if the focus of analysis shifts away from the investigation of the relationship between sign and 'reality' to that of the relationship between sign, the play of signification upon signification within a structural field of ideological relationships.[30]

Pykett recommends that we locate the 'structural field of ideological relationships' as the methodological field that Roland Barthes calls 'Text.' This, she writes, when considered alongside the 'concepts of discourse and discursive communities, reinstate history, economics and sociology in a new interdisciplinary formation.'[31]

In the recent reissue of his influential 'Bibliography and the Sociology of Texts,' D.F. McKenzie argues 'a book is never simply a remarkable *object*. Like every other technology it is invariably the product of human agency in complex and highly volatile contexts which a responsible scholarship must seek to recover if we are to understand better the creation and communication of meaning as the defining characteristic of human societies.'[32]   Mark Turner, although acknowledging the value of intertextual approaches, recognizes that the linguistic turn threatens to elide the politics inscribed in material culture. By invoking a more rigidly Foucauldian notion of discourse, Turner locates the interpretative strategies that constitute the 'sociology of the periodical text' in institutions including the gentleman's clubs of St. James's as well as the broader formations of editors and publishers.[33] Turner exploits Kristeva's notion of intertextuality to foreground the importance of discourse, rather than 'the comprehension of inherent textual structures and forms', as the creator of a text's meaning.[34] He cites John Frow, who writes that 'the identification of an intertext is an act of interpretation. The intertext is not a real and causative source but a theoretical construct formed by and serving the purposes of a reading.' 'What is relevant to textual interpretation is not, in itself, the identification of a particular intertextual source', Frow continues, 'but the more general discursive structure (genre, discursive formation, ideology) to which it belongs.'[35] As discourse includes both the material as well as the textual, it provides a suitable interpretive framework for the study of printed objects. 'In writing about periodicals', Turner argues, 'it is useful to move freely from textual criticism to material criticism in what might be seen as theoretical eclecticism; however, such turns allow for the cultural location of discourse, which bridges the gap between materialism and post-structural plurality.'[36] The interpretation of intertextual reference as cultural discourse is a way of reconstituting the historically contingent negotiations of meaning without opposing the signifier to an ontologically distinct realm of the signified.

However, even within the interpretive frame of discourse there is still a tendency to overlook the role the material plays in structuring the social world. John Frow argues:

> while a number of previously intractable theoretical difficulties about the structure of the social and its relation to the symbolic order are solved by the refusal of an ontological difference between moments of the social (between culture and the economic last instance or bottom line for example), this move nevertheless begs the question of the forms of constraint and determination which operate between a plurality of instances of the social – forms of structural pressure which can no longer be deduced from ontological qualities (such as materiality).[37]

Although there are undoubtedly cultural pressures that do not neatly reduce to ontological qualities, these are still manifested in material forms: in fact, all cultural phenomena depend at some level on the materiality of things for their manifestation in space and time. By suppressing the material aspects of culture we empower interpretative epistemologies while relegating the ontological to the bearer of signification. Well-intentioned efforts to counter this can produce a peculiar doubling which suppresses the materiality of culture even while insisting on the material location of the signifier.[38] Such strategies reduce culture to a signifying field, even while recognizing that it is made up of both texts and things. I suspect that this tendency partly results from the linguistic bias inherent within cultural studies; and that this is buttressed by a partial reading of the Marxist model of the commodity.[39] The division between use and exchange value inscribes a duality into the material realm that seems congruent with the division between ontology and social relations. For Marx, value is constituted entirely by exchange and, because 'not an atom of matter enters into its composition', the consideration of exchange-value overlooks materiality in favour of abstracted social relations.[40] The logic of the commodity fetish, in which the 'definite social relation between men' assumes 'the fantastic form of a relation between things', appears to operate without recourse to the material realm – in fact, these material relations become adopted by those who give their labour. Marx's language reiterates this: he describes one form being stamped upon another, and argues that the existence of things as commodities has 'absolutely no connexion with their physical properties and with the material relations arising therefrom.'[41] This categorical boundary, established at the moment of exchange, seems to divide the social from the material much as reflection models use ontology to posit a reality that can verify representation.

Marx, however, also identifies the labour necessary to create use-value. This he calls 'useful labour', and its mechanism is purely transformative, changing matter from one form to another.[42] As the 'social character of each producer's labour does not show itself except in the act of exchange', use-value is suspended in the moment of exchange and so is rendered secondary in cultural economies.[43] Yet this 'elementary value', which corresponds to human needs, dictates the material conditions in which commodities can be brought together in order to be exchanged. For instance, properties such as size and weight materially affect the role commodities can play in the market. In addition, Marx insists that labour is not synonymous with value, but can only become value 'in its congealed state, when embodied in the form of some object.'[44] Use-value thus becomes the medium for its opposite, exchange-value. These interconnected features of use-value – the material properties of a thing and their exploitation as a depository of value – reassert the importance of the material realm in the contingent moment of exchange. If, as Marx suggests, the work of history is to 'discover the uses of things', then this involves the relationship between moments of production and moments of exchange.[45] All things can become commodities in bourgeous society, but not all things are commodities at all times: the homogenizing networks of exchange that result from the quantification of value can displace the material conditions in which such exchanges occur, but such material conditions are nevertheless a determining prerequisite.

As Andrew King has shown, an analysis of the periodical as commodity fetish has considerable hermeneutic value.[46] It is when we apply this analysis to the modes of production of both its components and its resulting composite forms that conceptual difficulties arise. When W.T. Stead describes the periodical as a 'monthly market where authors sell their wares', he stresses its nature as vehicle for other objects.[47] The components of a periodical number are commodities that must be transformed from their various material forms into a single composite, which is then circulated anew. Each phase in the production process is historically contingent, and radically alters some aspects of the parts in order to make them compatible. However, this content still proclaims its independent existence, even while being subject to editorial control and constituting part of a combined object. Not only this, but some types of periodical content exploit the elision of the production process in order to invoke different spaces and times: news, for instance, elides the complicated changes it undergoes to establish the fiction of an unmediated account, linked to the event that it describes; and the rhetoric of openness that structures correspondence columns ignores editorial interventions and the radical transformations that transform handwriting into type. It is the relationship between the microhistories of these parts and their role in the whole that I wish to recover: as each part signals its heterdox origins, it seems to proclaim a separate status from the rest of the number's content, even while sharing its immediate ontological form. As it is often only textual features that differentiate contributions, the heterogeneous nature of periodical publication seems to confuse the boundaries between words and things.

Roland Barthes insists that 'it would be futile to try to separate out materially works from texts'; I argue that this boundary is constantly performed as a social act, and the periodical, because of its heterogeneous content, offers a highly visible (and variable) context through which to interpret the spatial and temporal construction of materiality.[48]   Henri Lefebvre argues that the dual nature of commodities creates a space that is at once unified and fragmentary. 'Exchange', he writes, 'with its circulatory systems and networks may occupy space worldwide, but consumption only occurs in this or that particular place.'[49]   As exchange is predicated on interchangeability, the movement of commodities tends towards homogeneity across the global span of commodity culture. However, the material aspect of the commodity insists that it has a location, that it is '*in space.*'[50] Consumption, although it can occur *en masse*, is always linked to a specific place; in addition, each commodity's 'particular traits become more marked once they become fixed' and, as they can deteriorate, tend towards a specificity dependent on location.[51]  As Lefebvre writes:

> The paradigmatic (or 'significant') opposition between exchange and use, between global networks and the determinate locations of production and consumption, is transformed here into a dialectical contradiction, and in this process it becomes spatial. Space thus understood is both *abstract* and *concrete* in character: abstract inasmuch as it has no existence save by virtue of the exchangeability of all its component parts, and concrete inasmuch as it is socially real and as such localized. This is a space, therefore, that is *homogenous yet at the same time broken up into fragments.*[52]

Just as the periodical number circulates through the homogenous space of its distribution networks, so it simultaneously participates in localized exchanges and moments of consumption. Equally, its composite parts are part of an economy of contributions and content, as well as being the products of localized practices. The material status of the text – whether it is abstract or concrete – seems to be a function of its location in space and time.

It was to account for the perplexing materiality of the periodical – this confusion between word and thing, text and work, poststructural plurality and materialism – that drew me towards science studies. The work of Bruno Latour, in following his own injunction to study 'science in the making', elaborates what has become known as actor-network-theory.[53] Latour rejects both nature and culture as exclusive domains, and instead studies the spaces where these are mixed, preferring to understand them as the products of historically contingent practices. Karen Knorr Cetina identifies the laboratory as the emblematic site for the cultural transformation of objects:

> What laboratory studies suggest is that the laboratory is a means of changing the world-related-to-agents in ways which allow scientists to capitalize on their human constraints and social cultural restrictions. The laboratory is an enhanced environment which improves upon the natural order in relation to the social order.[54]

Laboratories 'use the phenomenon that objects are not fixed entities which have to be taken as they are or left to themselves' and instead highlight the '*malleability* of natural objects.'[55] Latour (amongst others) develops these ideas to implicate the laboratory within its wider social context. It is this continual interface between 'culture' and 'nature' which disrupts them as absolute categories: words and things are no longer separated by impermeable ontological boundaries, but instead are hybrid forms bound together in complex networks.[56]

Latour's 'ethnomethodology of the text' is semiotic as it is predicated on the minimal space between representations that maintain signification despite changes in ontological form. This permits the existence of different textual objects (or indeed virtual objects) despite their ostensibly shared materiality. If the representations are accepted by others then the boundary between subject and object / words and things can be traversed. As Latour writes, science studies 'has always been an analysis of how language slowly becomes capable of transporting things themselves *without* deformation *through* transformation':

> Philosophers of science like to remind us, as if this were the epitome of good common sense, that we should never confuse epistemological questions (what our representation of the world is) and ontological questions (what the world is really like). Unfortunately, if we followed the philosophers' advice we would not understand any scientific activity, since confusing these two supposedly separate domains is precisely what scientists spend much of their time doing.[57]

In identifying the permeability of the boundary between words and things, Latour provides a fuller application of poststructural intertextuality. Just like the poststructural rejection of the ontological as the absolute domain of signification, so Latour denies that there 'are true statements that correspond to a state of affairs and false statements that do not, but only continuous or interrupted reference.'[58] Latour claims that truth value circulates 'like electricity through a wire'; Barthes, who despite his reluctance insists on a gap between the work and text, celebrates text as 'where languages circulate.'[59] The *jouissance* of intertextuality in Barthes relies upon the artificial suppression of the material world: the congruence of language and culture is based upon an act of assertion that elides the operation of power by denying the agency of things.[60]

Historians of science have long recognized that science is about things as well as texts, and the renewed emphasis on the history of the book in science studies is a useful extension of this. Jonathan R. Topham, in his introduction to a special section on book history and the sciences in the *British Journal for the History of Science*, writes that the object of book history is 'to reintroduce social actors, engaged in a variety of practices with respect to material objects, into a history in which books have too often been understood merely as disembodied texts, the meaning of which is defined by singular, uniquely creative authors, and is transparent to readers.' Topham reminds us that as 'much as any other historical artefacts, [books] contain not only physical evidence concerning the processes of their manufacture, but also physical evidence which is essential in constructing a history of their use – from the typography and layout to the paper and the binding.'[61] These aspects of the book are all culturally coded; but such meanings are inseparable from their ontological form.

For Topham, as for Turner, Brake, Pykett and Beetham, the material aspects of the printed object are all constitutive parts of its meaning. As such, they become sites for the struggle of conflicting interests. Topham claims 'by focusing on the practices of fabrication, distribution and use, book history continually reveals both the instability of meaning in printed objects, and the labour that is consequently expended by those seeking to establish universal claims through printed means.'[62] Scientific practice often exploits the behaviour of things to demonstrate theoretical concepts, and then uses objects and texts, often gathered and arranged in an institution, to convince others elsewhere of their validity. The last ten years have seen a renewed engagement with the mechanisms for the transmission of scientific knowledge. In what has become a classic article, Roger Cooter and Steven Pumfrey argue:

> From coffee houses to comic books and chemistry sets, from pulpits to pubs and picture palaces, from amateur clubs to advertising companies, from Science Parks to Jurassic Park, our ignorance both of the low drama and the high art of science's diffusion and modes of popular production and reproduction is staggering.[63]

When Topham places 'books, newspapers, magazines, almanacs and broadsides' alongside 'such apparently contrasting objects as gas-lamps, menageries and steam engines', he is deliberately (and provocatively) associating printed matter with other objects which are strategically used as part of scientist's wider ideological goals.[64]

It is because of this emphasis on the role of objects for the transmission of knowledge that I have drawn both my theoretical methodology and my examples from science studies. Although the use of different objects (including printed matter) for ideological purposes is readily accepted, scientific practice problematizes the material status of the objects that it discusses and circulates. Historians of science have explored how the products of laboratory science, in all their varying forms, are negotiated within wider cultural contexts. Instead of a top-down diffusionist model, with authority teaching its popular 'other', Cooter and Pumfrey argue for a 'less static model [...] in which the relations between science and its publics are configured in a more dynamic interactive fashion.'[65] They draw attention, for instance, to the fact that scientific knowledge is not presented in a form to be either accepted or rejected, rather it becomes 'developed by its recipients for different purposes.'[66] The existence of these recipients as an active audience reflexively 'reconfigures the cultural context of scientific activity and hence – conceivably – reconfigures the nature of the science itself.'[67] The history of science – and nineteenth-century science in particular – provides a suitably complex model of cultural transmission, in which audiences, producers and the things that move between them are linked in complex networks. As the recent collections of essays published by the Sciper project argue, the periodical was a key site for such negotiations.[68]

Cooter and Pumfrey claim that 'neither intellectual history, nor the sociology of (professional) science equip us for thinking about the history of the processes of scientific exchange, interaction, translation, and resistance.' However, they do concede that Latour's 'ethnomethodology of the text (semiotics)', as extended by Michel Callon and John Law, 'could also be applied to more popular writings with a view to recovering the power of scientific imagery in popular intellectual life.'[69] I suggest that it can do more than this. Through the application of this theory it becomes possible not only to follow the various components that make up the periodical through their ontological changes, but also to understand how aspects of these ontologies are deployed even though they have been changed into something new. In this analysis, news can signal its origins because it is accepted by readers that the various transformations it has gone through do not matter. This methodology allows me to trace both the production and circulation of the periodical and its constituent parts in all their material complexity: the periodical can now be read as a composite of objects – all with specific histories – and these can be conceived as on the page, the page itself, or as pages bound together. My work supplements existing approaches to the study of periodicals by insisting that the social meanings of texts do not exist outside of their materiality: in fact, their material status is often constructed and contested by the sociological frameworks about the texts themselves. In applying the 'semiotic turn' from sociology of science, I hope to reestablish the material side to the 'material turn' in cultural studies. Whereas a strict poststructural reading of the periodical text leads us only to other texts, I wish to locate these hybrid texts once more in a complicated network of both people and things.

**The 1890s and the Forms of Abundance**

Although both books and periodicals survive in large numbers, and both are subject to the same methodological problems of excess, it is periodicals that inscribe this into their material form. Unlike books, periodicals have many component parts, which appear at different times; they have many authors; they often cover a range of subjects; and the large numbers that survive account for a much larger expanse of letterpress. Such abundances, Laurel Brake suggests, 'provides a dramatic case for what scholars term "bibliographic control."'[70] It is for this reason that I have restricted myself to the late nineteenth-century, and specifically titles published in London. Ronald Schleiffer, in his *Modernism and Time: The Logic of Abundance in Literature, Science and Culture, 1880–1930*, picks up and expands on Kern's remark that there was a 'crisis of abundance' in energy in the late nineteenth century:

> The emergence of 'abundances' of social and class positions and of calculuses of private and social value accompanied, in the second Industrial Revolution, the abundances of commodities beyond the food, shelter, and clothing of the first Industrial Revolution. These included abundances of energy in the burgeoning of electrical and petroleum energies that replace the stable fixities of the material power of steam; the rise of the telephone that replaced the stable fixities of the epistolary culture of Enlightenment knowledge; and the remarkable explosion of imperialism in the last decades of the nineteenth century that replaced the experiential fixities of the time and space of that other element of Enlightenment culture, the nation state.[71]

Periodicals were part of this culture of abundance. As Kern writes, the 'technology of communication and transportation and expansion of literacy made it possible for more people to read about more distant places in the newspaper, see them in movies, and travel more widely. As human consciousness expanded across space people could not help noticing that in different places there were vastly different customs, even different ways of keeping time.'[72] It was the earlier emergence of the twin technologies of railway and telegraph that had, as Donald Read suggests, transformed physical and mental communication respectively.[73] These found a common material context in the periodical number: a commodity that was distributed across time and space, while also representing them. The unprecedented circulations claimed by titles such as *Tit-Bits* (1881) and the *Daily Mail* (1896) highlight the shared reading matter of the newly conceptualized masses. The periodical, as a mobile commodity, had always offered a discrete readership the same material to be consumed; but in addressing the 'mass' they foregrounded (and constructed) consensus in order to elide social difference and so offer unprecedented markets for the advertised goods in their pages. As mass-produced commodities are predicated on their constancy across space and time, so they bind together consumers in simultaneous experiences that challenge the contingencies of each act of consumption. Peter Broks suggests '"mass culture" conveys the ambiguous suggestion of, on the one hand, individual consumption of mass-produced goods, and on the other, of the consumption of goods *en masse*.'[74] Mass culture is thus predicated on the recognition of the same: not only are diverse individuals all consuming the same things, irrespective of who they are, but so too are the things the same, despite when and where they are made. The periodical, as a mobile, reproducible and disposable object, is thus both a commodity in its own right as well as serving as a space for the presentation of other, often mass-produced commodities.

The heterodox content of the periodical allows it to embody an abundance of times and spaces and present them simultaneously. Taking advantage of the colonial communications network to provide copy and imaginative resources that would interest readers, the periodical press could set stories in distant places and times, report on distant events, and provide panoptic surveys on global themes. This juxtaposition of narrative temporalities was furthered by the widespread practice of extracting copy from European, American, and sympathetic (or unknowing) domestic titles, thereby providing material clearly derived from a different textual space and time. The proliferation of photographic reproduction provided cheap, easily reproducible images which were marked with the original moment of capture. The exploitation (and so reaffirmation) of late nineteenth-century celebrity culture repeatedly presents the reader with the experience of recognizing individuals from other spaces and times. The interview and the photograph, two emblematic textual features of the late nineteenth-century periodical press, are thus intertwined in this politics of simultaneity: both the interviewer and the camera act as prosthetics, allowing the reader access to the (necessarily) exclusive space and time of the celebrity or the event that is captured.

It is not possible to separate the logic of abundance that structures the diversity of periodical content from that which determines periodical form, whether in terms of the number of titles, their size and shape, periodicity, or subject matter. I follow W.T. Stead in considering the periodical as 'everything that is published periodically.' However, Stead then refines his definition:

> The use of the term is, however, restricted in ordinary conversation to magazines and reviews appearing not less frequently than once a quarter, and not more frequently than twice a month. Weeklies, at least in Great Britain, have, with a few exceptions, ceased to be regarded as periodicals. As we have no fortnightlies, our periodicals may be said to be practically reduced to monthlies and quarterlies.[75]

Weeklies, as I go on to explore in Chapter Three, are uneasily situated between the timeliness of news and the more leisured, reflective rhetoric of the monthlies; by discounting them Stead can posit a distinction between periodical literature – and I use the word deliberately – and the more ephemeral products of the newspaper press. This piece, although originally written for the new edition of *Chamber's Encyclopedia*, was printed as a preface to his annual *Index to the Periodicals of the World* and, as such, identifies only those species of periodical that he perceives would be relevant for this periodicity. This bias towards the transcendence of literature is also apparent in his construction of the genre's origins:

> The genesis of the periodical can be traced back for centuries, but the earlier publications of the kind bear about as much resemblance to the magazines and reviews of to-day that the eohippus bears to the winner of last year's Derby. The evolution of the modern magazine is usually traced back to the *Philosophical Transactions of the Royal Society* which began to appear in 1665, but the true progenitors of our monthly miscellanies were the pamphlets which were spawned in such numbers in the heat of the revolutionary ferment of the 17th century.[76]

Although Stead identifies a scientific title as the ancestor of the current diversity of periodical forms, he displaces this history with an emphasis on the more literary qualities of the political pamphlets. Although these too are ephemera, their links to literary figures such as Swift and Milton establishes a transcendent tradition that relies less on the contingencies and esoteric nature of scientific research.

As my methodology is drawn from science studies, it is appropriate that my analysis of late nineteenth-century periodical culture consider scientific publications. If, as Latour argues, science is the clearest example of a cultural practice that manipulates materiality for social ends and, as I argue, this practice also underpins publishing, then the congruence between the two establishes continuities that are often obscured in considerations of other domains such as literature. However, my emphasis throughout this book is on the periodical as a publishing genre and so I am keen to both consider scientific culture across its diverse forms, while also maintaining its links with the wider culture that sustains it. As an exercise in bibliographic control, an emphasis on science allows me to consider a more manageable number of individual titles; however, such a methodological principle risks both distorting my conclusions through a focus on a distinct set of practices, and reducing science to one cultural subset amongst many. Science publishing was an important part of the periodical marketplace, and the titles themselves played a central role in both the communication of ideas and the consolidation of communities. By tracing the products of scientific practice as they move from specialized sites (which may or may not be those of institutionalized science) into the periodical press, I inevitably follow these things as they become incorporated into a medium that necessarily participates in wider economies. Science, of course, is shaped by its historical conditions; but when it becomes part of the periodical press it is explicitly juxtaposed against a wider world of things.

Stead, of course, was a close observer of scientific practice but, because he excluded weeklies, was indexing a partial version of science mediated through the monthly reviews. In 1895 he acknowledges this when he includes 'two geological and one or two other scientific periodicals which ought not in strictness to come within the scope of an index to general periodical literature.'[77]   Stead's late recognition of the value of weeklies for scientific publication (see Chapter Three below) reminds us of the continuities between different publishing contexts. Peter

Broks, in his *Media Science Before the Great War*, surveys long runs of seven periodical titles, and provides quantitative and qualitative analyses of his reading. Such an approach, despite allowing astute diachronic thematic interpretation, tends to elide the conditional differences between representations and does not consider the cultural debates which construct them. Broks, consequently sees science as part of a larger economy of signs:

> Common to all the periodicals was the presentation of science not as an approach to the world, but a collection of facts and feats. In the late Victorian consumer revolution science was another commodity, to be received, not participated in. It was not a process, but a product.[78]

As I will demonstrate, whereas this is undoubtedly true, it elides the different forms in which science is deployed, as well as constructing science as a unified practice perverted in its representation. Broks links this to the alienation of the reader by the scientific elite:

> In the end, it seems, 'Science' was best done by 'Scientists' and popular accounts of science reinforced the idea of a great gulf between the science and public. Inductive amateurs were to leave the 'real' work to be done by theorising professionals. Excluded from the process of science the common reader was left to consume the products of science.[79]

By positing science as a distant practice that occurs outside the text, Broks risks reinforcing the ideology of scientific popularization: in presenting science as an isolated signified, Broks reproduces the notion of science as uncontested extra-textual practice and depicts the reader as passive recipient of a represented discourse.

Throughout this book, I locate science within the various cultural codes which construct it. Science in the periodical press is not an isolated representation of a distant practice but rather an important part of that practice that also shares the vicissitudes of readership, processes of production, and relationship to the marketplace common to all periodicals. According to the contexts that report it, the same scientific event might have currency within elite research while also providing scandalous copy that makes a title more desirable. With each representation of science there is also an element of re-presentation, delivering an object to satisfy the perceived demands of readers. It is the potential for appropriation and reinterpretation of these different social aspects of science which create divisions and hint at its heterogeneous nature. In providing the reader with a tangible object, the presentation of fragmentary aspects of science also operates to elide such differences, provoking the reader to join the dots, and so reify science as unified social object. Textual representations of science are therefore both complicit in the construction of science as discourse and also constitutive of the periodical as text and commodity. Rather than replicate an idea of an essential science simply represented in a variety of ways depending on authorial or editorial discourse, I will demonstrate how science is a constitutive part of these discourses.

Science too participates in the logic of abundance, both as a diverse practice, and its many manifestations in the press. My emphasis on London partly results from a recognition of the importance of space in shaping practice, but also that it is in the urban centres that this logic of abundance is expressed. Not only was London the centre for British publishing, but it was also the centre of British science.[80] Although there were important scientific institutions (including the ancient and Scottish universities as well as the institutions federated as Victoria University) and scientists outside the metropolis, London contained the national (and by extension, imperial) museums, the learned societies and the largest concentration of educational institutions.[81] Additionally the sheer scale of the city ensured there were thriving amateur scientific communities which provided not only a market for scientific knowledge, but also a range of networks and opportunities for scientific practice. In a period where there were few scientific careers, the concentration of the print trade in London provided a further source of remuneration for those attempting to commodify scientific knowledge.

Although I argue that the periodical inscribes abundance into its form, and I follow Kern and Schleiffer in identifying the late nineteenth-century as a period of abundance, I do not recognize it as a *fin de siécle* marking the end of the Victorian era and introducing modernism. Schleiffer claims that a 'vast array of new commodities disrupted not only traditional experience of everyday life but, more importantly, the settled simple hierarchy – the Enlightenment hierarchy – between production and product, principle and example, the present and the past.'[82] The composite nature of the periodical inscribes this principle into its form, allowing it to present, in the same space, content that refers to different temporal and spatial sites. However, although Schleiffer's logic of abundance seems to challenge 'the settled simple hierarchy', its historical specificity risks reaffirming it as unique temporal break. What Schleiffer calls abundance does not mark a fundamental discontinuity with the past, allowing the creation of a 'modern' sensibility in contrast to that of the Enlightenment, but instead describes a process which is constantly at work. If the late nineteenth century is characterized by multiple abundances – whether commodities, people, information, texts, even want – in the urban environment, then the jostling of things signalling a range of spaces and times is inevitable. Schleiffer's thesis is that multiple temporalities, interjecting from a number of cultural positions, challenge linear conceptions of time, and the same applies to space. However, neither linear time not abstract space were extinguished in the twentieth century, and neither are stable across the centuries that preceded it. In positing the late nineteenth century as a '*fin de siècle*', as a discontinuity between two periods, we follow the modernists in constructing the past as Foucault's 'total history': the 'indispensable correlative of the founding function of the subject.'[83] Schleiffer claims that:

The 'moment' of the advent of the second Industrial Revolution, the moment of twentieth-century Modernism, is precisely when, in history, narrative, and science, the possibility of a view from nowhere, the possibility of forgetting time and temporality by reducing it to spatial figures – of reducing time simply to an accident that can *always* be disregarded – is lost.[84]

In conceding this one moment of transformation, historical analysis once more becomes 'the discourse of the continuous' and so restates 'human consciousness [as] the original subject of all historical development and all action.'[85] The modernists can only conceive of a radically temporalized present by positing an arbitrary break to create a stable past. By repeating it, Schleiffer introduces a modernist representation of the past into his own analysis which is not markedly different from the Enlightenment subject he claims is lost.

What became represented as cultural modernism were responses to an increasingly mobile world of things which forced the juxtaposition of spatialities and temporalities. Rather than discuss the role of time and space in shaping nineteenth-century culture, and so overdetermine a historical moment that is already represented as a transition, I explore a genre that clearly transcends this narrow cultural context. It is easy to claim the periodical, because of its spatial rendering of multiple temporalities, as an essentially modern (if not postmodern) medium. However, the long history of the periodical predates twentieth-century modernism, let alone the late twentieth-century explorations of postmodernity. Instead it seems more sensible to consider the periodical as premodern, as a form in which we can easily comprehend the complex and heterogeneous spatial-temporal coordinates of the things and people represented within it.

Throughout this book I argue that materiality is not prior to any cultural encounter but rather is part of it. Although periodical numbers are ostensibly single objects, their components gesture to a range of spatial-temporal origins, insisting on their presence within this composite. This book is accordingly divided into two parts – the first focusing on space and the second on time – with a transitional chapter that explores their interdependence. Chapter One considers the different publications of astronomy, and examines how the perception of reading audiences shapes both their respective textual spaces and the astronomical space described within them. It concludes with an account of Arthur Cowper Ranyard's photographic reproduction of astronomical photographs. By reprinting these images, Ranyard could claim access to the stars through the page of his periodical; the controversy this aroused demonstrates the politics of ascribing material form to textual objects. Chapter Two extends this account by considering the role of space in the *Strand Magazine*. Its pioneering editor, George Newnes, also exploited photographic reproduction; however, Newnes did so to present pleasurable spaces to his readers that were predicated on their co-presence in time. This informs the strategy underpinning both the *Strand*'s copious coverage of late nineteenth-century celebrity culture, and also its depiction of the weird microscopic realms revealed by science. Using H.G. Wells's comment that detective fiction provides a model form for science writing, this chapter considers how the *Strand*, like Conan Doyle, substitutes this eminently rational narrative form for one of pleasure.

Chapter Three is the transititonal chapter that opens Part Two. Focusing on weeklies, the chapter moves from a discussion of Bergson and Bakhtin to consider how contemporary space is used to invoke the present. Most weeklies were oriented around news content – i.e., the passing events of the present – and this chapter considers the means that the present is deployed in across titles. The chapter concludes with an account of the role of scientific news in this context: as late nineteenth-century attitudes to copyright and patent law demonstrate, neither news or science were considered property; however, to represent scientific events as news for a popular audience, it had to be mediated by an author and so was marked as their words.

Chapters Four and Five consider time more specifically. Chapter Four uses chemistry to investigate how the temporality of discovery functions, and the role the periodical plays in circulating the discovered objects so that they are recognized by the wider community. Chapter Five explores periodicity in more detail, setting the appearances of various weeklies against a calendar of the meetings of scientific societies. By mapping this, it becomes possible to see the different temporalities carved out by the various competing rhythms, and to trace the movement of scientific objects across textual domains and so into new spatial-temporal moments.

In the Conclusion I return once more to the role of electronic text in the digital age. If, as I argue throughout this book, the objects that constitute periodicals present their spatial and temporal origins in order to signal a materiality other than that of the number of which they are part, then it becomes important to record these relationships in this new medium. Just as textual critics might trace the differences between variant editions, and those in science studies might follow the progress of scientific objects from laboratories into texts, so we must understand what is at stake in the transformation of hard copy into electronic form. Opening with a discussion of the difference between words and things, this chapter argues that the electronic forms of texts are related to their paper predecessors. To demonstrate this, and to summarize the arguments of the previous chapters, I give an account of the materialization of an elusive substance, electricity, and explore how its presence or absence depends upon its context. The chapter, and the book, concludes by reiterating the constitutive role the material plays, even in the digital domain, and insists that we must recognize the politics inherent in any transformation of material form.

### Notes

1   'W.T.S.' [W.T. Stead], 'Introduction', *Index to the Periodical Literature of the World* (London, 1894), p. vii.

2   Henri Lefebvre, *The Production of Space*, trans. Donald Nicholson-Smith (1991; Oxford, 2001), p. 355.

3   Stephen Kern, *The Culture of Time and Space, 1880–1918* (Cambridge, MA, 1983), p. 2. As is explicit in this introduction and evident in the book as a whole, I differ from Kern's insistence on essential categories, even as a historiographic means to differentiate the historically contingent. See the 'Preface' to the second edition of *The Culture of Time and Space* (1983; Cambridge, MA, 2003), p. x–xxx.

4   Kern, *Culture of Time and Space*, p. 4.

5   For instance see Laurel Brake, 'The Discourse of Journalism: Authorship, Publishers and Periodicals', *Subjugated Knowledges* (London, 1994), pp. 63–82.

6   Kern, *Culture of Time and Space*, p. 4.

7   Lefbvre, *Production*, p. 7.

8   Anonymous, 'Tour the Waterloo Directory of English Newspapers and Periodicals', *Waterloo Directory of English Newspapers and Periodicals, 1800–1900*, ed. John S. North, www.victorianperiodicals.com [accessed 31 March 2006].

9   J.W. Robertson-Smith, 'Some Newspaper Men', in *Sell's Dictionary of the World's Press* (London, 1888), p. 118.

10  W.T. Stead, 'Preface', *Index to the Periodical Literature of the World* (London, 1893), p. 5, and W.T. Stead, 'Programme', *Review of Reviews*, 1 (1890): 14. For a further account of paper-based and electronic bibliographic tools since the nineteenth century see Chris Willis, '"Out flew the web and floated wide": An Overview of Uses of the Internet for Victorian Research', *Journal of Victorian Culture*, 7 (2002), 297–310 and James Mussell and Suzanne Paylor, '"Mapping the Mighty Maze": the Nineteenth-Century Serials Edition', *19: Interdisciplinary Studies in the Long Nineteenth Century*, 1 (2005) www.19.bbk.ac.uk [accessed 31 March 2006].

11  *Poole's Index to Periodical Literature*, ed. William Frederick Poole, 2 vols (London, 1882), also 5 supplements ed. William Frederick Poole (1888), William I. Fletcher (1893), William I. Fletcher and Franklin O. Poole (1897), William I. Fletcher and Mary Poole (1903, 1908) (London, 1888–1908). *Poole's Index Date and Volume Key*, eds Marion V. Bell and Jean C. Bacon (Chicago, 1957) and *Cumulative Author Index for Poole's Index to Periodical Literature, 1802–1906*, compiled and ed. C. Edward Wall (Ann Arbor, 1971).

12  See Geoffrey Cantor and others, 'Introduction', in *Culture and Science in the Nineteenth-Century Media*, eds Louise Henson and others (Aldershot, 2004), p. xix–xx. *Wellesley Index to Victorian Periodicals, 1824–1900*, ed. Walter E. Houghton, 5 vols (Toronto, 1966–1979).

13  Patrick Leary, 'Googling the Victorians', *Journal of Victorian Culture*, 10 (2005), 3.

14  Leary, 'Googling the Victorians', 10.

15  Margaret Beetham, 'Towards a Theory of the Periodical as a Publishing Genre', *Investigating Victorian Journalism*, ed. Laurel Brake, Aled Jones and Lionel Madden (London, 1990), pp. 23–4; Laurel Brake, *Print in Transition, 1850–1910* (London, 2001), pp. 20–51, 283–4.

16  Brake, *Print in Transition*, p. 27.

17  Brake, *Print in Transition*, p. 29, Beetham, 'Towards a Theory', p. 23.

18  Beetham, 'Towards a Theory', p. 23.

19  Joanne Shattock and Michael Wolff, 'Introduction', in *Victorian Periodical Press: Samplings and Soundings*, eds Joanne Shattock and Michael Wolff (Leicester, 1982), pp. xiii–xix and Cantor and others, 'Introduction', p. xx.

20  See for instance *Culture and Science*, eds Henson and others; *Science Serialized: Representations of the Sciences in Nineteenth-Century Periodicals*, eds Geoffrey Cantor and Sally Shuttleworth (Cambridge MA, 2004); Geoffrey Cantor and others, *Science in the Nineteenth Century Periodical* (Cambridge, 2004); Hilary Fraser, Judith Johnstone and Stephanie Green, *Gender and the Victorian Periodical* (Cambridge, 2003); *Nineteenth-Century Media and the Construction of Identities*, eds Laurel Brake, Bill Bell and David Finkelstein (London, 2000).

21  Consider the subtitles of the following: Andrew King, *The* London Journal, *1845–1883: Periodicals, Production and Gender* (Aldershot, 2004); John Plunkett, *Queen Victoria: First Media Monarch* (Oxford, 2003); Kate Jackson, *George Newnes and the New Journalism in Britain, 1880–1910* (Aldershot, 2001); and Mark Turner, *Trollope and the Magazines: Gendered Issues in Mid-Victorian Britain* (Basingstoke, 2000).

22  Geoffrey Cantor and Sally Shuttleworth, 'Introduction', *Science Serialized*, pp. 3–5.

23  Jerome McGann, 'Culture and Technology: The Way We Live Now, What Is to Be Done?', *Interdisciplinary Science Reviews*, 30 (2005), 181.

24  For instance at the time of writing Thomson Gale plan to publish hundreds of nineteenth-century periodicals, and Proquest are incorporating periodicals into a larger project that includes their existing electronic holdings and other important resources such as the *Wellesley Index* and the *Nineteenth-Century Short Title Catalogue*. Also, the British Library's *British Newspapers 1800–1900* plans to digitize two million pages (about 46 different titles) of newspapers.

25  See http://books.google.com/. The persistence of the codex as a model for print forms is reproduced in the language of GooglePrint. Not only is 'books' currently in their url, but their rhetoric of print is solely in terms of books. Even descriptions of selling and pricing mechanisms, as well as the current deliberations over copyright, are in terms of books.

26  Jerome McGann, *Radiant Textuality; Literature after the World Wide Web* (New York, 2001), pp. 18–19.

27  McGann, *Radiant Textuality*, p. 82.

28  McGann, *Radiant Textuality*, p. 82.

29  Lyn Pykett, 'Reading the Periodical Press: Text and Context,' in *Investigating Victorian Journalism*, eds Brake, Jones and Madden, p. 6. Turner, *Trollope and the Magazines*, p. 228. Tony Bennett, 'Media, "Reality", Signification', *Culture, Society and the Media*, eds Michael Gurevitch and others (1982; London, 1988), p. 287.

30  Bennett, 'Media, "Reality", Signification', pp. 307–8.

31  Pykett, 'Reading the Periodical Press', p. 16; Roland Barthes, 'From Work to Text', *Image, Music, Text*, ed. and trans. Stephen Heath (1961; London, 1977), pp. 156–7.

32  D.F. McKenzie, 'Foreward', in *Bibliography and the Sociology of Texts* (Cambridge, 1999), p. 4.

33  Turner, *Trollope and the Magazines*, p. 3, 229–30; Brake, *Subjugated Knowledges*, p. xi.

34  Turner, *Trollope and the Magazines*, p. 233; Julia Kristeva, 'Word, Dialogue and Novel', *The Kristeva Reader*, ed. Toril Moi (New York, 1986), pp. 35–61.

35  John Frow, 'Intertextuality and Ontology', *Intertextuality: Theories and Practices*, eds Michael Worton and Judith Still (Manchester, 1990), p. 46.

36  Turner, *Trollope and the Magazines*, pp. 235–6.

37  Frow, 'Intertextuality and Ontology', p. 50.

38  See for instance Lyn Pykett, 'The Material Turn in Victorian Studies', *Literature Compass*, 1 (2003–2004), available from http://www.blackwell-compass.com/subject/literature/.

39  In *Capital*, Marx describes the result of the imposition of value onto useful objects as 'social hieroglyphs', as much a product of social practice as language. Karl Marx, *Capital: An Abridged Edition*, ed. David McLellan (Oxford, 1999), p. 45. The linguistic bias within cultural studies is a result of the institutional links the discipline retains with literary studies.

40  Marx, *Capital*, p. 23.

41  Marx, *Capital*, p. 43.

42  Marx, *Capital*, p. 19.

43  Marx, *Capital*, p. 44.

44  Marx, *Capital*, p. 26.

45  Marx, *Captial*, p. 13.

46  King, *The* London Journal, pp. 3–5.

47  Anonymous [W.T. Stead], 'History of Periodicals', *Index to the Periodicals of the World* (London, 1892), p. 7. His *Review of Reviews* is 'a kind of clearing-house of periodical literature.'

48  Barthes, 'From Work to Text', p. 156.

49  Lefebvre, *Production*, p. 341.

50  Lefebvre, *Production*, p. 341. Emphasis is Lefebvre's.

51  Lefebvre, *Production*, p. 341.

52  Lefebvre, *Production*, pp. 341–2. Emphasis is Lefebvre's.

53  Bruno Latour, *Science in Action* (Cambridge MA, 1987). See Bruno Latour, *Reassembling the Social* (Oxford, 2005); and John Law's ANT website at http://www.lancs.ac.uk/fass/centres/css/ant/antres.htm.

54  Karin Knorr Cetina, 'The Couch, the Cathedral, and the Laboratory', in *Science as Practice and Culture*, ed. Andrew Pickering (Chicago, 1992), p. 116.

55  Cetina, 'The Couch, the Cathedral, and the Laboratory', p. 116.

56  See Bruno Latour, 'Drawing Things Together', in *Representation in Scientific Practice*, eds Michael Lynch and Steve Woolgar (London, 1990) pp. 18–60; Bruno Latour, *We Have Never Been Modern* (New York, 1993); Bruno Latour *Pandora's Hope* (Cambridge MA, 1999).

57  Latour, *Pandora's Hope*, p. 96, 93.

58  Latour, *Pandora's Hope*, p. 97.

59  Latour, *Pandora's Hope*, p. 70 and Barthes, 'From Work to Text', p. 164.

60  C.f. Latour, *Pandora's Hope*, p. 96: 'Disciplining men and mobilizing things, mobilizing things by disciplining men; this is a new way of convincing, sometimes called scientific research.'

61  Jonathan R. Topham, 'Introduction: *BJHS* Special Section: Book History and the Sciences', *British Journal for the History of Science*, 33 (2000), 155–6.

62  Topham, 'Introduction', 157.

63  Roger Cooter and Steven Pumfrey, 'Separate Spheres and Public Places: Reflections on the History of Science Popularization and Science in Popular Culture', *History of Science*, 32 (1994), 237.

64  Topham, 'Introduction', 158.

65  Cooter and Pumfrey, 'Separate Spheres', 252.

66 Cooter and Pumfrey, 'Separate Spheres', 249–50. There is a large body of work exploring the complex terrain of nineteenth-century science. See for instance James Secord, *Victorian Sensation: The Extraordinary Publication, Reception, and Secret Authorship of* Vestiges of the Natural History of Creation (Chicago, 2000); Anne Secord, 'Science in the Pub: Artisan Botanists in Early Nineteenth-Century Lancashire', *History of Science*, 32 (1994), 269–315; J.R. Topham, 'Beyond the "Common Context": the Production and Reading of the *Bridgewater Treatises*', *Isis*, 89 (1998), 233–62; Susan Sheets-Pyenson, 'Popular Science Periodicals in Paris and London: the Emergence of a Low Scientific Culture, 1820–1875', *Annals of Science*, 42 (1985), 549–72; Adrian Desmond, 'Artisan Resistance and Evolution in Britain, 1819–1848', *Osiris*, 3 (1987), 375–404.

67 Cooter and Pumfrey, 'Separate Spheres', 251.

68 *Culture and Science*, eds Henson and others; *Science Serialized*, eds Cantor and Shuttleworth; Cantor and others, *Science in the Nineteenth Century Periodical*.

69 Cooter and Pumfrey, 'Separate Spheres', p. 256. Michel Callon and John Law, 'On Interests and Their Transformation: Enrolment and Counter-Enrolment', *Social Studies of Science*, 12 (1982), 615–26.

70 Brake, *Print in Transition*, p. xiii.

71 Ronald Schleiffer, *Modernism and Time: The Logic of Abundance in Literature, Science, and Culture, 1880–1930* (Cambridge, 2000), pp. 131–2. It should be stressed that Schleiffer includes want as part of this logic of abundance.

72 Kern, *Culture of Space and Time*, pp. 34–5.

73 Donald Read, *The Power of News:Tthe History of Reuters* (Oxford, 1999), p. 71. See also Roger Luckhurst, *The Invention of Telepathy, 1870–1901* (Oxford, 2002), p. 143.

74 Peter Broks, *Media Science before the Great War* (London, 1996), p. 7.

75 Anonymous [W.T. Stead], 'History of Periodicals', p. 6.

76 Anonymous [W.T. Stead], 'History of Periodicals', p. 7.

77 W.T. Stead, 'Preface', *Index to the Periodicals of 1894* (London, 1895), p. iv.

78 Broks, *Media Science*, p. 37.

79 Broks, *Media Science*, p. 40.

80 It is important not to overlook 'regional' science, and indeed marginal scientific enterprises in London itself. See for instance Crosbie Smith, 'Nowhere But in a Great Town: William Thomson's Spiral of Classroom Credibility', in *Making Space for Science: Territorial Themes in the Shaping of Knowledge*, eds Crosbie Smith and John Agar (Basingstoke, 1998), pp. 118–46; Samuel J.M.M. Alberti, 'Amateurs and Professionals in One County: Biology and Natural History in Late Nineteenth Century Yorkshire', *Journal of the History of Biology*, 34 (2001), 115–47; Philip Lowe, 'The British Association and the Provincial Public', in *The Parliament of Science*, eds Roy MacLeod and Peter Collins (Northwood, 1981), pp. 118–44.

81 Aside from the university colleges of London Univeristy, the Royal College of Science, and the City and Guilds Institutions, there were also 11 polytechnics in London in 1898 at which 50,000 students were enrolled. D. S. L. Cardwell, *The Organization of Science in England* (1957; London, 1972), pp. 111–55.

82 Schleiffer, *Modernism and Time*, p. 48.

83 Michel Foucault, *The Archaeology of Knowledge* (1972; London, 2001), p. 12.

84 Schleiffer, *Modernism and Time*, p. 111–12. Emphasis is Schleiffer's.

85 Foucault, *Archaeology of Knowledge*, p. 12.

# PART 1
## Spaces

# Chapter One

# Astronomy and the Representation of Space

Astronomy is essentially a popular science. The general public has an indefeasible right of access to its lofty halls, which is the more important to keep cleared of unnecessary technical impediments, since the natural tendency of all sciences is to become specialized as they advance. But literary treatment is the foe of specialization, and helps to secure, accordingly, the topics it is applied to, against being secluded from the interests and understanding of ordinary educated men and women.[1]

Agnes M. Clerke suggests that because the stars are readily accessible to everybody, so the science of astronomy should be equally accessible. However, she also recognizes that sciences become more specialized as they progress, and so require technical expertise as they become more complex. Clerke's solution is to write an account of the latest advances in astronomical science in a form that would remove these 'technical impediments' for 'ordinary educated men and women.' What Clerke does not consider, however, is that although the stars can be seen by most people at night, astronomy is more than observation with the naked eye. In order to work with the stars, they must be translated into a form that can be handled, recorded, moved and compared. Instruments such as telescopes and spectroscopes not only bring the stars closer, they also provide quantifying measures of location and time. Although Clerke sees instruments and advanced practices as technical impediments, it is actually these mediating factors that constitute the science. Equally, her *System of the Stars* is a further impediment, an expensive text (21s) that interposes its representations of space between that of elite astronomy and the experiences of her readers. For the study of space, I suggest, we must turn to the study of spaces, textual and otherwise.

*System of the Stars* was published in November 1890, one month after the formation of the British Astronomical Association (BAA). This new society was explicitly aimed at the amateur astronomers who felt marginalized by the older, more prestigious Royal Astronomical Society (RAS). Throughout the nineteenth century astronomy had been represented by its totemic Grand Amateurs – men like John and William Herschel, Walter De La Rue, and the Earls of Rosse who used their private incomes to purchase and build their own equipment and fund their own research. These men constructed their homes as sites of scientific practice in which networks of men and women carried out astronomical research. The third and fourth Earls of Rosse, for instance, hosted scientific soirees for local tenants, organizations, and the British Association for the Advancement of Science whenever it was in Ireland.[2] Much like the country-house natural historians represented visibly by Darwin, these astronomers gained both celebrity and scientific authority as their scientific and social networks often coalesced. The new British Astronomical Association threatened to conflate the Grand Amateur tradition into a lesser one of dilettante astronomy, leaving the RAS as the society for elite astronomy in the hands of a class unclearly defined as non-amateur.

The RAS had been dominated by the Grand Amateurs since its foundation by the headmaster Revd Dr Richard Pearson in 1820. However, the increasing scale and cost of astronomical research meant that the majority of astronomical research was centred around a few, well-financed observatories. Not only were instruments becoming more expensive and more complex, but the latest observational work demanded institutional structures that would not only provide staff to use equipment and calculate data, but also to guarantee that any results were scientifically valid. The foundation of the Lick observatory in 1887, its giant 36" refractor the most powerful in the world, set a precedent within astronomical culture. Its position high up on Mount Hamilton in the United States, and the huge expense incurred by its foundation, demonstrated that only a well-funded observatory, staffed by full-time staff, would be able to compete at the cutting edge of astronomical research. This trend was confirmed when construction began in 1895 on the Yerkes Observatory at the University of Chicago that would house a 40" refracting telescope which remains today the largest in the world. Although the Fellowship of the RAS was held by both amateur and professional astronomers, the formation of the BAA implied that those practicing the elite astronomy that it represented were not amateurs. The increasingly expensive and complex structures required further aligned the category of non-amateur with professional.[3]

This chapter considers the way in which these astronomical communities were manifested through textual space. The accessibility of the stars, coupled with a long tradition of discovery by 'ordinary' people, meant that the astronomical community was both extraordinarily mixed while also sharing a strong sense of common purpose. However, the necessary mediating stages between the stars in the sky and the textual records that allowed astronomical discussion across space produced a diversity of practice. Through considering the way in which space – the stars in the sky – is represented in a form that allows it to move through space, it becomes possible to see how each title represents astronomical practice back to its intended audience. The chapter begins with a discussion of astronomy within the title in which the BAA was first mooted, the *English Mechanic*. Amateur astronomy also encompassed the researches of the 'paradoxers' – a heterodox mix of flat-earth theorists, anti-Newtonian believers in perpetual motion, astrologers, and other supporters of unorthodox scientific theories. The *English Mechanic* was predicated on its openness and, as such, provided room for those who were excluded from other astronomical publications. The journals published by the RAS were necessarily more exclusive: its *Monthly Notices* and annual *Memoirs* were distributed both to the Fellows and other influential observatories and scientific institutions around the world. These consisted of printed astronomical papers reporting research and, because they had institutional support, carried no advertisements. This community was also served by a commercial journal, *The Observatory*, published by Taylor and Francis and edited by Andrew Ainslie Common, a Grand Amateur, and Herbert Hall Turner, Chief Assistant at the Royal Observatory. Reliant on purchasers and subscribers, and containing a wider range of textual matter such as correspondence, reviews of publications and other societies, and astronomical papers, *The Observatory* provides a more nuanced sense of elite astronomical practice than the publications of the RAS. The *Journal of the British Astronomical Association* (*JBAA*), which was published to provide a textual space in which its geographically distributed members could meet, played a crucial role in shaping the identity of the new Association. Aimed explicitly at both men and women, it both structures practice and presents results in a hierarchical form that locates such work under the supervision of the masculine science of the RAS. The chapter ends by returning to the crucial mediating stages between the text on the page and the stars in the sky. The popular science journal *Knowledge* was intended for the interested, but not necessarily practicing, reader, yet, as it was edited by a succession of astronomers, it often sought to interject into scientific controversy. Its editor from 1888, Arthur Cowper Ranyard, championed the photographic reproduction of astronomical photographs, claiming this gave readers unprecedented access to the closed spaces of the observatory. Unsurprisingly, such a strategy was controversial, and the pages of *Knowledge* carried discussion over the status of astronomical images in the periodical press.

## The *English Mechanic* and the Periodical as Public Space

The *English Mechanic* was a 2d weekly edited by Ebeneezer Kibblewhite and owned by the philanthropist John Passmore Edwards. The epigram from Montaigne that headed each week's correspondence reflects the ideology of the title:

> I would have everyone write what he knows, and as much as he knows, but no more; and that not this only, but in all other subjects: for such a person may have some particular knowledge and experience of the nature of such a river or such a fountain, that as to other things, knows no more than what everybody does, and yet, to keep a clutter with this little pittance of his, will undertake to write the whole body of physicks, a vice from whence great inconveniences derive their original.[4]

By barring individuals arguing from their own 'particular knowledge', scientific progress becomes a communal enterprise owned by nobody. This principle is inscribed into the form of the *English Mechanic*: not only did correspondence take up six of its 24 pages, but these are followed by six pages of 'Queries' and 'Answers to Queries.' Apart from the serial articles – which only take up two pages of letterpress – the remainder of the title consists of 'Answers to Correspondents', which address unprinted queries by readers, and 'Our Sixpenny Sale Column', which is made up of readers' advertisements. Relying almost entirely on letterpress contributed by its readers, the *English Mechanic* presented its readers as its writers and the resulting sense of ownership was expressed in its nickname, 'Ours.'

This editorial policy was connected to the scientific culture embodied by the title. In 1889 the *English Mechanic* printed a number of letters discussing the supposed decline of astronomy within its pages caused by the unexpected success of the Liverpool Astronomical Society. This Society, whose failure in 1889 led directly to the establishment of the BAA, had recently outgrown its local roots and its *Journal* had displaced the *English Mechanic* as a focus for an increasingly national body of astronomers. P.F. Duke, a Fellow of the RAS and future secretary of the BAA, defended the *English Mechanic*:

> Experiences are given for what they are worth, and for readers to draw their own conclusions, or, if they choose, to respond and criticize. Mistakes may be made, but while there would be no honesty in describing imaginary observations, there would be no warrant in questioning the good faith of those who record to the best of their ability what they suppose they have seen.[5]

Duke identifies what differentiates the *English Mechanic* from its rivals: it is a space where the experiences of its readers are more important than their subsequent veracity. Like the extract from Montaigne, Duke's letter warns against purely invented contributions, but still stresses that it is the contribution itself – what readers 'suppose they have seen' – rather than any claims to essential truth that grant access to its text. This inscribes a formal dialogia into the *English Mechanic*, in which each contribution acts a partial utterance in an exchange across numbers which resists finalization.

Bakhtin / Medvedev claim that any work of science can only have a conditional end as 'one work takes up where the other leaves off. Science is an endless unity. It cannot be broken down into a series of finished and self-sufficient works.'[6] For Bakhtin / Medvedev, scientific publications impose an ending onto an ongoing process, dividing it up into separate works. However, these works are not homogenous units that represent an underlying ahistorical process, but rather culturally significant objects that are constitutive of moments of practice. Each act of closure is a political act that attempts to align thematic finalization with the conditional ending of a paper to inscribe a final truth claim in a fixed work that can be referenced in the future. Subsequent authors, in taking up the claims of others, use their works to both strengthen their own findings, and also situate themselves within a progressive, teleological process.[7] In specialist scientific journals like those described below, each paper has the final (although it is, of course, subject to further debate in the future) say in a narrative that stretches back over many other papers in a set of delimited textual contexts. In the *English Mechanic* this strategy is distributed over the whole title: rather than employ citations in individual articles, they all participate in an ongoing process that does not posit an end. In not only bringing this process into its text but also resisting 'truth' as a means of judging contributions, the *English Mechanic* redefines science as provisional, contemporaneous, and located in the dialogic exchange between contributors.

The formal structure of the *English Mechanic* was inherited from the miscellanies common in the early nineteenth century. Its proprietor, Passmore Edwards, owned the *Mechanics' Magazine* between 1857 and 1867, before returning it after acquiring the *English Mechanic* from George Maddick in 1866. Whereas the *Mechanics' Magazine* limped on until it was absorbed by *Iron* in 1872, Edwards, after buying it outright in 1869, increased the paper size of the *English Mechanic* and achieved a profitable circulation of 30,000 – an increase of over 20,000 copies a week.[8] Susan Sheets Pyenson argues that the *Mechanics' Magazine* was representative of the 'low' scientific culture that emerged in Paris and London. This culture, she argues, 'elaborated the ideal of an experiential, inductivist "low science" that could be understood and created by anyone' and, on occasion, 'vigorously opposed the "high" scientific establishment.' Its periodicals thus 'sometimes sought to establish their own canons of scientific investigation, criticism and explanation' that not only provided alternative methodological models, but also produced a space in which other scientific cultures could be discussed. Sheets Pyenson's influential article has been qualified by subsequent research but still serves to remind us of the plurality of scientific cultures, and the way such cultures are rooted in material practices. The *English Mechanic*, I suggest, functioned in a similar fashion with the rival cultures of astronomy: the creation of the BAA extended one model of practice over a diverse field of practitioners; as the formal structure of the *English Mechanic* was founded on principles that resist closure, it provided a space that could relativize the work of others.

An advertisement in *The Times* in 1895 seems to posit two distinct audiences for the *English Mechanic*. It claims it is 'THE PAPER FOR EVERY HOME AND WORKSHOP. Oldest, Cheapest, and Best Journal for Popular Science and Practical Mechanics.'[9] However, the text itself makes no distinctions between the home and the workshop, or between popular science and practical mechanics; rather it emphasizes that homes and workshops might be the same place, but different spaces, and that study might be for pleasure, as well as education or employment. Each number opens with an instructive technical serial article such as 'Practical Electric Bell Fitting' or 'Simple Exercises in Technical Analysis.'[10] These serials do not appear in every subsequent number, but are often – but not always – fortnightly. This means that they can overlap, readers are uncertain when they will appear, and sometimes pass between completely different topics. The serial articles are then followed by two or three extracts (fully acknowledged) taken from titles such as *Chemical News*, *La Nature*, and the *American Machinist*. Illustrations are woodcuts, and mostly technical drawings, further reflecting both the low price of the title and the practical inclination of its intended readership.

The epistolary format of the miscellany that constitutes the bulk of the title creates a curious space that bears little relation to events beyond the text. Although a few contributions are signed, the majority are pseudonymous and so restrict identity to within the text. Also, the textual space creates its own temporal narratives: as a weekly each number creates a sense of punctual time, with the number functioning as an event forwarding the debates; however, the arrangement of departments, with 'Letters to the Editor' and 'Replies to Queries' immediately after the serial articles and before the next batch of queries, stretches the discourse of the title over the time between numbers eliding this temporal discontinuity. All queries and letters are numbered within the *English Mechanic* (see Figure 1.1), so they create an elaborate network of cross references which span individual numbers. Its periodicity tends towards fragmentation: the next number will often appear before correspondents have a chance to write and send their contributions, splitting long-running controversies into various narratives that are pursued with each subsequent number. Correspondents often hope to reunite the various strands of a debate but, inevitably, their contribution will often coincide with another received that week, reigniting debate, and fracturing the narratives once more.

An example of this occurs in 1888 when the infamous flat-earth theorist John Hampden sparks a discussion about the curvature of the earth. Hampden had achieved notoriety when he lost £500 to Alfred Russel Wallace in 1870 in a wager that nobody could prove that the earth was flat.[11] 'Sigma', the pseudonym of the electrician John T. Sprague, refutes Hampden using astronomical principles.[12] This provokes the following from Hampden:

> I wish I could induce 'Sigma' or some other honest opponent to discuss the questions on my terms, instead of leading me into branches of Physics which have no sort of connection with the real question or issue. It is most unfair to force anyone into a debate on subjects which he candidly admits he is perfectly ignorant of. I am too old a controversialist to enter upon such a one-sided discussion.[13]

Hampden attempts to force the debate on his terms, denouncing Sigma's astronomy as an 'attempt to impose upon [him] the fanciful conjectures of Pagan astrologers' and demanding he first show the curvature 'on any part of the earth or ocean' before he will pretend 'to see it in the skies above our heads.'[14]

This refusal to answer the astronomical charges draws a rare interjection by the editor who declares 'Hopeless as usual. The above is hardly worth space, except as another proof of the inability of Mr. Hampden to respond to a direct challenge.' The editor, who must not be seen to interfere in the free exchange between readers, is drawn to comment because Hampden is transgressing the textual codes by refusing to continue to the debate. Despite this, Hampden's remarks are sufficiently provocative to elicit a number of responses. 'E.L.G.', a correspondent who frequently argues for parity between science and scripture, rather mischievously suggests Hampden prove his theory using a flat body of water – a reference to the 1870 canal experiment – before 'he should write again as on the

JUNE 24, 1892. ENGLISH MECHANIC AND WORLD OF SCIENCE: No. 1422. 409

Blakeley will perhaps be so kind to explain how he means it that my suggestion is not admissible, because his own observation only encourages my opinion.

The expectations I had for the return of the aurora for last week end or beginning of this week have, I regret to say, not been fulfilled, though I was very watchful. We have certainly had some most peculiar and beautiful sunsets lately, and noticed most remarkable arrangements of clouds.

Last Wednesday afternoon there was again a most beautiful halo round the sun of about 30° radius. The appearance of the sky was exactly the same as on the 30th of April (see Mr. Maclair Boneston's letter, 33449, and my own, 33483). But only *one* luminous spot, at the north extremity of the ring, was visible, the south-western and western portion of the halo being rather spoiled by the smoke hanging about this city. On the 1st of May last, the day after the occurrence of the beautiful solar halo and mock suns, I observed a modest display of aurora, and it is not improbable (and has often been suggested) that last Wednesday these remarkable strata of most delicate cirrus cloud were the means of an auroral discharge. I confidently expected the aurora that night, but with the disappearance of the halo at 7 p.m., rain clouds quickly gathered, and all observation was stopped for the night. The following day we had to burn gas at dinner time in town, and the temperature and aspect of everything was most dismal and winterly.

Manchester, June 19. **Albert Alfred Buss.**

### THE EVOLUTION OF ANGLING.

[33688.]—THE "contemplative man's recreation" is annually increasing in importance. We breed fish nowadays as we raise poultry, and the man with a full purse and a few acres of low-lying land, intersected by a rivulet, makes a loch, purchases a few hundred troutlets from a hatchery, and stocks his water. He introduces certain weeds which nourish aquatic snails, shrimps, and other piscine pabulum on which the finny tribe gorge themselves into weight and good quality. Thus he may obtain a high rate of interest on his investment after three or four years, by letting out the rod-fishing at per diem, or per annum. I know a Scotch landowner who has done all this; he has transformed a useless bog into a loch with a name to it, and boasts of his 5lb. trout—all in about five years time! I hear of many such improvers.

Then, again, *cæteris paribus*, what ingenious imitations of nature are being constantly invented in the shape of flies, and all manner of seductive insects, all kinds of lively little fishes, and every creeping thing admired by the scaly shoals. To-day I have received the latest novelty—artificial worms, the product of a Russian noble, who has just introduced them into the English market. They are remarkable imitations—red, soft, elastic, and semi-transparent; the rough concentric rings on the body from head to tail being closely executed. The box of two dozen cost me one shilling; it only remains to test their virtues in the river. There are highly-educated fishes in these days, originally pricked into the knowledge of a concealed hook; these are plentiful in all free waters, with sharpened instincts and acute perceptions. Such specimens I have frequently observed; but these wise, heavy inhabitants are very useful in a water as breeders.

**Eos.**

### THE VOTING MACHINE.

[33689.]—THE voting machine illustrated on page 288, letter 33521, condemns itself in several respects. The blind and the colour-blind would not be able to vote with certainty, and the communication from the voting box to the presiding officer would defeat the object for which secret voting was devised. An agreement with the officer would allow a voter to drop as many balls as he liked, and no Government would adopt a system of voting which did not provide some means of identifying the voter.

Mr. Maddison says: "The voter coming out of the cabin and intimating to the presiding officer that the vote is deposited, the official pulls a lever, the slide opens, and the ball drops into the ballot box, where they all accumulate; at the same time the knob goes back to its normal position." Then, I presume, the ball would remain visible, and the knob stand out whilst the voter is leaving the cabin, in which case anyone looking in could easily discover his vote.

Now I have planned a voting machine (very unlike Mr. Maddison's) which fulfils most, if not all, the requirements of the Ballot Acts—the identification of the voter with the vote given—putting a cross against the name of the person voted for, in sight of the voter, and all done by a simple act on the part of the voter himself.

My plan is very simple in operation, though the machine is complicated in itself, and is composed in a hut or voting box.

The officer in charge having satisfied himself that the person is entitled to vote, enters the voter's registered number in a place provided for that purpose; the voter then enters the voting-box, and by depressing a knob sees his vote registered. On releasing the knob his vote disappears, and a blank appears for the next comer. All necessary precautions are taken against his voting twice, &c. No one but the voter enters the box, and he cannot vote before closing the door. Both door and floor are brought into requisition in order to prevent a vote being taken without the voter being inside, so that if a person could reach the voting knob from outside he could not vote.

The voter's registered number is entered on a list of numbers corresponding to numbers on the voting list. None of the numbers are seen.

I believe this is the first time that voting by machine with the cross as required by the Ballot Acts has been thought of; but voting machines, using balls or other kinds of tokens, have been exhibited in the committee rooms of the House of Commons, and I have heard of one which counted the votes as they were deposited.

**Thos. T. Kemp.**

### "A DASH TO THE POLE."

[33690.]—IN reference to Mr. H. D. Ward's story that you are now publishing in the pages of the ENGLISH MECHANIC, some of your readers who are not posted in aëronautical matters will perhaps think the idea impossible; but the account he gives of the air-ship is really quite within the mark, as those which have been made and proposed are far more extraordinary. As long ago as 1844, M. E. Marey-Monge constructed a copper balloon which was inflated with hydrogen, and exhibited at Paris. Dr. Crestodoro in 1866 exhibited a model of a copper balloon intended to be 200ft. dia. and employed in commerce. Within the last twenty years several air-ship balloons have actually been made by Giffard, Dupuy de Lome, Dr. Wolfert, Koch, Campbell, and others. The American and French engineers have also proposed plans, in regard to which Mr. Ward's ideal machine must take a seventh-rate place. Sebillet, of Paris, proposed a line of steam Montgolfiers for commerce direct between Marseilles and Central Africa, which plan he patented in 1886. In America, Falconnet, of Nashville, has also patented an air-ship on an immense scale and of a distinctly novel type. The ideal balloon of the story in your columns is patented by a French engineer named Gloten. His air-ship is to be 162ft. long, 55ft. circumference, and is provided with four lifting propellers in addition to one at the stern. The whole machine is to be constructed of sheet metal, and driven by steam power.

The idea of driving by electricity originated with Tissandier. Perhaps as practical a method as any was patented by Lorrain in 1888. He proposes to drive the propeller by a Wimshurst machine used as an electrostatic motor. The flying balloon with an air-plane has been patented very frequently. The best is very likely that of Gaggino, patented in the year 1888.

There is also one important point which does not seem to be much understood even among engineers. When the size of a balloon is very much increased, the breaking strain also increases; but the sustaining power only increases in proportion to the surface, while the breaking strain increases in proportion to the weight carried.

In consequence, the carrying power is less in proportion to the cost in a large balloon than in a small one. And it would not pay to make balloons to carry over ten or twelve tons. In Giffard's great captive balloon the limit of safe strain on the network was nearly reached, for the balloon was over 100ft. diameter. If some of the large air-ships that have been proposed were made, in practice it would be found they could only lift their own weight, and would have no power to carry passengers and cargo.

**J. Sutcliffe.**

Gilbert Fields, Barkisland, near Halifax,
June 18.

[33691.]—IF it is permissible to ask questions suggested in the progress of your spirited dash into fiction, may I be allowed to call attention to page 377, middle column, and ask a question of our electrical experts?

"A powerful dynamo, which had filled the *storage* batteries."

"The wires carrying 500 *alternating* volts, &c."

(1) Could such a dynamo furnish such a charge? Mr. Bottone recently said it was impossible to store electricity with an alternating current.

(2) Could wires in any case afford protection?

Mark Twain, in "A Yankee at the Court of King Arthur," makes them offensive, as well as defensive—distance no object—whereas it occurs to me that a blow with a piece of wood would either break the wires, bring them into contact, or level them with the ground, so that one could easily step across.

(3) Would 500 volts kill? Mr. Preece, at the Institute of Electrical Engineers, 27th March, 1890, gave his experience of 2,000 volts and 1,200 volts, and Mr. Wyles of a 25-light Brush machine, where a pain across the chest was the only bad consequence.

**J. E. Harper.**

15, Henrietta-street, W.C., June 18.

### FIRE INSURANCE.

[33692.]—MY letter (33594) Mr. "A. E. B." thinks (33635) a rather uncalled for song. I venture to warn him that ere he finishes this century some far less called for will be heard. He probably fancies that A.D. 1900 may find as few landowners in England as now. That may turn out a huge mistake.

The existence of fire insurance companies, whether Satan or anyone else started them, we mean, by our God's help, to abolish. The first season that sees our people at all represented will be the last for a farthing to pass to or from any such company. A few other trains of thought that "A. E. B." cannot follow will, nevertheless, have to be followed utterly out before he ends the century.

**E. L. Garbett.**

### BACILLI THE CURATIVE AGENTS IN DISEASE.

[33693.]—FIRSTLY, I must thank Mr. Gerard Smith for having for the most part supported my argument throughout; but I would also point out, although I have not stated in so many words, that I believe "the ptomaine produced by the bacilli is the substance which confers after-immunity," yet I am decidedly of opinion that such is really the case; and I am further of opinion that eventually we shall have the process of vaccination instituted, not only as at present for the prevention of small-pox, but also for many other zymotic diseases.

With regard to the opening paragraph in letter 33655, permit me to point out that Mr. L. Hutchings *did* attack me in his previous communication, hence my reply; but as Mr. L. Hutchings in his present communication states he is "not discussing the subject with Mr. Davis, but with the public," I shall after this reply retire from the contest, as practically the public have my views upon vaccination, and nothing can be gained by repetitions. I hope, however, the subject will be thoroughly threshed out, and as I have previously stated, there is much to be said both for and against; yet with such enlightened correspondents as those of the "E.M." we may at least hope to arrive at something like a definite conclusion. I may mention I received through the post 200 letters dealing with this subject, and this will at once show the interest which the matter possesses for the public. Now although I cannot enter into detail with regard to the substance of these communications, I may mention the number upon either side is nearly equal; in fact, there are two in excess *for* vaccination. Most of those *against* vaccination are couched in language similar to letter 33672—namely, somewhat "rabid."

Mr. L. Hutchings (33655), in quoting from Carpenter, says: "There may be motion without life." I have mentioned this motion especially as a physical process in my previous articles under the title of "Brownian movements."

Finally, I may tell Mr. Hutchings that my whole life has been, and still is, engaged in studying and teaching the sciences, and therefore it is scarcely possible for me to omit to take into consideration the "natural chemistry of the land."

In conclusion, I should like to know Mr. L. Hutchings personally and shake hands with him, because if men hold different opinions, such is no reason they should be enemies, and I admire any one who holds to his convictions, whether politically, theologically, socially, or otherwise.

**Frederick Davis.**

26 and 28, Newington-causeway, S.E.

[33694.]—MR. L. HUTCHINGS mistakes his *ipse dixit* for proof of his assertions. Will he, apart from the question of vaccination, give any proof of "the position he has assumed"—viz., that bacteria are the products of, and do not cause, disease?

Of course, by "bacteria" is included the supposed ptomaines. Can he explain the fact that milk from a cow with a tuberculous udder will cause tubercle in those drinking it?

He says that the inoculation of sperm cells, when healthy and well formed, will not produce disease because they are not diseased, and follows this up by a warning not to try it, for sperm-cells in the eyes will destroy the eyeball! Persons who make statements purporting to be scientific facts must surely be expected to give some data upon which their assertions are made. Will Mr. Hutchings kindly say how the fact about sperm cells (I suppose spermatozoa) in the eyes was ascertained? That the Micrococcus gonorrhœa (derived from the urethra) will cause eye-disease is an aged fact; but spermatozoa are not micrococci.

Again, Mr. Hutchings says: "There is no proof that some species of bacteria have any life of their own." I want to fix Mr. Hutchings to one or two particular statements, and I hope he will not attempt, by vague generalities, to elude replying to my question specifically. I want to know what

**Figure 1.1 Page from the *English Mechanic*, 55, 24 June 1892, p. 409**

above page.' 'R.W.J.' describes his experiences of viewing the eclipse at the equator. He comments that 'only an idiot could have refused the evidence of his senses, for the truth of the natural phenomenon of a rotating earth was *felt* as palpably as it was *seen*,' thereby attacking Hampden using experiential evidence rather than astronomical theory. Thomas May acknowledges that Hampden 'only recognises one standard of authority – viz. *The Bible*' and so will, 'without further comment, refer him to Isaiah xl.22.' Hampden contributes in response to the editorial comment the previous week, writing that he does 'not for a moment suppose that any offence is meant' but as he is 'considerably in the minority' he ought to be granted 'every consideration.'[15] The following week F.S.S. echoes the editorial comment, suggesting that 'plain speaking is sometimes necessary. Mr Hampden *is* hopeless, as all paradoxers are.' He is concerned that May might have erred using scripture: 'as far as that verse goes', he writes, 'it might be quoted by Mr Hampden himself.' Sure enough, on the same page is a letter from Hampden that reads: 'Till I read Mr May's letter (28708) I would not have believed that any correspondent of the *E.M.* would have been so grossly ignorant of what he writes about as not to know a circle from a sphere [...] my opponents are certainly in a fog at present.'[16] The Isaiah reference operates within Hampden's domain, and so opens space for him to continue the debate alongside the various contributions of others.

This exchange thus operates in a number of spaces simultaneously. Hampden's flat earth theories, although long dismissed by astronomical science, shift into scriptural debates, philosophy and geography. The co-presence of these domains of knowledge not only denies a single authoritative standpoint, but also ensures that a single author cannot authoritatively pronounce on an issue. Captain Noble, the future President of the British Astronomical Association, submits pseudonymous panoptic astronomical letters under the pseudonym 'FRAS' which seek to participate in all current astronomical controversies and offer astronomical news and reviews of publications.[17] Noble's pseudonym signifies astronomical authority, but his letters form one part of a broader astronomical discourse, with correspondents often asking advice or disputing his opinions. 'FRAS' does not permit other voices simply to dismiss them in order to censor and so maintain his hegemony as the arbiter in scientific matters. For instance, in 1890 'FRAS' refutes the suggestion by 'Tempus' that the positions of the planets affect the weather ('Oh dear! Oh dear! Have we only got rid of the old woman's twaddle about the moon's influence on the weather, that the equally baseless and ridiculous astro-meteorological may be resuscitated?') and suggests that they banish 'such rubbish from the columns of the most widely-circulated scientific journal in England.'[18] This attempt to end a discussion which he believes is unscientific fails. A month later a correspondent returns to the subject, and asks 'FRAS', 'whose useful letters I much admire', for his opinion on the 'Planetary Influence on Weather' knowing that he will continue to refute the connection absolutely. The following number brings the expected response, but in doing so ensures that 'Tempus's' original remark remains part of the text of the *English Mechanic*.[19]

Although contributions are restricted to certain departments, the whole of the text of the *English Mechanic* is available for discussion. This reintroduces those narratives that are marked as owned by an author, and opens them up to the community. For instance, when Kibblewhite experiments by printing a serial novel by Herbert D. Ward in 1892 entitled *A Dash to the Pole*, correspondents treat it like any other item within the text by suggesting better endings and delighting in plot flaws and scientific mistakes (Figure 1.1). The editor only interjects when the terms of entry to the text are transgressed, the letter and comment – as in the example involving Hampden cited above – acting as a printed warning as to etiquette. For instance it is only when the debate over astronomical glasses between George Calver and Mr Linscott introduces personal correspondence into the *English Mechanic* that the editor interjects. When Calver reveals he has told Linscott 'plainly too, that he is "the greatest trumpet-blower on these matters that the *E.M.* ever had"', he is deemed to have violated the codes of the text and so Kibblewhite adds a note that they 'can spare no more space for these "warm" rejoinders' and that none of their readers 'are interested in the private correspondence of our correspondents.' [20] It is likely that editorial interventions determine the sort of contributions that are published, but the diversity of the 'Queries' suggests that a broad range of subjects were permitted. In the number for 2 March 1888 for instance, queries include how to play the piccolo ('Piccolo'); the chemical composition of didymium ('Didymium'); technical questions on how to build a boiler ('Copper Boiler'); 'Egg Problems' gives a mathematical problem, but challenges correspondents to solve it not by 'trial', but by 'arithmetic or algebra'; and even specific queries such as that by 'Minster', who asks 'some kind friend' to explain 'how to polish artificial eyes' as they 'must have a high polish or they are painful to wear' is granted space.[21]

The range of subjects under discussion suggests that it is not the content of each contribution, but rather its performance of community that is at stake. Jurgen Habermas, in his well-known definition of the public sphere, locates its emergence in the masculine spaces of the eighteenth-century bourgeois coffeehouses. These physical spaces allowed private individuals to meet, suspend their economic and institutional relationships, and so act as equals discussing, and so constructing, a 'common concern.' The periodical is a textual manifestation of this:

> In the *Tatler*, the *Spectator*, and the *Guardian* the public held up a mirror to itself; it did not yet come to a self-understanding through the detour of a reflection on works of philosophy and literature, art and science, but through entering itself into "literature" as an object.[22]

Readers of the *English Mechanic* literally were reading about themselves, and participating within the text: the title did not, as Habermas would suggest, embody *the* public, but suggests its own specific public posited on the congruence between its readers and its writers. The epistolary format that permits such a space structures the type of scientific culture that it represents: rather than locate authority within discrete bodies of knowledge or individual correspondents, it instead focuses on the moment of debate, displacing 'truth' as an ultimate end and foregrounding the contingent, immediate and provisional.

### Amateurs and Professionals: *The Observatory* and the *Journal of the British Astronomical Association*

When W.H.S. Monck called for the foundation of the BAA in the pages of the *English Mechanic*, it was because he felt that the RAS no longer fulfilled the needs of amateurs:

> Its subscription is too high, and many of its papers too technical for the amateur astronomers, who now form a pretty numerous body throughout the United Kingdom, while ladies (many of whom take an interest in the science, and have contributed to its progress) are practically, if not theoretically, excluded from the Fellowship of the Royal Astronomical Society.[23]

The Liverpool Astronomical Society (LAS) had provided an alternative model for the wider astronomical community, and its recent decline encouraged Monck, who was its Vice-President, to appeal through the pages of the *English Mechanic* for the establishment of a similar society on a national basis. The formation of the BAA does not repeat models of the professionalization of science with professionals replacing amateurs; rather, it was the means through which they were institutionalized within the discipline.[24] Its *Journal* was edited by E.W. Maunder, a professional astronomer employed in the Solar Section at Greenwich who had previously edited *The Observatory* and would go on to edit the popular science monthly *Knowledge*. The LAS had failed partly because its national ambitions overstretched its resources. The BAA recognized the importance of publications in constituting connections despite geographical distribution and its subscription of half a guinea – twice that of the LAS – largely went towards the cost of publications.[25]

Although half a guinea was considerably cheaper than the annual subscription to the RAS, it did not represent much of a saving on a year's subscription to *The Observatory*.[26] *The Observatory* was not an official publication of the RAS, but a shilling monthly owned and published by the commercial publishers Taylor and Francis. The definite article in its title emphasizes its spatial association with the Royal Observatory at Greenwich: it was founded in 1877 by W.H.M. Christie, who succeeded George Biddell Airy as Astronomer Royal in 1881 and who served as President of the RAS until 1889; and it declared itself 'an indispensable complement to the *Monthly Notices*.'[27] In 1890 it was edited by H.H. Turner and A.A. Common, an amateur and professional who together represent elite astronomy. Herbert Hall Turner was Chief Assistant at Greenwich, the same position as that held by Maunder, and he would become Savillian Professor of

Astronomy at Oxford in 1893. Andrew Ainslie Common was a sanitary engineer by trade who had stunned the RAS with his stellar photographs, winning their gold medal in 1884. He retired from Matthew Hall and Company in 1890, having made enough money to practice astronomy full-time from his home. Both men were well-regarded astronomers with a wide range of international astronomical contacts. They both had strong links with the RAS: Common was Treasurer from 1884–1895 and President from 1895–1897; Turner was on the Council and would serve as President from 1903–1904.

Unlike the *English Mechanic*, where writers and readers are merged within its pages giving readers access to the text and therefore the means for constructing truths within the textual field, *The Observatory* carefully regulates and controls access to its text. Both the *Monthly Notices* and *The Observatory* open with an account of the previous meeting of the RAS, with the latter a month in arrears. *The Observatory*, as a review of the progress of the science, only gives brief summaries of the papers read at the RAS, expecting its readers to either have been there or to have access to the *Monthly Notices*. It also regularly reports the LAS, the BAA and the Royal Meteorological Society, but only gives details for relevant papers and lists of those present. By subordinating the other societies while ensuring that the details of the RAS are only available to its Fellows or readers of the *Monthly Notices*, *The Observatory* acknowledges and aligns itself with the RAS as the source of astronomical authority. However, as its niche in the market was to supplement the papers of the RAS with further discussion and reviews, it had to ensure that those commenting within its textual space were part of the community of elite astronomers that it claimed to address. It did this by representing its authors as the same men who occupied the exclusive spaces of the learned societies and observatories that it discussed. As the editors assumed responsibility for unsigned material, their authority was attributed to the articles.[28]

However, as a review the exclusive space of *The Observatory* was constantly invaded by objects from outside. For instance, correspondence brings the texts of readers within the journal; and reviews, although keeping the object under discussion beyond its space, selectively quotes in order to demonstrate discursive discrimination. In July 1890, *The Observatory* printed an anonymous review of the second volume of George Frederick Chambers' *Handbook of Astronomy*.[29] Chambers was a barrister and Fellow of the RAS and had published extensively in the past twenty years. The review attacked the *Handbook* for its overemphasis on refracting telescopes and insufficient advice for the construction of small observatories. As the reflecting telescope was traditionally the instrument of choice for the amateur, and small observatories could be constructed by amateurs to house their instruments, the anonymous reviewer is challenging Chambers's authority to give them advice. Chambers objects to this criticism, and writes to the editors in an attempt to restore this authority. He includes two letters, duly reprinted, from the authors of the offending section on observatories, Frederick Brodie and T.R. Clapham. The two authors express surprise at the criticism levelled at them, as they claim to be a civil engineer and architect respectively. The editors reprint the letters in order to subvert these claims. Brodie's language is revealed as awkward: he claims that the 'arrangement of rings and grooves for balls of dome is far superior to anything in the shape of wheels so commonly used' and:

> How easy it is to say a thing is 'highly objectionable!' Why does critic not enlighten the public, and give those reasons? This perhaps is not so easy. But Critic has not seen such things before, and not being to him orthodox, they are of course bad.[30]

Brodie also quotes Latin and the editors cannot resist correcting 'Ne sutor crepidan' with the comment 'Supra in the original – Eds.'

The reprinting of Brodie's letter, and the editorial comments, give it an air of burlesque and invoke the caricature of the overeducated artisan. By challenging Chambers through the invocation of Brodie's social class, the editors both affirm their gentility and assert the 'higher' art of astronomy over the 'lower' technical craft of engineering. When Clapham suggests that while the critic 'may know something about a spectroscope or a speculum; [they] had better not pose an architect or a builder', the implication is that *The Observatory* would never do so.[31] The editors thus create a boundary between themselves and Chambers, suggesting that it is he who has violated the text of *The Observatory* by sending these letters. As the editors comment:

> The question as to who is now compromised we must leave [Chambers] to settle with these gentlemen [Brodie and Clapham]; it is due to Mr Chambers that they are now brought into the discussion at all.[32]

Not only then has Chambers weakened his own case by invoking the 'artisans' as authorities, but he has also betrayed himself as a gentleman by drawing them into the discussion. The editors still need to assert their own authority, on behalf of the title, to judge in these matters. They state they have passed on the name of the reviewer to Chambers in case he would like to take the issue further. Chambers does not, even though the following number of *The Observatory* attacks the next volume of his *Handbook*. This review, in the August number as well, is signed A.A.C., the initials of the editor, Common. This suggests that it was Common who wrote the first review: not only was he a former sanitary engineer, but was also a maker of high-quality silver on glass reflectors and his scientific reputation was based on the results he achieved, as an amateur, with a reflecting telescope. Common deftly employs his name as signifier of the appropriate scientific apprenticeship those outside 'high' science must observe before entering the culture espoused by the RAS.

Although *The Observatory* and the *Monthly Notices* mobilized accounts of spatially located practice, they imply that it is in such sites that astronomical practice occurs. Like these two monthlies, the *JBAA* also opens with an account of a meeting – in this case their own – but, as it claimed to represent a distributed community of amateurs, the actual proceedings of the Association were represented as beyond those in London. As Allan Chapman notes, the fact 'that it met on Wednesday afternoons at 5pm at Barnard's Inn, amidst the Inns of Court of London's barrister community, says something about the type of people who were expected to be able to attend the meetings.'[33] In March 1891, the BAA was receiving so many papers from respected amateur astronomers that only two of the 11 were read; the others 'would be more suitable for reading when in print in the *Journal* than for reading aloud in the meeting.'[34] The discussion is given for both of the two papers read, allowing readers access to both the papers and the criticism from the eminent astronomers on the Council. The number of papers published in the *JBAA* foregrounds it as the actual source of the Association, its proceedings almost relegated to a few pages at the beginning. However, the papers are not published in full: each is labelled as an 'Abstract' and, unlike the formalized abstracts described in Chapter Four, vary according to length and content. This disenfranchises the textual community in two ways: they are not provided with printed comments on all papers, and the material they have is severely edited.

The *JBAA* does not structure itself like the *English Mechanic* as an open dialogic field in which readers can participate in the negotiation and constructions of scientific truth. Its president, Captain Noble, had experienced the diversity of astronomical opinion as 'FRAS' in the *English Mechanic* and the BAA adopted a top-down institutional structure that would organize amateur astronomy under the scrutiny of astronomical expertise. In his first Presidential Address, Noble claims:

> The field of research has now become so illimitable that the individual observer must confine himself to a very circumscribed area of it if he is to do any useful work at all. All experience has shown the advantage of the division of labour; and assuredly, that advantage is nowhere more apparent than in the pursuit of observational Astronomy.[35]

The BAA was organized in a structure derived from its predecessor, the LAS. At the top of the BAA was an Executive (Council and Officers) which was composed of well-known astronomical figures. Noble stresses the close correlation between their Executive and astronomical authority invested in the RAS:

> Why, twenty-five out of thirty of our Executive are Fellows of that Society; and of the remaining five, one is officially connected with it, and three are ladies who are deprived by the wrongs of their sex, and, most emphatically, by those alone, from the enjoyment of its Fellowship [sic].[36]

The list of names on the Council and Officers of the BAA does show that most of these twenty five are amateur astronomers – they are not attached to an institution and do not derive an income from the pursuit of their research – however they are also inextricably linked with the RAS, and not just as Fellows.[37] The Vice-Presidents of the BAA, Downing, Roberts and Huggins, were all amateurs, but they were also serving as Secretary, Council Member and Foreign Secretary of the RAS respectively. W.H. Wesley, a scientific illustrator and engraver who had cooperated with Ranyard (the editor of *Knowledge*) on the highly acclaimed eclipse volume of the *Memoirs of the Royal Astronomical Association* of 1879, was on the Council of the BAA and also was Assistant Secretary of the RAS – a permanent post not subject to reelection. The overlap between senior members of both societies affirms the location of astronomical authority in the RAS and the presence of amateurs and professionals within the astronomical elite. For instance on the Council of the BAA are the amateur Sir Howard Grubb and professional Edwin Dunkin. Grubb derived his income from his company, which was one of the leading manufacturers of astronomical lenses in the world; and Dunkin had been Chief Assistant at Greenwich, alongside Turner and Maunder, since Airy's retirement in 1881. The Director of its Coloured Star Section, W.S. Franks, was employed between 1892 and 1904 by the Grand Amateur Isaac Roberts, and so could be described as a professional who produced amateur astronomical research.[38]

The presence of these astronomers at the head of the Association gave it a sense of legitimacy, but only in the terms dictated by the RAS. The structure of the Association, inherited from the LAS, was a top-down model in which areas of research were coordinated by astronomical sections and headed by a recognizable authority in that field. Each month the Directors, all of whom were Fellows of the RAS except Elizabeth Brown and David Booth, provided reports outlining their objectives and results.[39] This division of labour routinized idiosyncratic practices in order to produce large-scale results and, in 1893, the BAA issued its own *Memoirs*, based on those of the RAS. These were not the only way the combined efforts of the BAA would be presented. T.G. Elger, the Mayor of Bedford, former President of the LAS and current Director of the Lunar Section of the BAA, envisioned completing a series of monographs on the moon. Lunar work, according to Captain Noble, is 'an almost inexhaustible field for the younger observer' in which lunar structures 'can only be determined, if at all, by the most painstaking accumulation of detail.'[40] Elger sought to accumulate this detail by circulating a standard set of practices and nomenclature to his observers, and then reinscribing their results for presentation to elite astronomy through his weekly column in *The Observatory*. In December 1890 he wrote in this column that the 'new society promises to furnish more observers willing to take part in definite as distinguished from desultory Lunar observations; hence it may be hoped that ere long something may be accomplished which will be of permanent interest.'[41] Results of permanent interest, Elger suggests, are those that are quantifiable in the abstract space of science as represented by the readers of *The Observatory*.

The observers are being employed like astronomical instruments, producing raw data that must be standardized and tabulated before it can be understood. W.S. Franks, the Director of the Coloured Star Section, had great difficulty with this process. He attempts to regulate his observers, suggesting they 'avoid exposing the eyes to bright or strongly coloured artificial lights', use the same tables, do not observe within 20° of the horizon and, to avoid the colour of the previous star prejudicing the next, move through the list forward and backward so 'any errors arising from this cause would thus neutralise each other.'[42] He also recommends observers use Polaris as a reference star from which he could calculate their individual 'personal equation.'[43] This failed as the differences were even greater for the same observer on separate nights. Undaunted, Franks then uses this as a test for atmospheric conditions and issues his observers with a chart to map colours to numbers.[44] This standard nomenclature would then enable him to calculate a 'mean' colour for each star. In the March number, B.J. Hopkins laments that 'the estimation of star colours will never be placed on a scientific basis until some instrumental method has been adopted.'[45] Franks, conversely, suggests in the same number 'that what is more needed than a standard instrument is a "standard" observer.'[46] By controlling the individual idiosyncrasies of his observers, Franks hopes he can calibrate them sufficiently to replace astronomical instrumentation.

Philip. F. Duke, writing in support of the BAA in *The Observatory* in December 1890, claims it as a 'training-ground for future Fellows of the RAS.'[47] As the RAS was a strictly masculine space, Duke is implying that the BAA only provides an apprenticeship for its male constituents. The amateurs who have been ratified by the RAS and have become Fellows were distinguished from those who required guidance and control. Women were barred from becoming Fellows of the RAS until 1916, and so could only participate from a subordinate position outside the Grand Amateur tradition.[48] With the failure of the LAS, women were effectively disenfranchized from institutionalized astronomy. The formation of the BAA explicitly addresses this, welcoming women and stating 'no expression herein-after used shall be held to debar them from exercising any right or privilege of the Association, or even from filling any office to which they may be elected.'[49] Elizabeth Brown, the meteorologist, sun spot observer and Director of the Solar Section of the LAS, was one of the first correspondents to reply to Monck's letter in the *English Mechanic*.[50] She announces her resignation from the LAS as, now it is returning to a local organization, it ceases to offer 'the impetus of a common bond' and she cannot 'direct the section entrusted to me with any success without a regular and punctual organ such as the *Journal* was.'[51] Brown was swiftly appointed Director of the Solar Section of the BAA and, in the second number of the *JBAA* recommends her section to ladies as they 'have ample time at their disposal, and […] are often skilful in the use of the pencil.' Unlike the more nocturnal branches of the science, the 'sun is always at hand. No exposure to the night air is involved, nor is there need for a costly array of instruments.'[52] Like Franks and Elger, Brown issues directions to her observers to ensure that they produce knowledge in a standardized form. She instructs observers as to the correct paper size and quality, which pencils and colours to use, and directs those with equatorial mounts to use Thomson's discs and the tables issued in the 'Companion' to *The Observatory* to give heliographic longitudes and latitudes.[53] If observers do not have access to this equipment they should indicate the transit of the sun on a standard 8" circle. She is surprised more women do not take up solar observation, and believes that it is the first step 'to an occupation of absorbing interest, and would afford an ever-increasing pleasure previously little dreamed of.'[54] The reward for submitting to this standardization is pleasure, not hope of astronomical recognition.

The reading audience of the *JBAA* does recognize women and they are constructed as amateur in the same way as men. Unlike men, however, there is no way a woman astronomer could get the training through the BAA that led to ratification by the RAS and then perhaps to a Fellowship or an institutional post. Female observers could only remain subordinate to the interests of elite astronomy, even while being directed by its representatives. This division of labour, embodied in the institutional spaces of the BAA and the textual spaces of the *JBAA*, enforces the subordination of amateur astronomy. However, as I explore below, it also entails a risk: readers are not passive and, as Franks discovered, the construction of knowledge varies from space to space.

### *Knowledge* and the Production of Astronomical Space

*Knowledge* was established in 1881 as a cheaper rival to *Nature* but, unable to draw upon the financial support of Alexander Macmillan and the discursive weight of the scientific elite, became a monthly in 1885.[55] When founded as weekly, *Knowledge* was 2d, the same price as the *English Mechanic* but half that of the 4d *Nature*; as a monthly it was 6d, half of that of *The Observatory* but the standard price for late nineteenth-century, middle class monthly magazines.[56] Its editor and founder, Richard Anthony Proctor, opposed the specialization and professionalization of scientific research, and so *Knowledge*, as his mouthpiece, attempted to participate in elite scientific research while elaborating this within a wider audience, drawn from all classes.[57] Between 1888 and 1895, *Knowledge* was contested as a site for science. From a cheap monthly review which offered both an alternative to and criticism of the expensive and institutional publications of elite research, *Knowledge* became a magazine providing didactic scientific material for an interested, but not necessarily scientific middle class.

The advertisements in *Knowledge* from 1888 indicate the imagined interests of its predominantly middle class readership. Between 1888 and 1892, nearly every month carries full-page advertisements for Longmans, Green & Co., who published both *Knowledge* and Proctor before his death; W.H. Allen, the publishers who took on the title after November 1888; and Swan Sonnenschein & Co.[58] Occasionally these were varied with extra pages from publishing houses supporting new publications such *Tinsley's Magazine*. These advertisements, indicating a leisured, book-buying readership with both scientific and nonscientific interests are supplemented by others aimed at the practical needs of scientific readers. For instance the cover of the blue wrapper of *Knowledge* (Figure 1.2) carries advertisements for the famous telescope manufacturers Dollond's, the 'Watkin' barometer, and the lens manufacturer Browning, as well for *Webster's*

**Figure 1.2 Cover of *Knowledge*, 14, December 1891**

*International Dictionary.* These advertisements indicate the presence of a perceived market for astronomical goods, and often feature the same companies who advertise in the *JBAA*.[59]

At the time of his death, Proctor was anonymously contributing most of the content of *Knowledge* from the United States. There were other contributions, notably from his daughter, and extracts from American titles such as

*Cosmopolitan*, and Youman's *Popular Science Monthly*. Proctor so dominated the title that Edward Clodd, who was his subeditor in London, wrote in a hastily prepared obituary that the career of *Knowledge* 'must probably end with that of its conductor.'[60] However, the following month saw *Knowledge* appear as usual, but with a new publisher and editor. Arthur Cowper Ranyard was a friend of Proctor's and not only took over the editorship of *Knowledge*, but also finished Proctor's *magnum opus, Old and New Astronomy*, which he had been writing for 25 years and had just begun serial publication. Ranyard was a well-known astronomer and a regular attendee at the meetings of the RAS. He had made his astronomical reputation through his editorship of the highly acclaimed 1879 eclipse edition of the *Memoirs* of the RAS. Eight years in preparation and overseen by the Astronomer Royal, this illustrated volume summarized the information for every eclipse between 1715 and 1871. As the original diagrams and illustrations were in a variety of formats, Ranyard oversaw a complex negotiation between reproductive techniques to produce what Alex Soojung-Kim Pang describes as 'one of the few volumes that could serve as a tool for scientific research.'[61] Ranyard was a barrister, and therefore precisely the sort of amateur astronomer expected to take a leading role in the BAA.[62] However, although Ranyard attended meetings of the BAA, he did not report their proceedings or even note the formation of the society in the pages of *Knowledge*. Rather than align the journal with this amateur audience, Ranyard used it to provide an income for Proctor's family while establishing a scientific voice for himself.

Ranyard opens his first number of *Knowledge* with an address 'To Our Readers':

> The ablest exponents of science will be invited to contribute articles and letters to its pages, and more space than hitherto will be devoted to Physics and Physical Geography, and to Natural History, including Botany. The space devoted to Astronomy must be somewhat curtailed, but it will probably remain the leading feature of the magazine.[63]

The absence of Proctor and his frequent pieces on astronomy left a vacuum at the centre of the text which Ranyard fills by inviting other science writers to contribute articles. These would provide high quality, explicitly popular pieces which, by expanding the disciplinary scope of the title, could also expand its readership. The extension of higher education in the late nineteenth century, combined with the scarcity of scientific employment, produced a ready supply of authors who would contribute scientific articles for payment.[64] Ranyard shrewdly notes both the availability of these scientific writers, eager for incomes due to the scarcity of scientific jobs, and the potential for a large readership among those studying science, whether as students or as part of the wider market for scientific knowledge. It was these readers that Ranyard hoped would support *Knowledge* and enable him to use the astronomical sections as a medium to reach a more specialist audience of his own.

Ranyard's astronomical articles are consistently bitonal, acknowledging his inherited amateur audience while attempting to create discursive space through which to address the astronomical elite. The reconfiguration of astronomy, associated with the development of large instruments embedded in institutional structures, marginalized and subordinated amateur astronomy. Ranyard identifies these readers, but is careful to distance himself from them. In 'Automatic Recording Instruments at the Lick Observatory', an article which guides the reader around this newly completed space for professional astronomy, Ranyard writes that it 'has been thought worth while to describe [the instruments] in *Knowledge* as they are of so simple a character that they could easily be made by amateurs.'[65] Ranyard here facilitates his readers through his prose, allowing them to imitate the various technical inventions within the observatory, but he himself knows that imitation simply affirms the dominance and superiority of the elite observatory. As it is amateur readers who maintain the circulation of *Knowledge*, Ranyard ensures that this reading audience are present within his address, but not its main target. Ranyard, who made his astronomical reputation overseeing a publication that could substitute as object of study for the actual phenomena, once more attempts to use reproductive technology to shift the object of astronomical discourse from the stars in the sky to the images on the page.

In astronomy the phenomena that are observed are very distant. As Holly Rothermal writes:

> Accurate depiction of phenomena was an exceedingly difficult problem in the field of astronomy. The science was observational and mathematical; one could observe, record, calculate and theorize, but rarely could one experiment. Indeed, astronomy was often lauded as the most "ideal" science because of its non-reliance on laboratory experiments, and the intangibility and inaccessibility of phenomena. However, these same characteristics necessitated accurate reproduction and representation of these remote phenomena. Since astronomers could not rely on the replicability of an event or object in the laboratory, it had to be convincingly and carefully depicted.[66]

Photography, as a mechanical means of capturing an image, has been associated with astronomy from its inception.[67] Technological developments such as the dry plate in the 1860s negated many of the methodological difficulties (and indeed dangers) of photography and established the camera as a mechanical eye, not subject to the variations of the observer.[68] It was not long before photography began to surpass the eye as a tool for research: in 1884 the Henry brothers discovered the nebulosity of Merope through photography and, when E.E. Barnard discovered a comet with photography in 1890, even this traditionally amateur domain had been invaded.[69] By the 1890s a 'distrust of artistic judgement and interpretation', as well as a willingness to exclude the artisan from scientific practice, marked older reproductive techniques as old-fashioned and part of an amateur tradition.[70] Telescope size and power no longer provided astronomical authority, instead participation in the astronomical elite became associated with the institutionalization of a process that created uncontested, stable images that might be studied as scientific objects in their own right.

Bruno Latour, in his influential essay 'Drawing Things Together', further defines what he calls 'inscriptions.' If, in scientific debate, the side that triumphs is 'the one who can muster the most well-aligned and faithful allies', then this privileges a certain type of writing and imaging which makes *'this agnostic situation more favourable.'*[71] This evidence consists of 'objects which have the properties of being *mobile* but also *immutable, presentable, readable* and *combinable* with one another.'[72] These objects, the inscriptions, are the final stage in a process which gestures back to the original phenomena. Michel Foucault, in the *Order of Things*, politicizes resemblance as part of a discursively controlled practice rather than an unproblematic mimetic similitude.[73] Lynch and Woolgar argure that similarities are 'exposed in the way diverse texts are brought together' and so juxtaposition, rather than 'the inherent characteristics of an "original", provide the material basis for the disclosure of similitudes.'[74] Latour's notion of 'circulating reference' develops this further by locating truth value as circulating within a traceable chain:

> It seems that reference is not simply the act of pointing or a way of keeping, on the outside, some material guarantee for the truth of a statement; rather it is our way of keeping something *constant* through a series of transformations. Knowledge does not reflect a real external world that it resembles via mimesis, but rather a real interior world, the coherence and continuity of which it helps to ensure.[75]

By bringing the phenomena into the chain, instead of maintaining it in a distinct external ontological realm, Latour conceives of reference as the process of ensuring similarity through a culturally codified re-presentation. Scientists, Latour claims, 'start seeing something once they stop looking at nature and look exclusively and obsessively at prints and flat inscriptions.' If scientists – or readers generally – accept the stability of the links of the chain, then they also accept the presence of the phenomena, despite the evident transformations and translations it has undergone to reach them.[76]

In *Knowledge*, Ranyard attempted to mobilize the inscriptions of elite science in an otherwise popular periodical text. Ranyard had previously encountered the shifting status of various reproductive codes in his work on the eclipse edition of the *Memoirs,* and he exploited new reproductive technologies to provide a range of images within the text of *Knowledge.* Before 1888 most of the illustrations within *Knowledge* are wood-cuts but, almost immediately after assuming the editorship, Ranyard begins to experiment with photographic reproductions of engravings.[77] As these were cheaper, easier to size and set, and could be prepared more quickly than existing technologies, they were a much more convenient way of bringing images to the page. From April 1889 Ranyard began to print collotype reproductions that were not interspersed with the letterpress, but printed on higher quality paper and inserted into the journal on separate leaves.[78] The additional plates were included within the cost of *Knowledge* and did not illustrate the letterpress like those images interspersed within it, but instead were the subject for Ranyard's own astronomical discussions. Demarcated from the rest of the number but unmistakeably part of it, these images seemed to reproduce the 'aura' of the source image, uniquely situated in space and time.[79] It is through these photographic plates that Ranyard attempted to remain within elite scientific discourse: they are presented as the subject of scientific discourse, and so replace the phenomena they represent. By reproducing such high-quality images and then distributing them widely Ranyard is effectively removing the need for expensive instruments and displacing the observatory as the authoritative site for astronomical research.

It is the space between the reproduction and the source image that is important. They are collotype reproductions from either photographs, film or plates which are enlarged, reduced, reversed or reoriented in order to produce a standard image which can then be studied and compared with others. Both the production of the plates and the developments from them are the results of processes occurring at unique moments is space and time. Latour writes that 'it is not the inscription by itself that should carry the burden of explaining the power of science; it is the inscription *as the fine edge* and *the final stage* of a whole process of mobilization, that modifies the scale of the rhetoric.' The reproductions on the page are the result of a process that involves printers, photographic engineers, as well as the original negative from the observatory itself. Ranyard exploits this chain as a '*cascade* of ever simplified inscription that allow harder fact to be produced at greater cost.'[80] By appropriating the institutionalized cascade that produces the negative as stable scientific object, Ranyard places the space of scientific research onto the page.

In February 1889 Ranyard inserts a full-page wood-cut engraved from one of Isaac Roberts's famous photographs of the Andromeda nebula (Figure 1.3). This image was newsworthy, and Ranyard is careful to acknowledge the contribution of his amateur readers as he presents it to them.[81] He claims that this is the first time this image has been reproduced in the astronomical press, and he is keen to establish its status so that he can present his ideas to the whole of astronomical science. However, as an engraving, the image is immediately suspect: not only does it involve (and clearly show) an unacceptable amount of human interpretation in its preparation but, as a reproductive code relying on white and black line, it is not very effective at capturing the subtle gradations of nebulosity. To counter this Ranyard emphasizes Wesley's role in the drawing and engraving of the photograph, and states that it took him 'many days.'[82] This still leaves the question of nebulosity on the original photograph however, and Ranyard not only ensures that it is present, but that it has been verified by a second image.[83] Photography, although widely accepted as the only reproductive method to produce accurate scientific images, was still perceived as limited due to its spatial-temporal conditions: although composite drawings, which combine the results from a number of photographs, were now distrusted due to the human rendering of the image, the astronomical photograph, despite long exposure times, was still considered to represent the phenomena from a specific time and place.[84]

GREAT NEBULA IN ANDROMEDA.

*From an Original Negative taken by Mr. Isaac Roberts, F.R.A.S., December 29, 1888, with an Exposure of Four Hours.*

**Figure 1.3 'Great Nebula in Andromeda',** *Knowledge,* **12, February 1889, facing p. 75**

The following month Ranyard admits there has been 'great interest attaching to this photograph' and so it 'has been thought advisable to give this reproduction by a photographic process to compare with and check the woodcut given in our last number' (Figure 1.4).[85] By reproducing Roberts's photograph 'by a new process',

THE NEBULA IN ANDROMEDA

*From a Photographic Enlargement by* Mr. Isaac Roberts, *of his Negative of 29th December, 1888.*

**Figure 1.4 'The Nebula in Andromeda',** *Knowledge*, **12, March 1889, facing p. 108**

Ranyard hopes to buttress the authenticity of Welsey's engraving.[86] According to Ranyard, the differences between the photograph and the engraving are not serious: the block had been divided into two in order to speed the engraving and ensure it was ready for the February number of *Knowledge* but:

Unfortunately the block was not put together again with sufficient care, and a white line corresponding to the division between the two parts of the block shows across a part of the middle of the page, which corresponds to nothing on the photograph. Some white dots have also been put in by the engraver to increase the brightness of the southern end of the nebula, which have come out as small stars on the woodcut, and have no existence upon the photograph. But otherwise the woodcut gives a very satisfactory representation of the original negative, except that it was impossible to show the structure in the brighter central part of the nebula, which has a stellar nucleus, and the faintest regions of nebular light. The same difficulty has to be contended with in the photographic reproduction now given, and in addition the smaller stars shown in the original negative are lost.[87]

Ranyard argues that the two processes are equivalent, with each introducing its own flaws. However, by relying on his 'new process' to verify and validate the older one, Ranyard is implying that photographic reproduction is more successful in bringing the extratextual photograph to the page.

The original negative remains the inscription, but Ranyard is beginning to blur the distinction between it and the reproduction. By July 1890 he explicitly claims that the reproduction is equivalent to the negative. He inserts photographs of the Milky Way recently taken by E.E. Barnard at the Lick Observatory (Figure 1.5). Holden had announced these in the *Monthly Notices* the previous December, and Barnard had supplemented this paper with one of his own in March.[88] On seeing the image in the *Monthly Notices*, Ranyard wrote to Holden for permission to reproduce them.[89] These pictures, prepared by Barnard and then reproduced in *Knowledge*, actually surpass the observatory as a site for astronomy:

The exquisite photographic plates which illustrate this paper have been prepared from an enlargement and six contact copies from original negatives kindly made for our readers by Professor Barnard of the Lick Observatory. They are well worthy of close examination, for they afford the reading public an opportunity of studying the structure of certain rich portions of the Milky Way, such as only the possessors of the largest telescopes have hitherto enjoyed. Indeed, I am probably right in saying that that these plates show more of the structure of the milky way than can be seen by the eye with any telescope, for the gradations of brightness are accentuated, if smaller stars are not shown, and the eye can never grasp at one time, in the eye-piece of a telescope, as wide an area as that presented in these photographs.

Ranyard identifies his reproductions with negatives, the ambiguity of the word 'plate' eliding the difference between the two. He claims they 'bear examining with a hand magnifier, when it will be seen that many of the regions which appear to the naked eye to be tinted with a uniform tint, break up into a stippling of points corresponding to minute stars.' Ranyard is so confident of the quality of his reproductions that on 'such a close examination it will be evident that many streaks

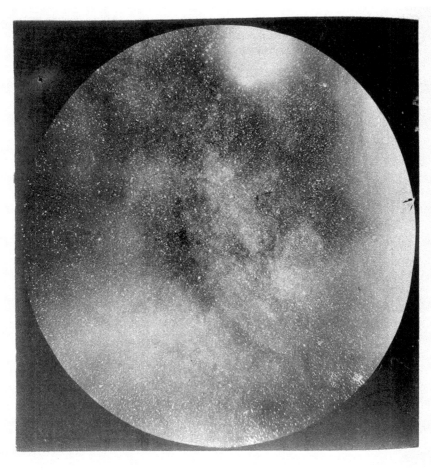

Region of the Milky Way to the South-west of the Trifid Nebula.

E    N

S    W

*From a Photograph taken at the Lick Observatory by Prof. E. E. BARNARD.*

The White patch at the top of the picture is the over-exposed image of Jupiter. The Trifid Nebula is just within the border of this patch nearest its lowest part. The dark patch referred to is near to the centre of the plate. Scale—1 inch = 1° 48'.

*Direct Photo Eng. Co., Limited, 9, Barnsbury Park, N.*

**Figure 1.5 'Region of the Milky Way to the South-west of the Trifid Nebula',** *Knowledge*, **13, July 1890, facing p. 174**

and markings which at first sight might be taken for photographic stains or imperfections are really due to groups of stars.'[90]

This merges the inscriptions with the text of *Knowledge*, wresting them from the closed spaces of the observatory or learned society and situating them on the page. This legitimates Ranyard's speculations, in this case that the Milky Way consists of many streams and structures which we are looking through and that these are complemented by some mysterious dark structures.[91] Holden, in his paper in the *Monthly Notices*, warns that the photographs are intended as '*diagrams*' and that 'successive copyings of the negative [...] have naturally injured the pictorial effect.'[92] Ranyard believes that *Knowledge*, because of these reproductive techniques, is an equivalent scientific resource: the following March, when discussing further the structure of the Milky Way, he cites both Barnard's paper in the *Monthly Notices* alongside his own article in *Knowledge*.[93]

It is this article, 'The Milky Way in the Southern Hemisphere', from March 1891, that provokes attacks upon Ranyard's photographic reproductions. He reproduces images of the Milky Way in the southern hemisphere taken by H.C. Russell, Director of the Sydney Observatory (Figure 1.6). These photographs, like Barnard's reproduced the previous July, were taken with identical apparatus in similar conditions. Just like Ranyard's earlier reproductions, these too 'bear close examination with a magnifying glass', but reveal much less nebulosity than Barnard's images. He suggests that perhaps Russell's images have been developed from the same negative, and the difference in brightness is 'due to inequalities in the sensitiveness of different parts of the film of Mr Russell's plates.' However, Mars is visible in only one photograph, so Ranyard concludes that there 'seems, therefore, to be no doubt that we have two independent photographs, and we seem to have evidence of a very rapid change in the brightness of the southernmost of these two star-clusters.'[94]

Ranyard claims that this rapid change of brightness is evidence of 'a resisting medium which occupies a vast region of the Milky Way' and that 'perhaps the whole nebulous circle which surrounds the sky is not one vast nebula.' This radical conclusion rests on the stability of photographic reproduction: although Ranyard elides the difference between his reproductions and those of the astronomers, he still carefully establishes that the differences are not due to the photographic process. From the images in *Knowledge*, Ranyard claims that the stars have changed. His reproductions provide 'evidence of the existence of a vast variable nebula which undergoes changes in the relative brightness of its parts with surprising rapidity.' This legitimates his speculative conclusion that the 'variability in brightness over so vast a region, if substantiated by future photographs, will need us to assume the existence of forces travelling far more swiftly than light or electricity, and giving rise to the synchronous dimming or glowing of light giving matter.'[95]

In May 1891 Ranyard prints a letter from Barnard, criticizing the reproductions:

> I have no hesitation in attributing the difference between these pictures (taken with instruments so similar) entirely to the development of the negative. As I have taken occasion to remark elsewhere (*Pub ASP* II 10), the utmost care must be exercised in the development of the Milky Way pictures to bring out the cloud forms clearly and strongly.

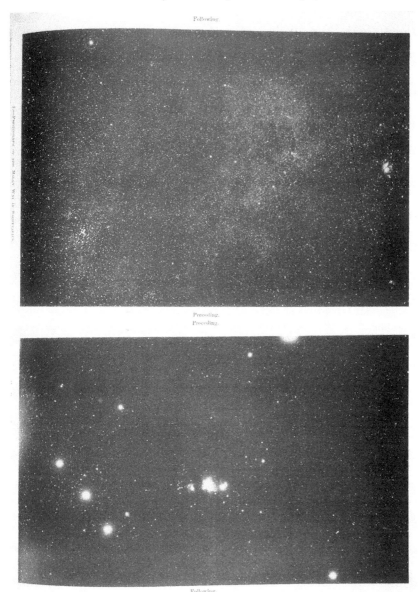

**Figure 1.6 'Photograph of the Milky Way in Sagittarius' and 'Belt and Sword of Orion Showing Great Nebula',** *Knowledge,* **14, March 1891, facing p. 50**

He warns that it 'is an extremely uncertain thing to compare two photographs like these', then overdevelops his own print to prove that the reproduction caused the differences. Ranyard prints this image, and Barnard confidently declares that the 'two photographs are identical in every respect, except that there are apparently several large stars near the middle of Mr Russell's picture which are not shown on mine, and which are undoubtedly defects in his plate.' He concludes with a final warning that:

> I would remark here, as a caution, that it is extremely unsafe to judge of the actual relative brightness of different surfaces, such as the Milky Way presents, from photographs which have been treated differently in point of time and development. A partially brought out configuration will have in many cases, a decidedly different aspect from that of a carefully and thoroughly developed one.[96]

Ranyard is forced to defer to Barnard, and admits that the stars that Barnard sees on Russell's plate were probably due to errors introduced during reproduction.

By conceding that his reproductive process is not a transparent stage in a chain which leads to the stars, Ranyard can no longer claim *Knowledge* as a site for elite scientific practice. When Russell's response arrives from Australia in September and vigorously defends his images, Ranyard supports Barnard:

> There is an intimate connection between the dark areas on Mr Barnard's photograph and the disposition of the stars that could not be due to chance, and the bright structures are altogether different in form from the patches in which fog shows itself on an overdeveloped picture. From my experience in reproducing pictures of nebulae, I can fully confirm Mr Barnard's statement that the density of the nebulosity and fainter cloud forms is very dependent on suitable development.[97]

Ranyard cannot claim more expertise in producing images than Barnard, and must agree with him in order to salvage his astronomical hypotheses regarding the structure of the stars, even at the expense of his more radical speculations which depend upon the validity of Russell's images. Although Ranyard continues to enthusiastically reproduce photographs in *Knowledge* (he even announces some more from Russell in the above editorial note), they are increasingly treated as illustrations and do not attract similar discussions from such eminent astronomers.

The authority to create inscription is once more located with the scientific elite. Like the representation of scientific practice in *The Observatory*, the process of generating inscription, and the inscriptions themselves, remain situated in the authoritative space of the observatory. Ranyard, using his reproductions to denote reality (which they can only do if they are inscriptions on the edge of a cascade that leads back to the observatory and up to the stars), threatens to situate scientific practice in his text and so make it available to his readers. By attacking the final stage in the chain, the astronomers restore the extratextual negative as the inscription and so sustain their position as final arbiter in astronomical matters.

**Conclusion: Power and the Paradoxers**

In the same number of *The Observatory* that reports the first meeting of the BAA, there is an article by the editor, H.H. Turner, entitled 'Paradoxers.' Turner gives details of a box at the Royal Observatory, 'Miscellaneous Science and Studies', which has a subsection 'Astrology, Squaring the Circle & c.' into which correspondence from paradoxers is placed. The Astronomer Royal and founder of *The Observatory*, W.H.M. Christie, answers all these letters, 'politely treating them as intelligent inquiries, though he knows that they actually deserve to be burnt as the product of crass ignorance.' Paradoxers are characterized as overzealous missionaries, whose enthusiasm has 'gone wrong' giving them 'pure self-confidence.' The Astronomer Royal, located in the preeminent authoritative site of British astronomy, humours these missives, literally sent from the margins, in order to politely patronize.[98]

Ranyard attempts the opposite. His use of reproductive technology mobilizes the resources from the observatory into his text. What is at stake is the material status of the images. The institutional structures located in the observatory allow the production of images that can operate as surrogates for the stars themselves. Ranyard asserts the same for his reproductions in *Knowledge*, in effect suggesting that the stars on the page are equivalent to the stars in the sky. This assumption of astronomical authority is also an assumption of property, and predictably it is rebuffed. However, while the controversy continues, the material status of the images is unresolved. For Ranyard they are the stars in the sky, constrained by the spatial-temporal conditions of their capture; for the astronomers, they are deficient copies from a superior source. The criticism that is levelled at Ranyard is not so much for his astronomy, but for his publication: *Knowledge* is no place for scientific objects, as its readers (not to mention its editor) are not capable of accurately judging their status.

This chapter has explored the way textual space configures objects, but also situates these textual spaces, and the objects they carry, within wider spatial configurations. The *English Mechanic*, which I return to in the Conclusion to this book, relativizes both its contributions and the ideas that they contain; *The Observatory* and the *JBAA* inscribe institutions within their textual spaces, but whereas the former locates a specific extratextual space as the origin of its authority, the latter is entirely constituted by the circulation of the texts themselves. Ranyard's experiments with visual technology in *Knowledge* foregrounds the mobility of space, and demonstrates that the final material status of the objects is not a pre-given, but must be established. My next chapter explores further the role of the visual in the mobilization of space, and discusses the disorientating capability for two spaces to coexist at the same time.

**Notes**

1   Agnes. M. Clerke, *The System of the Stars* (London, 1890), p. vii.
2   See Allan Chapman, *The Victorian Amateur Astronomer* (Chichester, 1998), p. 99.
3   The issue of professionalism is complex. For a good introduction see Jack Morrell, 'Professionalization', in *Companion to the History of Modern Science*, eds Robert C. Olby and others (London, 1990), pp. 980–89; Morris Berman, '"Hegemony" and the Amateur Tradition in British Science', *Journal of Social History*, 8 (1975), 30–50; A..M. Carr-Saunders and P.A. Wilson, *The Professions* (Oxford, 1933); and Anne Witz, 'Patriarchy and the Professions: The Gendered Politics of Occupational Closure', *Sociology*, 24 (1990), 675–90. For professionalism in astronomy see Chapman, *Victorian Amateur Astronomer*; Simon Schaffer, 'Astronomers Mark Time: Discipline and the Personal Equation', *Science in Context*, 2 (1988), 115–45; and John Lankford, 'Amateurs versus Professionals: The Controversy over Telescope Size in Late Victorian Science', *Isis*, 72 (1981), 11–28.
4   'Montaigne', *Essays*, cited in *English Mechanic*, 47, 20 April 1888 (1888), 167.
5   P.F. Duke, 'Planetary and Star Matters', *English Mechanic*, 49, 22 March 1889 (1889), 91.
6   M.M. Bakhtin / P.N. Medvedev, *The Formal Method in Literary Scholarship*, trans. Albert J. Wherle (1978; Baltimore, 1991), p. 129.
7   See Bruno Latour, *Science in Action* (Cambridge MA, 1987), especially chapter one, pp. 23–62.
8   See W.H. Brock, 'The Development of Commercial Science Journals in Victorian Britain', in *Development of Science Publishing in Europe*, ed. A.J. Meadows (Amsterdam, 1980), p. 112.
9   Anonymous, 'Advertisements', *The Times*, 23 March 1895 (1895), 2.
10  'F.C.A.', 'Practical Electric Bell Fitting', and 'An Analytical Chemist', 'Simple Exercises in Technical Analysis', both in *English Mechanic*, 47, 20 April 1888 (1888), 159–60, 60.
11  For the Bedford canal wager see Alfred Russel Wallace, *My life, a Record of Events and Opinions*, 2 (New York, 1905), pp. 381–93 and John Hampden and George Peacock FRGS, *Is the World Flat or Round?* (Gloucester, 1871).
12  'Sigma' [John T. Sprague], 'The Southern Heavens and a Flat Earth – The Moon's Heat – Dying By Effort of Will,' *English Mechanic*, 47, 20 April 1888 (1888), 168. Notice the string of narratives 'Sigma' hopes to address with his letter. For the identity of 'Sigma' see Brock, 'Development of Commercial Science Journals', p. 114.
13  John Hampden, 'The Southern Heavens and the Flat Earth', *English Mechanic*, 47, 27 April 1888 (1888), 190.
14  Hampden, 'Southern Heavens', 190.
15  'E.L.G.', 'Flat Earth v. Round Earth'; 'R.W.J.', 'The Late Lunar Eclipse'; Thomas May, 'Flat Earth v. Round Earth'; John Hampden, 'Gradients', *English Mechanic*, 47, 4 May 1888 (1888), 216–17.
16  'F.S.S.', 'Flat Earth v. Round Earth' and John Hampden, 'Flat Earth', *English Mechanic*, 47, 11 May 1888 (1888), 234, 235.
17  For instance see 'FRAS', 'American Criticism on the Lick Observatory – Books Worth Reading – Velocity of the Earth in her Orbit – Ordnance Datum – other Planetoids – Telescope – Adjusting Eyepiece', *English Mechanic*, 47, 20 April 1888 (1888), 167.

18  'Tempus', 'Weather Forecast', *English Mechanic*, 51, 30 May 1890 (1890), 294–5. 'FRAS', 'Stellar spectra: the Henry Draper Memorial – Erratum – Alioth and other Circumpolar Stars and the *Nautical Almanac* – Whether "Forecasts" are Worth Making? – Alcoholism – Eclipses – Aneroid Barometers – Rifle-Ball and Gravity – "Si Momentum Requiris" – Dr Terby and "FRAS" – Second Revolution (?) of the Earth – Pendulum – Achromatic Object-Glass', *English Mechanic*, 51, 13 June 1890 (1890), 334. For further discussion of this strategy, see Lynn Pykett, 'Reading the Periodical: Text and Context', *Investigating Victorian Journalism*, eds Laurel Brake, Aled Jones, Lionel Madden (London, 1990), p. 16.

19  A. Elvins, 'Planetary Influence on Weather', *English Mechanic*, 51, 8 August 1890 (1890), 512. For the response see 'FRAS', 'Errata – Saturn – Electricity and Photography: the Duration of a Lightning Flash – Planetary Influence on Weather – Huggins – Rain-Gauge – Deviation of the Magnetic Needle – The Liverpool Astronomical Society – Grant's "History of Physical Astronomy" – Astro-Meteorology – "Fellows" of Societies – Moonrise from Snowdon – Camera Lucida', *English Mechanic*, 51, 22 August 1890 (1890), 552.

20  G. Calver, 'The Telescope', *English Mechanic*, 51, 1 August 1890 (1890), 488.

21  'Flauto', 'Piccolo'; 'R.H.A.', 'Didymium'; 'R.A.B', 'Copper Boiler'; 'A.C.G.', 'Egg Problem'; 'Minster', 'Polishing Artificial Eyes', *English Mechanic*, 47, 2 March 1888 (1888), 20–21.

22  Jürgen Habermas, *The Structural Transformation of the Public Sphere*, trans. Thomas Burger with the assistance of Frederick Lawrence (London, 1989), p. 43.

23  W.H.S. Monck, 'An Amateur Astronomers' Association', *English Mechanic*, 51, 18 July 1890 (1890), 445.

24  Lankford, 'Amateurs versus Professionals', 11.

25  Chapman records 9s 6d went towards publications, *Victorian Amateur Astronomer*, pp. 243–71.

26  In 1890 the subscription was £2 2s. Anonymous, 'Report of the Council to the Seventieth Annual General Meeting of the Society', *Monthly Notices of the Royal Astronomical Society*, 50, February 1890 (1890), 142.

27  Anonymous, untitled advertisement, *Companion to the Observatory* (1889), unpaginated. See W.H. Brock and A.J. Meadows, *The Lamp of Learning* (1984; London, 1998), p. 140.

28  See 'Eds' [A.A. Common and H.H. Turner], 'Correspondence', *The Observatory*, 13, August 1890 (1890), 276.

29  Anonymous, 'Publications', *The Observatory*, 13, July 1890 (1890), 252–5.

30  Frederick Brodie, untitled correspondence, *The Observatory*, 13, August 1890 (1890), 279.

31  T.R. Clapham, untitled correspondence, *The Observatory*, 13, August 1890, (1890), 279.

32  Anonymous [A.A. Common and H.H. Turner], untitled editorial note, *The Observatory*, 13, August 1890 (1890), 279.

33  Chapman, *Victorian Amateur Astronomer*, p. 252.

34  Anonymous, 'Report of the Meeting of the Association Held March 25, 1891', *JBAA*, 1, March 1891 (1891), 296.

35  Anonymous, 'Report of the Meeting of the Association Held November 26, 1890', *JBAA*, 1, November 1890 (1890), 50.

36  Anonymous, 'Report of the Meeting of the Association Held November 26, 1890', 50.

37  Anonymous, 'Officers and Council,', *JBAA*, 1, October 1890 (1890), 8.

38  Chapman, *Victorian Amateur Astronomer*, p. 375, 377.

39  Brown was barred because of her gender, Booth probably because he was associated with the amateur astronomical discipline of meteor-spotting.

40  Anonymous, 'Report of the Meeting of the Association Held November 26, 1890', 50.

41  T.G.E. Elger, 'Selenographical Notes', *The Observatory*, 13, December 1890 (1890), 387–8.

42  W.S. Franks, 'Coloured Star Section', *JBAA*, 1, November 1890 (1890), 71.

43  Franks, 'Coloured Star Section', 72.

44  W.S. Franks, 'Coloured Star Section', *JBAA*, 1, December 1890, (1890), 123.

45  B.J. Hopkins, 'The Determination of Star Colours', *JBAA*, 1, March 1891 (1891), 304.

46  W.S. Franks, 'The Determination of Star Colours', *JBAA*, 1, March 1891 (1891), 302.

47  Philip F. Duke, 'British Astronomical Association', *The Observatory*, 12, December 1890 (1890), 391.

48  Or indeed from within the observatories themselves. Despite being a mathematics graduate from Girton, Annie Russell (as she was before she resigned from the Royal Observatory to marry E.W. Maunder in 1895) was paid £4 a month as a 'Lady Computer' – the same as the teenage boys on apprenticeships. Chapman, *Victorian Amateur Astronomer*, p. 156, 282.

49  Anonymous [E.W. Maunder], 'Rules of the British Astronomical Association', *JBAA*, 1, October 1890 (1890), 9.

50  For Brown see Mary Creese, 'Elizabeth Brown, solar astronomer', *JBAA*, 108 (1998), 193–7 and Mary R.S. Creese, *Ladies in the Laboratory? American and British Women in Science, 1800–1900: A Survey of Their Contributions to Research* (London, 1998), pp. 236–7.

51  E. Brown, 'An Amateur Astronomers' Association', *English Mechanic*, 51, 25 July 1890 (1890), 463.

52  E. Brown, 'Solar Section', *JBAA*, 1, November 1890 (1890), 59.

53  The 'Companion' was issued annually, cost 1s 6d, and consisted of tables detailing stellar statistics.

54  E. Brown, 'Solar Section', 59.

55  See Bernard Lightman, '*Knowledge* Confronts *Nature*: Richard Proctor and Popular Science Periodicals', in *Culture and Science in the Nineteenth Century Media*, eds Louise Henson and others (London, 2004), pp. 199–221.

56  For instance the *Strand* and *Review of Reviews*, as well as popular scientific monthlies such as the *British Naturalist*, were 6d.

57  Although Lancashire disputes any working class readership (p. 48), the *English Mechanic*, which was also a tuppeny weekly rival to *Knowledge*, had a readership which often proclaimed its working class status. See also Lightman, '*Knowledge* confronts *Nature*', p. 206–7.

58  Longmans also published Agnes M. Clerke, a contributor to *Knowledge* and Edward Clodd, for a time its subeditor.

59  For instance advertisements for Dollond's appear in both titles. See Anonymous, 'Dollond's', *JBAA*, 2, October 1891 (1891), unpaginated. The advertisements in *The Observatory* tended to be aimed at institutions, and made much of the status of their clients. See for instance anonymous, 'E. Dent & Co.', *The Observatory*, 13, December 1890 (1890), unpaginated. The *Monthly Notices* did not carry advertisements. For the *English Mechanic* see the Conclusion below.

60 Edward Clodd and Capt Noble, 'In Memoriam: Richard Anthony Proctor', *Knowledge*, 11, November 1888 (1888), 265.

61 Alex Soojung-Kim Pang, 'Victorian Observing Practices, Printing Technology, and Representation of the Solar Corona (I): The 1860s and 1870s', *Journal of the History of Astronomy*, 25 (1994), 267.

62 Not only were many of the founders of the BAA – such as Monck – in the legal profession, but they also met at Barnards' Inn in London as noted above.

63 A.C. Ranyard, 'To Our Readers', *Knowledge*, 12, November 1888 (1888), 1.

64 D.S.L. Cardwell, *The Organisation of Science in England* (1957; London, 1972), pp. 111–86. Cardwell claims there were only about 590 BSc graduates between 1880–1900 in the whole of the country, p. 161.

65 A.C. Ranyard, 'Automatic Recording Instruments of the Lick Observatory', *Knowledge*, 12, January 1889 (1889), 58.

66 Holly Rothermal, 'Images of the Sun: Warren De La Rue, George Biddell Airy and Celestial Photography', *British Journal for the History of Science*, 26 (1993), 146.

67 Larry J. Schaaf, *Out of the Shadows: Herschel, Talbot, and the Invention of Photography* (London, 1992), pp. 1–23.

68 Pang, 'Victorian Observing Practices (I)', 253–4.

69 D. Norman, 'The Development of Astronomical Photography', *Osiris*, 5 (1938), 590.

70 Alex Soojung-Kim Pang, 'Victorian Observing Practices, Printing Technology, and Representation of the Solar Corona (II): the Age of Photomechanical Reproduction', *Journal for the History of Astronomy*, 26 (1994), 71.

71 Bruno Latour, 'Drawing Things Together', in *Representation in Scientific Practice*, eds Michael Lynch and Steve Woolgar (London, 1990), p. 23. Emphasis is Latour's.

72 Latour, 'Drawing Things Together', p. 26.

73 Michel Foucault, *The Order of Things* (London, 1970), especially p. xx.

74 Michael Lynch and Steve Woolgar, 'Introduction: Sociological Orientation to Representational Practice in Science', in *Representation in Scientific Practice*, p. 7.

75 Latour, *Pandora's Hope* (Cambridge MA, 1999), p. 58.

76 Latour, 'Drawing Things Together', p. 39.

77 See for instance David Reed, *The Popular Magazine in Britain and the United States, 1880–1960* (London, 1997).

78 A collotype was a new reproductive technique which used a light sensitive albumen gel to create plates from which high quality copies could be made. See Pang, 'Victorian Observing Practices (I)', and A.C. Ranyard, 'The Collotype Process and Photo-engraving', *Knowledge*, 13, February 1890 (1890), 71–2.

79 See Walter Benjamin, 'The Work of Art in the Age of Mechanical Reproduction', *Illuminations*, ed. and trans. Hannah Arendt (Frankfurt, 1969) pp. 220–37.

80 Latour (1990), pp. 39–40. Emphasis is Latour's.

81 A.C. Ranyard, 'The Great Nebula in Andromeda', 12, February 1889 (1889), 75–6

82 Ranyard, 'The Great Nebula in Andromeda', 76. Wesley had also produced Huggins's eclipse images from the 1883 Royal Society expedition. See Barbara J. Becker, 'Priority, Persuasion, and the Virtue of Perseverance: William Huggins's Efforts to Photograph the Solar Corona Without an Eclipse', *Journal for the History of Astronomy*, 31 (2000), 230.

83 Ranyard, 'The Great Nebula in Andromeda', 75.

84 Pang, 'Victorian Observing Practices (I)', 256.

85  Anonymous [A.C. Ranyard], 'The Great Nebula in Andromeda', *Knowledge*, 12, March 1889 (1889), 108.
86  Anonymous [A.C. Ranyard], 'The Great Nebula in Andromeda', 108.
87  Anonymous [A.C. Ranyard], 'The Great Nebula in Andromeda', 108.
88  Edward S. Holden, 'On Some Features of the Arrangement of Stars in Space', *Monthly Notices of the Royal Astronomical Society*, 50, December 1889 (1889), 61–4; E.E. Barnard, M.A., 'On Some Celestial Photographs Made With a Large Portrait Lens at the Lick Observatory', *Monthly Notices of the Royal Astronomical Society*, 50, March 1890 (1890), 310–14. For the strained relationship between Barnard and Holden see Donald E. Osterbrock, 'The Rise and Fall of Edward S. Holden (1)', *Journal for the History of Astronomy*, 15 (1984), 81–127 and William Sheehan, *The Immortal Fire Within: the Life and Work of Edward Emerson Barnard* (Cambridge, 1993).
89  For the correspondence between Barnard, Holden and Ranyard see the Ranyard MS 3, Royal Astronomical Society, London.
90  A.C. Ranyard, 'On the Distribution of the Stars in the Milky Way', *Knowledge,* 13, July 1890 (1890), 174
91  Ranyard, 'On the Distribution of the Stars in the Milky Way', 175; Sheehan, *Immortal Fire Within*, pp. 264–77.
92  Holden, 'On Some Features of the Arrangement of Stars in Space', 64. Emphasis is Holden's.
93  A.C. Ranyard, 'The Milky Way in the Southern Hemisphere', *Knowledge*, 14, March 1891 (1891), 51.
94  Ranyard, 'The Milky Way in the Southern Hemisphere', 50–51.
95  Ranyard, 'The Milky Way in the Southern Hemisphere', 51.
96  E.E. Barnard, 'On the Comparison of the Photographs of the Milky Way in $\alpha$=17H 56M. $\delta$=-28° in *Knowledge* for July 1890, and March 1891', *Knowledge*, 14, May 1891 (1891), 93.
97  A.C. Ranyard, untitled editorial note, *Knowledge*, 14, September 1891 (1891), 173; H.C. Russell, 'On the Comparison of Photographs of the Milky Way', *Knowledge*, 14, September 1891 (1891), 172–3.
98  H.H. Turner, 'Paradoxers', *The Observatory*, 13, November 1890 (1890), 341–4.

# Chapter Two

# The Spectacular Spaces of Science and Detection in the *Strand Magazine*

> Those gaily proficient providers of serials and short stories for *The Strand* and other magazines were pedestrian writers in a non-derogatory sense. Their feet were firmly planted squarely on a common ground, where the surface was solid and familiar, where there was no need to look beyond the actual and the familiar.[1]

The periodical, as a fragmentary genre predicated on combinations of heterogeneous content, gestures to a range of different spaces simultaneously. The introduction of new imaging technologies in the 1890s, coupled with innovations in printing technology, permitted a further range of times and spaces into the text. George Newnes's *Strand Magazine* was the first and most successful of the sixpenny illustrated monthlies that dominated the late nineteenth-century trade. This chapter explores the *Strand* and demonstrates how, despite the much-proclaimed 'pedestrian' nature of its content, the genre it exemplifies actually compassed a wide range of material that was designed to seduce a middle-class readership. By exploiting new imaging and reproductive technologies, the *Strand Magazine* offered its readers access to an unprecedented array of subjects, presented in a range of formats, gathered together to be consumed simultaneously. Although critics have recognized Newnes's innovative publishing strategies, they often overlook the appeal of such a product for its middle-class readers. Reginald Pound suggests the *Strand* achieved its success as it 'faithfully mirrored their tastes, prejudices, and intellectual limitations' and so 'drew a large and loyal readership that was the envy of the publishing world.' Pound claims that Newnes provided mental comfort for his middle-class readers, and this perpetual reassurance ensured their continued support. He suggests the magazine 'radiated the "wonder of the world," that naïve, sincere, bright-moving quality which disarms sophistication and puts cynicism to flight. Responsible yet *dégagé*, developing its own ethos of dignity and popularity, it became as much a symbol of immutable British order as Bank Holidays and the Changing of the Guard.'[2] More recently Kate Jackson claims the *Strand* 'represents a unique example of the way in which the reflection model of periodical literature is more consistent with the method and character of some periodicals than of others' as it 'continued to confirm the familiar.' For Jackson, and to an extent Pound, it is this complimentary reflection that allowed the *Strand* to become 'a powerful cultural determinant.'[3]

In this chapter I will explore how 'solid and familiar' this 'common ground' is. I suggest that rather than simply reflect the middle-class world of its readers, the *Strand* uses the heterogeneity inscribed in its format to posit the coexistence of other realities. Reading the *Strand Magazine* is to be repeatedly reminded of these other times and spaces and, although they often signal the superiority of the middle-class world of the reader, they simultaneously offer the transgressive thrill of the strange. Science and technology play an important part in this: not only were the outcomes of scientific and technical endeavour often spectacular, but they also produced unexpected congruences of space and time. In the previous chapter I discussed the way Arthur Ranyard's use of photographic reproduction both presented his readers with the restricted products of the observatory while also claiming a link to the stars themselves. Similarly, by gesturing outside itself, the *Strand* continually presents its readers with exotic contexts that can be made subject to middle-class reading strategies. It is only by recognizing the strange that buttresses this stubbornly familiar text that we can understand why its readers returned, month after month, in such impressive numbers.

**Adventures of a Man of Science**

The *Strand* was one of the most successful of the sixpenny magazines that appeared in the 1890s, its first issue selling 300,000 copies.[4] Its success was due to the combination of attractive letterpress combined with generous illustration, a formula that the magazine retained until its demise in 1950. In the 1890s the magazine was about 120 pages a month, containing an average of 14 articles and was enclosed within about 100 pages of adverts selling a range of consumer goods. Each number of the *Strand Magazine* was relatively self contained: serial articles are scarce and rarely do narratives stretch between numbers. Reginald Pound claims that the 'middle classes of England never cast a clearer image of themselves in print than they did in the *Strand Magazine*.'[5] Indeed, the *Strand Magazine*, like the goods in its advertising pages, presented itself as a vital commodity through which to construct middle-class identities.

Newnes was able to provide a wide range of images by exploiting and developing new print technologies.[6] From its first issue the title promised a picture on every page, and Newnes exploited engravings, lithography and half-tone photography in order to invoke a highly visual world. Modelled on American monthlies such as *Scribners' Magazine*, but priced at 6d rather than a shilling, Newnes seized upon developments in both the production of paper and techniques in printing so that in the first six months of 1895, the 712 pages of the *Strand* featured 842 illustrated blocks, 44.7% of which were half-tones.[7] Not only then was Newnes exploiting the relatively new technology of half-tone reproduction to exceed his promise of a picture for every page, but he was also ensuring a large proportion of them were reproduced photographs. The *Strand*, using original drawings and agency photographs as source material for half-tones and engravings, was both a consumer and a manufacturer of images in the late nineteenth century.

It was not just the images that were commodified in the text of the *Strand*. Newnes gained a reputation for his financial dealings with his literary contributors. His payments were relatively generous (Arthur Conan Doyle initially received £4 per thousand words which was the same as his agent's better-known client Margaret Oliphant, but just below Eliza Lynn Linton, who earned £5) and were issued on acceptance rather than publication.[8] Payment varied according to who his contributor was: after just four months from their first appearance in the *Strand* in July 1891, Doyle could ask for £50 per Sherlock Holmes story, irrespective of length; when Newnes requested a further series of twelve in February 1892, Doyle demanded and received £1000.[9] This was the period when authorship itself became professionalized with the formation of the Society of Authors and the rise of the literary agent. Jackson deeply implicates the *Strand* in this process, claiming that in 'a period of crisis for established literary values and English literature, it offered a compromise between artistic quality and journalistic innovation, a combination of commercialism and professionalism, and thus a solution to the problem of literary succession: middle-brow literature.'[10] By paying substantial amounts for contributors' work and then championing his authors within the text, Newnes raised the social status of his authors. Increasing the social distance between magazine writing and journalism, Newnes could create a new professional role for his contributors which relied on an interplay between the representation of the writers and their letterpress. This strategy raised the magazine writer to a position of authority within the middle-class world constructed by Newnes, a strategy that relies on the blurring between this construction and the material object that was read.

The *Strand* was complicit in the ratification of the increasing number of professions that challenged existing hierarchies in the late nineteenth century. Newnes succeeded in this strategy because the *Strand* employed an iconography of notable figures. The presence of writers, lawyers, engineers and actors alongside more established notables such as the clergy, politicians and the aristocracy created a coterie of eminent social types. Regular serials such as 'Portraits of Celebrities at Different Times of their Lives' obfuscated individual differences and represented prominent individuals as examples of types. Newnes's use of the interview further enabled the individual to stand for the type: its voyeuristic gaze affirmed that the private life was as meritorious as the public.

This was not uncontroversial. Scientists were an established part of the iconography of notability employed within the *Strand Magazine*, appearing as both exemplars and objects of gentle satire in fiction, but this appropriation of the image of science aroused substantial anxiety with those who sought to manipulate it for their own ends.[11] In 1894 H.G. Wells compared the professional skills of the writer of fiction with those desirable for the scientific popularizer. In his article 'Popularising Science' in *Nature*, Wells, then a recent graduate of the Royal

College of Science, argues for the importance of popular science in the professionalizing context of the late nineteenth century. He writes 'that in an age when the endowment of research is rapidly passing out of the hands of private or quasi-private organizations into those of the State, the maintenance of an intelligent exterior interest in current investigations becomes of almost vital importance to continued progress.' Although Wells claims that he is 'a general reader' and 'a reviewer for one or two publications', his article actually conceals a vested interest. Recognizing that there 'is still a considerable demand for popular works, but it is met in many cases by a new class of publication from which philosophical quality is largely eliminated', Wells outlines a criteria for successful popular science written by scientifically-qualified writers such as himself. [12]

The appearance of this article in *Nature* further politicizes Wells's remarks. *Nature*, because of its weekly periodicity and network of high-profile contributors, had established itself, by the 1890s, as the leading review of scientific research. One of the recurring themes in its leading articles was for further state endowments of research. Its editor, J. Norman Lockyer was notoriously successful at securing government funding for his own work and campaigned eagerly for increased state funding for scientific enterprise.[13] Wells's contribution to *Nature* is part of this project: Wells identified the paucity of scientific positions in the late nineteenth century and sought to create another professional terrain, that of popular science writing, which could support those qualified as scientific workers. Wells, therefore, is not only addressing elite scientists, both professionals and amateurs, but also that generation of scientifically educated workers, of which he was one, who had passed through the expansion of university scientific education in the second half of the nineteenth century only to find a lack of opportunity to practice what they had learned.[14] Julie Ann Lancashire links this with the wider movement for the endowment of scientific research:

> Popularizations played an invaluable part in the acquisition of a broadly based acknowledgement of and popular support for science and its status as a profession [...] In their attempts to achieve this and thereby obtain status, recognition and rewards, professional scientists endeavoured to grasp control of this means of presenting science to various publics within society by ousting scientific writers and amateurs, and replacing them with professional scientists and their acolytes.[15]

Wells's article, strategically placed in *Nature*, must be read in this context. In appealing for a formalized popular science, Wells is complicit in the editorial ideology of *Nature* while seeking a discursive terrain of his own.

In order to affirm popular science as an enterprise for qualified scientists, Wells insists on a certain tenor of writing. He claims that 'scientific exponents who wish to be taken seriously should not only be precise and explicit, but also absolutely serious in their style.'[16] This seriousness would both allow science writing to be a 'proper' employment for the scientist and also be a way to dismiss those who traditionally contributed popular science to the periodicals. In attacking what he describes as 'Badgers and Bats' articles, Wells suggests that this sort of subject matter, chosen only for its alliteration, is unscientific and therefore not the domain of scientists. Unexpectedly, Wells then links the professionalization of science writing with short story writing. As well as 'seriousness', Wells calls for 'orderly progression and development.' This he calls 'inductive reading', and he believes this method underlies the success of detective fiction:

> The taste for inductive reading is very widely diffused; there is a keen pleasure in seeing a previously unexpected generalization skilfully developed. The interest should begin at Its opening words, and should rise steadily to its conclusion. The fundamental principles of construction that underlie such stories as Poe's 'Murders in the Rue Morgue,' or Conan Doyle's 'Sherlock Holmes' series, are precisely that should guide a scientific writer. These stories show that the public delights in the ingenious unravelling of evidence, and Conan Doyle need never stoop to jesting. First the problem, then gradual piecing together of the solution. They cannot get enough of such matter.[17]

It is tempting to read too much into this. Wells, in 1894, had published a number of short stories and essays in the *Pall Mall Gazette* and *Pall Mall Budget* but had only published scientific text books as monographs.[18] *The Time Machine*, Wells's first serial work and the story that would make his literary reputation, had been partly serialized as *The Time Traveller* in the *National Observer* before being aborted after its editor, W.E. Henley, left in March 1894. The *Time Machine* would appear in the *New Review*, which Henley began to edit at the end of 1894, between January and July 1895. Wells, at the beginning of his long career as an author of fiction, is here celebrating the parallels between two well-known short stories, both published in periodicals, and his projected model for science journalism.[19] Blurring the discursive boundaries between novel writing and journalism, fiction and nonfiction, science and detection, and periodicals and books, Wells seems to dissolve generic differences in a single narratorial strategy.

But Wells has a more specific goal here: the aspect of Poe and Doyle that he is identifying with is their method. In Poe's 'Murders in the Rue Morgue', the narrator, when describing the analytical method of the detective Dupin, states that 'the necessary knowledge is that of *what* to observe.'[20] The narrator ventriloquizes the entire narrative, from the details of the crime to Dupin's solution, to entertain the reader with the detective's methods. It is this controlled unveiling of the evidence that Wells praises. The popular science writer lacks not Dupin's abilities but the narrator's narrative method:

> He writes first of all about Badger A. 'We now come,' he says, 'to Badger B;' 'then another interesting species is Badger C;' paragraphs on Badger D follow, and so the pavement is completed. 'Let us now turn to the Bats,' he says. It would not matter a bit If you cut any section of his book or paper out, or shuffled the sections, or destroyed most or all of them.[21]

For Wells it is the performance of a scientific narrative, rather than representations of scientific observation, that provides the scientific value of popularisation.

This emphasis on method resembles the philosophy of science espoused by Karl Pearson in his *Grammar of Science*, published two years previously. For Pearson 'the scientific habit of mind' is 'an essential for good citizenship' and, as it 'may be acquired by all', 'the readiest means of attaining to it ought to be placed within the reach of all.'[22] As this habit can only be learnt through the practice of method Pearson, like Wells, criticizes contemporary popularizations that dwell overly on results. 'That form of popular science', he writes, 'which merely recites the results of investigations, which merely communicates *useful knowledge*, is from this standpoint bad science, or no science at all.' By distancing his version of popular science from the older discourse of utility, Pearson seeks to align popularization once more with science itself. 'The first work of any genuine work of science', he writes, 'however popular, ought to be the presentation of such a classification of facts that the reader's mind is irresistibly led to acknowledge a logical sequence – a law which appeals to the reason before it captures the imagination.'[23] Popular science, for Pearson, will civilize because it encourages the mind to acknowledge, follow and perform scientific method.

Pearson, in appealing to method, locates himself within a long tradition of such appeals by nineteenth-century scientists. When he claims that '[*t*]*he unity of all science consists alone in its method and not in its material*', Pearson is echoing the earlier well-known figures like Whewell, Mill, Jevons and Herschel who deployed method for a variety of discursive ends.[24] However, Pearson does not employ method discourse for institutional ends, but to claim society as an appropriate domain of scientific practice. He argues that the late nineteenth century is 'an era of rapid social variation [...] an era alike of great self-assertion and of excessive altruism' in which opposing traits jostle each other in the urban environment. However, this is not just sociological analysis as '[t]he same individual mind, unconscious of its own want of logical consistency, will often exhibit our age in microcosm.' Only by training the mind in scientific method can such mental contradictions be resolved:

> The scientific man has above all things to aim at self-elimination in his judgements, to provide an argument which is true for each individual mind as for his own. *The classification of facts, the recognition of their sequence and relative significance in the function of science*, and the habit of forming a judgement upon these facts unbiased by personal feeling is characteristic of what we shall term the scientific frame of mind.[25]

As discussed in Chapter One, this rational training was institutionalized in institutions marked by class and gender. Pearson, who believed all social conflicts arose from the want of logical reasoning, often, despite his intentions, assumed an arrogant masculinist contempt for those who disagreed with what was for him an unproblematic, essential subject position.[26] When he claims that the 'true aim of the teacher must be to impart a knowledge of method and not fact', Pearson is at once reclaiming science popularization as a province of a masculine discourse while simultaneously seeking to perpetuate an ideologically loaded politics under the guise of neutral scientific rationality.[27] This is exactly the same method that Wells describes as 'inductive reading', but Wells locates it in both the pedagogical texts of popular science and the popular texts of detective fiction.

Holmes dies in 'The Final Problem' in December 1893, but had such an impact on late nineteenth-century culture that Wells refers to him six months later and expects the readers of *Nature* to know who he was.[28] Holmes, a success from his first appearance in the *Strand Magazine* in July 1891, became one of its leading personalities and, famously, 'took on a greater reality than [his] creator.'[29] Peter McDonald warns:

> Yet if the character had a consistently unplanned influence over the course of his author's career, and a mythical life that went far beyond his creator's intentions, we cannot reduce this to a cartoonish postmodern struggle between a helpless creator and his mythopoetic creation. The contest was, more plausibly, between a strong, albeit never omnipotent, author and the new conditions of literary production in the 1890s.[30]

Doyle's presence in 'Portraits of Celebrities at Different Times of Their Lives' in December 1891 alongside Bismarck, Andrew Lang and Mary Alexander both establishes him as a 'real' person and also ratifies his importance to bourgeois society as represented in the *Strand*.[31] December 1891 marked the end of the first series of six Holmes stories, and Doyle was being admitted into the coterie of famous celebrities in recognition of their success. Equally, Doyle's appearance in a recognizable variation of the monthly 'Illustrated Interviews' called 'A Day with Dr Conan Doyle' in August 1892, comes at the end of the second series of six stories which complete the *Adventures of Sherlock Holmes*.[32] The last of the stories, 'The Adventure of the Copper Beeches', appeared in June 1892, and Newnes advertised the return of Holmes the following month.[33] 'A Day with Dr Conan Doyle' fills the space between this announcement and the eventual return of Holmes in December 1892 while also usefully maintaining his textual profile in order to encourage sales of the *Adventures of Sherlock Holmes*, published as the first volume of the *Strand Library* in October.[34] Doyle's presence in the resolutely nonfictional spaces of the *Strand* are, as McDonald suggests, connected to the technologies of literary production: however, functioning to further promote Holmes, Doyle, and the *Strand Magazine*, these spaces blur the boundary between the creator and his creations, subordinating both to the ideological ends of the title by representing them equally as part of its constructed world.

Ronald R. Thomas claims the *Strand* 'drew an indistinct boundary between truth and fantasy, imaginative literature and journalistic reportage, offering a context in which the Holmes stories occupied a special place.'[35] Like the individual mind in Pearson's *Grammar*, Doyle's stories capture the textual instability of the

*Strand* in microcosm and his narrative techniques portray a figure who sets about to resolve the boundaries between fact and fiction using the 'science' of detection. As Thomas writes, 'the great detective's task was to re-establish such boundaries by sifting out fact from fiction, transforming the lies and silences of criminals into the truth by measuring their words against the more authoritative voice of science with which he spoke.'[36] The success of the *Strand* was predicated on the presentation of images – often with an uncertain extratextual ontology – to be consumed as objects of middle-class desire; the Holmes stories enact, through their exposition of scientific method, the structuring of this fantastic space.

Doyle's use of Watson as a frame narrator for Holmes's adventures highlights the struggle for narrative agency that underlies both the detective's and, according to Wells and Pearson, the scientist's role in society. Holmes, as Thomas suggests, always 'points out the lie of the personal (as represented by Watson's narratives) over against the truth of the impersonal (as represented by his scientific methods).'[37] In 'The Copper Beeches', for instance, Holmes claims Watson has 'erred, perhaps, in attempting to put colour and life into each of your statements, instead of confining yourself to the task of placing upon record that severe reasoning from cause to effect which is really the only notable feature about the thing.'[38] Just as Pearson saw scientific method as a way to neutralize the contradictions inherent in the personal, Holmes claims his approach, because it depends on infallible method, allows him to perceive the truth behind the textual accounts in newspapers or the spoken accounts of his clients. However, Wells promotes Watson's versions of Holmes's adventures, rather than Holmes's method itself. If Holmes signifies scientific method, then Watson's frame narration popularizes the idea of that method into the textual space of the *Strand Magazine*.

There is a distinct difference between what Holmes claims he is doing and what Watson represents him doing. Holmes's various statements are a representation of scientific method, while Doyle's narrative, which melts into that of the fictional Watson, is an act of popularization. For Wells these narratives already embody enough scientific method for him to recommend them as a model for popularization. The tales therefore work on two levels: they represent a man claiming to 'do' science, while also embodying that method in their structure. Pearson claims scientific method consists of the classification of facts and the recognition of their sequence: Holmes, who represents the 'facts' of science, often discourses on this method for the benefits of the reader, who is textually embodied in Watson; Doyle's narrative structure, which is again represented through Watson, is a second translation of method – this time a demonstration which fits structurally into the generic spaces of the *Strand*.[39] If Doyle does not 'play fair' with the reader, failing to give all the clues or allowing Holmes to operate outside of the narrative, it is because his popularization, appealing to the reason *and* the imagination, demands it. Neither the representations nor the narrative method can be described as strictly scientific, but both, in different ways, perpetrate the myth of unified scientific method that was so often espoused by scientists.

Holmes does not actually practice science; instead it is signified through his utterances and actions.[40] This has led many commentators to see his science as a sham.[41] His science of observation and classification, the judicious selection and ordering of facts which allow him a privileged view of the truth, often relies on a culturally constructed Huxleyan typology. In 'A Case of Identity' Holmes reads the body of Mary Sutherland and, finding plush on her sleeves, a mark on her wrist, 'the dint of a pince-nez at either side of her nose', ventures 'a remark upon short sight and typewriting, which seemed to surprise her.'[42] The signs of her labour have marked themselves upon her body: the machine which provides part of her income by marking blank pages has also rendered her legible.[43] Appealing to a lexicon of feminine work, Holmes then reads Mary's social position and connects her to the sexual economy that drives the plot.

The success of the Holmes stories encouraged Newnes and his literary editor Herbert Greenhough Smith to pursue others of the same type. These subsequent detective stories maintained the generic features introduced by Doyle and exploited by the *Strand*. In July 1892, after the first series of twelve Holmes stories had ended, a series called 'A Romance from a Detective's Casebook' by 'Dick Donovan' begins. 'Dick Donovan' was both the name of J.E. Preston Muddock's hero, a special constable from Glasgow, and also the pseudonym under which much of his crime fiction was published. The editorial note in the same number (see above) reassures readers that Holmes will return and that meanwhile 'powerful detective stories by other eminent writers will be published.'[44] Although the detective 'Dick Donovan' predates Holmes, it was only after the demonstrable acceptance of the genre by the readers of the *Strand* that he appeared in the magazine.[45]

Thomas claims that the body 'presented itself to an empirical culture as a material expression of the individual person at a moment when the nature of the subject was as contested and undetermined as it was.'[46] The detective represented a privileged expert, a professional who could decode the body and uncover the hidden truth of identity. The first story in the new 'Donovan' series demonstrates this clearly. Donovan, who narrates the tale himself, is investigating the theft of an antique skull from a seemingly locked room. Unlike Holmes, he is interested in the wealth the skull represents, rather than the idiosyncrasies of the case, but he nevertheless adopts Holmes's characteristic pose 'to make a study' of his client the Colonel. When Donovan visits the scene of the crime he 'reads' the countenances of the Colonel's servants but nothing strikes him; the Colonel's son, however, 'seemed to suffer from an unconquerable lassitude that gave him a lifeless, insipid appearance. He was very dark, with dreary languid eyes, and an expressionless face of a peculiar sallowness.' Employing the familiar iconography of the opium eater, with the feminized appearance usually associated with Asiatic foreigners in 'oriental' discourse, Donovan's description quickly reveals to the reader who the guilty party is.[47]

The reading of bodies had become almost a cliché in the late nineteenth century. The belief that the middle-class virtue of character was legible in the physiognomy of the subject established a strong tradition of observation that detective fiction thrived upon. Just as morality could be read in the brow of the observed, there was also the familiar notion that any moral deviation would indelibly mark the body. In 'Adventures of a Man of Science', which began publication in July 1896, L.T. Meade and Clifford Halifax claim to have taken down verbatim the words of the protagonist, Paul Gilchrist.[48] Gilchrist is very much a scientific amateur, and his private income means that he need not solve crimes for profit. In '5 – At the Steps of the Altar', the entire plot revolves around Gilchrist's identification of purity and vice from the bodies he encounters. Standing in as an anaesthetist, Gilchrist opens the patient's shirt and notices 'a large violet patch nearly the size of the palm of the hand; it was red near the edges, and looked inclined to ulcerate.' He does not mention this to anybody, and the next time he encounters the patient, Colonel Normanton, he is wooing a 'dark eyed slender girl of about twenty.' She is of striking appearance, 'dressed, very simply, in white, and gave an instant impression of great purity and innocence.' This overdetermined symbolization contrasts her with the Colonel, to whom she is engaged to marry. Arriving at the church just in time, Gilchrist reveals that the Colonel is a leper and so prevents the now racialized marriage. This disease, which hints at illegitimate racial contact in the past, lies concealed from all but the medical man and so becomes subject to his scientific / imperialist authority.[49]

Gilchrist demonstrates the easy overlap between the detective and the scientist, and these tales affirm Thomas's conviction that the detective, anthropologist, or the criminologist 'read in the body the scientifically predetermined identity of the person, a skill that was developed at the very moment when Great Britain needed to secure its identity as the predestined ruler of a great global empire.'[50] For instance in the first of the stories, '1. The Snake's Eye', a valuable diamond has been stolen. Gilchrist does not share the suspicions of the police and believes Laurence Carroll, the former lover of the owner of the diamond, innocent. When it appears that Carroll will be imprisoned, the Indian guard of the diamond appears in Gilchrist's laboratory:

> I glanced up at him, and was immediately struck with the great change in his appearance. When last I had seen him he had appeared as a strikingly handsome specimen of his race – thin and wiry, upright as a dart, with beautiful, supple limbs. Now his face was emaciated, his eyes had the expression of anguish which one sometimes notices in a suffering dog, his figure was bowed, and at intervals long, shuddering sighs escaped his lips.

Gilchrist confirms his guilt with the twin technologies of racial knowledge ('men of Gopinath's nationality had swallowed precious stones before') and X rays. The alliance of science with the imperial project converts the previously private location of the laboratory into a component of imperial surveillance. When Gilchrist speculates whether his X rays 'might be the means of discovering crime, and so save an innocent life', he displaces the original colonial theft of the diamond in India with the later theft, this time by Gopinath, which it has provoked.[51]

The man of science rarely uses his science to solve the various crimes he comes across. Instead – like Holmes and Donovan – it is his highly developed powers of observation that allow him to detect the aberrant. Although Gilchrist, Donovan and Holmes are dilettantes, operating outside of institutionalized science or the police, they are all privileged observers of the body and so participate in the rise of a masculine forensic science.[52] An article on police anthropometry in the *Fortnightly Review* claims that when the policeman 'learns to trust nothing to the eye, and relies on the inflexible laws of mathematics to decide for him', then cases of mistaken identity will disappear.[53] The eye is no longer trustworthy; instead only the rigid laws of science, embodied in the scientific rational observation of the detective, can perceive the essential truth of character.

Yet these stories are also part of the *Strand Magazine*. As well as gesturing to larger extratextual discursive formations, they also present a way of reading that enables readers to decode the visual world of the *Strand*. As mentioned above, the *Strand* participated in the commodification of images within its pages: Newnes, exploiting new reproductive techniques, made images that were available externally on the market a component of his sixpenny text. This is especially true of portraiture: as John Plunkett has shown, the proliferation of *cartes-de-visites* at the end of the nineteenth century both democratized and commodified notions of celebrity.[54] Actors, sportsmen and women and singers were all commodified alongside more traditional representatives of the social hierarchy. Newnes's monthly 'Portraits of Celebrities at Different Times of Their Lives' transformed the quotidian nature of the *cartes* and instead rendered it part of the larger commodity of the periodical.[55]

Catering to what Walter Benjamin calls the 'desire of contemporary masses to bring things "closer" spatially and humanly', 'Portraits of Celebrities', like the studio window, presented a national bricolage which celebrated the contemporary prominence of a range of different figures in an accessible, commodifiable and quotidian material form (see Figure 2.1).[56] Whereas portraits in the National Portrait Gallery were only admitted after the death of the sitter, 'Portraits of Celebrities' was predicated on their contemporary fame. However, unlike the *cartes*, which featured photographic portraits, the engraved reproductions distance the viewer from the subject. Newnes's choice to use engravings is revealing: they were far more expensive than half-tone reproductions and, unlike the half-tone, were difficult to enlarge to incorporate with text on the page; but, as an older reproductive medium, had a connection with art that photography did not.[57] As each portrait was marked as to its source, most being photographs, Newnes decided to sacrifice the utility of photographic reproduction and its potential to link the image on the page with the sitter in the studio, instead choosing to render all the original source portraits in a common medium.[58]

### LORD KELVIN.

#### Born 1824.

WILLIAM THOMSON, LORD KELVIN, was born at Belfast on the 26th of June, 1824. His father was a distinguished mathematician, and was Professor of Mathematics, first in Belfast, and afterwards in Glasgow University. At a very early age, Lord Kelvin showed extraordinary mathematical ability; and he passed with great distinction, first through the University of Glasgow, and then through Cambridge, where

AGE 45.
*From a Photo by John Fergus, Largs.*

have done good service to seamen. His electrical instruments are the standards all over the world. He is President of the Royal Society and member of every important scientific society at home and abroad. In January, 1892, the Queen conferred upon him his peerage. He held the Colquhoun Sculls, at Cambridge, for two years. He is a sailor at heart and an enthusiastic yachtsman; and, among amateurs, a more keen lover of music it would be difficult to find.

*From a)*          AGE 28.          *[Photograph.*

he gained the Second Wranglership and the first Smith's Prize. He became Professor of Natural Philosophy in the University of Glasgow in 1846, at the age of twenty-two; and he still holds that office. He was one of the pioneer band who laid the first successful Atlantic cable, in 1858. In 1866 Her Majesty conferred the honour of knighthood on him for his distinguished services to the science and practice of submarine telegraphy. Lord Kelvin is the author of many inventions. His mariner's compass and sounding machine

PRESENT DAY.
*From a Photo. by W. & D. Downey*

**Figure 2.1 'Lord Kelvin', 'Portraits of Celebrities at Different Times of their Lives', *Strand Magazine*, 5, June 1893, p. 590**

This strategy highlights the visual parity of these disparate portraits and renders up their temporal narrative to the scrutiny of the reader in the present. As all copy for the *Strand Magazine* had to be ready four weeks before publication, the *Strand* presented a peculiar, ahistorical contemporaneity.[59] The series of portraits which make up 'Portraits of Celebrities' lead up in a teleological sequence to this present, and the final portrait totalizes the past of the sitter. In engraving the portraits, Newnes and his art editor, W.J.K. Boot, present a series of images in which certain physiognomical aspects would change whereas others would remain the same. By perceiving these changes over time, readers would be able to trace developing faculties, spot the origins of that person's talents, or even rarely trace a gradual decline. The genre of detective fiction, with its traditions of disguise and deception, both challenges and reaffirms this reading strategy. Drawing upon representations of scientific practice, stories such as 'The Adventures of Sherlock Holmes', 'A Romance from a Detective's Casebook' and 'Adventures of a Man of Science' provided readers with a method with which to gaze upon the reproduced portraits of prominent figures, to discern their inner-qualities through their physiognomy, and affirm the character described in the written testimonies that accompany the portraits.

Doyle's stories do more than elaborate a technology of surveillance that can render the body legible. Holmes is rarely confronted with a body; instead, he must use his talents to recreate the narrative despite its absence. In 'The Boscombe Valley Mystery', Holmes identifies a stone as the murder weapon and claims the murderer is 'a tall man, left-handed, limps with the right leg, wears thick-soled shooting-boots and a grey cloak, smokes Indian cigars, uses a cigarette-holder, and carries a blunt penknife in his pocket.' It is the things that remain that allow Holmes to read the body: the footprints and their spatial arrangement furnish Holmes with information regarding the unusual boots, the limp and the height of the suspect; the ash and the stump of the cigar allow him to deduce the use of the cigarette holder and the blunt penknife. Holmes's method is the 'observation of trifles', i.e., the overlooked histories of things, and it is from the intersections between these that he can construct the history of the body.[60]

In some Holmes cases there is no body, whether of murderer or victim. 'The Blue Carbuncle', a seasonal Holmes story in the January 1892 number of the *Strand*, opens with a hat. Unlike Watson who, 'too timid in drawing [his] inferences' finds nothing, Holmes reveals that the man is intellectual, was wealthy but has fallen on bad times, has had a moral retrogression which suggests drink, and that his wife has ceased to love him.[61] Each of these deductions is drawn from the hat, and it is the hat's shared history with its owner that Holmes actually narrates. The plot follows a blue gem from the Hotel Cosmopolitan to Baker Street, via the inside of a goose. In tracing this passage (necessarily in reverse), Holmes uncovers the history of the carbuncle from the moment it was taken. He identifies the thief because he too is trying to trace the history of the gem (he took the wrong goose) and their paths (their histories) intersect. 'The Blue Carbuncle' offers a case study in the 'intimate hybridization between humans and artefacts, which [suggests] that social networks are unable to cohere without the delegated intentionality and agency of things.'[62] In all the stories Holmes consistently demonstrates to Watson and the reader the presence of other histories connected to the objects around which we structure society. Holmes does not so much convert bodies into texts, as relativize the history of the body with the objects that surround it.

This too finds its analogue elsewhere in the *Strand*. Whereas 'Portraits of Celebrities' plays to the politics of physiognomy, 'Illustrated Interviews', with longer biographies and a wider range of illustration, must establish character from a broader cultural repertoire. The interview was a highly intrusive mode that transgressed the boundary between the public and the private in order to bolster each. The private text, as read in the domestic surroundings of the interviewee, is presented to the reader so that they can ratify that person's public prominence. The chatty tone of Harry How's interviews in the *Strand* is contrasted with reproduced photographs that present the interior of the home, complete with bric-à-brac, and encourage the reader to partake in the intrusion along with the interviewer. Often the interviewee's artworks are photographically reproduced, destroying the uniqueness of the image by making it simultaneously available to the reader.[63] However, the relationship between reproduction and original is still maintained – it remains the possession of the celebrity – and so the reference to its location bolsters the status of the celebrity while raising the cultural status of the magazine. In explaining the past histories of the various ornaments, artworks and bric-à-brac, Harry How, just like Holmes, recreates the biography of the individual through the objects they surround themselves with. 'Illustrated Interviews', just like the Holmes stories, suggest that individuality can only be delimited through the delegated agency of things.

These two departments, 'Portraits of Celebrities' and 'Illustrated Interviews' are brought together in the *Strand* in December 1892. This number not only featured the return of Sherlock Holmes after the publication of the first twelve stories as the *Adventures*, but also had George Newnes in 'Portraits of Celebrities' and the offices of the *Strand Magazine* in a derivative of the 'Illustrated Interview.'[64] Newnes's portraits, which were produced 'in consequence of the repeated wish of readers of *Tit-Bits* and the *Strand Magazine*', complement those that we learn hang in the *Tit-Bits* office and its 'inner room.'[65] These (specifically located) portraits are only partially reproduced in the engravings that accompany the 'Interview' – the letterpress reveals that they are there – and so 'Portraits of Celebrities' both imitates its poetics, provides the actual image, and presents Newnes as both owner and constitutive part of the *Strand Magazine*. In this number the method of Sherlock Holmes, represented and enacted in 'The Adventure of Silver Blaze', is fully implicated in the commodification of self contained in the interaction between 'Portraits of Celebrities' and 'Illustrated Interviews.'

**Science, the Strange and the *Strand***

The Holmes stories in the *Strand* function as archetypes for a form of reading that is conservative, reaffirming and identified as scientific. Kate Jackson claims that the 'magazine offered a confirming, conciliatory rigidity that was based on social and professional distinction, corporate identity, individual example, and commercial viability, and was comforting to a middle class audience who, beset by anxiety, change and uncertainty, sought reassurance in its pages.'[66] Newnes's text was fully complicit in the ideological recognition of a scientific normalization of observation: its fiction provided countless archetypal demonstrations and references to an advanced form of 'reading' that would provide a sound basis for the interpretation of the various textual objects rendered up by the other aspects of the magazine. However, this sterile, reassuring code was not only about interpreting the world of people and things; it also functioned as a rigid guide to the taking of pleasure.

In identifying science writing with detective fiction, H.G. Wells links two cultural discourses that are predicated on explaining the strange in the terms of the familiar. Wells praises Doyle for the way in which he handles his evidence: no matter how inexplicable the situation, Doyle, through Watson, reveals the mundane truth of the crime by revealing the logical steps through which Holmes progresses. Equally, Wells suggests, science writers should use this narrative strategy to explain the often weird natural phenomena that they address. Implicit in both are spatial movements: just as Holmes moves across London, or reads the various people and things that come to him at 221b Baker St, so scientists use their instruments to reveal hidden realms, or examine ancient and hidden objects, now divorced from their context in the space of the laboratory. In communicating these activities, the reader is necessarily distanced from the pleasurable voyages that they imply. The pleasure inscribed in the narrative is thus of an altogether different variety than that of scientific practice or detection: rather than the embodied experience of disorientation and movement, the reader, positioned outside the space described, is encouraged to experience a more cerebral appreciation of the author's deductive method.

In 'The Engineer's Thumb', Dr Watson defends his retelling of Holmes's adventures in language that predicts Wells's description of the scientific popularizer:

> The story has, I believe, been told more than once in the newspapers, but, like all such narratives, its effect is much less striking when set forth *en bloc* in a single half-column of print than when the facts slowly evolve before your own eyes and the mystery clears gradually away as each new discovery furnishes a step which leads on to the complete truth.[67]

Rather than simply relate the events, Watson's version displaces the voyeuristic pleasure derived from observing them into the narrative process that reveals them.

Watson's narrations depict the detective's actions until Holmes (via Watson of course) can reveal the full 'truth.' Slavoj Žižek claims that there 'is a certain self-reflexive strain in the detective novel: it is a story of the detective's effort to tell the story, i.e., to reconstitute what "really happened" around and before the murder, and the novel is finished not when we get the answer to "Whodunnit?" but when the detective is finally able to tell "the real story" in the form of a linear narrative.'[68] It is through Watson's account that we encounter the events of the story: he structures the narrative so that it embodies the method of Sherlock Holmes (and Wells, and Pearson) while simultaneously guarding against its illicit pleasures.

The practice of detection is pleasurable, but these pleasures must be mediated for the reader. Poe's Dupin takes 'an eager delight in its exercise – if not exactly in its display – and did not hesitate to confess the pleasure thus derived.' The narrator of the 'Murders in the Rue Morgue' goes further:

> As the strong man exults in his physical ability, delighting in such exercises as call his muscles into action, so glories the analyst in that moral activity which *disentangles*. He derives pleasure from even the most trivial occupations bringing his talent into play.[69]

Holmes too, famously, relies on his detection to 'escape from the commonplaces of existence' that he otherwise combats with drugs.[70] The exercise of his abilities affects a physical transformation in Holmes from that 'quiet thinker and logician of Baker Street' into a wild animal:

> His face flushed and darkened. His brows were drawn into two hard, black lines, while his eyes shone out from beneath them with a steely glitter. His face was bent downwards, his shoulders bowed, his lips compressed, and the veins stood out like whipcord in his long sinewy neck. His nostrils seemed to dilate with a purely animal lust for the chase, and his mind was so absolutely concentrated upon the matter before him, that a question or remark fell unheeded upon his ears, or at the most only provoked a quick, impatient snarl in reply.[71]

Yet this visceral experience is not that which is communicated to the reader. Watson makes no secret of the pleasure that he derives from observing Holmes at work, but this pleasure is of a different nature from Holmes's all-consuming passion. In 'The Adventure of the Crooked Man', Holmes 'in spite of his capacity for concealing his emotions' is 'in a state of suppressed excitement', whereas Watson 'was tingling with that half-sporting, half intellectual pleasure' that he invariably experiences accompanying Holmes on a case.[72] Watson displaces his own bodily pleasure into a combination of the respectable masculine codes of sport and intellectual challenge. For the reader a further displacement occurs: in 'The Adventure of the Speckled Band' he claims he has 'no keener pleasure than in following Holmes in his professional investigations', but this pleasure is from 'admiring the rapid deductions, as swift as intuitions, and yet always founded on a logical basis, with which he unravelled the problems submitted to him.'[73] The pleasure that the reader is invited to share is thus the pleasure derived from the reconstruction of a satisfying narrative.

The mystery story dramatizes the process of reinterpreting events until they reveal what really happened. The detective uses his or her powers of observation to isolate the relevant 'facts' and then order them in the proper temporal sequence to present them for the space-time of the reader. This is precisely what Karl Pearson describes as a scientific law. 'Men study a range of facts – in the case of nature the material contents of their perceptive faculty – they classify and analyze, they discover relationships and sequences, and then they describe in the simplest possible terms the widest possible range of phenomena.'[74] This scientific law is not associated with civil or moral law as it is descriptive rather than prescriptive. Instead it operates in a similar way to Bruno Latour's cascade of inscription: the law is so persuasive as it is built upon layers of stabilized, and therefore incontestable, 'facts' mobilized from authoritative sites.[75] Roger Caillon claims the crime 'must be enigmatic, and seem to mock natural law, verisimilitude, and good sense' and the 'ingenuity of the *author* is demonstrated in the preparation of such a situation and in its simple and surprising resolution.'[76] As everything in the novel obeys the author, there are as many different possible stories as there are possible explanations as to how the crime happened. In revealing the 'how', the final description of events, the author reveals their genius while explicating a model scientific law.

Žižek claims that the crime scene predicates deception. This is 'why it is totally misleading to conceive of the detective's procedure as a version of the procedure proper to "precise" natural sciences: it is true that the "objective" scientist also "penetrates through false appearance to the hidden reality," but this false appearance with which he has to deal *lacks the dimension of deception.*'[77] Should the scientist be confronted with deception, Žižek suggests, we would have to posit a dishonest God. However, as I have argued, the detective is not the scientist but the agent of scientific exposition. The scientific author must, in order to interest the reader, act as both murderer and detective – must deliberately stage a manoeuvre that renders the familiar strange before resolving it through scientific knowledge. If, as Žižek claims, the scientist confronts 'a traumatic shock, an event that cannot be integrated into symbolic reality because it appears to interrupt the "normal causal chain"', it is because he or she has presented it this way. Therefore both the detective and the scientific author attempt to 'resymbolize the traumatic shock to integrate it into symbolic reality.'[78] This is the source of power for the popular scientific author and also the cause of Wells's anxiety: because the scientific expositor, like the author of detective fiction, must both stage the 'crime' as well as solve it, they must take responsibility for the illicit pleasures of the uncanny scenes they create.

This narrative movement is explicitly revealed in the *Strand's* colonial fiction. The series 'Shafts from an Eastern Quiver' by Charles J. Mansford BA appeared from July 1892, helping to fill the space left by Holmes.[79] The stories revolve around a pair of British explorers at the fringes of the empire. In each number their

Arabic guide relates a tale, the truth of which is then seemingly proven by the events that unfold. However, at the resolution of each story one of the men, Denviers, produces a rational explanation to counter the 'primitive' narratives which almost convince the narrator. The imperial context here functions as a space which legitimizes both the buccaneering behaviour of the British and permits the rival constructions of 'truth' to be tentatively indulged.[80]

Just as the colonial adventure opened new spaces in order to rule them, so nineteenth-century science was both responsible for opening new worlds and accounting for what was found there. For both, the reproductive technologies employed by editors such as Newnes allowed these spaces to be placed directly onto the periodical page, emphasizing their contemporary existence with the reader. Alfred W. Porter's 'The New Photography' and William Fitzgerald's 'Some Wonders of the Microscope' are in the July and August 1896 numbers of the *Strand* respectively. Both articles exploit Newnes's eagerness to employ photographic reproductions in order to expose the reader to unsettling and strange images. Porter's article deals with the new technology of X rays and is in the same number as Meade and Halifax's story on the same theme (above). Porter begins in recognizably popular style by giving the phenomenon he is describing a human history as a prelude to an accessible account of the science. As an inquiry 'into the secrets of Nature', this is delivered, as Wells recommended in 1894, in a serious tone, and slowly builds up from the relatively familiar ('an ordinary medical or "shocking" coil') to the increasingly sensational images themselves. However, this is where the narrative ceases, instead becoming commentary on the radiographs. Whereas Wells requires these images to be explained rationally, Porter instead treats them as spectacle. The tone becomes lighter ('there is no need to put a bullet in one's hand to test the point') and that of the showman ('we willingly turn to less gruesome specimens'). Eventually the spectacle entirely drives the narrative, even to the expense of the objects: the frog, we read, '*was made for the process*' and the image 'kindly hides the fact that he had been dead several days' (Figure 2.2). Even when Porter writes that the medical aspect of the images 'is more suited to the pages of a medical journal – we prefer not to look on ghastly things' he proceeds to reproduce them. His final images are of an exploding book and a hand, the veneer of scientific explanation in the narrative there to justify the inclusion of these sensational images. Just like the detective, Porter, a professional scientist at University College London, has constructed a letterpress purely to share with readers the normally hidden world beneath the surface.[81]

Fitzgerald's 'Some Wonders of the Microscope' even more flagrantly transgresses Wells's instructions. Fitzgerald was a regular contributor of light articles and from the beginning his tone is not serious, invoking 'the young man who wears spectacles and talks of diatomacæ […] who can find Paradise in a Hampstead pond.' The narrative then recounts an amusing anecdote ('I once attended a lecture on the microscope; everything was microscopic – even the audience') before proceeding to discuss the photographs. Each image, for Fitzgerald, offers an opportunity to disgust and amuse: when discussing a fly's

Spectacular Spaces of Science and Detection

But for magnificence nothing can compare with the common frog (Fig. 10). *He was made for the process.* His skeleton is strong but graceful : built up of innumerable small bones, each of which is so fine that the radiation partly penetrating

*From a Photo. by]*  FIG. 9.—NEWT.  [*A. W. Porter.*

it reveals its internal structure, and yet it stands boldly out in the midst of its almost spiritual covering of flesh. The radiograph kindly hides the fact that he had been dead

Fig. 11 is by Professor Hicks, of Sheffield. (We must remark that all the examples by Professor Hicks which we have seen are of remarkable sharpness and distinctness, and we would have been glad of examples from him on a *variety* of subjects.) This figure served to locate a needle which had become embedded in the ball of a thumb.

Fig. 12 (*a* and *b*) is another similar instance where the needle is in a more difficult position. It illustrates how entangled such an intruder can become in the

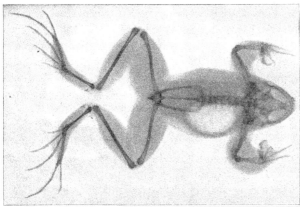

FIG. 10.—GERMAN FROG.
*From a Photo. by A. W. Porter.*

several days when this last memorial of his earthly career was obtained. The only indication of the fact is the abnormally expanded lung, which shows of a light shade in the figure.

We turn now to the severely practical side of the subject—the utility of the process as an aid to the surgeon. This aspect of the subject is more suited to the pages of a medical journal — we prefer not to look on ghastly things. A few illustrations will serve to emphasize its vast importance.

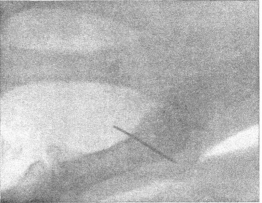

*From a Photo. by]*  FIG. 11.—PORTION OF HAND  [*Prof. Hicks, F.R.S.*
(SHOWING NEEDLE EMBEDDED IN THE BALL OF THE THUMB).

**Figure 2.2 From Alfred W. Porter BSc, 'The New Photography', *Strand Magazine*, 12, July 1896, p. 112**

foot, magnified and reproduced on the page, he invites the reader to 'fancy this awful looking thing being laid lightly on your face at all hours of the day.' He delights in both the grotesque and the sublime nature of the microscopic world, providing statistics and information which further render the objects strange. In a startling reversal, Fitzgerald concludes with a discussion of vision and reproduces a portrait taken through a beetle's eye (Figure 2.3). The resulting image, pluralizing the face, is eerily reminiscent of 'Portraits of Celebrities', but this time the reader is aligned with the beetle, rather than the middle-class consumer of middle-class celebrity culture.[82]

Porter's narrative accompanies the reader into the unfamiliar invisible world and attempts to explain what is seen there. It acts a resymbolization of these startling images, providing a safe set of codes through which to view them. Fitzgerald's piece is like an unsolved crime: his narrative, perhaps because microscopic images were not that unusual by the late nineteenth century, makes no attempt to resymbolize the reproductions. It delights in the unusual uncanny nature of the objects, and takes the reader from one unconnected, isolated fragment of the real to another. Both articles are in stark contrast to Lubbock's serial 'Beauty in Nature' of 1892. This presents a completely symbolized account of the natural world in which science, feminized and familiarized as 'our fairy godmother', opens up new worlds to see by guiding us as to 'what we *look for.*' 'For our greater power of perceiving', Lubbock writes, 'and therefore of enjoying Nature, we are greatly indebted to science. Over and above what is visible to the unaided eye, the two magic tubes, the telescope and microscope, have revealed to us, at least partially, the infinitely great and the infinitely small.' [83] Scientific instruments may play a part in this, but they do not plunge the viewer into alien realism. Instead, we are situated alongside Lubbock, his literary techniques and scientific knowledge accounting for their oddities from a fixed scopic site that is resolutely familiar.

Lubbock's series in the *Strand* pronounces definitively on nature, and carefully delimits the reader's mediated experience of it. In this familiar anthropocentric world, the naturalist is the privileged subject at its centre as 'to him the seasons come round like old friends, to him the birds sing, and as he walks along, the flowers stretch out from the hedges and look up from the ground.'[84] It is the position of these articles in the *Strand* that is important: three of Lubbock's contributions are positioned immediately after a Sherlock Holmes story and the fourth precedes one. The dynamic of detective fiction restores the stability of the social world after the psychological shock of the real that usually results from an illicit criminal act. Lubbock's articles provide a safe space, known through science, in which nothing is strange and alien natural objects are unmistakeably part of the human, social world. In resisting such fantasies of complete socialization of the natural world Fitzgerald, and to an extent Porter, use their science to provide an unsettling image of the grotesque and unusual, and so thrill readers with their bewildering novelty.

The success of the *Strand Magazine* was the result of more than the reassurance that it gave to its middle-class readers. It actually presents the world as an object of

top are also visible (No. 18). Next come four hairs from the whiskers of a lioness. You are looking vertically down on to these latter, and the tops of the hairs were cut off to give a better result in the photograph (No. 19).

NO. 20.—THE FINEST FRENCH CAMBRIC.

Under a powerful microscope, even the most delicate specimen of human workmanship looks astonishingly coarse. Look at this photograph (No. 20). The fabric shown is not a rough Harris or Sutherland tweed, such as shooting suits are made of, but a piece of the most exquisitely fine French cambric, which cost twenty shillings a yard.

The various microscopical societies throughout the world are in no danger of a famine in subjects — or objects. Swift told us that " great fleas have little fleas upon their backs

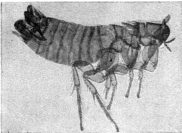

NO. 21.—BLIND FLEA OF A MOLE.

to bite 'em"; and then, again, " little fleas have lesser fleas, and so *ad infinitum.*" Here is an extraordinary example of what I might call the physiological sympathy which the parasite has for its "host." The mole, as we all know, is not remarkable for keenness of vision, and it has a special kind of flea all to itself. Well, that flea is also blind, although you wouldn't think so on looking at the photograph (No. 21).

It may be some satisfaction to the victims of the ordinary house-fly to know that that

provoking insect is in turn preyed upon by these little parasites (No. 22); whether these, too, "have lesser fleas" I can't say—probably they have. At any rate, the beetle has its parasite, with lancets 700 times finer than a human hair; and an exceedingly minute flea has been found upon the flea of a hedgehog. The eye of a water-beetle is made up of many facets; there are about 24,000 of them in the two eyes of a dragon-fly. Each of these facets acts as a lens to convey to the insect's brain some small portion of the object

NO. 22.—PARASITES OF THE HOUSE-FLY.

that is being looked at; at the same time, I want to illustrate a peculiar phenomenon in connection with these facets. If an image be placed between a luminant body and one of these sets of lenses, that image will be represented entirely in each individual facet. A really wonderful microscopic photograph has been specially taken to illustrate this (No. 23). It shows a portrait in every facet of the beetle's eye. The eye was first of all dissected and placed on the stage of the instrument. The portrait—on glass and, of course, exceedingly small—was then interposed and the photograph taken through the microscope.

NO. 23.—PART OF A BEETLE'S EYE, WITH PORTRAIT IN EVERY FACET.

**Figure 2.3 From William G. Fitzgerald, 'Some Wonders of the Microscope', *Strand Magazine*, 12, August 1896, p. 216**

desire while simultaneously educating the reader how to perceive it. Žižek, following Lacan, describes fantasy as 'a scenario that realizes the subject's desire' but not the satisfaction. If anxiety is 'the danger of our getting too close to the object and losing the lack' then the codes of the *Strand* carefully position the reader and teach them how to apprehend the object of desire. Žižek continues:

> The fundamental point of psychoanalysis is that desire is not something given in advance, but something that has to be constructed – and it is precisely the role of fantasy to give the coordinates of the subject's desire, to specify its object, to locate the position the subject assumes in it. It is only through fantasy that the subject is constituted as desiring: *through fantasy, we learn how to desire.*[85]

The detective fiction of the *Strand*, especially Doyle's Sherlock Holmes stories, acts as a model for two constructions of desire: the actions of Holmes popularize the notion of perception as a way to read the faces that are rendered up for scrutiny and emulation; and the method of science legitimizes the production of the grotesque and the voyeuristic pleasure in the thrill of the strange. Just as Doyle used the text of Newnes's publications to provide material for his plots, so his published stories provide a model for readers to interpret both the texts that they are reading and the world around them.[86] The *Strand* guides its readers through diverse spaces via a single narrative structure that offers pleasurable movements while resituating them in a single scopic site. Newnes's *Strand Magazine* is more than a mirror of the middle classes, it instead participates in the construction of desire in the middle-class subject.

## Conclusion

H.G. Wells's 'Popularising Science' identifies a model for scientific popularization in the texts of detective fiction. However, the poetics of these stories is embodied in the periodical forms that carry them. Serialization necessarily foregrounds the orderly development of a theme; Doyle's innovation, following Poe, was to contain this dynamic within a single narrative. Rather than rely on the serial nature of the periodical to derive suspense they internalized the plot into a single number. For Doyle, who believed himself foremost an historical novelist, this was a result of George Newnes's editorial policy: Sherlock Holmes was the product of the space of the *Strand Magazine*.[87]

But this is to conflate two spaces. Periodical form is predicated on heterogeneity: even those older journals that systematically elide multiple authorship such as the quarterly reviews inevitably posit multiple references through their constituent parts. I have used Doyle to suggest that there was an accepted way of reading these fragmentary texts, of conceptualizing their spatial reach from a relatively stable subject position. Holmes, and his analogues in the man of science and the various other detectives who entered the *Strand* in his wake, operates as a spokesperson for a scientific method that can uncover the truth beneath the sometimes uncanny, but often banal, circumstances of surface reality. Whether reading the bodies of those around him or tracing the unexpected histories of objects, the detective is a privileged observer who can use the masculine codes of science to preserve social order. These spokespeople – the professionalizing experts of scientific exposition or forensic science – are situated on the borders of the representational spaces of the magazine and the world of its readers. Holmes is manipulated by Doyle / Watson so that, through him, the true story can be told against the various rival narratives that mask the crime. The frame narratives of Watson provide space for these misreadings as well as guarding against the bodily pleasures of detection. In slowly unveiling the true narrative, the plot sequence substitutes a different pleasure, that of a guarded voyeuristic pleasure in the strange accompanied by a due appreciation of the author's ingenuity. These stories provide the regulatory codes through which the text constructs desire, rendering an otherwise repetitive textual format a space of guarded fantasy.

Just as Doyle writes such ideological structures into his narratives, so too does George Newnes inscribe them into the form of the *Strand Magazine*. With its solid middle-class ideology, the *Strand* provides a variety of textual spaces for the exercise of this interpretive method. The widespread use of photographic reproduction enables Newnes to present images that both confirm the value of its celebrities and, in revealing the strange worlds of the invisible and microscopic, demonstrate the versatility and stability of these codes in the realms of the strange. In the previous chapter I demonstrated how Arthur Cowper Ranyard did not simply use his photographic reproductions to represent space, he actually deployed them to produce certain exclusory spaces within his text. Equally, George Newnes presents his content in order to posit spaces far removed from the middle-class world of his readers. However, in simultaneously providing a reading strategy with which to negotiate the spatial politics of the *Strand*, Newnes grants his readers with the agency to enjoy plural representations of space while also maintaining a middle-class spatial hegemony that is based on the codes of class, empire and capital.

Rather than simply mirror the world of its readers, the *Strand*, like all periodicals, is predicated on the distance, the space, between representational space and the space-time of reading. Each number of a periodical takes up its content, and combines it to form a new object which circulates through culture. My next chapter explores the dynamic of this relationship, and considers the various strategies employed to make these two space-times coalesce. Even though periodicals exploit a variety of spaces and times, this interaction occurs in the present. As serial texts, in which editors and publishers refine their concept of their readers, this process is iterative, and so the present is enunciated in different temporal moments. It is this complex dynamic, which links linear time with the duration of the present, that I discuss in Chapter Three.

**Notes**

1   Reginald Pound, *The Strand Magazine 1891–1950* (London, 1966), p. 105.
2   Pound, *Strand Magazine*, pp. 7, 9.
3   Kate Jackson, *George Newnes and the New Journalism in Britain 1880–1910* (London, 2001), pp. 116, 117.
4   See Jackson, *George Newnes*, p. 92; Pound, *Strand Magazine*, p. 32; 'W.T.S.' [W.T. Stead], 'Introduction', *Index to the Periodical Literature of the World* (London, 1893), p. vii.
5   Pound, *Strand Magazine*, p. 7.
6   For an account of Newnes's printing technologies see anonymous, 'A Description of the Offices of the *Strand Magazine*', 4, December 1892 (1892), 594–606. Newnes employed a Rotary Art Press ('the only one in Europe'), a Web Press, and a Cylinder Press for the *Strand*, 604.
7   David Reed, *The Popular Magazine in Britain and the United States, 1880–1960* (London, 1997) p. 95.
8   Peter D. McDonald, *British Literary Culture and Publishing Practice, 1880–1914* (Cambridge, 1997), p. 140 and note 147, p. 205 and Jackson, *George Newnes*, p. 107.
9   McDonald, *British Literary Culture*, p. 141. By 1892, only a year after he began writing full time, Doyle could command over three times his previous fee.
10  Jackson, *George Newnes*, p. 117.
11  In 1891, for instance, Huxley, Lubbock and Owen feature in 'Portraits of Celebrities' and Doyle's anonymous short story 'The Voice of Science' revolves around the gendering of science and the politics of romance and the conversazione. See anonymous, 'Portraits of Celebrities at Different Times of their Lives', *Strand*, 1, January 1891 (1891), 47; 1, February 1891 (1891), 160; 2, September 1891 (1891), 274; and anonymous [Arthur Conan Doyle], 'The Voice of Science', *Strand*, 1, March 1891 (1891), 312–17.
12  H.G. Wells, 'Popularising Science', *Nature*, 50, 26 July 1894 (1894), 300.
13  See A.J. Meadows, *Science and Controversy: A Biography of Sir Norman Lockyer* (London, 1972).
14  See Roy M. MacLeod, 'Resources of Science in Victorian England', in *Science and Society 1600–1900*, ed. P. Mathias (Cambridge, 1972), pp. 160–66; Roy M. MacLeod, 'Education: Science and Technical', in *The 'Creed of Science' in Victorian England* (London, 2000), pp. 196–225.
15  Julie Ann Lancashire, 'An Historical Study of the Popularization of Science in General Science Periodicals in Britain 1890–1939' (Unpublished PhD thesis, University of Kent at Canterbury 1988), p. 75.
16  Wells, 'Popularising Science', 301.
17  Wells, 'Popularising Science', 301.
18  The books are *Textbook of Biology* (London, 1892) and, with R.A. Gregory, *Honours Physiography* (London, 1893). See J.R. Hammond, *Herbert George Wells: An Annotated Bibliography of His Works* (New York, 1977), pp. 59–62.
19  'The Murders in the Rue Morgue' was initially published in *Graham's Magazine*, 18, April 1841 (1841), 166–79. There were many editions of Poe in the 1890s including *The Works of Edgar Allan Poe* (Edinburgh, 1890) and *The Murders in the Rue Morgue and Other Tales* (London, 1893).

20  Edgar Allan Poe, 'The Murders in the Rue Morgue', *Great Short Works of Edgar Allan Poe*, ed. G.R. Thompson (1841; New York, 1970), p. 275.

21  Wells, 'Popularising Science', 301.

22  Karl Pearson, *The Grammar of Science* (London, 1892), pp. 9–10. For science as part of common sense see also T.H. Huxley FRS, *The Crayfish: An Introduction to Zoology* (London, 1880), p. 1.

23  Pearson, *Grammar*, p. 12.

24  Pearson, *Grammar*, p. 15 and Richard R. Yeo 'Scientific Method and the Rhetoric of Science in Britain, 1830–1917', in *The Politics and Rhetoric of Scientific Method*, eds John A. Schuster and Richard R. Yeo (Dordrecht, 1986), pp. 259–97. See also Richard Yeo, 'Scientific Method and the Image of Science 1831–1891', in *The Parliament of Science*, ed. Roy Macleod and Peter Collins (London, 1981), pp. 65–88 and David Philip Miller, 'Method and the "Micropolitics" of Science: The Early Years of the Geological and Astronomical Societies of London', in *Politics and Rhetoric*, pp. 227–57.

25  Pearson, *Grammar*, pp. 4, 7–8.

26  See for instance Judith Walkowitz, 'The Men and Women's Club', *City of Dreadful Delight: Narratives of Sexual Danger in Late-Victorian London* (London, 1992), p 146.

27  Pearson, *Grammar*, note 1, p. 8.

28  Arthur Conan Doyle, 'Adventures of Sherlock Holmes: XXIV. The Final Problem', *Strand*, 6, December 1893 (1893), 559–70. The latter is the only story to open the *Strand* and, because the opening article usually provides the full-page fine engraving for the number, includes a Paget engraving of Holmes's final struggle with Moriarty to mark both the end of the volume and the Holmes stories.

29  Martin Fido, *The World of Sherlock Holmes* (London, 1998), p. 51. Fido gives Holmes a biographical timeline alongside that of Doyle, and describes himself as a 'Sherlockian', part of an intellectual game which treats Holmes as a real person.

30  McDonald, *British Literary Culture*, p. 142.

31  Anonymous, 'Portraits of Celebrities', *Strand*, 2, December 1891 (1891), 600–607.

32  Harry How, 'A Day with Dr Conan Doyle', *Strand*, 4, August 1892 (1892), 182–8.

33  Newnes also advertises the interview, claiming it contains 'amongst other interesting matter, some particulars concerning Mr Sherlock Holmes.' Anonymous, untitled editorial note, *Strand*, 4, July 1892 (1892), 82.

34  The *Adventures of Sherlock Holmes* was 6s with a light blue cloth cover in royal octavo format thus 'marketed as a *de luxe* book version of the *Strand Magazine* itself.' McDonald, *British Literary Culture*, p. 119.

35  Ronald R. Thomas, *Detective Fiction and the Rise of Forensic Science* (Cambridge, 1999), p. 75.

36  Thomas, *Detective Fiction*, p. 75.

37  Thomas, *Detective Fiction*, p. 78.

38  Arthur Conan Doyle, 'Adventures of Sherlock Holmes: XII The Adventure of the Copper Beeches', *Strand*, 3, June 1892 (1892), 613.

39  Pearson, *Grammar*, pp. 7–8.

40  Although Holmes's chemistry is mentioned in passing. See Doyle, 'Adventures of Sherlock Holmes: III. A Case of Identity', *Strand*, 2, September 1891 (1891), 253 and 'Final Problem', 559–70.

41  Rosemary Jann, *The Adventures of Sherlock Holmes: Detecting Social Order* (New York, 1995), p. 56.

42  Doyle, 'Case of Identity', 253.

43  Thomas, *Detective Fiction*, p. 81.

44  Anonymous, untitled note, 82.

45  The Donovan stories collected in *The Man-Hunter* and *Caught at Last!* (1888 and 1889) are more sensational and dwell overly on the details of the crime. See for instance 'Dick Donovan' [J.E. Preston Muddock], 'The Tuft of Red Hair', *The Man-Hunter: Stories from the Notebook of a Detective* (London, 1888), pp. 77–94.

46  Thomas, *Detective Fiction*, p. 89.

47  'Dick Donovan' [J.E. Preston Muddock], 'A Romance from a Detective's Casebook: The Jewelled Skull', *Strand*, 4, July 1892 (1892), 71, 73. The 'locked room' scenario is a generic reference to 'The Murders in the Rue Morgue.' Holmes customarily listens with his eyes half-closed and his fingertips together: see for instance Doyle, 'Adventures of Sherlock Holmes: VIII. The Adventure of the Speckled Band', *Strand*, 3, February 1892 (1892), 145. Donovan does not do this in the earlier stories.

48  Meade had previously published anonymously 'Stories from the Diary of a Doctor' from July–December 1893 of the *Strand*. The name of the hero, Clifford Halifax, was chosen as the pseudonym of Edgar Beaumont, her co-author for 'Adventures of a Man of Science.'

49  L.T. Meade and Clifford Halifax, 'Adventures of a Man of Science: V. At the Steps of the Altar', *Strand*, 12, November 1896 (1896), 530–31.

50  Thomas, *Detective Fiction*, p. 239.

51  L.T. Meade and Clifford Halifax, M.D., 'The Adventures of a Man of Science: I. The Snake's Eye', *Strand*, 12, July 1896 (1896), 67, 68. This appears in the same number as an article on X-Rays. See below.

52  In the early Donovan stories he is a 'special constable' but this is silenced in the *Strand* to make Donovan a gentleman.

53  Edmund R. Spearman, 'Mistaken Identity and Police Anthropometry', *Fortnightly Review*, 46, March 1889 (1889), 366.

54  John Plunkett, 'Celebrity and Community: The Poetics of the Carte-de-visite', *Journal of Victorian Culture*, 8 (2003), 69.

55  The combination of these two commodities was not new. The cabinet photograph and the periodical were physically combined in Cassell's *Cabinet Portrait Gallery* (1890–94).

56  Walter Benjamin, 'The Work of Art in the Age of Mechanical Reproduction', *Illuminations*, ed. and trans. Hannah Arendt (Frankfurt, 1969), p. 223.

57  Reed, *Popular Magazine*, p. 18.

58  For the intrusion of the viewer into the studio see Plunkett, 'Celebrity and Community', 72–9. For the politics of photographic reproduction see Chapter One above.

59  Jackson, *George Newnes*, p. 116; Pound, *Strand Magazine*, p. 64.

60  Arthur Conan Doyle, 'Adventures of Sherlock Holmes: IV. The Boscombe Valley Mystery', *Strand*, 2, October 1891 (1891), 411, 413.

61  Doyle, 'Adventures of Sherlock Holmes: VII. The Adventure of the Blue Carbuncle,' *Strand*, 3, January 1892 (1892), 75.

62  Dick Pels, Kevin Hetherington and Frédéric Vandenberghe, 'The Status of the Object: Performativity, Mediations and Techniques', *Theory, Culture and Society*, 19 (2002), 4.

63  John Berger, *Ways of Seeing* (London, 1972), p. 19.

64   Doyle, 'Adventures of Sherlock Holmes: XIII. The Adventure of Silver Blaze', *Strand*, 4, December 1892 (1892), pp. 645–60; anonymous, 'Portraits of Celebrities', *Strand*, 4, December 1892 (1892), 589–93; anonymous, 'Description of the Offices', 599–604.

65   Anonymous, 'Portraits', 593; anonymous, 'Description of the Offices', 599–600.

66   Jackson, *George Newnes*, p. 92.

67   Doyle, 'The Adventures of Sherlock Holmes: IX. The Engineer's Thumb', *Strand*, 3, March 1892 (1892), 276.

68   Slavoj Žižek, *Looking Awry: An Introduction to Jacques Lacan through Popular Culture* (Cambridge, 1991), p. 49.

69   Poe, 'Murders in the Rue Morgue', pp. 278, 273.

70   Arthur Conan Doyle, 'Adventures of Sherlock Holmes: II. The Red-Headed League', *Strand*, 2, August 1891 (1891), 204. For a rare reference to drugs in the *Strand* stories see Doyle, 'Adventures of Sherlock Holmes: XV. The Adventure of the Yellow Face', *Strand*, 5, February 1893 (1893), 162.

71   Doyle, 'Boscombe Valley', 411.

72   Doyle, 'Adventures of Sherlock Holmes: XX. The Adventure of the Crooked Man', *Strand*, 6, July 1893 (1893), 29.

73   Doyle, 'Speckled Band', 142.

74   Pearson, *Grammar*, p. 119.

75   Bruno Latour, 'Drawing Things Together', in *Representation in Scientific Practice*, eds Michael Lynch and Steve Woolgar (London, 1990) p. 41.

76   Roger Caillon, 'The Detective Novel as Game', in *The Poetics of Murder: Detective Fiction and Literary Theory*, eds Glenn W. Most and William W. Stowe (San Diego, 1983), p. 3. Emphasis his own.

77   Žižek, *Looking Awry*, p. 55. Emphasis his own; quotations are unattributed.

78   Žižek, *Looking Awry*, p. 58.

79   Charles J. Mansford, 'Shafts from an Eastern Quiver: I. The Diamond of Shomar's Queen', *Strand*, 4, July 1892 (1892), 21–8.

80   See for instance Charles J. Mansford, 'Shafts from an Eastern Quiver: IV. Darak, the Scorn of the Afghans,' *Strand*, 4, October 1892 (1892), 407–14 in which they are told of a woman turned to crystal who turns out to be the victim of a freak glacier.

81   Alfred W. Porter, B.Sc., 'The New Photography', *Strand*, 12, July 1896 (1896), 107, 111–12. Emphasis his own.

82   William G. Fitzgerald, 'Some Wonders of the Microscope', *Strand*, 12, August 1896 (1896), 210.

83   Sir John Lubbock, 'Beauty in Nature: I. Introduction', *Strand*, 3, February 1892 (1892), 167, 158

84   Lubbock, 'Beauty', 159.

85   Žižek, *Looking Awry*, pp. 6, 8, 6. Emphasis his own.

86   See Richard Lancelyn Green, 'Explanatory Notes', in Arthur Conan Doyle, *The Adventures of Sherlock Holmes*, ed. Richard Lancelyn Green (Oxford, 1993), pp. 297–389.

87   See for instance, Ian Ousby, *Bloodhounds of Heaven: The Detective in English Fiction from Godwin to Doyle* (Cambridge MA, 1976), pp.156–63 for the way the character of Holmes alters from the novels to the *Strand*.

# PART 2
## Times

# Chapter Three

# Representing the Present

We cannot compare a process with "the passage of time" – there is no such thing – but only with another process (such as the working of a chronometer).[1]

Times, of necessity, are local; and this goes too for the relations between places and their respective times.[2]

In *Tractatus Logico-Philosophicus*, Ludwig Wittgenstein disputes the essential existence of an underlying linear time. For Wittgenstein 'we can describe the lapse of time only by relying on some other process.'[3] In gesturing towards the ticking hand of a chronometer, Wittgenstein reveals the constituent role that nonhuman objects play in the construction of temporality. Henri Lefebvre, arguing for the primacy of space, insists that time is only ever realized in discrete locations. In this section of the book I argue that the periodical becomes a key site for these analyses. As composite objects, periodicals both gesture to a range of space-times through their textual narratives, and incorporate these within their material forms. As mobile, reproducible objects, they also have an existence in space and time, moving to reach readers and appearing at predetermined intervals. Stuart Sherman suggests '[c]locks tell time, narratives tell what transpires in time': periodicals, it seems, do both.[4] In this chapter I compare the text's capacity to represent time with the periodical's sequential appearance in it.

Chapter One demonstrated how textual objects correspond to different space-times, and the cogency of their links to these moments shapes their ontological form. Chapter Two explored how editors exploit the mobile nature of space in order to posit the coexistence of multiple realms. Both chapters establish that the simultaneous spatial arrangement of things presents a complex range of spatial-temporal moments on the periodical page. Bruno Latour insists that we have 'always sorted out elements belonging to different times,' and that is '*is the sorting that makes the times, not the times that make the sorting.*'[5] As readers conceive of themselves not only in physical spaces and times, but also through configurations of social space and time, so editors attempt to produce material that corresponds to both. As periodicals are serial texts, temporality is also inscribed in their material form. By combining periodical appearance with the other signifying features, editors and publishers attempt to identify and cohere reading audiences according to both cultural determinants such as class and gender, as well as the social spaces and times through which readers move.

Each periodical number necessarily conceives itself as speaking to the present, but how this present is conceived, and linked to the quotidian lives of its readers, varies both between periodicities and from title to title. Weeklies, positioned uneasily between the contemporaneity of the newspaper and the more reflective pace of the monthly, often exploit public events to identify their represented temporality with the perceived experiences of the readers. However, these news events are predicated on transience – they are deemed significant as they are exceptional – and so they have an ambiguous material status. What is at stake in this context is the role of the author: whereas in the monthly press the event has already become assimilated into (recent) history and so available for discussion; the weekly is predicated on passing events, whose status is unresolved. In the copyright debates of the late nineteenth-century, the status of news as writing was highly contested: traded over the wires from the agencies, it was clearly commodified, but the value of news was located in its contemporaneity and accuracy, both of which were not seen to be properties of the text. For scientific news stories this problem was exacerbated: not only was there a difference between 'finished' science, and that played out week by week in the scientific press; but the necessity to render science accessible to a more general readership introduced metaphor and analogy into scientific discourse, moving it away from news and towards fiction. The chapter concludes by suggesting that the scientific writer thus became an author – even though science itself was unpatentable, and news was not deemed writing – and that this role was determined by the necessity of bringing external events into the periodical press.

## Space, Form and Time

In *Time and Free Will*, Henri Bergson insists on a spatial dimension to all conceptions of time except that of immediate, transitory experience. For Bergson, any temporal sequence relies upon the preexistence of a homogenous realm in which successive occurrences can be comprehended simultaneously. Using numerical sequences as an example, Bergson demonstrates that 'counting material objects means thinking all these objects together, thereby leaving them in space':

> For though we reach a sum by taking into account a succession of different terms, yet it is necessary that each of these terms should remain when we pass to the following, and should wait, so to speak, to be added to the others: how could it wait if it were an instant of duration?[6]

Space, therefore, is integral to any concept of quantitative time. 'When I follow with my eyes on the dial of a clock the movement of the hand which corresponds to the oscillations of the pendulum,' Bergson writes, 'I do not measure duration, as seems to be thought; I merely count simultaneities, which is very different.' In duration there is only ever one position of the hand, so a space is required in which to arrange simultaneities into a sequence. Bergson writes, "we create for them a fourth dimension of space, which we call homogenous time, and which enables the movement of the pendulum, although taking place at one spot, to be continually set in juxtaposition to itself.'[7] Not only does space establish linear time, but it also provides the means that this temporality can be shared.

The recognition of subjective temporality as opposed to abstract, linear time is frequently posited as modernist but, as I suggested in the introduction, what became represented as literary modernism were responses to an increasingly mobile world of things which forced the juxtaposition of spaces and times. For Bruno Latour, the modern notion of time results from an intellectual standpoint that structures time according to temporal discontinuities. The moderns, who for Latour are those who obfuscate the hybrid nature of reality, choosing instead an absolute division between an essential nature and historical culture, can only perceive time as an 'irreversible arrow – progress or decadence' which 'stems from an ordering of quasi-objects, whose proliferations [they] cannot explain.' This results in a present 'outlined by a series of radical breaks, revolutions, which constitute so many irreversible ratchets that prevent us from ever going backwards.' Julia Kristeva calls this 'monumental' time: 'time as project, teleology, linear and prospective unfolding: time as departure, progressions and arrival – in other words, the time of history.'[8] Patricia Murphy argues that the nineteenth century presented this as a 'natural order of time' to 'cope with the relentless and unnerving pace of change brought about by myriad scientific, technological, material and philosophical developments throughout the century.'[9] This time is not an inherited cultural resource however, but the result of cultural practice: as Latour suggests, it is 'the result of a retraining imposed on entities which would pertain to all sorts of times and possess all sorts of ontological statuses without this harsh disciplining.'[10] As Bergson argues, we need a space to comprehend the simultaneous existence of these things, and this space is the space of power.

In *The Production of Space*, Lefebvre suggests that the spatialization of time is the product of capitalist modernity:

> With the advent of modernity time has vanished from social space. It is recorded solely on measuring-instruments, on clocks, that are isolated and functionally specialized as this time itself. Lived time loses its form and its social interest – with the exception, that is, of time spent working. Economic space subordinates time to itself; political space expels it as threatening and dangerous (to power). The primacy of the economic and above all of the political implies the supremacy of space over time.[11]

Modernity – for Lefebvre the period of high capitalism – conceives of time spatially in order to render it quantitative, regular and exchangeable. 'Time may have been promoted to the level of ontology by the philosophers,' he writes, 'but it has been murdered by society.'[12] Like Wittgenstein and Bergson, the clock face becomes the emblematic instrument for the portioning of time, and this spatialization identifies homogenous time with the dominating codes of abstract space.

Although the serial publication of periodicals seems to correspond to this spatial conception of time – even to the extent that they are arranged sequentially on the library shelf – there is an element of *durée* present through the notion of gap. Many critics and historians have noted the ways in which periodicity and content interact according to both the perceived interests of readers and the various interests that produce the periodical.[13] As Margaret Beetham writes, periodicals are the 'first date-stamped commodity [...] designed both to ensure a rapid turnover and to create regular demand.'[14] As markets became increasingly competitive in the late nineteenth century, sophisticated strategies were developed to reach readers. Beetham notes 'the reader is addressed as an individual but is positioned as a member of certain overlapping sets of social groups; class, gender, region, age, political persuasion or religious denomination – to name only the most important.'[15] Time and space play a part in this: readers did not just purchase according to their social position, but also according to the various roles that they performed (or wished to perform) throughout their day. As times and spaces are both socially demarcated and not exclusive, they become important mechanisms to further delimit readers.[16]

There is a tension inherent in the reappearance of numbers. As Mark Turner notes, 'the natural state of being for periodicals is change and movement, and newspapers and periodicals rely, to a greater or lesser degree, on the 'new' and on the very modern concept of advancement, of moving forward, of futurity.'[17] The demand for novelty requires that each number of a periodical repeats its 'address' – whether this be in terms of who it considers its readers to be, or where and what they're doing – in the same terms despite different content. The unit within which this must be achieved is the space between numbers: this predetermined gap is the period within which the number must be relevant. Turner notes that 'built into the notion of seriality is necessarily some conceptualization of waiting.'[18] If the ticking hand of the clock is the appearance of the next number, and so participates in spatialized time, the moment between ticks, when the hand is still, is part of Bergson's *durée*. By conceiving the seriality of periodicals as imposing linear form on a more complex representation of temporality, we risk eliding this gap. This pause between numbers, which corresponds to the temporality addressed by the journal, is not congruent with either the time of reading or the events that might unfold within it. In order to link the lived experiences of readers with the space-times represented in the journals, editors and publishers deploy content that explicitly signals certain temporalities in the moment of reading. In this way periodicals interconnect their represented worlds with those of the readers, and they do this by constructing a present that will pass with the publication of the next number.

The competition between titles ensured that the periodical press, rather than provide a synchronic pulse, dictating and constructing public, linear time, instead operated like multiple chronometers, all marking different times. The overall effect, despite the regular rhythms of individual titles, and the similarities of rhythms between titles with the same periodicity, is cacophony.[19] However, it is a cacophony that is built upon a shared emphasis on the present. As the market in the late nineteenth century was dominated by certain periodicities (daily, weekly, monthly), there are certain discernible patterns that underpin the representation of the present. Weekly periodicals, because they appear more often, can create a sense of the present in the interval between numbers which is interpenetrated with recent events. Monthlies, with more 'time to pause, reflect and remember', construct a more distanced conception of the present which reflects upon a sense of the communal past.[20] In each case public events are selected that are perceived to be of interest to readers, but the way in which they signal their contemporaneity depends upon the space in which they must do so.

Mikhail Bakhtin's concept of the chronotope, 'where spatial and temporal indications are fused into one carefully thought-out, concrete whole', usefully provides a framework to understand the relationship between the world represented in the periodical, the world of 'public' events, and the quotidian lives of readers.[21] As all narratives embody a temporality, this chronotope must also be re-presented through a series of transformations from authors manuscript to periodical page. Bakhtin, with his emphasis on the literary, traces this chain:

> The text as such never appears as a dead thing, beginning with any text – and sometimes passing through a lengthy series of mediating links – we always arrive, in the final analysis, at the human voice, which is to say we come up against the human being.[22]

Here Bakhtin seems to be describing something similar to what Latour calls 'reference', 'our way of keeping something *constant* through a series of transformations.'[23] However, unlike Latour, Bakhtin posits a 'sharp and categorical boundary' between the 'world as source of representation and the world represented in the work.' It is the presence of this boundary that permits material transformations as long as they do not interfere with the processes of signification within the text. Yet Bakhtin maintains that to confuse these worlds leads to naïve realism, biography and dogmatic interpretation and evaluation. 'All such confusions are methodologically impermissible,' he writes:

> But it is also impermissible to take this categorical boundary line as something absolute and impermeable (which leads to an oversimplified, dogmatic splitting of hairs). However forcefully the real and the represented world resist fusion, however immutable the presence of that categorical boundary between them, they are nevertheless indissolubly tied up with each other and find themselves in continual mutual interaction; uninterrupted exchange goes on between them, similar to the uninterrupted exchange of matter between living organisms and the environment that surrounds them.[24]

The relationship is symbiotic: 'the work and the world represented in it enter the real world and enrich it, and the real world enters the work and its world as part of the process of its creation, as well as part of its subsequent life, in a continual renewing of the work through the creative perception of listeners and readers.'[25] Bakhtin recognizes that it is materiality that permits movement between the realms but, because he overlooks the malleability of material form, this movement is one-way. The work can circulate through culture because it is an object, but can only signify through its text. Equally, the work is only influenced by acts of reading, but the text remains isolated on the page.

Previous chapters have shown that material form also bears a chronotope: by altering its form, an object might present the history (and so chronotope) of its production alongside those that it more conventionally represents. In Chapter One, for instance, the controversy over Ranyard's astronomical photographic reproductions can be read as a dispute over whether or not they produced the space-time of the stars, or the space-time of their reproduction. Bakhtin concedes that chronotopes are 'mutually inclusive, they co-exist, they may be interwoven with, replace or oppose one another, contradict one another or find themselves in ever more complex interrelationships.'[26] However, because material form is not part of the represented world, its chronotopes do not interfere with it. For Bakhtin, matter and language are distinct: 'inscription and books in any form already lie on the boundary line between culture and a dead nature,' he writes, 'if we approach these items as carriers of the text, then they enter into the realm of culture and [...] the realm of literature.' It is only as material containers that objects feature, hence the absolute presence of the boundary despite its permeability. However, if we grant objects a social role, then their materiality plays a part in representation too. Bakhtin writes:

> Every work has a *beginning* and an *end*, the event represented in it likewise has a beginning and an end, but these beginnings and ends lie in different worlds, in different chronotopes that can never fuse with each other or be identical to each other but that are, at the same time, interrelated and indissolubly tied up with each other.[27]

With objects participating in the world represented in the work, and the represented world altering the nature of the objects through which it moves, the boundary between them is revealed not only as permeable, but performed. If a representation can posit transparent links to a referent, then its ontology is both presented on the page and further defined beyond it. If, however, any of these links are disputed – or even noticed – then a space is opened up between chronotopes and the boundary established. By signalling incursions into the work from the world, and vice-versa, periodicals attempt to bring the beginnings and ends together in order to establish the present as the same both within the text and without.

**Authorship, Science and the *Illustrated London News***

The *Illustrated London News* (*ILN*), like many weeklies, combined news items with more reflective pieces. At sixpence, it was expensive when compared to the cheap penny weeklies that imitated George Newnes's *Tit-Bits*. However, it was lavishly illustrated and, like the *Strand Magazine*, used photographic reproduction to bring a variety of illustrative techniques to the page. Published on a Saturday, the title reported the week's events through a combination of regular departments, notes and discussion in more discursive columns by named writers. Each number opens with a large engraving of something noteworthy that occurred during the week. This is then followed by James Payn's weekly 'Our Note Book', which takes a sardonic glance at the week's often more curious events; and the letterpress accompanying the engravings is on the third page. The items that follow survey events in the courts and theatre, before listing any outstanding news items in a miscellaneous list. 'Foreign News' has its own department, and this is followed by the features 'The Silent Member', 'Science Jottings' and 'Ladies Column.' The final sections of each number contain an instalment of a serial novel, and then a chess problem and some advertisements. Although this order privileges news content, it also highlights the diverse sources considered news by the title. Just as the opening engraving and accompanying letterpress are explicitly identified as news, it is the 'new' that is discussed by all the other departments in the title, and underpins the temporal address of the advertisements. For instance, the 'flu epidemic is discussed in the news items, in James Payn's notebook, in Andrew Wilson's 'Science Jottings' and in Florence Fenwick Miller's 'Ladies Column.' Through this repetition, the 'flu is given a sustained representation in the title from beginning to end that ensures that an intangible physical object has a very real social presence; the repeated variations in this representation allow it to demarcate social groups while maintaining its link to the present.[28]

Each section explicitly addresses the week's events, but their treatment thus varies according to the address of the department. For instance the annual meeting of the British Association for the Advancement of Science (BAAS) was a major news story every summer. Its peripatetic nature meant that each meeting provided the chance to survey the local venue, as well as demonstrate the integration of science with the public good. When the BAAS visited Nottingham in 1893, the *ILN* began its coverage on the 9 September 1893 with 'Meeting of the British Association'. The meeting actually began on the 13 September, but this article 'makes an occasion for presenting some views of that important provincial town and its neighbourhood.' These are presented in photographs, and the accompanying letterpress gives local histories and descriptions. The text only refers directly to the BAAS in the last paragraph, where it compares the list of papers unfavourably with that of the last meeting in Nottingham in 1866. Although 'it promises not to fall behind those of more recent meetings', the claim for scientific importance is not really the focus of the article, rather it is the reporting of an important occasion in the annual rhythm of the nation.[29]

The coverage of the meeting of the BAAS demonstrates how contemporary events are represented as passing into the past. In 1890, the BAAS met in Leeds from the 3 to 10 September, and coverage appeared in the *ILN* on the 6 September. The first mention comes at the beginning of the number with a profile of the new President, Frederick Abel. The notice opens with a reference to his opening address, and refers readers to 'another page' of the number. The letterpress and accompanying photograph establish Abel as an important public servant: we are told he 'is one of the most distinguished chemists of the present day, his researches having been applied more especially to explosives, and the use of electricity for igniting them, with great practical service to our War Department.' The 'our' here ensures that Abel is represented as a public servant as well as a scientist to the *ILN*'s British readers, and that his honours – both scientific and civil – are part of this public service. Like the equivalent biographical notices in the *Strand*, Abel's life is presented as significant to the present; however, whereas the *Strand* posits a broad sense of the contemporary, the *ILN* signals a much more delimited temporality by linking biography to a transient event.[30]

The account of the address itself is given in the middle of the number. Even though the BAAS circulated the address as part of its advance publications, the *ILN* do not quote from it verbatim, preferring to let readers know that it 'was an elaborate review of progress made in the practical application of scientific discoveries' and give a précis with some general descriptions of Leeds and the proceedings of the meeting. The scientific papers that are described tend to be those of the Presidents, and they are conspicuously rewritten for the *ILN*'s readership: for instance Lyon Playfair, in his Presidential Address to Section E (Geography), praises the management of the French colony of Algiers as emblematic of good imperial practice around the Mediterranean; the *ILN* notes 'he gave a splendid survey, in which he commended Corsica to tourists as an epitome of everything that makes travel delightful.' Such rewriting, coupled with the absence of any discussion after the event, emphasizes that it is the meeting – and specifically its Presidential Address – that is newsworthy, rather than its scientific content.[31]

This can be seen through a comparison with *Nature*. As the leading scientific weekly, *Nature* was predicated on scientific news, its 'Notes' and correspondence columns providing a valuable way to signal current research, track controversy and mark intellectual property. Whereas the *ILN* might cover the BAAS in two numbers, for *Nature* it is both a major scientific event and, as it occurs while the scientific societies are in recess, an important source of copy. The first mention of the Leeds meeting is a request for abstracts printed in the number for 7 August 1890. Notices then reappear on the 14 and 28 August, the latter advertising the published materials that accompany the meeting. Abel's Presidential Address was on Tuesday 2 September, and it was reported in *Nature* that Thursday. The item is headed 'The British Association, Leeds, Tuesday Evening', the temporal marker emphasizing the item's role as breaking news. As the dailies also published the Presidential Address on the 4 September, this meant *Nature* was as current as the daily press. Unsurprisingly, the item gives the address in full, and also contains the Section Presidential Addresses of T.E. Thorpe and A.H. Green.[32] The rest of the Section Presidential Addresses appear in a notice 'The British Association, Wednesday Morning' the following week. This article appears after the correspondence in *Nature*, towards the review section of the journal and the text itself is review-like: the author notes it has been 'universally admitted that no more successful lectures have ever been delivered at an Association Meeting than those of Mr Poulton on Friday, on "Mimicry", and Prof. Boys on Monday, on "Quartz Fibres." The large audiences were really entranced.'[33] The days indicate the span that this article encompasses: rather than the moment of the Address, it summarizes the developments throughout the week from the perspective of the last day, and the focus is thus switched to the success of the event as a whole.

*Nature* continues to publish the proceedings of the BAAS long after it finishes. The following week's item is entitled 'The British Association' – the absence of temporal marker indicating the finished nature of the event. Further details are given in specialized reviews such as 'Chemistry at the British Association' or 'Physics at the British Association.'[34] Also, selected papers are reprinted: the two mentioned above by Poulton and Boys appear in the *Nature* on the 2 October and 16 October respectively; and Spencer Umfreville Pickering's paper, identified as a paper read to Section B, is printed the following week.[35] These later reports are no longer about the BAAS: as I discuss in the following chapters, as they are written up as academic papers, their nature as objects changes. These reports and papers are no longer about an event that has passed, but rather an ongoing discussion of science in the present.

Although both *Nature* and the *ILN* note the proceedings of the BAAS as newsworthy, their representation of it is different both in terms of content, and treatment over time. For both titles, events are news for as long as they are current; as they are both weeklies, the temporal period for which this applies is a week. The *ILN* identifies a diverse range of newsworthy institutions, from the theatre to fashion, and its commodification of these passing events ensures that it addresses the present of the readers, while ensuring that the moment it inscribes will pass before the appearance of the next number, taking the current number with it. As such, there is nothing about the BAAS that can be discussed retrospectively, as its social function is based upon its contingent spatial-temporal moment. For *Nature*, however, the BAAS is both a social event, containing a public address on behalf of science, a source of scientific news that could provoke further responses, and a repository of more stable copy such as lectures. With each number the BAAS becomes decreasingly newsworthy, and the attention of *Nature* shifts from its novelty, to the different temporal narrative of scientific progress.

**Authorship and Editorship in the Weekly Periodical Press**

None of the reports about the BAAS in *Nature* or the *ILN* are signed. Signature posits an originary source for the text, implying that it was written by an individual somewhere beyond the title. However, authors can also write themselves into their texts. Mikhail Bakhtin argues that the 'novelist stands in need of some essential formal and generic mask that could serve to define the positions from which he views life, as well as the position from which he makes that life possible.'[36] This applies equally to writers within periodicals: the combination of editorial metanarratives, departmental divisions, as well the generic constraints of individual items, all ensure that a wide range of performative textual identities are deployed in order to advance careers. These textual personae influence the perception of the name appended to the text while also positing a different set of represented chronotopes within it. By signalling a presence within the text, its temporality is represented as being the moment of writing, rather than posited somewhere beyond the number as a whole. This space is manipulated for temporal effect: in fiction, the distance is exploited to display artistic skill; in reflective essays the events are often placed in the past, but the commentator shares the present, however defined, of the reader; and in the interview the signed author and textual persona are seen as the same, in order to allow them to substitute for the reader in the space-time of the interviewee.

The evangelical penny weekly *Great Thoughts* exploits the space between represented chronotopes and the times and spaces of reading to produce a present that is both nuanced toward different types of reader while also offering sustained moral guidance. However, although it is constituted by a miscellany of signed quotations, extracts and articles, these names are rarely granted authorial status. Instead its editor, the Reverend Robert P. Downes, exploits the publishing process to insert a new time of writing that displaces that of the original authors in its resultant textual space. *Great Thoughts* was situated at the apex of a number of periodical discourses: as a miscellany, containing various 'great thoughts from master minds', it was similar to early nineteenth-century 'scissors and paste' journalism but, from its first number, it was also a clear imitator of George Newnes's *Tit-Bits*.[37] By 1893 *Great Thoughts* was clearly identified with the New Journalism: the title page for the 14 October (see below Figure 3.1) carries a travel insurance policy and advertises an interview by Raymond Blathwayt (who was also a contributor to Stead's *Review of Reviews*) by reproducing the portrait on the cover. These features are linked to the journal's wider commercial position: the insurance policy is also an advertisement for Ocean Accident and Guarantee Corporation Ltd; the strip down the left advertises Blathwayt's *Interviews*, collected from the journal and sold by its publishers; and the 'Literary Circle', advertised in the advertising wrapper and offering a £50 prize, is actually a course of study that focuses on books distributed by the publishers, A.W. Hall, two of which are by Downes himself.

**Figure 3.1 Cover of *Great Thoughts*, 20, 14 October 1893**

*Great Thoughts* complicates Mathew Arnold's dismissal (and gendering) of the New Journalism as 'feather brained.'[38] Downes, a Wesleyan Methodist 'minister without pastoral charge', follows Arnold in endorsing 'the knowledge of the best which has been said or written' against the debilitating effects of modern life: [39]

> The necessity for our existence was never greater than in the present hour, since amid the fierce competitions of our busy and restless age, men are in constant danger of over-valuing the world of sense and undervaluing the world of spirit, or forgetting that noblest part of our complex nature, the inner life, because the calls to the outer life are so loud and unceasing. [40]

Denying the link between form and content suggested by Arnold, Downes employs such 'calls' – both in the 10 pages of advertisements that surround each number and more widely in the journal's format – in order to provide literary, religious and cultural heritage in a manner compatible with urban working life. The fallen state of the present is due to the abundant pace of late nineteenth-century life. In the preface to volume 18, Downes quotes a 'recent writer':

> We have, depend upon it, lost something by the desuetude of the fine old practice of our wiser parents of 'reading a chapter' morning and night. Like most old fashions, it was based on the needs of our nature. The spirit should have its meals 'regular' no less than the body; but alas! While we would not miss our dinners, our 'devotions' come off but badly these breakneck days. [41]

But, the writer continues, 'on those rum days when we have taken, say, one fine line with us to town, how strongly complete the day has seemed, how the little discords have been harmonised by that one commanding chord.' *Great Thoughts*, Downes suggests, is a periodical designed to easily furnish such a 'fine line':

> The charm of such a volume as this arises from the fact the busy man may take it up in a brief interval of leisure, and read a sentence or a paragraph which will linger in his mind like deep, divine music, and go with into the place of his toil. [42]

Identifying the archetypal reader of New Journalism, the 'busy man', Downes offers him a text that operates like a surrogate Bible tailored specifically to his needs. [43]

The way *Great Thoughts* does this is by quoting from its 'master minds', while not attributing them ownership of their words. Like *Tit-Bits*, the rhetoric of *Great Thoughts* is one of Christian Democracy: he encourages his readers to wander 'through this mansion reared by hands which have planned and tongues which have uttered wisdom [...] and count anything which is rare and precious in it as their own.' [44] When authorship is ascribed in the title, the only information given is a name, and there is no textual gloss to provide context. This disassociates the words from their originary time-space, and allows them to be recontextualized by editorial discourse. For instance, the passing seasons are represented through the juxtaposition of articles: in October 1892 there are a number Autumn-specific articles; and at Christmas, Downes themes the title accordingly. [45] More newsworthy events are also accommodated: the death of Tennyson on the 6 October 1892 is commemorated well into November.[46] The emphasis is continually placed on the content of the statement, rather than where it comes from, and this divests it of the personality of the author and the contingency of its utterance. The indexes given as supplements further emphasize this by providing cross references that stress genre rather than source. The categories indexed are 'Prose', 'Poetry', 'Illustrations', 'Children's Page', 'Index to Authors' and 'Index of Scripture Texts'. Although it is possible to trace all the quotations by a single author, references are only to the pages of *Great Thoughts*. Even the 'Index to Scripture Texts', although ordered as per the Bible, will guide the reader to 'the Article in *Great Thoughts* by which the same is illustrated.'[47] *Great Thoughts*, in mobilizing the words of the past, insists on the primacy of the present, with all its temptations and potential dangers.

As these dangers depend on the location of the reader, *Great Thoughts* configures its temporal-spatial references accordingly. It was published on a Saturday and so, even though it was aimed at those travelling to work, it also provides reading suitable for Sunday. Although an increasing number of women worked in the city, the working body in *Great Thoughts* is always male. Its textual spaces are thus gendered accordingly, and then contrasted: just as the periodical provides sustenance on the journey from domestic space into the world of work; so it also contains items directed at these domestic spaces. Its address here is double: it both mobilizes a representation of domestic space for men to take with them, while also providing reading for domestic space, aimed primarily at the family, women, and children. This feminized reading thus operates as a contrast to material aimed at working men warning of the dangers of the city, while also guiding women readers in the appropriate domestic behaviour.

For *Great Thoughts* the city contains 'the seduction of impure delight', so many of the articles aimed at men provide masculine fortifying content.[48] The regular 'Counsels For Young Men', which runs throughout the 1890s, provides a moral framework for the secular workplace. This department betrays the title's wider concerns over how time is spent either beyond the home or its mobile surrogate *Great Thoughts*. For instance in 1892 Downes combines an excerpt from Cicero ('To live long it is necessary to live slowly') with another from Johnson ('Life, however short, is made still shorter by waste of time').[49] In January 1894, Downes provides extracts from Charles Bray's *The Science of Man* under the headings 'The Love and Power and Approbation', 'The Company We Keep' and 'A Plea Against Selfishness.' He then ventriloquizes Bray with an unsigned piece of his own, 'Inexperience of Youth', which encourages rising early, exercise and study.[50] These extracts exhort 'young men' to create more spaces and times outside of work, preferably in the home, and suggests that *Great Thoughts* can help fill them safely.

These departments are contrasted with others such as the 'Children's Page', 'Poems for Recitation', and 'Deep Sea Soundings for Christian Teachers', which cater to other categories of imagined readers. These ostensibly pedagogic departments construct women as teachers within the home, complementing any schooling children might receive outside. However, the co-presence of these departments, so vital for the ideology of *Great Thoughts*, belies an anxiety over the feminization of men. The article 'Manly Boys' nicely demonstrates this: defending the 'home boys', 'mother boys' and 'babies' who are 'led by a mother's apron strings', the article recommends this mother-son relationship by justifying it with the more conventional masculine tropes of war and honourable death.[51] Even the melodramatic serial fiction, heavily coded with tropes of female sin and redemption through heterosexual love, affirms the domestic as a site for femininity.[52]

Even though its form is contemporary, *Great Thoughts* rarely addresses passing events because its text is intended for the 'inner life'. *Great Thoughts* is not a newspaper: if anything it mobilizes the space of 'Sunday', the temporal demarcation in which public events are replaced by a static domestic space. The journal achieves this by distancing its texts from their external origins, preventing these times and spaces from obfuscating the meanings that Downes overwrites onto them through their spatial configuration. As such, news rarely penetrates *Great Thoughts*, but when it does, Downes's editorial strategy allows him to ventriloquize events so that they too address the 'inner life' of readers rather than the contemporary moment. When John Tyndall died on the 4 December 1893, Downes ran a sequence of articles that make Tyndall into a 'master mind' by ignoring his death while making his life speak to the themes of redemption and the responsible pursuit of knowledge. Downes was not against science, but he felt that its increasingly imperial reach encroached upon moral and spiritual domains: the death of Tyndall provided an opportunity to rehearse this lesson for the guidance of his readers.[53]

The sequence opens with a page that contrasts a poem called 'The Dying Year' with an unsigned piece purportedly by T.H. Huxley (Figure 3.2). The verse, by Gover Shaw, addresses the passing of the old year, and asks for God's guidance for the New Year. However, the piece by Huxley reflects upon his life's work and so complements the anonymous note under the column 'Thoughts on Love' that suggests sincerity is the sacrifice of oneself for principle. In this context the passage into the New Year is both about death and sacrifice, as well as the search for truth in the darkness of the unknown. The next page continues this theme. Arthur Smith's 'Grave of the Cynic' describes how the author stumbles over a forgotten grave that belongs to one who has committed 'the crime of indifference towards all that is exalting, all that is divine in life.' This man is the worst kind of scientist: in a parody of Karl Pearson, Smith alleges that 'for thee, science pointed to *order in development, and to unity in law.* Didst thou not then perceive a grand purpose to underlies life, flooding the universe with energy?' As night falls the narrator lingers over the desolate grave until God's mercy is revealed by a patch of light that falls upon the 'cold grey stone':

## ➤ Thoughts on Love. ◄

NOTHING is so fierce but love will soften, nothing so sharp-sighted in other matters, but it throws a mist before the eyes on it. L'ESTRANGE.

Love is a bad tenant for one's bosom ; for when compelled to quit, he always leaves the mansion more or less out of repair. C. F. HOFFMAN.

To love in order to be loved in return is man ; but to love for the pure sake of loving is almost the characteristic of an angel. LAMARTINE.

OF all the joys we can experience in the present, or hope for in the life to come, love is the only one worth our care and solicitude. W. ALEXANDER.

Love and friendship exclude each other : love begins by love, and the strongest friendship could only give birth to a feeble love. DU CŒUR.

ALL brave men love ; for he only is brave who has affections to fight for, whether in the daily battle of life or in physical contests. N. HAWTHORNE.

THERE is no permanent love but that which has duty for its eldest brother ; so that if one sleeps the other watches, and honour is safe. STAHL.

HE who has fostered the sweet poison of love by fondling it, finds it too late to refuse the yoke which he has of his own accord assumed. SENECA.

WHEN love is well timed, it is not a fault to love ; the strong, the brave, the virtuous, and the wise sink in the soft captivity together. ADDISON.

LADIES, lovers, lawyers, loafers, draymen, and drunken men are equally interested in the solution of the little word of one syllable—love. R. D. OWEN.

IN love we never think of moral qualities, and scarcely of intellectual ones ; temperament and manner alone, with beauty, excite love. HAZLITT.

Love is like what is called the Milky Way in heaven, a brilliant mass formed by thousands of little stars, of which each perhaps is nebulous. H. BEYLE.

WE can receive anything from love, for that is the way of receiving it from ourselves ; but not from any-one who assumes to bestow. R. W. EMERSON.

HOWEVER dull a woman may be, she will understand all there is in love ; however intelligent a man may be, he will never know but half of it. MME. FEE.

THE only conclusive evidence of a man's sincerity is that he gives himself for a principle. Words, money, all things else, are comparatively easy to give away ; but when a man makes a gift of his daily life and practice, it is plain that the truth, whatever it may be, has taken possession of him.

### THE DYING YEAR.

NOW, Lord, as softly breathes the wind
The requiem of the dying year,
Our mingled thoughts we cast behind,
As night's black pall falls o'er the bier ;
Accept our praise from heart's sincere,
For mercies through another year.

Upon the New Year's threshold, Lord,
With throbbing, anxious hearts we stand,
Fearing to tread " the unexplored "
Without Thine own Almighty hand
To guide ; O Lord, we pray to Thee
To guide and guard us constantly.

If it should be Thy will that we
Should scale affliction's sterile steeps ;
Bear sorrow and adversity,
With none to cheer the heart that weeps ;
Still we our prayer would raise to Thee,
" Thou 'Man of Grief,' our solace be."

Thou, who alone the wine-press trod,
Who uttered the forsaken cry,
Bore meekly persecution's rod
Without a murmur or a sigh ;
Thou " Man of Sorrows " be our stay
While trav'ling life's perplexing way.

Lord, we are blind !—be Thou our sight ;
Lord, we are weak !—be Thou our strength ;
Oh, shed Thy ever-radiant light
Upon our path until at length
We grasp the hands—life's wand'rings o'er—
Of the " beloved ones gone before."
GOVER SHAW.

### PROFESSOR HUXLEY ON THE WORK OF HIS LIFE.

THE last thing that it would be proper for me to do would be to speak of the work of my life, or to say at the end of the day whether I think I have earned my wages or not. Men are said to be partial judges of themselves. Young men may be ; I doubt if old men are. Life seems terribly foreshortened as they look back, and the mountain they set themselves to climb in youth turns out to be a mere spur of immeasurably higher ranges when, with failing breath, they reach the top. But if I may speak of the objects I have had more or less definitely in view since I began the ascent of my hillock, they are briefly these : To promote the increase of natural knowledge and to forward the application of scientific methods of investigation to all the problems of life to the best of my ability, in the conviction, which has grown with my growth and strengthened with my strength, that there is no alleviation for the sufferings of mankind except veracity of thought and of action, and the resolute facing of the world as it is when the garment of make-believe by which pious hands have hidden its uglier features is stripped off.

It is with this intent that I have subordinated any reasonable or unreasonable ambition for scientific fame which I may have permitted myself to entertain to other ends ; to the popularisation of science ; to the development and organisation of scientific education ; to the endless series of battles and skirmishes over evolution ; and to untiring opposition to that ecclesiastical spirit, that clericalism, which in England, as everywhere else, and to whatever denomination it may belong, is the deadly enemy of science.

**Figure 3.2 Page from *Great Thoughts*, 20, 30 December 1893, p. 268**

Behold! beneath the rays of that light the creeping lichen shrinks away, and from under its folds are revealed the words: 'In my Father's house are many mansions.' How luminous now this spot so dark before: how each letter sparkles and glitters on the cold grey stone.

The salvation of the cynic signals the appropriation of science by religion, and so guides the reader as to the correct interpretation of Bütschli's experiments to synthesize protoplasm, given directly beneath. After the cynical scientist has been chastized but forgiven, Bütschli's emulsions are cast as presumptuous folly rather than disturbing new discovery.

The introduction of the most recent attempt at proving the spontaneous generation of life enlists Tyndall on the side of religious orthodoxy against radical science.[54] It is this context that frames the anonymous biography of Tyndall that is presented as his obituary on the following page. It immediately sets out the title's anxiety over scientific endeavour, recognizing that it has 'greatly widened the boundaries of knowledge' but also 'has been wielded to the lessening of our belief in Divine providence.'[55] Tyndall's life is presented as a mixture of expositor and expert, a servant of the reading public and a responsible guardian of scientific progress. This is important as the increasing specialization of science makes it harder to monitor whether science is lessening belief:

> He works at the crucible, the retort, or the telescope, works for the most part behind the veil. And yet those who stand without earnestly desire to know the conquest which science is achieving, and the results of those conquests on the whole body of accepted truth.

Tyndall becomes a late nineteenth-century Moses, bringing interpretations of God's work from 'where the snows linger and the eagle finds its eyrie' to 'come forth to prepare the world for its reception.'[56]

Tyndall is not just depicted as a popularizer – which is a common theme running through most of his obituaries – but a popularizer for the ends of religion. The subheading 'Battle for Life' relates the addiction to gambling with railway shares that he indulged while working as a railway engineer. The subsequent 'Study in Germany' intertwines the established apprenticeship of the laboratory researcher with the protestant poetics of fall and redemption through work. It is at this point that they print an anonymous engraving of Tyndall, taken from a photograph by Barrand (Figure 3.3.). The portrait does not invoke his profession and, as an engraving, does not establish his co-presence in time and space. Instead we are given a likeness of a 'master mind', with the contrasts between light and dark reflecting the narrative that established Tyndall, despite his early moral lapse, as a contemplative but responsible man of science.

This narrative rewrites Tyndall's life as one of selfless devotion to knowledge. Even the most controversial moment of Tyndall's life, his notorious Belfast Address in 1874, is made to testify to his sense of responsibility. Not only is it credited as 'the first clear and unmistakable public utterance as to the aims of modern science', but Tyndall 'endeavoured to soothe down the excitement by assuring the world that the address had not all the materialistic and agnostic bearings which on the surface it appeared to possess.' It is not his death that is the focus here, but rather the way in which he lived his life: the gravestone that marked

GREAT THOUGHTS. 271

STUDY IN GERMANY.

TYNDALL meantime had been devoting what spare time he had to the study of science, and in 1847 exercise of thrift managed to save some two or three hundred pounds, and the following year, along with Dr. Frankland, proceeded to the University of Mar-

THE LATE PROFESSOR TYNDALL, PH.D., LL.D., D.C.L., F.R.S.
*From a Photograph by Barraud's, Limited, 263, Oxford Street, London, W.*

he accepted a post at Queenswood College, Hants, where Dr. Frankland was chemist. He had by the burg, in Hesse Cassel, to study chemistry under Bunsen. There, he said, he was able to work without weariness for

**Figure 3.3 'The Late Professor Tyndall, PhD, LLD, DCL, FRS', from *Great Thoughts*, 20, 30 December 1893, p. 271**

the passing of the scientist in 'Grave of a Cynic' was eloquent despite its silence; the account that memorializes Tyndall's life makes a lesson of his passing by ensuring that his life is interpreted. Although obituaries do provide an extratextual temporal reference, *Great Thoughts* subsumes them within its wider system of intertextual reference.

In *Great Thoughts* the gap between numbers is a source of anxiety. In providing moral, religious reading in a form that can easily be consumed during the week, the journal sought to fill this space with nourishing content. Its dominant temporality is the present but, as this is predicated on a stable internal spiritual and moral life, it is not anchored in depictions of passing events shared by the readers. Even the death of Tyndall is reinscribed into a longer history that can testify to good practice in the present. Parasitically thriving off the words of others, *Great Thoughts* can use almost any textual source to communicate its message. The potential for polysemy, and its attendant spatial-temporal diversity, is regulated by Downes's judicious editing. His semivisible presence seeks to guide the production of meaning by the reader so these heterogeneous linguistic fragments produce a concentrated focus on living well in the present.

**Authorship, News and Science**

The death of John Tyndall is also covered in the *Illustrated London News*. Published 12 days after his death, the number for 16 December contains a lengthy item by the Keeper of Printed Books at the British Museum, Richard Garnett. Like the notice in *Great Thoughts*, the piece establishes the reasons for Tyndall's renown while countering the more notorious aspects of his life. Garnett writes that although science has a far greater importance 'in the world of thought than it held in the days of a Newton or even of a Davy', it is also well-served for scientific expositors. Tyndall, he argues, was an expositor of ideas, and the 'man who circulates scientific ideas animates then with moral purpose, and brings them into relation with the best thoughts of his time.' By establishing Tyndall as a moral philosopher, Garnett displaces Tyndall's controversial scientific utterances with a poetic sensibility that sometimes leads him astray. He claims that Tyndall's 'talent for imperceptibly conducting his reader into his own conclusions [is] so irresistible' that it becomes the text, rather than the ideas, that are communicated.[57] This is a necessary manoeuvre: as a number of obituaries note, his scientific achievements are not enough to merit his fame, and so it is his popularizations that are admired.[58] Whether as an expositor of science or of ideas, Tyndall is positioned as a mediator, standing between the elusive and unpatentable idea and works that are stable, owned and reproducible.

Garnett's role as author is similar to this: his textual persona operates to fill the space left by Tyndall's death with a testimony to his importance. It is for this reason that obituaries, even though they mark time, are not really news. Because the event that passes signals an absence, they require the presence of a mediating subject to interpret the significance of that which has passed and so secure a place for it in history. News, however, does not need an author as it contains nothing that is 'written.' Sidney Low, writing in the *National Review*, expresses incredulity that, since 1842, the law treats newspapers as books in terms of copyright.[59] For Low, the demarcation between books and newspapers is based on permanence, with books – in the words of the judgement – being 'literary works of lasting benefit to the world', and newspapers being 'essentially ephemeral.'[60] He writes that the courts have 'decided that it is the literary expression, not the ideas, in a book which can be most easily and suitably protected; and the test of an infringement of copyright is the piracy of the author's words rather than of his thoughts.'[61] This creates the possibility of copyright in news as long as it is written in a striking manner. Low dismisses this as absurd:

> There are occasions, as, for example, some famous special correspondent sends a striking description from a field of battle, in which, even in a Newspaper, literary form gives its whole value to the composition; and, of course, novels, stories, and those literary articles which are happily becoming more common in Newspapers, stand on a footing of their own. But much of the most commercially valuable part of the every newspaper is valuable quite irrespective of its form.[62]

The majority of newsprint concerns timely reporting of facts, and this is the product of the staff of a newspaper, toiling away anonymously to capture the essence of the event itself. If copyright be at all applicable to news, Low argues, it should be for the short time in which such writing is relevant; literary writing, of course, aspires to be timeless. This distinction was enshrined in the recent Berne Convention, which established copyright in periodicals but not in 'articles of political discussion, or to the reproduction of news of the day or current topics.'[63] Time, then, not only determines whether something is news, but also whether something is authored.

Andrew Wilson's 'Science Jottings Column' in the *ILN* employs a similar generic temporality that is structured by authorship. Wilson does note Tyndall's death, but not until the number for the 23 December 1893, a week after Garnett's piece. Wilson reiterates many of the same themes, referring to Tyndall's skill as a popularizer and his moral character, but he also introduces a number of personal reflections. He recounts 'his eloquent defence of a rational Sunday delivered at Glasgow, an occasion when I had the felicity of taking part in the proceedings over which Professor Tyndall presided.' Also, Wilson ensures that his presence in this account is linked to the passing moment: when discussing Tyndall's works, he recommends that readers read his *Forms of Water* as 'an attractive Christmas study of frost and ice.'[64] Like Garnett, Wilson directs readers to Tyndall's literary remains; however, Wilson does so on the basis of personal recommendation: this is not so much an obituary of Tyndall, as a column about Wilson's reaction to his death.

Despite its title, 'Science Jottings' is not a scientific news department like the 'Notes' sections of scientific publications such as *Nature*. Instead, it offers anecdotal comments about science, with Wilson acting as author and narrator. It is oriented towards the present, but this is not the present structured by passing events and is often located in the represented chronotopes of Wilson's textual persona. For instance, 'A Corner of Kent' begins, 'Strolling from Herne Bay towards Reculvers the other day, I found myself on a coast which is geologically classic as regards the action of the sea on the land'; and his 'The Way of Growth' with 'From where I sit I can see the elm-trees day by day throwing forth their leaves, and the limes and the aspens making a leafy screen in front of the brook.'[65] These introductory sentences preface scientific essays that are aimed at a nonscientific readership. Even his 'Our Monthly Look Around' does not survey the month's events in a systematic way, instead preferring to ruminate on curiosities, odd publications, and occasional events.[66] Although these are within the 'recent' defined within the item's monthly periodicity, it does not claim to present the latest results of scientific research, nor does it survey any of the newsworthy scientific institutions.

Wilson does not even comment about the annual meetings of the British Association, even though they represent an ideal opportunity to present science in an accessible fashion. In the same number that carries the report of Abel's Presidential Address to the Association in 1890 (6 September), Wilson's 'Science Jottings' – one of his 'Monthly Look Around' items – opens: 'What is this one hears about the higher apes and their powers of imitating humanity?' The piece quotes a report from *Nature* that states that 'a large ape is undoubtedly acting as a signalman (*sic*) under direction on a railway in Natal.' Wilson appeals to 'any South African reader' of the *ILN* to furnish details of species, age, habits and disposition and what it actually does on the railway.[67] This might seem like news – Wilson responding to recent scientific reports – and by opening it to his readers appears to create a temporal narrative that could complement that unfolding in *Nature*; however, the article in *Nature* was published six weeks previously (24 July 1890) and was part of a longer controversy prompted by Stanley's verification of Emin Pasha's claim that apes were serving as torch bearers.[68] This sensational story, which combines late nineteenth-century evolutionary tropes with a promethean myth located at the limits of empire, is not pursued.

The reason Wilson does not record scientific news in 'Science Jottings' is because of his audience. In *Visualizing Deviance: A Study of News Organizations*, Richard Ericson, Patricia Baranek and Janet Chan argue that 'the journalistic search for procedural strays and signs of disorder is a means of charting the consensual boundaries of society and acknowledging order.'[69] This certainly applies to the *ILN*'s more familiar news coverage; but because of the necessary distance between scientific research and the 'consensual boundaries of society', science cannot function as a newsworthy institution in its own right. Scientific practice is predicated on a withdrawal into a private space in order to isolate complex phenomena and record results. This spatial politics, and the method that safeguards, in turn informs the cultural stereotype of the disinterested scientist, abstracted from society. This can clearly be seen in the representations of science as an introverted amoral practice during the debates over vivisection, but it also underpins James Payn's ironic treatment of scientific pronouncements upon public affairs and broader caricature of the scientist as cold and inhuman.[70] Andrew Wilson recognizes the need for a mediating figure to explain scientific research in 'Science Jottings.' In an account on 'A Display of Energy' he writes:

> To certain minds the words 'force' and 'energy' are meaningless terms: and I sympathize with the mind which, accustomed to the practical details of life, and to the realities of pounds, shillings and pence, refuses or is unable to assimilate the abstractions or transcendentalisms in which the scientific mind delights. But most ideas in science are easily mastered, if one can but think in terms of things rather than of names.[71]

This movement from names to things is an argument in favour of analogy and metaphor in scientific popularization. In a curious reverse, it is the introduction of things to stand in for the concepts that underlie them that is the abstraction here and, in order to retain the link between them, this move requires the presence of an author

There is a further element to this. The notion that ideas cannot be property was well-established in law, and this also applied to scientific ideas.[72] Under nineteenth-century patent law, a scientific principle 'cannot form the basis of a valid patent unless its application to a practical and useful end and object is shown.'[73] Sidney Low links the abstract idea with the abstract event:

> To call it copyright of news seems misuse of language; copyright is the exclusive right to multiply copies of your own artistic or literary work, not the right to debar other people from describing certain circumstances or events. It would be as if one could secure by letters patent the sole and exclusive use of a natural principle; or as if one could copyright a particular train of ideas in philosophy or metaphysics and forbid anyone else so much as to refer to them.[74]

An accurate rendering of an idea or event could not be property, and so would not be marked as the work of an author. However, the temporal dynamics informing each are direct opposites: an idea cannot be patented as it is timeless, but its application can as it will be superseded; an event is contingent and will pass, but a literary rendering has the potential to preserve it. What connects the two is the introduction of an object that can manifest the marks of property in time and space in place of the abstract event or principle.

The presence of the author in a text signals its derivation as somewhere beyond it. As both science and the news are predicated on transmitting events occurring elsewhere, the author figure is displaced onto nature, institutions, or the mediating journals themselves. In *Visualizing Deviance*, Ericson et al. suggest that 'journalists offer accounts of reality, their own versions of events as they think they are most appropriately visualized.'[75] This involves a necessary degree of interpretation, in which cultural resources are deployed in order to create a frame that can accommodate otherwise exceptional events. When the *ILN* discusses scientific events as news – for instance in its reports of the BAAS – it can do so only by invoking science as an institution, and its sole terms of reference are the wider social world that it occurs within. To discuss the science itself would necessarily involve recourse to Wilson's methods of analogy and example, and such manifestly literary creations, clearly invoking an author, cannot be deemed either news or science.

## Conclusion: Authorship, Illness and Proprietary Medicines in the *Chemist and Druggist*

Like other weekly titles, trade journals such as the *Chemist and Druggist* deploy selected passing events in order to signal their link with the present. In the 1890s the *Chemist and Druggist* was a 4d weekly which consisted of just over 50 pages of letterpress, including about 22 pages of advertising material.[76] It was aimed at druggists, those who had completed the Minor examination of the Pharmaceutical Society and who were consequently marginalized from both the pharmaceutical elite and academic science more generally. However, through a policy of active opposition to the Pharmaceutical Society, the *Chemist and Druggist* presented itself as the alternative voice of the entire industry, taking in pharmaceutical chemists (who had passed the Major examination), analytical, and industrial chemists. The regular departments however betray its main audience: the 'Metropolitan' and 'Provincial Reports', 'General and Provincial News', 'Bankruptcy Reports', 'Gazette', 'Trade Report', 'Patents', 'Practical Notes and Formulae', 'Medical Gleanings' and 'Dispensing Notes' clearly place the reader in a shop, part of a community of druggists in competition with each other but united against the traders on the street.

The *Chemist and Druggist*, although a specialist title, shares certain generic features with other weeklies. It begins by focusing on the week's events, organizing these spatially with an emphasis on the capital that acknowledges events beyond it while simultaneously labelling them provincial. Like other weeklies, the leading articles tend to be in the middle of the journal, and these were followed by correspondence and information relevant to the community like bankruptcies, births and deaths. At the end of each number are the market reports, this explicitly commercial information leading to advertising on the numbered letterpress and then onto the wrapper. Also, the *Chemist and Druggist* was published on a Saturday, linking its periodicity with the weekly wages of the druggists, while giving the journal a sense of weekly retrospection that also looks forward to the resumption of trade on Monday.

The *Chemist and Druggist* attempts to assert itself as a source of guidance to the druggist according to the weekly rhythms of the trade. Features such as the 'Trade Reports' positioned at the end of the number, insert up-to-date financial reports to guide the druggist for the forthcoming week. However, the shop-keeping druggist was in danger of being conflated with (and put out of business by) the tradesman, and so the *Chemist and Druggist* sought to identify a professional identity through the practice of dispensing rather than trade. This was problematic as the objects that druggists passed over the counter were subject to substantial scrutiny but often had dubious histories. In his *Chronicles of Pharmacy*, A.C. Wootton, the editor of the *Chemist and Druggist*, claimed pharmacy was 'an acquirement which must be almost as ancient as man himself on the earth.' This ancient history conveniently displaces the origins of drugs for the moment they are sold:

> Of the hundreds of drugs yielded by the vegetable kingdom, collected from all parts of the world, and used as remedies, in some cases for thousands of years, I do not know of a single one which can surely be traced to any historic or scientific personage. It is possible in many instances to ascertain the exact or approximate date when a particular drug was introduced to our markets, and sometimes to name the physician, explorer, merchant, or conqueror to whom we are indebted for such an addition to our materia medica; but there is always a history or a tradition behind our acquaintance with the new medicine, going back to an undetermined past.[77]

Wootton's purpose is to restore this past, to 'trace back to their authors the formulas of the most popular of our medicines, and to recall those which have lost their reputation.'[78] However, Wootton's task is doomed to failure: by defining the practice as the 'manipulation of drugs, the conversion of the raw material into the manufactured product' he confuses authorship, and its related myth of origin, with manipulation.[79]

Wootton's *Chronicles of Pharmacy* attempts to establish a noble history for the trade, yet his accounts consistently confuse this with the contingent moments of dispensing advocated in the *Chemist and Druggist*. For instance in the section 'Familiar Medicines and Some of Their Histories' his narrative struggles to maintain the coherence of these familiar medicines over time. Joseph Ince's tincture of quinine is reported to consist of 1 grain of sulphate of quinine in one drachm of compound spirit of ammonia. This was not approved and Mr Bastick produced an Ammoniated Sulphate of Quinine by dissolving 32 grains of sulphate of quinine in 3½ ounces of proof spirit. This too was deemed inadequate and the British Pharmacopœia, attempting to install a standard, insists on less ammonia and the use of alcohol instead of proof spirit. 'Anderson's Scots Pills' were 'invented' in 1635 (although Dr Patrick Anderson claimed he had obtained the formula in Venice) and patented in 1687. This patent was then passed on within the family until it was sold to the present proprietors, Raimes Clark and Co., in 1876. Despite the existence of the patent, Wootton claims formulas for Anderson's Scots Pills 'will be found in all the manuals of pharmacy published in Europe and America, but they differ considerably.' The history of the 'Chelsea Pensioner', an 'electuary for rheumatism', is even more uncertain. Wootton reveals he 'has not been able to discover where or when or with whom it originated' and as the compilers of books of formulas naturally copy from each other 'a legend once started is likely to become crystallized.' The apocryphal origin of the drug – that the recipe was given to either Lord Anson or Lord Amherst by a Chelsea Pensioner for the sum of between £300–£500 and an annuity of £20–30 – has become accepted. Wootton reveals how his previous attempts to find the truth failed and an appeal in the *Chemist & Druggist* resulted in 'a number of old formulas.' Wootton ruefully concludes '[i]t rather looks as the fiction was concocted as an advertisement in the days when the electuary was a proprietary medicine, if it ever was.'[80]

Wootton's failure to trace the histories of drugs prevents the evocation of their past in the present. Instead, the practice of pharmacy necessarily pluralizes these narratives, preventing the creation of an over-arching temporal narrative and confusing any myths of origin. The *Chemist and Druggist* is caught between these temporal moments: the 'Practical Notes and Formula' and 'Dispensing Notes' attempt to standardize practice in order to establish the correct way of doing things; yet because of the existence of local names, recipes and ingredients, variation is repeatedly emphasized through the named correspondence and submitted notes. When John Findlay, speaking at the Edinburgh Chemists' Assistants' and Apprentices Association, suggested that synonyms be inserted into the British Pharmacopœia as 'there is great variation in the appearance and composition of many articles regularly sold under the same name', Wootton responds the following week with a strenuous rebuttal.[81] The Pharmacopœia was not only an authoritative list, inscribed in the common pharmaceutical Latin of the trade, but, as a book, it provided a more stable source of reference than the reiterated present of the *Chemist and Druggist*.

It is perhaps unsurprising then that the druggists reserve most of their fury for the manufacturers of patent medicines. Though Virginia Berridge and Griffith Edwards claim that 'patent medicines appear to have been enjoying a vogue at the end of the century' there were actually very few patent medicines in the 1890s.[82] A patent medicine was exempt from the Pharmacy Act of 1868 and so did not have to be marked as a poison. This allowed manufacturers to keep controlled substances such as morphine and opium within their products without having to advertise the fact or have the retail of their products strictly curtailed. However, a patent medicine would have to declare its constitution in order to get a patent, thereby allowing imitators to adapt its recipe. What claimed to be patent medicines were often proprietary medicines.[83] These were manufactured products which paid the medicine duty under the Medicine Stamp Act. As they were not patented, manufacturers could keep their ingredients secret whilst using the confusion surrounding the Stamp to evade the Pharmacy Act. These secret objects, explicitly locating their origins with their manufacturers, removed any agency pharmacists had in dispensing. Authorship signals an origin, a derivation in time and space; the trade weeklies emphasized the contingent moment of preparation, linking it with the passing events of news. The names on proprietary medicines invoked a distant space-time, stable despite local conditions and contexts, that elided the knowledge of the pharmacist and turned him or her into a shopkeeper.

When the influenza epidemic struck over Christmas 1889, the *Chemist and Druggist* made much of both the elusive nature of medicine, and the constructed nature of the infection. While reluctant to celebrate an international epidemic, the correspondents express a uniform relief that trade, and interest in the druggists among customers, has increased.[84] The instability and textuality at the heart of this network is demonstrated by a poem printed in the *C&D* in January 1890. It opens

> 'The influenza germ, we hear, is bounding on its way',
> Said every daily paper for a month from day to day;

The virus, with its uncertain materiality, is given substance by the reiterated reports in the press. The rise of the epidemic is consequently measurable by column inches:

> And then the little paragraph to half a column grew;
> Next day the *Standard* gave a col, and the *Telegraph* gave two;
> For somebody at Hammersmith 'twas said had gone 'Atchoo.'

> And soon Lord Salisbury kept his bed, and Mr Labouchere
> Prescribed for all the world in *Truth*, and helped along the scare
> Four columns now we get per day in *Times* and *Daily News*
> The *Pall Mall* sneaked prescriptions from MacKenzie, Clayton, Roose.

The implication, with some irony, is that the medical names cited here are, by the very act of their presence in other texts, lending their authority to this insubstantial virus.

> Now Mr Blank, the pharmacist, whom all our readers know,
> Was looking out for something live to make his physic go.
> So when he read about the germ, says he, 'I am on the track;
> I'll offer something, first of all, that's bound to keep it back.
> A cure for when it comes stands next; and lastly I will sell
> A tonic, to take afterwards, until the patient's well.'
> With that the sly old fox withdrew into his private den,
> And studied hard the *C.&D.* for twenty minutes, when
> He wagged his head, sardonic smiled, and, seizing a quill pen
> Scribbled a handbill boldly headed, 'Cure for Influen-
> Za'; sent it to the printers, and ordered thousands ten.

Blank's act of authorship, inspired both by the increasing column inches of reportage as well as the recipes and advertisements of the *Chemist and Druggist*, further testifies to the materiality of the virus. His triple treatment, which we are left to assume is fairly innocuous, is also authored by him, and named (admittedly only as a 'Cure for Influenza' – but notice how the line break mocks the druggist's authorship) upon the reproducible, mobile handbills. The verse concludes:

> And this went on week after week, for people took all three,
> The prophylactic and the cure, and the tonic (A.B.C.)
> And Blank himself was the only man, 'tis said, in all the town,

Who never took a single dose, and still he is not down.[85]

Here it is uncertain whether the 'flu has created the news, or the news has created the 'flu. In the midst of the uncertainty of what has authored what we have Blank, the author with no name, whose own works – handbills and medicines - capitalize on prior acts of dubious authorship by more authoritative figures in both science and the news.

Both science and the news fall beyond property laws as neither posits the existence of an author. It is only when the abstract idea or event is inscribed into an object, and so can circulate through culture, that ownership is acknowledged. The weekly press, so dependent on transient events to link itself with the temporality of its readers and, in turn, render itself obsolescent prior to the appearance of the next number, constantly negotiates whether a textual object is news or literature. What Andrew Wilson, and indeed many of the popular science authors in monthlies such as *Knowledge*, demonstrate is the belief that to communicate science it must be contextualized within the quotidian material realm. The introduction of literary techniques such as metaphor and analogy preclude such reports from functioning as news. Chapter Four explores a similar topic, investigating how scientific discoveries are communicated to scientific audiences. These are also a type of news and, because scientific phenomena are both located in contingent space-times and present in an essential underlying realm, also negotiate the border between text and object.

## Notes

1   Ludwig Wittgenstein, *Tractatus Logico-Philosophicus* (London, 1997), p. 69.
2   Henri Lefebvre, *The Production of Space*, trans. Donald Nicholson-Smith (1991; Oxford, 2001), p. 175.
3   Wittgenstein, *Tractatus*, p. 69.
4   Stuart Sherman, *Telling Time: Clocks, Diaries and English Diurnal Form, 1660–1785* (Chicago, 1996), p. viii.
5   Bruno Latour, *We Have Never Been Modern* (New York, 1993), p. 76.
6   Henri Bergson, *Time and Free Will*, trans. F.L. Pogson (1910; London, 1971), pp. 77, 79.
7   Bergson, *Time and Free Will*, pp. 109–10.
8   Julia Kristeva, 'Woman's Time', in *The Kristeva Reader*, ed. Toril Moi (New York, 1986), p. 192
9   Patricia Murphy, *Time Is of the Essence: Temporality, Gender, and the New Woman* (New York, 2001), pp. 2–4.
10  Latour, *We Have Never Been Modern*, p. 72.
11  Lefebvre, *Production of Space*, p. 95. See also E.P. Thompson, 'Time, Work-Discipline, and Industrial Capitalism', *Past and Present*, 38 (1967), 91.
12  Lefebvre, *Production of Space*, p. 96.

13  Laurel Brake, *Print in Transition, 1850–1910* (London, 2001), pp. 11–26; Mark Turner, 'Periodical Time in the Nineteenth Century', *Media History*, 8 (2002), 187.

14  Margaret Beetham, 'Towards a Theory of the Periodical as a Publishing Genre', in *Investigating Victorian Journalism*, eds Laurel Brake, Aled Jones and Lionel Madden (London, 1990), p. 26.

15  Margaret Beetham, 'Open and Closed: The Periodical as a Publishing Genre', *Victorian Periodicals Review*, 22 (1989), 99.

16  Turner, 'Periodical Time', 191.

17  Turner, 'Periodical Time', 184.

18  Turner, 'Periodical Time', 193.

19  Brake, *Print in Transition*, p. 11; Turner, 'Periodical Time', 186, 188–9.

20  Turner, 'Periodical Time', 193.

21  Mikhail Bakhtin, 'Forms of Time and of the Chronotope in the Novel: Notes Towards a Historical Poetics', in *The Dialogic Imagination*, ed. Michael Holquist, trans. Michael Holquist and Caryl Emerson (1981; Austin Texas, 1996), p. 84

22  Bakhtin, 'Forms of Time and of the Chronotope', p. 212.

23  Bruno Latour, *Pandora's Hope* (Cambridge MA, 1999), p. 58.

24  Bakhtin, 'Forms of Time and of the Chronotope', pp. 253–4.

25  Bakhtin, 'Forms of Time and of the Chronotope', p. 254.

26  Bakhtin, 'Forms of Time and of the Chronotope', p. 252.

27  Bakhtin, 'Forms of Time and of the Chronotope', p. 255.

28  James Payn, 'Our Note Book', *Illustrated London News* (*ILN*), 96, 18 January 1890 (1890), 66; James Payn, 'Our Note Book', *ILN*, 96, 25 January 1890 (1890), 98; Andrew Wilson, 'Science Jottings – Our Monthly Look Round', *ILN*, 96, 1 February 1890 (1890), 146; and Florence Fenwick Miller, 'The Ladies Column', *ILN*, 96, 1 February 1890 (1890), 154.

29  Anonymous, 'Meeting of the British Association at Nottingham', *ILN*, 103, 9 September 1893 (1893), 323–4. The coverage of the meeting itself includes a portrait of the president, John Burdon Sanderson, giving the Presidential Address flanked by local dignitaries. See anonymous, 'The British Association at Nottingham: Professor Burdon Sanderson Delivering the Inaugural Address', *Illustrated London News*, 103, 23 September 1893 (1893), 387, 371.

30  Anonymous, 'Sir Frederick Abel, C.B., FRS', *ILN*, 97, 6 September 1890 (1890), 292.

31  Anonymous, 'The British Association', *ILN*, 97, 6 September 1890 (1890), 302. The BAAS published a journal, the Presidential Address, and 'other printed papers', all of which were available by post for 2s 6d up until the first day of the meeting. See anonymous 'British Association for the Advancement of Science', *Nature*, 42, 28 August 1890 (1890), xxxviii.

32  Anonymous, 'The British Association, Leeds, Tuesday Evening', *Nature*, 42, 4 September 1890 (1890), 456.

33  Anonymous, 'The British Association, Wednesday Morning', *Nature*, 42, 11 September 1890 (1890), 463.

34  Anonymous, 'Chemistry at the British Association', *Nature*, 42, 25 September 1890 (1890), 530–31; anonymous, 'Physics and the British Association', 'Biology at the British Association', 'Geography at the British Association', and 'Anthropology at the British Association', *Nature* 42, 9 October 1890 (1890), 570–81.

35  E.B. Poulton, 'Mimicry', *Nature*, 42, 2 October 1890 (1890), 557–8; C.V. Boys, 'Quartz Fibres', *Nature*, 42, 16 October 1890 (1890), 604–8; and Spencer Umfreville Pickering,

'The Present Position of the Hydrate Theory of Solutions', *Nature*, 42, 23 October 1890 (1890), 626–31.

36  Bakhtin, 'Forms of Time and of the Chronotope', p. 161.

37  The first number of *Great Thoughts* offered a guinea for the best contribution, identical to *Tit-Bits*. See anonymous, 'Prize Competition', *Great Thoughts*, 1, 5 January 1884 (1884), 1.

38  Matthew Arnold, *Culture and Anarchy* (Cambridge, 1970), p. 70. See also Laurel Brake, *Subjugated Knowledges*, pp. 83–103.

39  Anonymous [Robert P. Downes], '£50 Cash Prizes', *Great Thoughts*, 20, 14 October 1893 (1893), unpaginated. Such 'calls' were not unique to Downes: see also W.T. Stead, 'Programme', *Review of Reviews*, 1, January 1890 (1890), 14.

40  'The Editor' [Robert P. Downes], 'Preface to Vol. XX', *Great Thoughts from Master Minds*, 20 (1894), unpaginated. For Downes see George J.H. Northcroft, 'Robert Percival Downes, LLD.: Father and First Editor of *Great Thoughts*', *Great Thoughts*, 81, May 1924 (1924), 85.

41  Robert P. Downes LLD., 'Preface to Volume XVIII', *Great Thoughts*, 18 (1893), unpaginated.

42  Downes, 'Preface to Volume XVIII', unpaginated.

43  The 'busy man' is the addressee in Stead's *Review of Reviews*. See the advertisement in his *Index to the Periodicals of the World* (London, 1892), unpaginated and his 'Programme', 14.

44  Downes, 'Preface to Volume XVIII', unpaginated.

45  Anonymous, 'Autumn Revelations', *Great Thoughts* 13, 15 October 1892 (1892), 42; James Rigg, 'October', and Richard Jeffries 'The Sunshine of an Autumn Afternoon', *Great Thoughts* 13, 15 October 1892 (1892), 24, 32. The number for 24 December has an engraving of a robin, poetry from Wordsworth, an anecdote from Krummacher, and an anonymous poem 'Christmas Hospitality', *Great Thoughts*, 200–202.

46  Tennyson is commemorated in anonymous, 'Tennysoniana' and S. Trevor Francis, 'Tennyson', *Great Thoughts*, 22 October 1892 (1892 and 1892), 71–2; and anonymous [John Richard Vernon], 'Clevedon and A.H.H', *Great Thoughts*, 18, 12 November 1892 (1892), 106–7.

47  Anonymous, 'Index', *Great Thoughts*, 20 (1893), 500.

48  Anonymous, 'Threshold of Manhood', *Great Thoughts*, 13, 4 January 1890 (1890), 7.

49  Anonymous, 'Counsels for Young Men', *Great Thoughts*, 18, 12 November 1892 (1892), 106.

50  Anonymous, 'Counsels for Young Men', *Great Thoughts*, 20, 27 January 1894 (1894), 359.

51  W.W. Totheroh, 'Manly Boys', *Great Thoughts*, 13, 8 February 1890 (1890), unpaginated.

52  Each number of *Great Thoughts* contained an instalment of a serial novel. See for instance, Edith Gray Wheelwright, *The Vengeance of Medea* serialized in *Great Thoughts*, 20 (1893) or Maxwell Gray [Mary Gleed Tuttiett], *The Last Sentence* in *Great Thoughts*, 18 (1892). Both of these were later published as 3-volume novels.

53  See Robert P. Downes, *Pillars of Our Faith: A Study in Christian Evidence* (London, 1893), p. 20.

54  The debates over the spontaneous generation of life had been carried out very publicly since 1870 by Henry Charlton and his opponents in the X-Club. See John Tyndall, 'Spontaneous Generation', *Nineteenth Century*, 3, January 1878 (1878), 1–21 and H.C.

Bastian, 'Spontaneous Generation: a Reply to Professor Tyndall', 3, February 1878 (1878), 261–77. See also J.E. Strick, *Sparks of Life: Darwinism and the Victorian Debates Over Spontaneous Generation* (Cambridge MA, 2000).

55  Anonymous, 'Professor Tyndall', *Great Thoughts*, 20, 30 December 1893 (1893), 270.

56  Anonymous, 'Professor Tyndall', 270.

57  Richard Garnett LLD., 'The Late Professor Tyndall', *ILN*, 103, 16 December 1893 (1893), 759–60.

58  See Grant Allen, 'Character Sketch: Professor Tyndall', *Review of Reviews*, 9, January 1894 (1894), 21–6. Both Allen's and Garnett's piece use the same engravings, which are conspicuous for their depiction of Tyndall's home (and even his coat), but not picturing Tyndall himself.

59  Sidney Low, 'Newspaper Copyright', *National Review*, 19, July 1892 (1892), 649.

60  Low, 'Newspaper Copyright', 650.

61  Low, 'Newspaper Copyright', 655.

62  Low, 'Newspaper Copyright', 663–4.

63  Low, 'Newspaper Copyright', 665.

64  Andrew Wilson, 'Science Jottings', *ILN*, 103, 23 December 1893 (1893), 806.

65  Andrew Wilson, 'Science Jottings', *ILN*, 96, 17 and 24 May, (1890), 626, 662.

66  For instance see Andrew Wilson, 'Science Jottings – Our Monthly Look Around', *ILN*, 96, 1 March 1890 (1890), 267.

67  Andrew Wilson, 'Science Jottings – Our Monthly Look Around', *ILN*, 97, 6 September 1890 (1890), 310.

68  'J.F.', 'Chimpanzees and Dwarfs in Central Africa', *Nature*, 42, 24 July 1890 (1890), 296.

69  Richard Ericson, Patricia Baranek and Janet Chan, *Visualizing Deviance: a Study of News Organization* (Toronto, 1987), p. 8.

70  Consider for instance Benjulia in Wilkie Collins's *Heart and Science* or the Physiologist in Conan Doyle's 'The Physiologist's Wife.' Wilkie Collins, *Heart and Science: A Story of the Present Time* (1883; Peterborough Ontario, 1996). Arthur Conan Doyle, 'A Physiologist's Wife', *Blackwood's Edinburgh Magazine*, 148, September 1890 (1890), pp. 339–51. For Payn mocking science, see James Payn, 'Our Note Book', *Illustrated London News*, 96, 17 May 1890 (1890), 610.

71  Andrew Wilson, 'Science Jottings – A Display of Energy', *ILN*, 96, 26 April 1890 (1890), 530.

72  See Joseph Loewenstein, *The Author's Due: Printing and the Prehistory of Copyright* (Chicago, 2002).

73  A.W.R [Alexander Wood Renton] and T.A.I. [Thomas Allan Ingram], 'Patents', *Encyclopaedia Britannica*, 20, 11th ed. (Cambridge, 1911), p. 903.

74  Low, 'Newspaper Copyright', 663.

75  Ericson, Baranek and Chan, *Visualizing Deviance*, p. 4.

76  For the origins of the *Chemist and Druggist* see W.H. Brock, 'The Development of Commercial Science Journals in Victorian Britain', in *Development of Science Publishing in Europe*, ed. A.J. Meadows (Amsterdam, 1980), pp. 115–22.

77  A.C. Wootton, *Chronicles of Pharmacy*, 1 (London, 1910), p. v.

78  Wootton, *Chronicles*, 1, p. vii.

79  Wootton, *Chronicles*, 1, p. vii.

80  Wootton, *Chronicles*, 2, pp. 153, 169, 169–70, 123–4.

81  John Findlay, 'Note on Synonyms', quoted within anonymous, 'Edinburgh Chemists' Assistants' and Apprentices Association', *Chemist and Druggist*, 36, 18 January 1890 (1890), 71 and anonymous [A.C. Wootton], 'The Pharmacopœia Addendum', *Chemist and Druggist*, 36, 25 January 1890 (1890), 117.

82  Virginia Berridge and Griffith Edwards, *Opium and the People: Opiate Use in Nineteenth Century England* (London, 1981), p. 125.

83  Anonymous, 'What is a Patent Medicine?', *Pharmaceutical Journal*, 1 March 1890 (1890), 714–15.

84  See for instance anonymous, 'Metropolitan and Provincial News', *British and Colonial Druggist*, 17, 4 January 1890 (1890), 5–10 and anonymous, 'Provincial Reports', *Chemist and Druggist*, 36, 11 January 1890 (1890), 30–33.

85  Anonymous, 'Blank and the Epidemic', *Chemist and Druggist*, 36, 18 January 1890 (1890), 78.

# Chapter Four

# Discovery and the Circulation of Names

> More and more, as time goes on and co-operation increases, is this the case with science. Nobody can really say in one word who invented the steam-engine, the locomotive, photography, the telephone. People who know nothing about it will tell you glibly enough: Watt; Stephenson; Talbot or Daguerre; Bell or Edison. People who know more about it know that many separate inventions contributed many separate parts to each of these inventions: and most of these parts could only be explained to technical readers.[1]

> The printing-press which multiplies the words of the thinker; the steam-engine, which both feeds the press and rushes off its product, and the electric telegraph, which carries thought around the globe makes this an age in which mental force assumes an importance which it never had before in the history of mankind.[2]

In his 'Character Sketch' of John Tyndall, Grant Allen challenges the 'foolish Carlylese view of the Great Man as the sole maker of human progress' in order to find space for the contribution of scientists like Tyndall in the 'onward march of the human mind.' Although he offers a more complicated history of invention than those 'who know nothing about it', this history still sustains a grand narrative of scientific progress. Tyndall's role in this, Allen claims, has not yet been revealed: 'he led up towards those great developments in physical and electrical knowledge which have not yet been made, and towards practical inventions which have not yet been invented.' This unresolved aspect to discovery, in which the names of 'Great Men' are attributed in retrospect, ensures that Tyndall is both part of the collaborative scientific project, while still retaining the possibility of his as yet unacknowledged genius.[3]

The retrospective allocation of credit relies upon material traces that testify to actions in the past. Florence Fenwick Miller, here writing about the genius of Harriet Martineau, attributes the increased influence of the writer to the technologies that reproduce and distribute his or her words. This utopian form of authorship, in which the mind of the writer can touch that of the reader in an unmediated fashion, requires the technologies which facilitate it to remain silent and transparent. However, as I have argued in previous chapters, this silence is itself socially attributed, as all these technologies work by radically altering material form: the printing press can only multiply the words of the thinker once they are set in type; the steam engine distributes the type once the ink is captured on flat, portable and lightweight paper; and the telegraph requires knowledge of another linguistic code entirely and involves two acts of translation before the requisite technologies are employed to capture and distribute thought as immutable mobile object.

The individual who wishes to disseminate his or her thoughts must negotiate with the range of institutions that can translate his or her words into stable, reproducible and portable forms. These negotiations are socially and ideologically controlled: they occur between people and are often regulated by the forces of the market. This social dimension is silenced in Miller's celebration of the emancipatory potential of the mobilized human mind. For her, technology offers the solution to thwarting social constructions of gender, yet technology too is a socialized entity and derives in part from the same social constructions. In order to publish, the author must negotiate with the institutions of the press, and ally him or herself to them. Each transformation is marked by the cultural location of the institution which facilitates it and so with each transformation the object becomes increasingly distanced from the author. The author's discourse, inscribed within an object that also signifies, is no longer a simple imprint from their mind but bears the marks of its passage through culture.

In this chapter I suggest that it is precisely these 'mediating' forms that interject between writers and readers that constitute the space of scientific discovery. In order that credit be attributed, the contingent moments of scientific practice – often located in private laboratory spaces – must be presented in material form so that they can be assessed by the relevant authoritative public. A number of temporalities therefore intersect: the original moments in the laboratory are represented in the text; the texts themselves interact and are read in the present; and the result of this is that the discovery is inserted into linear historical time and esteem allocated to the discoverer as appropriate. I suggest that the periodical is the key site for this intersection, its pages both representing activity in the past while providing the possibilities for the production of a newly discovered object. As discovery suggests the preexistence of the discovered object prior to the moment of discovery, this is an extremely powerful process that is responsible for populating the essential forms that make up the world in the present. As a result, this process is subject to considerable scrutiny, and the various institutional procedures that structure scientific publication are designed to ensure that only ratified objects are permitted a place in the universe, and their discoverers a place in history.

However, this scenario is complicated by the notion of authorship. As I discussed in the previous chapter, a scientific principle cannot be the basis of a patent, and scientific writing does not have the requisite style necessary to lend it the protection of copyright. The market value for scientific content is predicated on the extent of authorial intervention: an expositor could be well paid for a skilful piece of writing that makes a complex idea simple; but an experimental account would be unremunerated as the figure of the author must withdraw in order to provide unmediated access through the text to the laboratory. There are therefore two economies at work for scientific writers, and they intersect. Writers of research papers accrue esteem through the public display of their research, and this then allows them to capitalize on their reputations through the profile of their names. It is not just the career of the thing they write about that is at stake in the circulation of texts, but also the reputation of the scientist as author. Their names, both projected from the letterpress and signified by its signature, become a form of currency which is commodifiable in both of these intertwined economies. Although the publication of their scientific research accures only esteem, the high-profile researcher might demand a high fee for an article on some aspect of science outside of their own professional research, or as an expert representing science in a nonscientific context.[4]

In this chapter I conceive of authorship broadly as any act of language-use intended to be commodified in the market. This focus on the act of writing necessitates the inclusion of both the object that is written upon and the resulting hybrid that is created. This emphasis is important as what is at stake is the material status of an idea. In Donaldson vs Beckett, the legal case which questioned the status of legal copyright in common law in 1774, Sir John Dalrymple claimed that ideas could be property as long as they were kept private. The Lords narrowly found that the Statute of Queen Anne superseded any claim to property in common law: as Joseph Loewenstein writes, 'the idea of "natural" property was checked by an idea of property as artificial, as the product of deliberate social will.'[5] Scientific writing, I argue, attempts to inscribe ideas, in the forms of natural principles and scientific phenomena, into material objects, periodical texts, in order to mark them as property. In a process analogous to patent law, it is the application of ideas that marks their interaction with society and so necessitates the attribution of an owner.

Michel Foucault's 'author function' is a partial recognition of this. Foucault identifies the author function as a discursive construction resulting from the various institutions which facilitate the circulation of the author's own discourse as a disembodied work. The rise of the systems of copyright and ownership in the late eighteenth century necessitated the identification of an author in order to commodify, censor and regulate the circulation of texts. As Foucault says, the author's name 'is functional in that it serves as a means of classification. A name can group together a number of texts and thus differentiate them from others. A name also establishes different forms of relationships between texts.'[6] By attaching different texts to a single name an author becomes an oeuvre, and a diversity of texts, independent of form or content, can be objectified as a whole. This allows both the author, the texts, and the links between them to be stabilized, and retain their relationship across time and space. By identifying the author of a work, that author is then constructed as the unifying force behind multiple texts, becoming both responsible for any inconsistencies and also for the subsequent progress of the texts as they are constantly reinterpreted by readers.

Joseph Loewenstein admits that '[t]he notion that individualizations are back formations of institutionalizations is a useful etiological model' but that 'we need more institutional divinities in the myth of origins. The Author is a censorship-effect, and also a book-effect, a press-effect, a market-effect.'[7] This recognition of the plurality of author functions recognizes the plurality of roles that texts must perform in order to be read. It also shifts the emphasis from text, which is the prevalent category in Foucault's work, to the object. Texts themselves, being located in readers' interpretation of signifying codes on the page, cannot traverse space and time. As mentioned above, it is instead the inscription of these codes into material things which allows, in a modified form, the words of the writer to reach the reader. Each ontological transformation, therefore, threatens to introduce different signifying codes which would thereby prevent the creation of a similar text. The author function, projected from the object itself, insists on its similitude, and so seeks to counter the erosion of authorial control necessary in the dissemination of 'text.'

The connection between public reputation, authorship and ownership was well-recognized in the period. William Crookes, editor of *Chemical News*, used a leading article to defend his 1889 Presidential Address to the Chemical Society against the criticisms of Lecoq de Boisbaudran. Crookes's address contained an overview of the recent controversy concerning the rare earths, but had also touched on the French practice of sealed papers. Writing as 'W.C', Crookes maintains that the two issues were separate, but Lecoq de Boisbaudran disputed both in the *Bulletin de la Societé Chimique de Paris*. The system of sealed papers allows scientists to lodge expected results in a sealed envelope with a learned society in order that priority be established when the research was completed. Crookes, in his address, had described this secretive practice as 'something which borders unpleasantly on fraud.'[8] In a second article Crookes, this time writing anonymously, explains why. He claims that the British system of preliminary papers – in which a brief notice marking the general area of research is circulated in the press in advance of carrying it out – is preferable as it is public. He claims that nobody 'can deny that "sealed papers" do not lend themselves to dishonourable, if not formally dishonest practices; and, as the German proverb says, "opportunity makes thieves."' As the French system is not open to scrutiny, the establishment of a stable narrative that links the discovery with its discoverer can only be retrospective, and the nonexistence of other, incorrect papers, must be taken on trust. The British system ensures that each step of research is ratified publicly:

> The subjects which a chemist thus appropriates for his further study are not 'vast questions', but are generally well defined in their scope, as anyone may see who will look over the 'preliminary notices' published in various scientific journals [...] Their memoirs come at once under the notice of their colleagues, and if they are found to be dishonest or superficial, or if they are not worked to some definite conclusion, they speedily find their own level.[9]

The role of 'colleagues' here is vital: it is to them that research is offered up and, in exchange for their scrutiny, it is from them that the right to exclusively work in an intellectual domain is granted. Rather than the retrospective allocation of priority through a single act of authorship committed in the past but 'published' in the present, the system of preliminary notices is predicated on a distributed series of acts of authorship, in the present, that can be retrospectively connected by a linear narrative once research is complete.

The system of preliminary notices corresponds to late nineteenth-century patent law. Patents grant a monopoly to their owner for 14 years within which time they can enjoy remuneration from their exclusive property. The 1852 Patents Act introduced the Provisional Specification to grant a temporary monopoly while continuing work on the invention. Both the Provisional Specification and preliminary notice reserve an area for future work, and in both cases are only acceptable if the ends are clearly declared. For a patent to be awarded the Final Specification it has to be close enough to the aims set out in the original Provisional Specification as set out by the Patent Office. Equally, a preliminary notice will succeed or fail on the fidelity of subsequent research as judged by the scientific community. In both cases it is periodicals that bring the initial notice into the public sphere, and in both validity is established retrospectively.

The adoption of anonymity in the second piece displaces Crookes's public persona – he was speaking as the head of British chemistry – with a more generalized public consensus. When he claims that it 'must not be supposed that the objection to "sealed papers" is a peculiarity of Mr Crookes', he is disguising his own interests in the debate. In his Address as President of the Chemical Society, Crookes had also criticized those who send their paper to a (usually foreign) journal prior to reading it at the Chemical Society. As the Society took at least three months to publish papers in its *Journal*, this would ensure the prompt appearance of a written record that could testify to its author's ownership of the science. Although he claims otherwise, his own interests are clearly at stake: not only was his own research being challenged by Lecoq de Boisbaudran but, as an editor of a weekly scientific periodical, a portion of his livelihood was threatened by rival systems of authorship and attribution that did not need a prompt vehicle for preliminary notices. The two portions might have addressed different topics, but they correspond to different aspects of Crookes's public persona.

'Authorship', writes Hannah Gay, 'implies possession of intellectual property, a form of capital in the economy of science.'[10] This has been long recognized in scientific periodical publishing. From the late eighteenth century titles such as the *Philosophical Magazine* and *Annals of Science* consisted of a series of scientific papers, with the name and often institution of the author clearly marked. These contributions are thus marked as property before being picked up in other texts, reproduced, and distributed further. This is what is at stake in the periodical context: the rival claims of other authors, the dominating editorial discourse, and the endless reproduction, transformation, reference and proliferation that fuels the production of copy, all threaten the link between the author and his or her ideas. I want to suggest that it is the construction of the author, their name attached to the idea, that allows intellectual property, with its uncertain materiality, to maintain integrity across this uneven textual terrain. Focusing not just upon the text as the property at stake, but the various material forms it can take, I will suggest that the notion of authorship is vital in considering the status of things. The marking of a text with a name signals its derivation as an object with its origin outside the contingent material form of the periodical. The naming of a thing or an idea also suggests an origin independent of the text that names it, and so grants it the permission to thrive beyond the mind of its nominator.

The act of writing, and particularly the act of naming, are constitutive acts in the production of a 'discovery.' Scientific authorship is not attributed through the skill of writing – although of course this is acknowledged and has value – but rather through the other things, beyond the text, that are authored. In 'What is an Author', Foucault suggests that names are not needed in science as an index of truthfulness as 'scientific texts were accepted on their own merits and positioned within an anonymous and coherent conceptual system of established truths and methods of verification.'[11] If scientific 'texts' are the vehicle for scientific ideas and observations then they are an ontological transformation of the discourse of the scientist into a textual work. Scientific writing, as demonstrated in the previous chapters, draws upon inscription in order to overwhelm dissenting readers with the resources and allies it has amassed. As Lorraine Daston explains, scientific objects 'grow more richly real as they become entangled in webs of cultural significance, material practices, and theoretical derivations.'[12] It is this ontological gain which grants scientific objects their independent place in nature even while linking them more elaborately with the sites of their construction. In packing these webs, these layers of ontology, into a name, the author of a scientific paper can translate the object once more, liberating it from its textual representation and giving it an independent being of its own.

To demonstrate the relationship between periodical literature and discovery, this chapter focuses on the publications and institutional practices of the Chemical Society. The objects of study in chemistry are not readily available to the scientist: chemicals do not simply appear within nature as things to be observed; instead, in order to be perceived, they must be forced to undergo reactions in a controlled setting. This introduces a level of mediation which is not as marked in sciences such as astronomy or natural history. Chemicals are not encountered in nature in any pure, unrefined forms, only as mixtures and compounds. This means that the theoretical foundation of chemistry, the level of the basic components that dictate and underpin the behaviour of more complicated structures, is a projection. It is when chemicals are in their simplest forms, as elements, they are also at their most contrived: even when purified, collected, and made available to the chemist, their purity is only a socially accepted approximation.

Chemistry is a science that is both explicitly performed and constructed. It deals with 'virtual objects', whose traces are read and retold in a social process. John Law describes a virtual object as 'an object that appears to be real, to be solid and to be out there [...] An object that is both created, and at the same time warrants the process of representing within which it is created.'[13] Joost Van Loon claims that as 'the existence of a virtual object itself is a performative effect of locally interactively accomplished specific decisions', it must be retold in a process of articulation which renders the manifold manifestations produced by different techniques of enframing and revealing into a single point.[14] The phenomena witnessed in the laboratory, themselves the result of a contrived and regulated situation, are then made the proof of a single underlying cause. This causal substance is rarely glimpsed, is known only through its traces, but it is this that is named, and it is this that is given a history.

Although there was an expansion in the numbers of academic, institutionally-based chemists in the late nineteenth century, these were only a small minority of those with chemical knowledge. The utility of chemistry was widely recognized and was well-established within the academy (including the polytechnics, technical colleges and schools), industry, and medicine, as well as being a prerequisite for posts within government as analysts and inspectors. Although their numbers were few, there were a diverse range of potential social roles for practicing chemists to adopt.[15] Academic, 'pure' chemical research was represented by the prestigious Chemical Society (1841) and the Institute of Chemistry (1877) and Society for Chemical Industry (1881) that it sponsored. Chemists could also work within pharmacy: the Pharmaceutical Society was established the same year as the Chemical Society but, as mentioned in the previous chapter, functioned primarily as an examination body. The Society for Public Analysts (1876) represented those chemists who, either independently or as part of a government department, analyzed the products of manufacturing and pharmaceutical chemistry. These various roles were not exclusive, and many chemists combined multiple roles and belonged to many societies in order to accrue both scientific capital and a financial income.[16]

Through an analysis of the role that the laboratory plays in both the practice of chemistry and the authorship of chemical papers, this chapter explores the textual basis of discovery. Each paper that is published produces sets of names – those of the chemicals, and those of the chemists – that are then reprinted elsewhere. The name of the chemical is more than a signifier of structure and ownership, it actually becomes an object in its own right that, as it is reproduced, carries with it the name of its discoverer. Scientific practice, therefore, is linked to scientific authorship; and the allocation of scientific esteem depends on the public visibility of the private events that happen in the contingent moments in the laboratory. It is the process of transforming the objects of chemistry – whether authored articles or the things that are described within them – into flat, mobile, textual forms that maintain enough integrity to be reproduced across culture that allows the essential existence of chemical phenomena to be established. The independence of an aspect of their materiality – they are both of the page and beyond it – permits them to have an existence in other spatial-temporal realms. Just as the paper describes laboratory events in the past, so the things described within them are also established independently in history. Social ratification of these acts of authoring create the author, granting him or her esteem for liberating scientific phenomena from past events in the closed spaces of the laboratory. By following the movement of names through print culture, it becomes possible to trace the history of authorship as well as the history of discovery. It is these contingent moments that produce the myth of the moment of discovery: the reproduction of names grants them authority, establishing them with a cultural significance that transcends their immediate material context; in this way, the mediating stages are overlooked, testifying to the existence of Allen's Great Men, and Miller's silent technology.

## 'In that mysterious region, "The Lab"': Nomination and the Location of Chemical Practice

In their classic *Introduction to Chemical Nomenclature*, R.S. Cahn and O.C. Dermer claim that the 'aim of systematic chemical nomenclature [is] to describe the composition, and insofar as practicable the structure, of compounds.' The term 'composition' not only implies that chemical names describe what compounds are made of, but also how these components are combined in certain structural features. Chemical nomenclature is therefore not simply a sign representing an absent substance; instead, it is part of a systematic grammar which claims to be predicated by the substance itself. 'Chemists are fortunate', Cahn and Dermer write, 'biologists, geologists, and astronomers have no such convenient way of associating scientific names with the things, or classes of thing, that they describe.'[17] The chemical name strives to describe the very constitution, at the level of its most simple parts, of even the most complicated organic substance. Not only are these parts listed, but they are also given a structure, a spatial location at the molecular level, far beyond the observing eye of the chemist. This knowledge can only be deduced from observations of the chemical's behaviour under controlled conditions. The laboratory then, 'that mysterious region' with its array of resources, becomes the space within which chemicals act and are then named.[18]

The laboratory was not a stable category across nineteenth-century chemical culture. Whereas it was both the site of production and legitimization of chemical knowledge for academic chemists, it was seen as 'a necessary nuisance, an institution only of use to us to ascertain if we get full value in our raw materials, and that our finished products are sent out up to strength' by John Morrison, a manufacturing chemist from Tyneside.[19] The range of ideological power associated with the laboratory is a crucial index of the relative configurations within chemical culture. It is of paramount importance to the academic chemists as it is the site from which they read chemical behaviour, pronounce the reality of the virtual object, and then inscribe it into text: as we shall see, the laboratory is vital for the construction and then stable translation of the referent into a form which can circulate in the cultural economy. With industrial chemistry, which operates foremost in the capital economy, the laboratory is largely oriented to ensure good commercial practice, i.e., efficient production and a consistently reliable product. More than simply, 'the place where scientists *work*', the laboratory is a resource whose role depends on its social configuration.[20] It is a space that allows scientific objects to be modified, whether gaining more layers of ontology as in the case of academic chemists, or becoming reified into a packaged product as in the work of the industrial chemists. Its relative status is variable as it is determined by the contingent evocation of a configuration of geographical, physical and social codes.

The Chemical Society was dominated by a metropolitan, academic oligarchy that institutionalized a specific idea of the laboratory. When founded in 1841, the Society was 'for the general advancement of Chemical Science, as intimately connected with the prosperity of the manufactures of the United Kingdom' and 'for a more extended and economical application of the industrial resources and sanatory conditions of the community [sic].'[21] However, the Society represented a gentlemanly, disinterested form of chemical research and, when similar amateur traditions were becoming institutionalized within the academy at the end of the century, attempted to establish the academic research laboratory at the head of all chemical practice.[22]

The Chemical Society was dominated by its Council, which consisted of the President, the Vice Presidents and twelve Ordinary Members. Every President of the Chemical Society became a Vice President and, from 1890, there were between 14 and 16 of them.[23] This oligarchy at the centre of the Society was well recognized, and partly provoked the various outbreaks of blackballing by Fellows who disputed the credentials of those offered for Fellowship.[24] Its constitution meant that it tended toward conservatism. Both Vernon Harcourt and William Ramsay's attempts to allow women access to the Society, in 1883 and 1888 respectively, were overruled, the latter attempt as 'it being judged inexpedient to recommend any such change at present.'[25] As Presidents tended to be eminent male academic chemists the Council perpetuated the identification of the Society with the ideology of disinterested research and consolidated this gendered stance at the centre of chemistry. The collection of eminent names also granted the Society an international reputation, encouraging links with individuals and societies in Europe and America and further forwarding itself as the forum through which to speak to British chemistry.

The Council also extended its control over the publications of the Chemical Society as the President (or the Vice President in his absence) chaired all meetings of the Publication Committee. The remainder of its members were eminent research chemists who doubled as referees. Of the 11 members in 1890 (not including the President or the Editor), 6 were Fellows of the Royal Society and all of these had PhDs, suggesting a heavy bias towards European laboratory research.[26] The Committee met at least monthly, but in busy periods fortnightly, to hear referees' reports and recommend any changes prior to publication in the society's monthly *Journal* or fortnightly *Proceedings*. In 1889 refereeing was made anonymous with referees' names recorded only in the minutes and not announced at the meetings. In order to ensure authority was exercised by these established Fellows, it was ruled that no paper could be rejected solely on the recommendation of the Secretary or Editor. This negated the influence of the two Officers and asserted that of the recognized scientific authorities. Rejected papers were usually referred to Council but, in a move that further buttresses the authority of the referees, not until two different Fellows had reported to the Committee.[27]

In 1890 the editor of the *Journal* was C.E. Groves. Groves had edited the *Journal* since 1884 and, in 1890, received a salary of £300 for the task. Groves was typical of many late nineteenth-century scientists in that he combined a number of jobs in order to earn a reasonable income and to participate as widely as possible in scientific culture. As well as the editorship of the *Journal*, he was a lecturer at St Guys Hospital, Secretary to the Institute of Chemistry, and a consulting chemist to the Thames Water Board. He was assisted by A.J. Greenaway who was paid £150 for his work as Sub Editor. The *Journal* was distributed monthly free of charge to Fellows and was consequently run at a substantial loss. In 1890 the *Journal* cost £2724 and only raised £383 through 'adverts and commissions.' The print run was 2350 and, as there were 1698 Fellows in 1890, suggests that just over 650 copies a month were distributed to laboratories and other learned societies around the world.[28] These extra copies allowed smaller societies access to the expensive texts of the Chemical Society, while allowing the Society to further its influence and consolidate its position at the centre of scientific culture.

The rigorous editorial process was designed to ensure that papers admitted into the text of the *Journal* met the ideological criteria of the Society. As periodicals are mobile, it distributed this model of 'correct' chemistry around the world, allowing those who could not attend the meetings to keep up to date with the results of other researchers. Between 1878 and 1925 there were two parts, with separate pagination, to every monthly number of the *Journal*, which were then bound into separate volumes at the end of the year. The 'Transactions' were full versions of papers read at the Society and the 'Abstracts' gave brief summaries and bibliographic details for the contents of other major chemical publications from around the world. These two components complemented each other: the papers translated the constructed events in the laboratory, elided their contingency, and announced the existence of new scientific objects; the abstracts took up these named objects and ensured their passage across texts, linking them with the names of their respective authors. The *Journal* thus fulfilled three roles: it distributed results and suggested domains for further research; operated as a model of authorship and scientific practice; and marked scientific knowledge and phenomena as the property of the authors.

Access to the text of the *Journal* was to be granted the power to construct and then 'possess' the independent and essential phenomena of chemistry. Papers had to articulate a certain form of language to both convince the reader and be ratified by the Society: the contingent events within the laboratory had to be translated in such a way to grant reality to the phenomena described within; and this act of translation was then stabilized through the ideological position of the Chemical Society, inscribed into the *Journal* by the editorial process. When Spencer Pickering submitted his paper 'Nature of Solutions' to the Chemical Society in the beginning of 1889, its length and reliance on graphical illustration immediately caused its referee, in this case the Professor of Chemistry at the University of

London, William Ramsay, to recommend that it be valued. The report from the printers Harrison and Sons stated that the text and the tables would cost £125 and the lithographed plates a further £101. This was about 8% of the total annual cost of the *Journal* and consequently the Committee wrote to Pickering advising him that they were not prepared to reproduce his illustrations. However, their decision was not strictly on economic grounds. They did not require Pickering to reduce the number of tables in his text, a typographical device which was also highly expensive, on the grounds that 'no-one carefully reading such a paper will draw any conclusion from printed diagrams, but will certainly reproduce from the numerical results those portions which he wishes to study.'[29] It is the second order illustrations, those that represent an authorial translation of inscripted results, that are deemed superfluous.

Pickering, eager to have his text published within the *Journal*, initially agreed on the condition that the final arrangement was the result of a committee consisting of himself, Groves and Ramsay. The Committee however were not convinced 'as to the value of the method which it was the object of the paper to display' and so commissioned another report, this time by T.E. Thorpe and A.W. Rücker, to address the relative merits of publishing it.[30] Their judgement again focused on the merits of the expensive, second order graphs. They conclude:

> Many of the minor bends or discontinuities found by Mr Pickering are so slight that we believe that he himself admits that taken alone they only suggest a faint probability of a real change at the point at which they are alleged to occur. We do not think it is possible to form an independent opinion as to their meaning and value without going into every detail of the individual observations and graphical methods from which they are deduced, and we think that in many cases different persons would arrive at different results.[31]

They do not dispute the validity of his experimental results, it is not Pickering the scientist they suspect, but instead his deployment of textual resources and the conclusions that he draws from them. They recommend Pickering be permitted to publish his analysis of sulphuric acid solutions (as it is the strongest portion of his research) and grant him 100 pages of the *Journal*. It is his authorship that the referees feel is unreliable: by permitting Pickering to publish his paper they are giving him the opportunity to let his solutions 'speak' for themselves.

Pickering's paper was eventually published in the *Journal* in April 1890 after further negotiations with Harrison & Sons.[32] The final version consists of 120 pages, 24 tables, 16 lithographed figures and 2 inserted plates.[33] The protracted process before publication demonstrates how closely intertwined economic considerations were to questions of authorship. Pickering was a graduate in science at Balliol College, Oxford, a former lecturer of chemistry at Bedford College, the Director of the Woburn Experimental Fruit Farm and a Fellow, member of the Council, referee, and member of the Publication Committee of the Chemical Society. The economic costs certainly dissuaded the Committee from publishing his paper, yet it was the need to maintain a certain form of authorship that ultimately determined their actions. Pickering's paper, because it did not conform to the codes of authorship required by the Society, threatened the successful writerly codes of the *Journal*.[34]

The way scientific objects are created is demonstrated more successfully in other papers published by the Society. In the *Journal* for February 1890 there is a paper by W.H. Perkin Jr. and his colleague at the new Herriot Watt College, Stanley Kipping.[35] The minutes of the Publication Committee show that this was approved by the Committee on 19 December 1889 and was refereed by Groves.[36] Bruno Latour describes an experiment as 'a text about a nontextual situation, later tested by others to decide whether or not it is simply a text.'[37] Scientific papers attempt to convince readers that the phenomena they describe are not contingent upon the conditions of their making but have an ontological existence beyond the spatial and temporal moment of the experiment. The papers in the *Journal* are texts that seek to elide the distance between their representation of the experiment and the actual experiment itself, occurring in the authoritative space of the laboratory. Through deploying a combination of mimetic representation and inscription, the authors seek to inscribe the experiment into the text, forcing the reader to recognize its ontology despite its presence as purely linguistic code. As Latour says, '[t]he dissenter will be unable to oppose the text to the real world out there, since the text claims to bring within it the real world "in there."'[38] If the paper succeeds, then the referent simultaneously exists within the text and is identified as an essential object independent of it.

According to these terms, Perkin and Kipping's 'Action of Dehydrating Agents on αω-Diacetylpentane. Synthesis of Methylethylhexamethylene' demonstrates a classic laboratory process.[39] Latour argues that the resources gathered in the laboratory provide extreme conditions that force an as-yet unknown entity to act in certain ways. He claims it 'is possible to go from a nonexistent entity to a generic class by passing through stages in which the entity is made of floating sense data, taken as a name of action, and then, finally, turned into [an] organized being with a place in a well-established hierarchy.'[40] Perkin and Kipping's paper outlines precisely this process: from a disparate collection of actions, recorded and mathematicized as results, the nonexistent entity becomes a 'name of action', a posited essence which they cannot yet name. Each stage is an increase *'from one ontological status to the next'* through which the thing itself comes into being.[41] Its independent ontological existence is structured by the social configurations and textual strategies it simultaneously elides.

The paper begins with a discussion of a previous paper in which the authors recap the preparation of αω-diacetylpentane and αω-dibenzoylpentane. They hypothesize the results of a dehydration of αω-diacetylpentane and attempt to predict its structure, claiming they will do the same for the second compound in a subsequent paper. The reaction itself is a straightforward dehydration:

$$C_9H_{16}O_2 - H_2O = C_9H_{14}O$$

However, the authors note that '[c]onsiderable difficulty has been experienced in determining the constitution of this interesting substance' as it may 'in accordance with the present views on the structure of organic compounds' have one of eight possible structures.[42] In order to differentiate between these, Kipping and Perkin subject their resulting compound to a series of reactions in order to identify its structure through the behaviour of the resulting experimental products. In the paper they list, in the perfect tense, the results of these experiments and explain how the behaviour of the products precludes certain projected structures. The structure that concurs with the experimental results is their number 'VIII' and they confidently name it '$\Delta^1$-orthomethylacetyltetrahydrobenzene.' They then 'clean up' this name so that it names the parts of the compound according to the codes of the Chemical Society, re-branding it '$\Delta^1$-orthomethyltetrahydrobenzene methyl ketone.'

At present the authors have only argued this structure by analogy, comparing its behaviour with other known structures under similar conditions, and so have not established its existence as a referent within the text. They do this through a quantitative analysis of the formation of the compound coupled with descriptions of its physical behaviour. They give the weight of the starting product (the diacetylpentane), and describe the most accurate method for the addition of the dehydrating agent, the concentrated sulphuric acid. They give a description of the resulting product:

> The resulting solution, which varies in colour from brownish-red to dark brown, is kept in a loosely stoppered flask at the ordinary temperature from one or two days, during which time it darkens in colour, and a slight evolution of sulphurous anhydride occurs.

The authors now use the simple past tense to indicate the unresolved nature of the events. The solution, they write, is then poured into cold water to allow a precipitation and the precipitate shaken with ether and allowed to evaporate. Once more they describe the product:

> A yellow mobile oil, smelling strongly of peppermint, is obtained; the yield of the crude product is, on the average, 85–90 per cent. of the diketone employed.

Throughout this description the authors have stepped back away from the paper, their textual presence as agents (describing actions, smells, tastes, colours, results etc...) is reified to an objective tone which states what 'is.' The implication is now that the substance is acting of its own volition and that it no longer needs the human actors to speak for it. The paragraph that follows merely provides the stage upon which the substance performs:

> When this oil is distilled under the ordinary pressure, a small quantity passes over between 120° and 190°, but the principal portion distils between 190° and 210°; [...] The fraction 190–210° still contains traces of unchanged diketone; pure orthomethyltetrahydrobenzene methyl ketone, boiling constantly at 205°-206°, can only

be obtained by again treating this product with sulphuric acid and fractionating two or three times under the ordinary pressure.

This is also the first time the authors name orthomethyltetrahydrobenzene methyl ketone in this portion of their paper. Now an independent entity, with its behaviour determined by its structure rather than its conditions, it demands to be named. It is at this crucial stage in their text that the authors then introduce an inscription, 'folding' experimental data into their description to create a stable link back to the laboratory:

0.1855 gram of substance gave 0.5294 gram $CO_2$ and 0.1720 gram $H_2O$.

|           | Calculated for: |               |
|-----------|-----------------|---------------|
|           | $C_9H_{14}O$    | Found         |
| C......   | 78.26 per cent. | 77.84 per cent. |
| H......   | 10.14 '' ''     | 10.30 '' ''   |
| O......   | 11.60 '' ''     | 11.86 '' ''   |

The similitude between the projected figures and those obtained by experiment links the narrated account by the authors with the events in laboratory by presenting the substance as a mathematicized inscription that is seemingly independent of human interpretation. Orthomethyltetrahydrobenzene methyl ketone is consequently posited as an essential substance, with an independent materiality that is beyond that of an authorial representation. The paper has folded the list of trials and the resultant mathematical results into its narrative, presenting the compound as an entity which is independent of the text. This is demonstrated once more in conclusion by a final list, immediately below the inscription. This list is not, as before, of its actions but of its properties:

> Orthomethyltetrahydrobenzene methyl ketone is a colourless, mobile oil with a strong odour of peppermint and a sharp, somewhat bitter taste. The compound boils at 205° - 206° (about 755mm.) without decomposition, and is readily volatile with steam. It is insoluble in and specifically lighter than water, but it is miscible with the ordinary organic solvents in all proportions.[43]

Latour argues that we 'cannot even claim that [...] it is only the author, the human author, who is doing the work in the writing of the paper, since what is at stake in the text is precisely the reversal of authorship and authority.'[44] Kipping and Perkin are only present as part of the resources of the laboratory: they have become one of many instruments through which the compound is 'authoring' itself. By lending their own ontological status to the substance, they are compelled to speak on its behalf.

The poetics of the chemical paper are constituted by the ontological exchange between the name of the author and the name of the compound. In order for the substance to become articulated in such a way as to break free from its articulation, the subject that articulates it must itself be annihilated. Perkin's papers, according to his biographer Jocelyn Field Thorpe, are 'chiefly interesting because, for the first time, indications are afforded of Perkin's power of expression in his descriptions of the substances he isolated.'[45] Yet the possibilities of personal expression are restricted due to the demands of the ontological exchange. Perkin may be able to describe 'beautiful, slender, pale-yellow needles' but this does not bring them into being. Descriptions such as 'this solution, on cooling, deposited beautiful, colourless, feathery crystals'[46] only work within the context of the scientific paper because the signifying description of the crystals, which necessarily evokes the arbitrary connection between signifier and signified, is countered by the re-presentation of the event in the form of inscription. Perkin's rhapsodic accounts, in which his own style threatens to embody his personality in the run of signifiers, cannot be tolerated in scientific discourse as it signals the presence of the author and raises the spectre of signification. As soon as the paper is recognized as a representation then the experiment, and the phenomena which are born within it, remain firmly extratextual. It is only with this somewhat different death of the author, and the birth of a distinct 'scientific' author function, that scientific writing can mobilize objects across space and time, placing the moment of practice onto the periodical page.

In these papers ontological status flows between two poles, the name of the scientist and the name of the chemical. Both are acknowledged as entities 'out there' but both undergo a translation via their textually mediated link with the laboratory. At the moment the chemical is given an essential existence it becomes simultaneously a name on a page. Equally the scientist, in the process of articulating that chemical name, also becomes reified, translating his / her being as author into an immutable mobile, a marker on a page that will hopefully appear on other pages and so accrue cultural capital. The construction of these two linguistic items is, however, slightly different. Because the scientist loses ontological status as the representation of the experiment progresses s/he becomes reified, located as a name which is outside the laboratory but associated tangentially with it. The chemical name, on the other hand, actually embodies both the processes and ideological status of the laboratory, and it is these extra ontological layers which allow it to exist outside the text.

The name 'orthomethyltetrahydrobenzene methyl ketone' is more than just a signifier of a thing in a lab, it reveals the constitution of that thing at the level of laboratory process. The whole of Kipping and Perkin's experiment leads up to the triumphant moment of nomination. They know the empirical content of the dehydration, and can give it an empirical formula '$C_9H_{14}O$.' Yet as Cahn and Dermer point out, 'assemblies of symbols, not being words, are literally unspeakable.'[47] Primo Levi describes these 'so-called raw formulae" as "a raw, incomplete language [...] which has the sole value (precisely typographical) of fitting neatly into the printed line.'[48] The name orthomethyltetrahydrobenzene methyl ketone is (just about) speakable and it also, crucially, describes the structure derived from the laboratory that is elided in the empirical formula. Levi describes structural formulae as 'a portrait, an image of the miniscule molecular edifice.'[49] This personification of the chemical is retained in the chemical name as it renders the portrait into linear form. The word 'ortho' gives the location of the methyl group and the methyl ketone on the carbon ring, and the 'tetrahydrobenzene' gives the structural details of the ring, using bezene as an analogy.[50] As these are the active groups in the compound, their nature and proximity dictate its possible behaviour. The name, which grants the new object the ability to traverse different texts and so establish its place in nature, is fully inscribed with the codes of the laboratory: it is its behaviour within this artificial environment that allows the deduction of its structure; and it is also within the laboratory that the chemists can predict the substance's behaviour and so affirm its essential preexistence.

Chemical nomenclature has its roots in Enlightenment philosophy. In the *Méthode de nomenclature chimique* Lavoisier claims that '[l]anguages are intended, not only to express by signs, as is commonly supposed, the ideas and images of the mind; but are also analytical methods, by means of which, we advance from the known to the unknown, and to a certain degree in the manner of mathematicians.'[51] Lavoisier claims that 'algebra is in fact a language: like all other languages it has its representative signs, its methods, and its grammar [...] thus an analytical method is a language; a language is an analytical method, and these two expressions are, in a certain respect, synonyms.'[52] As Jonathon Simon has shown, this evocation of the philosophy of Condillac was a deliberate strategy on the part of the French chemists to claim the authority of nature for their imposition of an artificial chemical nomenclature. For Condillac 'languages were analytical methods that approached more or less closely to a naturally ordained ideal.'[53] Foucault, in the *Order of Things*, understands this as a constituent part of his Classical episteme:

> But if all names were exact, if the analysis upon which they are based had been perfectly thought out, if the language in question had been 'well made,' there would be no difficulty in pronouncing true judgements, and error, should it occur, would be as easy to uncover and as evident as in a calculation in algebra.[54]

In echoing Lavoisier's goal of a mathematical grammar, Foucault foregrounds the determining logic of mathesis that underlies the organization of representation in the Classical episteme. Chemical nomenclature, based upon this same episteme, also claims a determining grammar, but derives its logic from the events in the laboratory. Inscribing these performances into the name, chemistry can appropriate its own mathesis in the form of chemical names and formulae, allowing its language to do the work of the laboratory.

In the Classical episteme, as in chemistry, to name is an act of great power. Foucault writes:

> One might say that it is the Name that organizes all Classical discourse; to speak or to write is not to say things or to express oneself, it is not a matter of playing with

language, it is to make one's way towards the sovereign act of nomination, to move, through language, towards the place where things and words are conjoined in their common essence, and which makes it possible to give them a name.[55]

Each chemical name strives to be a perfect fusion of form and content. Each describes the spatial arrangement of an absent substance, but in doing so dictates both its behaviour and potential. In translating the contingent events of the laboratory into a name, the authors of scientific papers seek to create more than a signifier of the absent substance, they seek to establish a fully realized substitute, cast out into culture, which can then affirm the essential existence of the elusive substance it names. Yet Foucault claims the 'name is the *end* of discourse', as soon as it is spoken all the language which led up to it, which oscillates around its potential, is absorbed within it.[56] In the moment of translation the rhetorical strategies and the contingent events they capture are absorbed within the name, removing the distance between textual representation and essential being. This is why the authorship of papers for the *Journal* is such a regulated practice: it is part of an ongoing process which seeks to create an allegedly timeless, gendered realm of chemical reality that claims to underpin the empirical nature of all things.

## Abstracts and Abstractors: the Propagation of Chemical Names

Chemical nomination in the nineteenth century was the preserve of a male academic elite situated within the research laboratory. However, the act of nomination depends upon a network and is therefore protected at a number of points. Although the poetics of the chemistry paper are not in themselves exclusory (the extinguishing of the author removes, for instance, the gendered subject), the projected author function as name is strictly regulated according to the institution that allows authorship.[57] Discursive boundaries connected with education and qualification, class and gender, operate to monitor who was permitted to work within the walls of the laboratory, as well as determining what role one would play there. The institution creates its authors; and the Chemical Society, for instance, rarely recognized the status of female chemists in the laboratory as female authors of chemical papers.[58] Chemists sought publication in the *Journal* to exploit its exclusive codes and lend their work prestige. A paper appearing in the *Journal* had been ratified by a consortium of the leading chemists of the day and was then circulated through a distribution network that acknowledged this fact. Yet the Chemical Society was only one such network operating in the culture of chemistry. In order to preserve its position as the source of chemical authority, extending its monopoly over the posited chemical realm being mapped by the chemists who wrote the papers in its journal, it had to allow the authors to disseminate their results while remaining associated with the things described therein.

The *Proceedings of the Chemical Society* was one of the means the Society employed to maintain authority over its texts. Published as quickly as possible after the meetings of the Society, the *Proceedings* participate in the weekly, fortnightly and monthly rhythms of nineteenth-century science and science publishing. Consequently, I deal with this publication in some detail in the following chapter. They were prepared from author's abstracts, and so posit a link back to the laboratory; however, their focus is on the events in the meeting rather than the events in the laboratory; and their abbreviated style makes them more of a summary of results than a description of unfolding events. Paradoxically, the completed nature of reported experiments is linked to their uncertain status within the science as a whole: although, as mentioned above, a paper read to the Society was often considered as refereed; the chemistry within it was not ratified until published in the *Journal*. Even though the reported science of the abstracts is placed in the past, it is not until they are rewritten into the present that they can argue for the essential existence of the phenomena that they describe. As the *Proceedings* were reproduced widely in the weekly periodical press, they function to mark scientific terrain as the provisional property of a chemist. However, as Crookes points out (above), it is only when colleagues accept such work, signalled by its publication in full in the *Journal* or an equivalent publication, that priority is retrospectively awarded and the phenomena is deemed to have always existed.

The reports of the proceedings of societies help disseminate the names of both the substance and the authors in the wider cultures beyond that of the original textual objects, but the provisional nature of the events described, and the focus on the meeting rather than the laboratory, locates the authoritative text elsewhere. However, the circulation of abstracts, which are compiled from published papers, provides a different model of circulation. Although abstracts were used in a range of disciplines, chemistry was the most prescriptive in terms of form and content.[59] Periodicals also included a range of notes and reviews which reproduced (and anteceded) the form of the abstract. The presence of the author in this form of writing is expressed mainly in the choice of what to include, the brevity of the form restricting individual expression. Yet in chemistry, because the career of the chemist depended on the career of the chemical, the abstract was a highly codified practice. It had to convince readers of the reality of the chemical, mobilize that reality whilst marking it as the property of the chemist, and ensure that the name of the author remained linked with it.

The Chemical Society led the way in the regulation of abstracts. Since 1847, the year in which the predecessor of the *Journal*, the *Quarterly Journal of the Chemical Society*, had been founded, the preparation of abstracts had been part of the Editor's remit. By 1862 the text of the *Quarterly Journal* had become swamped with this material and the Society opted to reconfigure its format. The abstracts had been collected as an annual alphabetical list of all chemical papers published. This had grown so much since 1847 that it occupied a quarter of the title's annual 12 sheets. They decided to drop the list, make the title monthly (it now was known as the *Journal*) and increase its annual size to 30 sheets. In order to get through the abstracts and papers the Publication Committee also began to meet monthly. Still however, the form of the abstracts remained at the discretion of the author: as the role was still undefined the editor Henry Watts was not in a position to assert himself over the sometimes more eminent authors who submitted abstracts.[60] It was at this point that the category of Abstractor was evolved, answerable to a newly enlarged Publication Committee (from 4 to 22). This solution, however, was unsuccessful as there were frequent disagreements over the substance of abstracts between the Abstractors who did the work and the Committee that ratified it. This left an enormous burden on the Editor and elicited trenchant criticism from the *Chemical News*. In 1877 Groves joined the editorial staff as Sub-Editor and the *Journal* adopted the mode of separate pagination for the abstracts that would continue into the twentieth century.

The abstracts were one of the most popular features of the *Journal* and their cost was comfortably accommodated by increases in membership of the society.[61] In terms of pages, the abstracts dominated the title: for the year 1890 the *Journal* consisted of 71 papers occupying 1106 pages and 1479 abstracts occupying 2324 pages. These showed substantial rises from 1889 (773 pages and 2174 pages respectively) but, as Groves announces, his Abstractors are up to date and coping.[62] He had 29 Abstractors on his staff drawn from the younger Fellows. In 1890 only 9 had PhDs, suggesting that few had yet worked in the prestigious laboratories in Germany – a rite of passage for the high-flying researcher. The position of Abstractor was paid, but was mainly seen as good training. H.E. Armstrong, then Professor of Chemistry at the Central Technical College, wrote anonymously in the memorial volume to celebrate the Society's jubilee that:

> in point of fact, the training which the younger English chemists acquire as Abstractors for the Society's Journal, is of no slight value, and the Society may properly claim on this account that it has rendered a considerable educational service, and that it has done much to promote the literary studies of a large number of the more active of its Fellows.[63]

Becoming an abstractor allowed one to read widely but, more significantly, become trained in the art of writing abstracts. There was no shortage of interest: in February 1890 Groves was forced to close his waiting list.[64]

Abstractors were required to use a certain method. From 1890 Groves published his 'Instructions to Abstractors' as an annual preface intended for the bound volume of abstracts collected at the end of the year. This allowed readers to learn the forms of abstracts and also served to disseminate the Chemical Society form as the standard. The abstract, Groves suggests, 'should mainly consist of the expression, in the abstractor's own words, of the substance of the paper.' It should 'be made as concise as possible, consistently with an accurate statement of the author's results or theories, due regard being paid to their import.' This emphasis on results and theories, the elusive 'substance', is important: as mentioned above, both patent and copyright law only recognize the application of an idea, not the idea itself. The form of the abstract rewrites the intellectual property of the author in a standardized language that allows it to be reattributed to them. Details of method and preparation are omitted 'unless such details are essential to the understanding of the results, or have some independent value.'[65] This, as well as further distancing the author, also divorces the phenomena described within the paper from the contingent circumstances of its existence. Much like the reported papers considered above, the abstract presents an independent named thing, acting autonomously, and the chemist who named it, reified into a mere name.

The 'Abstracts' are chiefly vehicles for the circulation of chemical and authorial names. Rule 4 of Grove's 'Instructions' requires abstractors to reproduce any references within the paper and to supplement these with references to similar work of which they might be aware.[66] To safeguard this material, Groves also outlines an ideal nomenclature. The guidelines give standard names for chemical groups, thereby helping to progress towards Condillac's utopian natural language that underpins Foucault's model of the Classical episteme.[67] These standard names infuse the language of the abstract with chemical logic, allowing reactions to be understood at a glance. The names embody their own grammar, dictating the potentialities of the substances they claim to embody. Equations, which explicitly demonstrate chemical logic, are made superfluous and are either omitted or, if included, merged with the text.[68] Not only were they expensive to set, and took up much needed space, but they also, as mentioned above, presented an unspeakable name. Although structural formulae and equations are seemingly advantageous in the advance toward a 'well-made' language, they tend too much to mathesis and threaten to damage the ontology of the name by restricting its rearticulation by other speakers, both textual and nontextual.

Through publishing the 'Instructions' and training a cadre of chemists who would go to work in research schools, Groves, as editor, furthered the reach of the Chemical Society. Its hegemonic stance at the centre of chemical research was predicated on precisely such an approach. Its various codes of authorship were determined by the ideology of the Society, and the texts produced translated these codes into a form that was easily disseminated. Through the circulation of chemical names, always insisting on the reality of the substance that they capture, and the attendant signifying names of the chemists, an economy is set up which rewards the authorial practice of the chemist and helps to construct an ideal, masculine realm of chemical reality. However, just as the translation of the referent and the scientist into mobile things (of differing ontology) allows their circulation within the cultural economy, so too does it permit the taking up of these things, whether in the form of plagiarized articles or the respective names, and their rearticulation in the discourse of the other.

## Conclusion: the Rival Domains of Chemical Names

In his *Chronicles of Pharmacy*, the editor of the *Chemist and Druggist*, A.C. Wootton, criticizes '[t]he ingenious laboratory devisers of synthetic products' for 'a nomenclature which it is impossible to use.' From his position as a representative of the druggists, preparing drugs from chemist's shops, it is essential that names be convenient and easy to use. However, Wootton admits that the inventors of a product are 'are always ready to meet this requirement with a more or less expressive title which can be protected as a trade mark.' As these names are proprietary, they are signifiers of ownership rather than elements of scientific schema. 'This forces other manufacturers to devise others distinct for the same article' Wootton continues, 'so that among the new chemicals which have become popular within the last thirty years there are sometimes a dozen designations for the same substance.'[69] In renaming the substance, manufacturers reconfigure it as object, eliding its origins in the laboratory and marking it as a product of a company. Often an element of the chemical name will be retained – for instance 'antipyrin' is actually phenyl dimethylisopyrazolone and 'sulphonal' is dimethyldiethylsulphone-methane – but this is only to signify the scientific properties of the product, not to invoke the Classical grammar of the chemists.

Ideally chemical nomenclature should provide one name for each compound and, depending on the system in use, this name is the only one possible. As chemical names approximate to chemical logic, and scientific ideas themselves cannot be patented, such names cannot be marked as property. The elaborate institutional publishing practices derived by institutions such as the Chemical Society exist to verify the accuracy of nomenclature and allocate credit where it is due. However, as the pharmaceutical trade demonstrates, their influence was limited. In *Chemical News* in 1890, J.W. Slater suggests the chemical community stop using the suffix '–ine' in organic chemistry as '[w]e find the inventors of so-called proprietary medicines, &c., using it as a tail piece to the names of their nostrums, though these are mere mixtures, not chemical individuals […] Not long since I saw a disinfectant advertised as "Listerine"!'[70] By appropriating chemical nomenclature, Slater implies, the chemical manufacturers have sullied it by rendering it inaccurate and associating it with the world of commerce.

Grant Allen's notion that the myth of discovery is sustained by those 'who know nothing about it' is both accurate and disingenuous. It is accurate in that it demonstrates that rival publics attribute origins in different ways. However, his use of technology as a metaphor for discovery elides the crucial temporal distinction between the two practices. Whereas the examples he gives are applications of an idea, and therefore can be patented and the inventors credited as their authors, scientific discoveries claim to reveal something that was always there. As the discovery predates the discoverer, they can have no ownership over it, but instead be credited for bringing it to public notice. In both cases discovery is an eminently social practice, but the temporal operations differ: whereas the technological invention is not given a prehistory, the scientific discovery is granted a place in the ahistorical realm of nature.

Both technological invention and scientific discovery involve the retrospective displacement of a complex, nonlinear process with a single defining moment. As I mentioned in the previous chapter, the writing of science as news is complicated by the need for an author to interpret the importance of the scientific event for a nonscientific public. This figure, interposing between the author of scientific papers and the things they describe, repositions both within different histories. Allen recognizes that the history of technology 'could only be explained to technical readers', and so the public are presented with a different narrative that is oriented towards what are perceived to be their own interpretive frameworks.[71] However, just as scientific credit can only be accrued through the circulation of objects to the scientific community for ratification, so too does public acknowledgement of credit rely on the circulation of objects for their scrutiny. Each translation of an object for a new context relies on the assent of those within its intended space, and so runs the risk of being misinterpreted and appropriated. The next chapter explores how the objects of specialist research move into wider cultural domains, and considers how the periodic appearance of such objects structures temporal patterns.

## Notes

1  Grant Allen, 'Character Sketch: Professor Tyndall', *Review of Reviews*, 9, January 1894 (1894), 25.
2  F. Fenwick Miller, *Harriet Martineau* (London, 1888), p. 222. See also Barbara Onslow, *Women of the Press in Nineteenth-Century Britain* (London, 2000), p. 12.
3  Allen, 'Character Sketch', 25–6.
4  Katherine D. Watson, 'The Chemist as Expert: The Consulting Career of Sir William Ramsay', *Ambix*, 42 (1995), 143–59.
5  Sir John Dalrymple, *Cobbett's Parliamentary History*, 17, col. 962. Cited in Joseph Loewenstein, *The Author's Due: Printing and the Prehistory of Copyright* (Chicago, 2002), p. 17.
6  Michel Foucault, 'What is an Author?', *Screen*, 20 (1970), 20.
7  Loewenstein, *The Author's Due*, p. 12.
8  William Crookes, cited in anonymous [C.E. Groves], 'Annual General Meeting', *Journal of the Chemical Society*, 55 (1889), 253. See also 'W.C.' [William Crookes], 'M. Lecoq de Boisbaudran on the Rare Earths', *Chemical News*, 61, 7 March 1890 (1890), 111.
9  Anonymous [William Crookes], 'Sealed Papers', *Chemical News*, 61, 14 March 1890 (1890), 123.
10  Hannah Gay, 'Invisible Resource: William Crookes and His Circle of Support, 1871–81', *British Journal for the History of Science*, 29 (1996), 335.
11  Foucault, 'What is an Author?', 20.
12  Lorraine Daston, 'The Coming into Being of Scientific Objects', in *Biographies of Scientific Objects*, ed. Lorraine Daston (Chicago, 2000), p. 13.
13  John Law, 'Organizing Accountabilities: Ontology and the Mode of Accounting', in *Accountability: Power, Ethos and the Technologies of Accounting*, eds Rolland Munro and Jan Mouritsen (London, 1996), p. 298.
14  Joost van Loon, '"A Contagious Living Fluid:" Objectification and Assemblage in the History of Virology', *Culture, Theory and Society*, 19 (2002), 111.

15  See D.S.L. Cardwell, *The Organisation of Science in England* (1957; London, 1972), pp. 156–86.

16  For the Society for Public Analysts see R.C. Churnside and J.H. Hamence, *The Practising Chemists: A History of the Society for Analytical Chemistry 1874–1974* (London, 1974). For the government laboratories see P.W. Hammond and Harold Egan, *Weighed in the Balance: A History of the Laboratory of the Government Chemist* (London, 1992), pp. 1–99.

17  R.S. Cahn and O.C. Dermer, *Introduction to Chemical Nomenclature*, 5th ed (1959; London and Boston, 1979), p. 2.

18  Jane Hume Clapperton, *Margaret Dunmore, or A Socialist Home* (1888; London, 1892), p. 152. In this novel the harmony of the socialist utopia of *La Maison* is threatened as two of the characters enjoy an intimacy encouraged by the privacy of the laboratory. Not only do they jeopardize their wider relationships, but they also indulge an illegitimate egotistical pleasure.

19  John Morrison, 'On the Manufacture of Caustic Soda', *Chemical News*, 31, 26 February 1875 (1875), 87. Cited in R.F. Bud and G.K. Roberts, *Science versus Practice: Chemistry in Victorian Britain* (Manchester, 1984), p. 99.

20  Bruno Latour, *Science in Action* (Cambridge MA, 1987), p. 24.

21  'Charter of the Chemical Society' (1848), cited in Tom Sidney Moore and James Charles Philip, *The Chemical Society 1841–1941: A Historical Review* (London, 1947), p. 179.

22  Bud and Roberts, *Science versus Practice*, p. 107. They find 84 academics joined the Society from 1850–1870 and between them published over 1200 papers. Three quarters of them had published at least one paper by 1883.

23  Moore and Philip, *Chemical Society*, p. 85.

24  For the blackballing see Moore and Philip, *Chemical Society*, chapter 4, esp. p. 51.

25  Anonymous, *Chemical Society: Minutes of Council Meetings 19 April 1883–27 March 1893*, unpublished minute book, Royal Chemical Society (1893), p. 103. There was a further attempt in 1892 but women were not admitted until 1920. See Mary R. S. Creese, 'British Women of the Nineteenth and Early Twentieth Centuries Who Contributed to Research in the Chemical Sciences', *British Journal for the History of Science*, 24 (1991), 298.

26  The 6 were H.E. Armstrong, F.R. Japp, Hugo Müller, W.H. Perkin, W. Ramsay and T.E. Thorpe. Of the remainder, J. Millar Thomson was Secretary and W. R. Dunstan, W. P. Wynne, and H.F. Morley held academic posts at the Pharmaceutical Society, Royal College, and Queens College respectively.

27  See Anonymous, *Minutes of the Publication Committee 27 January 1887–21st December 1893*, unpublished minute book, Royal Society of Chemistry, 19 December 1889 (1893), unpaginated.

28  Moore and Philip, *Chemical Society*, p. 83, 190; anonymous, *Chemical Society*, p. 127, 111, 134.

29  Anonymous, *Minutes*, 9 May 1889, unpaginated.

30  Anonymous, *Minutes*, 21 May 1891, unpaginated.

31  Anonymous, *Minutes*, 14 November 1889, unpaginated.

32  Anonymous, *Minutes*, 19 December 1889, unpaginated.

33  Spencer Umfreville Pickering MA, 'The Nature of Solutions, as elucidated by a Study of the Density, Electric Conductivity, Heat Capacity, Heat of Dissolution, and Heat of Sulphuric Acid Solution', *Journal of the Chemical Society*, 57 (1890), 64–184.

34  The Committee declined to publish the second portion of the paper, 'Nature of Solutions as elucidated by a Study of the Density, Electric Conductivity, Heat Capacity, Heat of Dissolution, and Heat of Calcium Chloride', but kept the manuscript as evidence of priority. Pickering appealed to Council (16 April 1891) who called for a report from the Committee. Groves and Armstrong provided a report on 21 May 1891 and Council suggested Pickering resubmit the paper. It was rejected on 17 December 1891. Pickering maintained the public profile of this research however: he read 'The Present Position of the Hydrate Theory of Solution' at the Leeds meeting of the BAAS in 1890, and then summarized the discussion and resulting interventions in *Chemical News* in 1891. See Spencer U. Pickering, 'Discussion on the Theory of Solutions', *Chemical News*, 63, 26 Mar 1891 (1891), 147–51; 2 April 1891 (1891), 157–9; and 9 April 1891 (1891), 169–71.

35  For Perkin see Jack Morrell, 'W.H. Perkin, Jr., at Manchester and Oxford: from Irwell to Isis', *Osiris*, 8 (1993), 104–26.

36  Anonymous, *Minutes*, 19 December 1890, unpaginated.

37  Bruno Latour, *Pandora's Hope* (Cambridge MA, 1999), p. 124.

38  Latour, *Science in Action*, p. 49.

39  F. Stanley Kipping, PhD., D.Sc. and W.H. Perkin, Jun., PhD., 'Action of Dehydrating Agents on αω-Diacetylpentane. Synthesis of Methylethylhexamethylene', *Journal of the Chemical Society*, 57 (1890), 13–28.

40  Latour, *Pandora's Hope*, p. 122.

41  Latour, *Pandora's Hope*, p. 122. Emphasis is Latour's.

42  Kipping and Perkin, 'Action of Dehydrating Agents', 13.

43  Kipping and Perkin, 'Action of Dehydrating Agents', 16–17.

44  Latour, *Pandora's Hope*, p. 132.

45  Jocelyn Field Thorpe, 'Section II', *The Life and Work of Professor William Henry Perkin MA, ScD, LLD, PhD, FRS*, by A.J. Greenaway, J.F. Thorpe and R. Robinson (London, 1932), p. 39.

46  W.H. Perkin, Jun., PhD., FRS, 'Contributions from the Laboratories of the Heriot Watt College, Edinburgh: On Berberine. Part II', *Journal of the Chemical Society*, 57 (1890), 1046.

47  Cahn and Dermer, *Chemical Nomenclature*, p. 1.

48  Primo Levi, 'The Language of Chemists (I),' in *Other People's Trades*, trans. Raymond Rosenthal (1989; London, 1999), p. 103. For a semiotic analysis of the adoption of Berzelian formulae as 'paper tools' earlier in the century see Ursula Klein, 'Paper Tools in Experimental Cultures', *Studies in History and Philosophy of Science Part A*, 32 (2001), 265–352.

49  Levi, 'Language of Chemists', p. 103.

50  I have not been able to establish why Kipping and Perkin use benzene as a structural unit here. It seems that they are using it as a shorthand to indicate a ring of six carbon atoms despite the fact that it is not, nor was, benzene.

51  Louis Bernard Guyton de Morveau and others, *Method of Chymical Nomenclature*, trans. James St. John (London, 1788), pp. 4–5. For the *Méthode of nomenclature chimique* see Maurice P. Crosland, *Historical Studies in the History of Chemistry* (London, 1962), pp. 153–214.

52  de Morveau and others, *Method of Chymical Nomenclature*, p. 5.

53  Jonathon Simon, 'Authority and Authorship in the *Method of Chemical Nomenclature*', *Ambix*, 49 (2002), 221.

54  Michel Foucault, *The Order of Things* (London, 1970), p. 116.

55  Foucault, *Order of Things*, p. 117.

56  Foucault, *Order of Things*, p. 118.

57  The unmarked author is, of course, never neutral: see Donna Haraway, 'Modest_Witness@Second_Millennium', in *The Haraway Reader* (New York, 2004), pp. 223–50.

58  Creese gives 33 papers authored by women in the *Journal* between 1880 and 1900. Sixteen are co-authored by men and often the gender of the author is concealed beneath initials. See Mary R.S. Creese, *Ladies in the Laboratory: American and British Women in Science, 1800–1900* (London, 1998), pp. 415–17.

59  A.J. Meadows, 'Access to the Results of Scientific Research: Developments in Victorian Britain', in *Development of Science Publishing in Europe*, ed. A.J. Meadows (Amsterdam, 1980), p. 49. Abstracts were also constituent parts of periodicals in the humanities, medicine and social science. Bruce M. Manzer, *The Abstract Journal 1790–1900* (Metuchen NJ and London, 1957), p. 136.

60  For instance in 1862 the Professor of the Royal College of Chemistry, Augustus Hofmann, submitted a 22-page abstract. Moore and Philip, *Chemical Society*, p. 25.

61  Moore and Philip, *Chemical Society*, p. 48.

62  Anonymous, *Minutes*, 6 February 1891, unpaginated. Groves is however, struggling to find Abstractors familiar with Italian to abstract from the *Gazetta*.

63  Anonymous [H.E. Armstrong], *The Jubilee Chemical Society of London 1891: Record of the Proceedings Together with an Account of the History and Development of the Society 1841–1891* (London, 1896), p. 248.

64  Anonymous, *Minutes*, 13 February 1890, unpaginated.

65  Anonymous [C.E. Groves], 'Instructions to Abstractors, giving the Nomenclature and System of Notation Adopted in the Abstracts', *Journal of the Chemical Society*, 58 (1890), liii.

66  Anonymous [C.E. Groves], 'Instructions', liii.

67  Although organic chemistry was not considered in the *Méthode de nomenclature chemique*. Standardized nomenclature for organic chemistry was not adopted until the Geneva Congress in 1892.

68  Anonymous [C.E. Groves], 'Instructions,' lv.

69  A.C. Wootton, *Chronicles of Pharmacy*, 2 (London, 1910), p. 278.

70  J.W. Slater, 'Scientific Terminology', *Chemical News*, 61, 9 May 1890 (1890), 228.

71  Allen, 'Character Sketch', 25.

# Chapter Five

# Periodicity and the Rhythms of Nineteenth-Century Science

At the anniversary meeting of the Chemical Society, 27 March 1890, the President, William Russell, singled out the Society's *Proceedings* in his Presidential Address:

> I cannot leave the subject of our publications without calling your attention to the *Proceedings*. They have now existed for nearly six years, and are a most valuable adjunct to our *Journal*, serving to give as wide and as important a publicity to a paper as the 'Transactions', and at the same time to afford a rapidity of publication not exceeded by that of any scientific journal.[1]

Although such occasions are often marked by hyperbole, Russell here signals an important aspect of this publication. Whereas the *Journal of the Chemical Society* provided a repository for the ratified research of the society's Fellows, the *Proceedings*, published rapidly on preprinted sheets after each meeting, mobilized a different set of spatial-temporal coordinates. Founded in 1885 in order to keep those Fellows living in the country in touch with the society's business, the *Proceedings* were not so much a textual adjunct to the *Journal*, as Russell suggests, as a mobile version of the space of the meeting. Russell's emphasis on speed however is apt: the papers circulated via the *Proceedings* are not the finished science of the *Journal* but instead provisional reports of work in progress. It is their position at the forefront of scientific progress that predicates their importance, and so the relevance of the *Proceedings* is determined by the proximity of its publication date to the date of the meeting.

There is a further aspect to this. The previous chapter showed how the papers published in the *Journal* create two objects, the name of the chemical and the name of the scientist, that can be distributed through culture in order to mark intellectual property. Papers read at the meetings of the Chemical Society operate in a similar way, with a speaking scientist proclaiming their ownership over a scientific domain by literally giving it voice. The risk that audience members might appropriate the results of a paper is offset by the gentlemanly, fraternal codes of scientific practice. This logic also motivates the *Proceedings*: authors are willing to publish abbreviated reports of research in order to mark their work as their own through the act of sharing it. However, the Fellows of the Chemical Society were not the only audience of the *Proceedings*. As part of intellectual culture, involving the activities of recognizable public figures, the proceedings of scientific societies were newsworthy. By circulating a sanctioned version of these proceedings, the Society could control the form in which they reappeared in other titles. The circulation of textual objects, whether on the page or as a work in their own right, always risks their appropriation: as Russell notes, the *Proceedings* affords authors the means to further their work in order that it might accrue publicity without the attendant loss of authorial control.

The learned societies all met according to their own temporal rhythms. The Chemical Society met fortnightly, and its *Proceedings* approximated this periodicity in order to fill the space between a paper being read and its eventual publication in the *Journal*. The weekly scientific press provided a further mediating context, reaching different readers in a quicker temporal rhythm. Titles such as *Nature* and *Chemical News* were predicated on providing writers with a medium in which results could be announced quickly and readers kept abreast of current developments. By reprinting proceedings, these titles provided access to those debarred from the spaces of scientific practice. As Chapter One demonstrated, the readership for science was much more varied than those permitted to become Fellows of the learned societies, and the relatively cheap weeklies allowed women, students, and those who did not live within easy reach of the metropolitan societies, access to the knowledge that was located there.

The movement from spoken paper, to society's proceedings, to their republication in the weekly periodical press, demonstrates how objects can remain stable across different contexts without manifesting ontological deterioration. Reading the proceedings in the weekly periodical press allows access on the condition that the reader recognize the exclusivity of the originary space, whether laboratory or learned society. In this way ownership is attributed to the scientist despite the heterodox contexts in which accounts might appear. It was through the reiteration of this connection that a scientist could combine the roles of expert, consultant (for both commerce and the courts), entrepreneur, academic, and gentleman. Although the actual content of their research would allow them to accrue scientific esteem, it is the reportage of their activity in the public medium of the press that attributes broader cultural authority. In this way, well-known chemists such as William Crookes and William Ramsay amassed sizable sums through exploiting a body of knowledge they were simply associated with.

This chapter explores the connection between the different rhythms that structure scientific practice. Mark Turner, in his article 'Periodical Time in the Nineteenth Century' argues that, although segments of time are artificial, they are not simply arbitrary. As such, what 'media historians need to do is find out exactly for whom particular temporalities are meaningful, and this needs to be undertaken by considering a range of cultural determinants – social position and gender most obviously, but also important differences which emerge according to location.'[2] The periodicity of the press determines one set of temporal demarcations but, as Turner recognizes, this rhythm participates in a whole set of wider cultural routines. By tracing the overlapping rhythms of learned societies, their publications, and the reports of their proceedings in weekly periodicals, I map the segmented temporal zones that emerge, and explore the spatial movements of the objects that cut across them.

It is important to recognize that the influence of any originary space for these movements is not inherent within its location, but rather in the way that it is invoked. Although a report of the proceedings of the Chemical Society does signal the Society's authority, it does so from the context in which it appears. It is the references to the Society, invoked from the context of the journal, rather than anything about the Society itself that structures its influence. Any origin is always posited, and it is the social acceptance of the references to it that allows it to influence the present. It is when we forget the influence of the social – which allows things to move while granting them a source – that we lapse into the diffusionist model. Bruno Latour describes this as a world of 'black boxes', finished objects that by their own means move through culture: 'spewed out by a few centres, new things and beliefs are emerging, free floating through minds and hands, populating the world with replicas of themselves.' This ideology, which informs the logic of popular science, makes it seem 'that the behaviour of people is *caused* by the diffusion of facts and machines. It is forgotten that the obedient behaviour of people is what turns the claims into facts and machines; the careful strategies that give the object the contours that will provide assent are also forgotten.'[3] Movements, as I demonstrated in Chapter One, do not just occur through space and take time; rather they are moved by things that happen in those spaces, and their path is often the result of how they are presented on arrival.

The remainder of this chapter is based around an analysis of a calendar of the years 1890 and 1891 upon which I have mapped these periodicities. The calendars, one of which I have provided as an appendix to the chapter, is marked with the publication dates of three weeklies – *Athenaeum*, *Nature* and *Chemical News* – each of which listed and reported on the proceedings of scientific societies. Using these lists I have juxtaposed their overlapping weekly rhythms with the dates and times of the meetings of the various scientific societies. Although I have interpreted science widely, including medical institutions and scientific lectures, I have deliberately excluded nonscientific meetings and events in order to make clearer their various rhythms. In order to show the durations between the moment of reading a paper, and its manifestation in paper form, I have also noted when each weekly publishes the proceedings of a meeting. As each title reports on organizations that it believes its readers are interested in, I have included all the societies here. As the dates of meetings are also given, it is still possible to reconstruct the fuller calendar.

Not only does this map mark a selection of the different rhythms of scientific life, but it also indicates the passage of textual objects from one space-time to another. To demonstrate this, I have included the dates of publication of the *Journal* and the *Proceedings of the Chemical Society*. As I have mentioned, although the 'Transactions' and the 'Abstracts' that make up the *Journal* create a repository of names that can be circulated through society, the *Proceedings* were conceived to represent the space of the Chemical Society in different textual contexts. As the calendar shows, the meetings of the Society determine when the *Proceedings* is published, and these in turn structure when the proceedings can be reported further. By exploring the manifestation of chemical papers in these different moments (albeit via material forms that are marked with a time), it becomes possible to see how time and space interact in the gaps created by overlapping rhythms.

Although monthlies such as the *Journal of the Chemical Society* seek to present the results of scientific endeavour, there is always an unresolved aspect to their temporality. It is the possibility of restaging an event that grants it ontological value, and the poetics of laboratory accounts provide both the details for actual laboratory reconstructions and surrogate laboratory conditions of their own. Phenomena restricted to one spatial-temporal moment are then recreated – either in the minds of readers or in their actual laboratories – and these multiple emergences are reified to posit a clear narrative of discovery through the body of the original scientist / author. As Chapter Four showed, at the heart of experimental science is a site where authors can withdraw, point to the reality of the phenomenon staged in the laboratory, and speak on its behalf. Isabelle Stengers argues in *The Invention of Modern Science* that the sciences 'do not depend on the possibility of representing something it would be the task of philosophy to ground; they invent possibilities of representing, of constituting a statement that nothing a priori distinguishes from a fiction, as the legitimate representation of a phenomena.'[4] These 'possibilities of representing' are created by what happens in the laboratory, and are the context in which they must be judged. Stengers calls this the 'event': the reported phenomena gathers together interested fellow authors who then decide if the event is a fiction or not; and every affirmation of its reality further brings it into existence.

The emergence of nonhuman things, whose actual history is suppressed, is an event whose meaning is constructed retroactively by a collective of people who, in turn, have been brought together in the terrain produced by it. The event, according to Stengers, 'establishes a difference between the before and after [...] A great number of actors, all of whom have been, in one way or another, produced by the text, undertake to draw lessons from it. All are situated in the space it has opened; none can claim to have a privileged relation of truth within it.' This is because 'as the creator of difference, the event is not for all that the bearer of signification.' Its meaning is constructed by the actors, and their testimonies will reify its materiality and establish its history.[5]

Although Stengers locates the event within the laboratory, if this space can be mobilized then the spaces in which an event will be ratified become much more distributed and diverse. For instance they might be physical locations such as the meeting rooms of a learned society, or spaces created in the act of reading a scientific paper. In the traditional history of the sciences these events are described as a series of epistemological breaks or Copernican revolutions that, in turn, constitute a linear narrative of scientific progress. Latour claims that this creates two histories, 'one dealing with universal and necessary things that have always been present, lacking any historicity' and 'the other focusing on the more or less contingent or more or less durable agitation of poor human beings detached from things.'[6] The past thus becomes a series of discontinuous moments, arranged sequentially, with absolute demarcations between periods preventing any illegitimate return.

This dynamic also informs the periodicity of the press. Each number of a periodical is just such an event, and its effect is that it opens a space for the redefinition of past, present and future. The appearance of the latest number of a periodical differentiates it from the last, rendering its back issues as a new coherent history. The practice of continuous pagination and the numbering of volumes suggests that most nineteenth-century periodicals aimed at the status of books, if not libraries, encyclopaedias, galleries, or museums as many of their subtitles suggest. However, as has often been noted, the 'time-stamped' nature of the genre marks it as ephemeral, linked to a moment that passes, and so only a fraction of titles were actually bound into volumes and kept.[7] For scientific publications, these bound volumes constituted an important archive through which to discuss events in the present. However, the current number of a periodical reconfigures those that precede it as part of its history. As Chapter Three explained, the latest periodical number must re-perform all its connections with the present and it does so by referring to and representing objects, times and spaces which intersect with the lives of its imagined readers. This duration only exists between the latest number and the one before it, the temporal spaces between issues in the more distant past being elided as the archive is once more reformed as history.

As the creator of difference, the event demarcates a before and after. Meetings of societies and the publication of periodical numbers are events that gather interested actors together to judge their significance. The situation is complicated as there are at least two different orders of event: the scientific event represented within the text (whether heard or read); and the actual manifestation of that text in the appearance of the number or the gathering of a society. As the latter will vary according to the medium through which the event is related – including its spatial location and temporal moment – not all interpretations of the scientific event will be identical. Instead, it becomes pluralized according to its context: rather than witness scientific activities moving through culture, we have individual, contextualized acts that posit these movements from specific spatial temporal frames. It is the co-presence of these two events that introduces the possibility of appropriation, and it is the plurality of these frames that I have mapped below.

## The Rhythms of 1890 and 1891

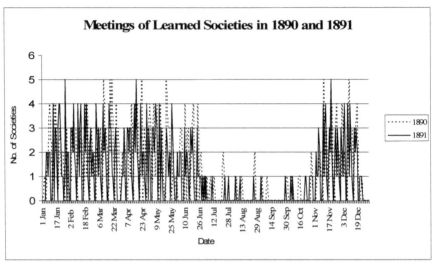

**Figure 5.1 The Meetings of Learned Societies 1890 and 1891**

There are a number of obvious rhythms that shape the calendars for 1890 and 1891. Of course, these are themselves suggested by the frame I have chosen: had I plotted this data over ten years, I may have found larger temporal structures. I used two years to compile my data as I wanted to verify the recurrence of the annual rhythm determined by the summer recess. Figure 5.1 plots the number of scientific societies meeting per calendar date (I have excluded the various lectures) in order to better display this annual structure. The most striking features are the the Christmas and summer recesses. Between July and October very few of the metropolitan societies met, both reflecting and affirming the London 'season.' Those that did were the societies whose activities depended on the weather: the Horticultural Society, Botanical Society, Entomological Society and the Photographical Society. The peaks are higher in 1890 as the *Athenaeum* stops listing the Horticultural Society in 1891. As I mentioned in Chapter Three, the recess restricts the amount of scientific material available to be reproduced in the various interested periodicals, and the events surrounding the annual meeting of the British Association in September were an important source of copy. There are also annual pauses dictated by the recurrence of religious festivals. The break for Christmas occupies two weeks, with the majority of scientific activity focused around the juvenile lectures at the Royal and London Institutions. At Easter, no society met from Good Friday to Easter Monday, and many tried to avoid meeting that week altogether: in 1891, for instance, the Chemical Society moved their anniversary on to a Wednesday to avoid having the occasion on the Thursday before Easter; and William Crookes's *Chemical News* was regularly published on a Thursday in order to avoid appearing on Good Friday.

The societies themselves meet either weekly, fortnightly or monthly. Like the cacophonous rhythms of the press, the societies jostle together on a crowded calendar, trying to establish their own rhythms and avoid awkward clashes. The monthlies include the Entomological Society, Royal Microscopical Society, Royal Meteorological Society, Quekett Club, Royal Astronomical Society, Royal Statistical Society, Society of Engineers, and the British Astronomical Association. Although it is difficult to generalize, these tend to be the more prestigious, well-established institutions. That said, the fortnightly societies include the Linnean Society, Chemical Society, Geological Society, Physical Society, Zoological Society, Anthropological Institute, Photographic Society, Society for Chemical Industry, Royal Botanical Society, Pathological Society of London, and the Royal Medical and Chirurgical Society. This is the most common periodicity, and these societies are a mix of the dilettante, professional, and prestigious. There are few weeklies, but this frequency includes the oldest and most prestigious organization, the Royal Society, the oldest medical organization, the Medical Society of London, and the relatively new Institution of Electrical Engineers.[8]

In the calendar I have also given the dates of any scientific lectures that were delivered at the Royal Institution, London Institution, Society of Arts, Victoria Institute and the Sunday Lecture Society. These lectures were an important source of copy for scientific publications, as well as a source of lucrative income for the lecturers who would often lecture at more than one institution, and publish the lectures in more than one title. For instance in 1890 C.V. Boys gave lectures on the 'Heat of the Moon and Stars' on the 17, 24 April and 1 May at the Royal Institution, and then repeated them in December at the London Institution. By giving lectures in these institutions, scientists offered themselves as public representatives of the topics under discussion while also participating in late nineteenth-century celebrity culture. Just as the repetition of proceedings in the weekly press exposed closed proceedings in a public place, so these lectures, occurring physically in public space prior to being mobilized further in the press, represent science as part of public life.

I have noted the times when all these various organizations met. Eight o'clock is the most common time, with the remainder being usually either half past seven or half past eight. The major exceptions to this are the meetings of the Royal Society at half past four, the afternoon and evening lectures at the Royal Institution at three and nine respectively, the Entomological and Meteorological Societies at seven, and the Physical Society and the British Astronomical Association at five. There are reasons for these: the Royal Society met in the afternoon to avoid clashing with the other societies, and to give Fellows the opportunity to get to London. These exceptions aside, the common time indicates the necessity of meeting after the close of the working day, and emphasizes just how pressing the demands on scientists' time were. However, the overlapping periodicities meant that Fellows and members of more than one society could probably attend some of their respective societies' meetings. For instance, a Fellow of the Entomological Society who was also a geologist would face a clash once a month on a Wednesday, but could attend the other fortnightly meeting of the Geological Society. Although only a minority of the audiences of scientific lectures are likely to be members of learned societies, should a lecturer commit to a series of lectures at the Society of Arts or London Institution, they would miss a swathe of meetings. Of course, the lecturer at the Royal Institution would not have this problem to the same extent, as his or her lectures would be either in the afternoon, or begin at nine in the evening. However, the presence of lecturers, Fellows and audience members at all of these events in the evenings makes the activities of learned societies and institutions part of the London evening scene, with their audiences mixing with the pleasure-seeking crowds on the street, rushing for the last trains after their proceedings close.

It is important to note that these listings are neither authoritative nor exhaustive. They are compiled from the weekly listings in *Nature*, *Chemical News*, and the *Athenaeum*: as mentioned above, I have only included the scientific societies; consequently, these lists represent the particular scientific biases of each title. The purpose of the calendar is to juxtapose segmented temporal periods with the movement of material across these contexts. It is therefore appropriate that the lists are predicated on the societies that each title thinks its readers should know is meeting. Against the weeklies, I have also mapped the publications of the Chemical Society. The *Journal*, although ostensibly a monthly, was notoriously irregular; equally the *Proceedings* did not quite approximate the more regular fortnightly rhythm of the Society. The latter publication was published on prepared sheets in order to facilitate a prompt publication, but varied in size from 2 to 32 pages according to content. Usually it took about two weeks to appear after a meeting, but this could vary in either direction. For instance the number containing proceedings for the 20 November 1890 was published on the 26 November; but the number containing proceedings for the 19 Jun 1890 was eventually published on the 14 August. By comparing the irregular publications of the Chemical Society with its more regular fortnightly meetings and the rigidly regular temporality of the weeklies, a variable temporal dimension is created as proceedings are reprinted across them.

The weeklies were all published on different days. The *Athenaeum*, the well-established high-culture 3d weekly, was published on a Saturday. Its broad sweep of interests represents the learned amateur approach of its readers and, at 48 pages a week, contains a great deal of matter, mostly consisting of reviews of recent publications and events. Its scientific content was published in a department called 'Science', which appeared after the first department, 'Literature', but before 'Fine Arts', 'Music' and 'Drama' This weekly department consists of a series of notes for a particular discipline – for instance 'Astronomical Notes' – a sub-section devoted to 'Societies', and a 'Science Gossip' column. The 'Societies' section contains both a list of forthcoming meetings and a series of accounts of proceedings. Despite being in the 'Science Department', this list is not restricted to science. The *Athenaeum* notes a wide range of societies, including the Numismatic Society, Shorthand Society, Aristotelian Society, Society of Antiquities, Society of Biblical Archaeology, the Huguenot Society, Philological Society and the New Shakspere Society. This esoteric selection of institutions are listed alongside most of the major scientific societies: as the calendar shows, the 19 April 1890 number of the *Athenaeum* includes reports from the Royal Astronomical Society, the Chemical Society, the Institution of Civil Engineers, the Society of Engineers, the New Shakspere Society, the Hellenic Society and the Aristotelian Society. Frank James has indicated the decline of science reporting in the *Athenaeum* in the 1860s, and speculated that this might be related to the creation of a specialist scientific weekly press.[9] However, in the 1890s reports of scientific societies, including the lectures at the Royal Institution, are very much part of its wider survey of the capital's learned societies. Although this diversity might reflect the lingering presence of a 'intellectual common context', it more probably represents the fields of endeavour of sections of the title's perceived readership which, taken as a whole, reflect the title's conception of culture more generally.[10] None of the reports are particularly detailed, and often the sheer number of them prevent them consisting of more than lists of papers given.

As the leading scientific weekly, *Nature* was the authoritative space for an overview of the proceedings of scientific societies. At sixpence it was twice as expensive as the *Athenaeum* yet contained half the number of pages. Its coverage of 'Societies and Academies' was positioned towards the back of the number, after any material reprinted from other sources and following a department called 'Scientific Serials.' 'Societies and Academies' consists of a list of recent meetings, arranged by city: London is always first, then any other British cities, then cities abroad such as Paris, Berlin, Stockholm, Amsterdam, Sydney and Göttingen. This international survey by city suggests that science is a collaborative enterprise across national boundaries. Not only does it provide information to British readers about distant scientific events, but it also signals *Nature's* role as an international title, informing foreign readers about science in Britain and circulating valuable advertising space for Macmillan and his advertisers. These reports are followed by a 'Diary of Societies' listing all meetings from the day of publication (Thursday) through to the Monday eleven days later. As *Nature's* reports were substantially more detailed than the *Athenaeum's*, it devotes more letterpress but at the cost of being less up-to-date.

*Chemical News* was a four penny weekly published on a Friday. It is the shortest of the three, consisting of only 12–14 pages, and is the most focused in its listings. Like *Nature*, the coverage of societies is towards the back of the number, and it lists the meetings for the coming week (Monday to Friday) in 'Meetings for the Week' on its back page. The only societies that are regularly reported on in *Chemical News* are the Chemical Society, Physical Society, and the monthly meetings of the Royal Institution. However, it lists many more, including various medical and pharmaceutical societies that are excluded from the other titles. As 'A Journal of Practical Chemistry in all its applications to Pharmacy, Arts and

Manufactures', *Chemical News* perceived all of these exponents of chemical knowledge as potential readers. *Chemical News* was founded in 1859 and, for a while, was in direct competition with *Nature* before the latter's price rise in 1878. *Nature*, well-resourced through Macmillan and able to rely on its supportive network of scientists for purchasers and contributors, quickly identified a specialist audience of well-placed scientists.[11] Crookes, on the other hand, already had a specialized title that necessarily relied on a broader readership.[12] As his coverage of societies is thorough, space limits those he could include: by printing the proceedings of the Chemical and Physical Societies he both represents his own scientific interests, while providing access to societies that excluded the bulk of his readers.

The representations of these meetings share certain features across the titles. All three, for instance, are surprisingly inaccurate. The *Athenaeum* fails to list the Physical Society's meeting in Cambridge on the 9 May 1891. This might be because, as a London weekly, the meeting was seen as irrelevant to its readership. However, in 'Societies' for 23 May 1891 they give full details. This occurs again with the regular meeting of the Physical Society in the same month: the meeting on the 22 May is not noted in the list printed in the 16 May number of the *Athenaeum*, but the proceedings of that meeting are given in 'Societies' for the 6 June 1891.[13] Errors such as these may be due to a failure on the part of the Society to inform the journal, but sometimes they are the result of internal inconsistencies. In 1891 the Royal Society had its anniversary on the 30 November at 4pm. The *Athenaeum* announced this in their summary of the Royal Society meeting on the 19 November, listed it as a forthcoming meeting in the number for the 28 November, but then recorded that the meeting occurred on the 1 December in their report published on the 5 December 1891.[14] On the 5 March 1890 *Chemical News* mistakenly lists a fortnightly meeting of the Geological Society, even though they had recorded the previous meeting the week before. Also, *Chemical News* lists the monthly meetings of the Royal Microscopical Society incorrectly from 12 March 1890 onwards until after the summer recess (they actually met the following week). The inaccuracies in *Nature* are mainly due to its eleven day listings (Thursday to the Sunday of the following week). As they have two opportunities to list meetings on Thursdays, Fridays, Saturdays and Sundays, they often overlook meetings of the Royal Society (Thursdays) or Physical Society (Fridays) on the first notice, before inserting them the week of publication.[15] Of the three titles, *Nature*'s coverage of lectures is the most inconsistent: although they are the only title to list the Sunday Lecture Society, their coverage of the London Institution and Victoria Institution is extremely sparse and they do not notice the activities of the Society of Arts, even when they are scientific. Although *Nature* had a dual role of serving the specialist scientific community and providing a platform for scientific opinions within public discourse, these popular lectures do not seem to be worth listing for its readers.

However, these lectures were reprinted in both *Chemical News* and *Nature*, suggesting that it is the content, rather than the event itself, that is deemed important. Lectures were generally protected by copyright (except when delivered in public institutions), and lecturers would often publish them in multiple titles to maximize their revenues. As lectures were newsworthy events, they were often published as soon as possible. For instance Frederick Abel's lectures 'On Smokeless Explosives', delivered at the Royal Institution on the 31 January 1890 was printed in *Nature* a week later on the 6 February.[16] The letterpress clearly signals its derivation, and makes a point of highlighting the date on which the lecture was delivered to emphasize its timeliness. This lecture was also published in *Chemical News*, but not until 21 March 1890, two months after it was delivered and so no longer news. Instead, Crookes stresses its scientific merit; although the letterpress is identical, he emphasizes the eminence of his author, and places the second half of the lecture on his front page.[17]

*Nature* is not always the first to publish lectures. When T.E. Thorpe gave 'The Glow of Phosphorous' at the Royal Institution on Friday 14 March 1890, Crookes published it in *Chemical News* the following Friday. The lecture was clearly of value to *Nature* as Lockyer found room for an identical paper in the number for 3 April 1890, three numbers later.[18] Although this latter report is anonymous – as were many of the lectures (and indeed contributions generally) published in *Nature* – its provenance is once again signalled in a footnote. There are occasions when both titles publish lectures concurrently. Vivian Lewes gave a course of five Cantor lectures 'On Gaseous Luminants' at the Society of Arts on Mondays from the 24 November until 22 December 1890. *Chemical News* was the first to publish these lectures, also over five weekly parts, from 2 January to 6 February 1891. These were presented as abstracts '[c]ommunicated by the author' and indicate their derivation. They were also serialized anonymously (although Lewes is referred to in the third person throughout the text) in *Nature* from the 8 January, but were condensed into only three weeks. As there are portions omitted in *Nature*, they are not reprinting material from *Chemical News* but rather editing it for their readers: the version in *Nature* is completed by the 22 January 1891, two numbers before it is finished in *Chemical News*, and occupying four fewer pages.[19]

A revealing difference between the two titles is in their treatment of the Chemical Society's Jubilee in 1891. The meeting, to celebrate its fiftieth anniversary, was spread over two days: delegates would meet at the Society of Arts from 3 to 5pm on the 24 February to hear speeches and addresses, before attending a reception at 8:30pm at Goldsmith's Hall; on the 25 February there was a banquet from 3 to 5pm at the Hotel Metropole. The meeting was first noticed in *Chemical News* on the 30 January 1891, but *Nature* is the first of the titles to print the Presidential Address, appearing in 'The Chemical Society's Jubilee' on the 12 March, a week before *Chemical News*.[20] Aside from a further report in the following number of *Nature* detailing the proceedings of the rest of the occasion, there is no further coverage. In *Chemical News*, Crookes gives details about the event in the very next number, three days later. This report gives details of the various gifts exhibited, and notes that '[i]t is our intention to give a full report of the above proceedings in an early number.' However, each subsequent number before the publication of the Presidential Address contains yet more details of the exhibits, and when the Address is finally published on the 20 March, it follows a report of the Chemical Society's next ordinary meeting (5 March 1891). As the event itself is newsworthy, it received substantial coverage in the daily press.[21] Instead, the titles memorialize and contextualize the event differently: for *Nature* the public nature of the Presidential Address is the most important part; for *Chemical News*, it is the more specialized details of the proceedings, particularly the catalogue of exhibits, that take precedence.

Each title lists societies and reprints proceedings according to the perceived interests of its readers. The scientific societies included in the *Athenaeum* are diverse: as the appendix shows, it lists most of the major scientific societies, yet it excludes the more professional societies such as the Pharmaceutical Society or any of the medical societies. *Nature* also overlooks these domains, although it too includes the Institution of Civil Engineers. Unlike the *Athenaeum*, *Nature* does cover the Society for Chemical Industry, perhaps because of its ties to the more-established Chemical Society. *Nature* also includes the Essex Field Club, indicating a provincial bias as well as a metropolitan focus, and the inclusion of the University College Biological, Chemical, Physical, and Photographical Societies signals its connection to the London universities. The only nonscientific society is the Aristotelian Society, which is also listed in the *Athenaeum*, and perhaps indicates science's link with natural philosophy and the university backgrounds of many of its practitioners. *Chemical News* contains a wider selection of scientific societies, including the Pathological, Medical, Pharmaceutical, and Royal Medical and Chirurgical Societies. As *Chemical News* was relatively specialized, Crookes needed to attract readers beyond chemistry, hence his notice of other branches of science that employ chemical knowledge. As photography relies on both chemistry and a supply of chemicals, this, as well as his own experience with photography, informs his regular inclusion of the Photographical Society and the Camera Club. This slant towards chemistry, albeit broadly defined, is evident in his exclusion of natural science societies such as the Anthropological Institute, Linnean Society, Zoological Society, and the Entomological Society, all of which are listed in the other titles.

The way in which the proceedings of societies are recorded also varies according to title. The *Athenaeum's* reports offer little more than the lists that advertise forthcoming meetings: although they often provide the titles of the papers under discussion, it is not what goes on in the meetings that the title notes, but rather that the meeting has occurred. Any other newsworthy detail is reported in the 'Science Gossip' column: for instance, when T.H. Huxley was awarded the Linnean Medal at the Anniversary Meeting of the Linnean Society on 24 May 1890, it was noted in 'Science Gossip' on the 31 May, but not recorded in the reports of societies until the 21 June, which notes both the Anniversary and the subsequent meeting on the 5 June. *Nature* does not report on as many societies as the *Athenaeum*, but it does so in more detail. Not only were the readers of *Nature* distributed around the country, but they were also likely to be interested in more than one province of science, and relied upon these notices to keep abreast of papers read in London. However, the need for accuracy and detail in these reports means that they are often delayed, both due to their preparation and a lack of space within *Nature*. For instance, most proceedings were published within a month, but the copy generated by the weekly meetings of the Royal Society disrupt the chronology of their publication. On the 9 January 1890 Lockyer prints proceedings from the 19 December 1889; on the 23 January from the 5 December 1889; on the 30 January from the 9 January 1890; on the 6 February from the 3 January; and on the 13 February 1890 from the 19 December 1889. Not only is the order of these reports inconsistent, but they are also not particularly punctual. For instance, in the first few months of 1890, *Chemical News* gets its proceedings into press a week faster than *Nature*; however, as the weeks proceed, a larger space opens up until the summer recess. Even after the recess *Nature* is behind *Chemical News* by two weeks for the Physical Society and even more for the Chemical Society. The reports are identical in both titles, and in the case of the Chemical Society, are drawn verbatim from its *Proceedings*. For Crookes, these reports have a different status than for Lockyer: whereas many readers of *Nature* would have access to this material, whether through institutions or membership of societies, the more diverse readership of *Chemical News* probably would not, and needed it immediately. This is reiterated by the treatment of the listings by these two titles. Lack of space in *Nature* often forces Lockyer to print the 'Diary of Societies' on the advertising wrapper at busy periods. As the 'Diary' is the most ephemeral of *Nature's* content, this move to the margins seems sensible; however, the decision to retain it at the cost of advertising revenue reveals the importance of this item, despite its transient nature. This is not the case in *Chemical News*, where 'Meetings for the Week' does not even appear in the wrapper if there is no room in the letterpress. In *Nature* then, readers are always provided with a schedule of metropolitan meetings, in *Chemical News*, readers are promptly kept up to date after those meetings have taken place.

During the recess neither title prints a listing and, after catching up with any backlog, do not notice the proceedings of any societies (with the exception of the Entomological Society for *Nature*). However the *Athenaeum*, with its more inclusive but less detailed reportage, does record whenever there is a meeting of a society. It is also the only title to print a list to notify readers of a forthcoming meeting. The three titles all fill the space differently. The *Athenaeum* expands its science reviews and notes, thereby devoting the same amount of letterpress to science even without the proceedings of societies. *Nature* continues its coverage of foreign societies, and simply extends its other departments – especially 'Scientific Serials' – to take advantage of the space. Much of the copy in *Chemical News* is derived from American and European sources not protected by copyright. The supply of this material continues throughout the recess, and Crookes can clear space for the increase of material that ensues after the meeting of the British Association and the resumption of the societies' publications.

The summer recess also affects the publications of the Chemical Society. Although the *Journal of the Chemical Society* was ostensibly a monthly, with a publication date of the first of the month, it was rarely produced on time. In 1890 for instance, the *Journal* was published in the second week of the month 8 times (9 January, 12 April, 12 May, 13 June, 9 July, 9 August, 11 October, 8 November) and the third week twice (19 March, 19 December); in 1891 they are more successful, the *Journal* appearing in the second week three times (9 June, 8 July, 10 December) and the third week twice (19 January, 30 April). Although the dates of publication of the *Journal* are given in the *Proceedings*, it is difficult to judge how long it takes for papers to appear as the bound *Journal* effaces any textual marks that would signal the end of a number. The *Minutes of the Publication Committee* reveal that they met fortnightly, usually the week after an Ordinary Meeting of the Society. However, the refereeing process could take time and, after 1889, a rejection was referred to the Council, which only met once a month. The *Minutes* do give the dates when a paper was approved for publication and, using the first papers within a number as those likely to be in the first number, it seems to take up to three months. For instance although Kipping and Perkin's 'Action of Dehydrating Agents on $\alpha\omega$-Diacetylpentane. Synthesis of Methylethylhexamethylene' was approved at a meeting on the 19 December 1889 and appears as pp. 16–28 of the volume for 1890, suggesting it was published on the 9 January 1890 and therefore coming into press in three weeks, William Tilden and Charles Beck's 'Some Crystalline Substances Obtained From the Fruits of Various Species of *Citrus*' was read at the Society on 6 March 1890, published in the *Proceedings* on the 12 March, ordered for publication by the Publication Committee on the 13 March, and probably appeared in the *Journal* on the 12 May 1890.[22]

The delays between reviewing or reading a paper and its (unpredictable) appearance in the *Journal* made the *Proceedings* even more important. In each year there were 15 numbers of the Proceedings covering 16 meetings, with the April number usually covering the normal meeting and the March AGM. As the *Proceedings* was intended to fill the gap between the first public announcement of research at the fortnightly meetings of the Society and its memorialization in the *Journal*, the editors endeavoured to publish it as quickly as possible, and so approximate a fortnightly periodicity. However, as I have already noted, some numbers were substantially delayed, and there was no need for the *Proceedings* to appear over the recess. As the *Journal* was still being published throughout the summer, usually with papers that had been read earlier in the year or were being refereed, the editors summarized what had been published in the *Journal* in the first number of the *Proceedings* to appear after the recess. As Fellows would already have this information, this list appears to be aimed at those others who make use of the *Proceedings* beyond the Society.

All the reports of the proceedings of the Chemical Society are identical to those published in the *Proceedings*, although editors did standardize some features. For instance in *Chemical News* for 16 May 1890 Crookes amends a citation that reads '(these 'Proceedings,' 1886, 255)' in the *Proceedings* to '(*Proc. Chem. Soc.*, 1886, 225).'[23] As a report is never published in the weekly press prior to its appearance in the *Proceedings*, it seems likely that these are the source of this material. The proceedings of the Chemical Society usually appear in *Chemical News* the week after the publication of the *Proceedings*; as a Friday weekly, this usually means a gap of over a week. However, sometimes a report is published in *Chemical News* in a matter of days. In *Chemical News* for the 14 March 1890 is a report from the 6 March, yet the *Proceedings* containing this material was only published on the 12 March. Also, *Chemical News* published the reports of the AGM on 25 March and the Ordinary Meeting on the 2 April 1891 on the 1 May, but the *Proceedings* were only published the day before, on the 30 April 1891. This suggests a common source from the two publications rather than a reliance of one upon the other: the *Proceedings* are prepared from author's abstracts and, as Crookes was President of the Chemical Society in 1888–1889 and so had chaired the Publication Committee, he might have had access to material prior to publication.

The republication of authors' abstracts in the *Proceedings* and then the weeklies presents a different version of the events described in the papers published in the *Journal*. In providing a summary of results, the papers in the *Proceedings* elide the experimental details in favour of a reified description of properties. For instance, Francis R. Japp and G.H. Wadsworth's '*p*-Desylphenol', which was read on the 1 May 1890, is only one page in the *Proceedings* but occupies nine in the *Journal*. Statements such as:

> *p*-Desylphenol was heated in a sealed tube with acetic anhydride for three hours at 150°; the excess of the anhydride was distilled off on the water-bath under reduced pressure, and the last traces destroyed by evaporation with alcohol. The product was twice recrystallised from light petroleum (b.p. 90-120°), from which it was deposited in slender, white needles melting at 106-107°.[24]

are rendered in the *Proceedings* as 'When heated with acetic anhydride it yields a monoacetyl-derivative, $C_{20}H_{15}(C_2H_3O)O_2$, which forms aggregations of slender, white needles melting at 106-107°.'[25] This elides the narrative through which the various compounds unfold, instead providing a list of essential properties for substances that have always existed. The shift in tense alters the temporal frame of the narrative: in the *Journal* the events have occurred in a specific moment, and it is the resources gathered there that allow it social agency; in the *Proceedings* however, the present tense removes the phenomena from a contingent spatial-temporal frame and grants it autonomy. Even though the papers in the *Proceedings* have not yet been refereed, they aspire to relate the essential properties of things, and these are always encountered in the present.

Whereas the papers in the *Journal* memorialize a contingent, but repeatable, moment in the laboratory, the *Proceedings* memorialize an equally contingent – but this time unrepeatable – moment at the meeting of the Chemical Society. The inclusion of the discussion that followed the reading of papers in the versions disseminated through the *Proceedings* provides a contingent frame for the essentialized events described within the papers. As the reports in the *Proceedings*,

*Chemical News* and *Nature* reproduce an original and unique authorial performance, connected with a scientist and a laboratory, the discussions introduce, as names of eminent Fellows, more signifiers of scientific authority. This operates slightly differently in the *Journal*: although names and institutions are given in the titles, the reader is granted access to this exclusive space; as the reading of a paper, like the author's manuscript, is considered prior to the 'final' form published in the *Journal*, any discussion is excluded from the published form in order to provide access to what appears to be an uncontested event. The famous names that comment on the papers operate both as scientific celebrities, performing for the reader, and signifiers of scientific authority. Whereas in the *Journal* the reader is encouraged to enter the laboratory (through the text) and judge for themselves, in the *Proceedings* and the weeklies, the Fellows judge for them.

### Conclusion: The Spatial-Temporal Conditions of Before and After

The investment of scientific judgement in an exclusive elite is compensated by privileged access to their deliberations. However, this shift from laboratory event to meeting of society changes the conditions of what Stengers calls the 'possibilities of representing.' In the *Journal* the reader is invited to become one of the spectators who can judge the meaning of the laboratory event. As I discussed in Chapter Four, there are elaborate institutional strategies inscribed into the text that condition the terms of entry, but it is necessary to admit the reader for the phenomena to have a social presence. The event itself is inextricably linked to its spatial-temporal conditions, but these are predicated on their reproducibility both in the laboratory and in the act of reading. As such, the *Journal* memorializes the experimental event in a relatively permanent state. These carefully written, institutionally ratified papers are circulated in a periodical which, with its irregular days of publication, varying size and two separately paginated sections, is designed to be bound in an annual volume. The *Journal*, which is predicated on persuading readers of the permanence that belies the contingent events that it narrates, not only aspires to the status of the book, but also to constitute a permanent archive in its own right.

In the reports in the *Proceedings*, access is granted not to the laboratory but to the meeting of the society. This too is an event that must be judged but, unlike the laboratory event, it is not repeatable. Each event is based around the co-presence of author, paper and audience, and these change from meeting to meeting. Although one can read the proceedings as often as one likes, their inclusion in the *Proceedings* and the weekly press inscribes them into a much more ephemeral form. With the exception of the Athenaeum, which numbers its monthly parts and issues semi-annual indices, the other two weeklies and the *Proceedings* include textual apparatus that allow them to be bound into annual volumes. Although this produces a more stable, book-like form, the use of the reports of societies is to memorialize events that will pass. The dual role of the *Proceedings* is to provide an archive of the Society's activities while occupying the temporal space between the reading of a paper and its publication in the *Journal*: whereas the first function is more permanent, the second is necessarily transient. The weeklies exploit both properties of this publication, but due to the logic of their periodicity, they redefine them again. Their coverage of the scientific societies is to survey scientific progress and testify to the intellectual life of society. The incorporation of the reports associates them with the many other links with the present that I described in Chapter Three. For *Nature* and *Chemical News*, the reports provide a means to announce results and mark research territory, but they also threaten to turn science into news, making it once more ephemeral. The meetings themselves, however, are granted a social presence: their multiplication across titles grants them cultural authority by repeating the abnegation of judgement, while their recurrence over time forecloses intervention by locating them in the recent past. Therefore, although science does become ephemeral news content in this context, it still plays a role in structuring the institutional authority of the learned societies.

### Appendix: Calendar of Meetings and Publications for 1890

The following table lists the dates and times of the meetings of the scientific societies that are listed in *Nature*, *Chemical News* and the *Athenaeum* in 1890. Against these I have also plotted the dates of publication for these three weeklies, plus those for the Chemical Society's *Journal* and *Proceedings*. In this column you can see if a number of a title notes the proceedings of any London society, and the date on which the proceedings occurred. For instance on the 23 January 1890 the Royal Society met at 4:30pm and the Institute of Electrical Engineers met at 8pm. On that day *Nature* published a report of the proceedings on the Royal Society from the 5 December and a report of the Mathematical Society from the 9 January. Also, a number of the *Proceedings of the Chemical Society* was published containing details of the meeting held on the 16 January. For clarity, only scientific societies are marked in the first column, but all societies are recorded in the second. I have only included the lectures at the Society of Arts, London Institution, Royal Institution, Sunday Lecture Society and Victoria Institute when they have scientific content. As the key below demonstrates, I have interpreted science as widely as possible.

*Periodicals:*

| | |
|---|---|
| *Athenaeum* | *Ath* |
| *Chemical News* | *CN* |
| *Nature* | *N* |
| *Proceedings Chemical Society* | *PCS* |
| *Journal of the Chemical Society* | *JCS* |

*Societies:*

*Science:*

| | |
|---|---|
| Anthropological Institute | Anthro |
| British Astronomical Association | BAA |
| Camera Club | Cam |
| Chemical Society | Chem |
| Entomological Society | Ent |
| Geological Society | Geol |
| Geologists' Association | GeolAssoc |
| Horticultural Society | Hort |
| Institution of Civil Engineers | Civil |
| Institute of Electrical Engineers | IEE |
| Institution of Mechanical Engineers | Mech |
| Linnean Society | Linn |
| London Amateur Scientific Society | LonSci |
| London Institution | LI |
| Medical Society | Med |
| Mineralogical Society | Min |
| Pathological Society | Path |
| Philosophical Society | Phil |
| Photographic Society | Photo |
| Physical Society | Phys |
| Quekett Club | Quek |
| Royal Academy | RA |
| Royal Astronomical Society | RAS |
| Royal Botanical Society | Bot |
| Royal Geographical Society | Geog |
| Royal Institution | RI |
| Royal Medical and Chirurgical Society | RMC |
| Royal Meteorological Society | Met |
| Royal Microscopical Society | Micro |
| Royal Society | RS |
| Royal Statistical Society | Stat |
| Society of Arts | SA |
| Society for Chemical Industry | SCI |
| Society of Engineers | Eng |
| Sunday Lecture Society | SLS |
| Victoria Institute | VI |
| Zoological Society | Zoo |

*Nonscience:*

| | |
|---|---|
| Archaeological Institute | ArcheI |
| Aristotelian Society | Aris |

| | |
|---|---|
| British Archaeological Association | Arche |
| Folk-Lore Society | Folk |
| Hellenic Society | Hell |
| Historical Society | Hist |
| Hugenot Society | Huge |
| New Shakspere Society | Shaks |
| Numismatic Society | Num |
| Philological Society | Philol |
| Royal Society of Literature | RSLit |
| Shorthand Society | Short |
| Society of Antiquities | Anti |
| Society of Biblical Archaeology | Bibl |
| Society of Antiquaries | Anti |

| Date (1890) | Day | Societies | Publications / Reports of Societies |
|---|---|---|---|
| 1 Jan | W | | |
| 2 Jan | T | RI 3 (juvenile) | *N*: RS 5; Met 18; Phys 6; Math 12 |
| 3 Jan | F | GeolAssoc 8 | *CN*: no reports |
| 4 Jan | S | RI 3 (juvenile) | *Ath:* Geol 18 Dec; Numismatic 19 Dec; Linnean 19 Dec; Micro 11 Dec; Chem 19 Dec |
| 5 Jan | S | SLS 4 | |
| 6 Jan | M | SCI 8 | |
| 7 Jan | T | RI 3 (juvenile); Anthro 8:30; Path 8:30 | |
| 8 Jan | W | Geol 8; Micro 8 | |
| 9 Jan | T | RI 3 (juvenile); RS 4:30; LI 6; Math 8; IEE 8 | *N*: RS 19 Dec; Geol 18 Dec; Linn 19 Dec<br>*JCS* |
| 10 Jan | F | Civil 7:30; RAS 8; Quek 8 | *CN:* no reports |
| 11 Jan | S | Bot 3:45 | *Ath*: Aristotelian 20 Dec, Shorthand 22 Dec |
| 12 Jan | S | SLS 4 | |
| 13 Jan | M | Med 8:30 | |
| 14 Jan | T | Civil 8; Zoo 8:30; Photo 8; RMC 8:30 | |
| 15 Jan | W | Ent (annual) 7; Met 7 (AGM); SA 8 | |
| 16 Jan | T | RS 4:30; Linn 8; | *N*: Chem 19 Dec; Micro 11 Dec |

|         |   | Chem 8; Zoo 4                                              |                                                                                                                                                                                              |
|---------|---|-----------------------------------------------------------|----------------------------------------------------------------------------------------------------------------------------------------------------------------------------------------------|
| 17 Jan  | F | Phys 5                                                    | *CN*: no reports                                                                                                                                                                             |
| 18 Jan  | S |                                                           | *Ath*: RS 9 Jan; RAS 10 Jan; Geol 8 Jan; Anti 9 Jan; Civil 14 Jan; Math 9 Jan; Bibl 14 Jan; Huge 8 Jan                                                                                     |
| 19 Jan  | S | SLS 4                                                     |                                                                                                                                                                                              |
| 20 Jan  | M | LI 5; SA 8; Geog 8:30; Med 8:30                           |                                                                                                                                                                                              |
| 21 Jan  | T | RI 3; Stat 7:45; Civil 8; Path 8:30                       |                                                                                                                                                                                              |
| 22 Jan  | W | Geol 8                                                    |                                                                                                                                                                                              |
| 23 Jan  | T | RS 4:30; IEE 8;                                           | *N:* RS 5 Dec; Math 9 Jan<br>*PCS*: 16 Jan                                                                                                                                                  |
| 24 Jan  | F | Civil 7:30; RI 9; Quek 8                                  | *CN*: Phys 17 Jan                                                                                                                                                                            |
| 25 Jan  | S | RI 3; Bot 3:45                                            | *Ath*: RS 16 Jan; Geog 20 Jan; Antiq 16 Jan: Arche 15 Jan; Num 16 Jan; Zoo 14 Jan; Ent 15 Jan; Chem 16 Jan; Met 15 Jan; SA 17 Jan; Hist 16 Jan; Phys 17 Jan; Aris 20 Jan                  |
| 26 Jan  | S | SLS 4                                                     |                                                                                                                                                                                              |
| 27 Jan  | M | LI 5; SA 8; Med 8:30                                      |                                                                                                                                                                                              |
| 28 Jan  | T | RI 3; Civil 8; Anthro 8:30 (anniversary); RMC 8:30       |                                                                                                                                                                                              |
| 29 Jan  | W |                                                           |                                                                                                                                                                                              |
| 30 Jan  | T | RS 4:30;                                                  | *N:* RS 9 Jan; Phys 17 Jan; Geol 8 Jan                                                                                                                                                      |
| 31 Jan  | F | RI 9                                                      | *CN*: Chem 16 Jan                                                                                                                                                                            |
| 1 Feb   | S | RI 3                                                      | *Ath*: RS 23 Jan; Geol 22 Jan; Anti 23 Jan; Stat 21 Jan; Linn 16 Jan; Micro 8 Jan; Philol 24 Jan; SA 27, 28, 29 Jan.                                                                       |
| 2 Feb   | S | SLS 4                                                     |                                                                                                                                                                                              |
| 3 Feb   | M | RI 5 (monthly); Eng 8; SA 8; VI; SCI 8; Med 8:30         |                                                                                                                                                                                              |
| 4 Feb   | T | RI 3; Civil 8; Zoo 8:30; Path 8:30                       | *JCS*                                                                                                                                                                                        |
| 5 Feb   | W | Ent 7; Geol 8                                             |                                                                                                                                                                                              |
| 6 Feb   | T | RS 4:30; Chem 8 (election); Linn 8;                      | *N:* RS 23 Jan; Geol 22 Jan; Ent 15 Jan; Linn 16 Jan; Micro 8 Jan;                                                                                                                         |

| | | | |
|---|---|---|---|
| | | | Chem 16 Jan; Zoo 14 Jan |
| 7 Feb | F | Phys 5; Civil 7:30; GeolAssoc 7:30; | *CN*: no reports |
| 8 Feb | S | RI 3; Bot 3:45 | *Ath*: RS 30; Anti 30; Civil 4; RI 3; Eng 3; Aris 3 |
| 9 Feb | S | | |
| 10 Feb | M | LI 5; SA 8; Geog 8:30; Med 8:30; Photo 8 (anniversary) | |
| 11 Feb | T | RI 3; Hort 3 (annual); Civil 8; Anthro 8:30 | |
| 12 Feb | W | SA 8; Micro 8 (annual); Pharm 8 | |
| 13 Feb | T | RS 4:30; IEE 8; Math 8 | *N*: RS 19 Dec, 30 Jan; Met 15 Jan. |
| 14 Feb | F | RI 9; RAS 3 (anniversary); LonSci 7:30 (agm) | *CN*: Phys 7 Feb |
| 15 Feb | S | RI 3 | *Ath*: RS 6 Feb; Geog 10 Feb; Geol 5 Feb; Anti 6 Feb; Arche 5 Feb; Archel 6 Feb; Zoo 4 Feb; Ent 5 Feb; SA 7, 10, 11, 12 Feb; Phys 7 Feb; Huge 10 Feb; Short 5 Feb |
| 16 Feb | S | SLS 4 | |
| 17 Feb | M | SA 8; Med 8:30 | *PCS*: Feb 6 |
| 18 Feb | T | RI 3; Stat 7:45; Civil 8; Zoo 8:30; Path 8:30 | |
| 19 Feb | W | Met 7; SA 8; | |
| 20 Feb | T | RS 4:30; IEE 8; Linn 8; Chem 8; Zoo 4 | *N*: RS 30 Jan, 6 Feb, 13 Feb; Phys 7 Feb; Ent 5 Feb; Zoo 4 Feb; Geol 5 Feb |
| 21 Feb | F | Geol 3 [1 in *CN*] (anniversary); Phys 5; Civil 7:30; RI 9 | *CN*: Chem 6 Feb |
| 22 Feb | S | RI 3; Bot 3:45 | *Ath*: RS 13 Feb; RAS 14 Feb; Linn 6 Feb; Chem 6 Feb; Civil 18 Feb; SA 17, 18, 19 Feb; Math 13 Feb; Shaks 14 Feb; Aris 17 Feb |
| 23 Feb | S | | |
| 24 Feb | M | SA 8; Geog 8:30; Med 8:30 | |
| 25 Feb | T | RI 3; Civil 8; Anthro | |

| | | 8:30; RMC 8:30 | |
|---|---|---|---|
| 26 Feb | W | Geol 8 | |
| 27 Feb | T | RS 4:30; IEE 8; LonSci 8 [*Ath*] | *N*: Linn 6 Feb; Zoo 18 Feb; Met 19 Feb; Anthro 11 Feb; Math 13 Feb |
| 28 Feb | F | LonSci 8 [*Nature*]; Quek 8 (anniversary) | *CN*: Phys 21 Feb |
| 1 Mar | S | RI 3 | *Ath*: RS 20 Feb; Geog 24 Feb; Anti 13 Feb; Num 20 Feb; Stat 18 Feb; Linn 20 Feb; Zoo 18 Feb; Chem 20 Feb; Met 19 Feb; Philol 21 Feb; Phys 21 Feb; Hell 24 Feb |
| 2 Mar | S | SLS 4 | |
| 3 Mar | M | RI 5 (monthly); Eng 7:30; SA 8; Med 8:30 | |
| 4 Mar | T | RI 3; Civil 8; Zoo 8:30; Path 8:30 | |
| 5 Mar | W | Ent 7; Geol 8 [*CN*] | |
| 6 Mar | T | RS 4:30; LI 6; Linn 8 | *N*: RS 20 Feb; Linn 20 Feb |
| 7 Mar | F | Phys 5; GeolAssoc 8; RI 9; Civil 7 | *CN*: Chem 20 Feb |
| 8 Mar | S | RI 3; Bot 3:45; SA 8 | *Ath*: RS 27 Feb; Geol 21, 26 Feb; Anti 27 Feb; Civil 4 Mar; RI 3 Mar; Eng 3 Mar; Bibl 4 Mar; Hist 20 Feb; Aris 3 Mar |
| 9 Mar | S | SLS 4 | |
| 10 Mar | M | Geog 8:30; Med 8:30 | |
| 11 Mar | T | Hort 11, 3 lecture; RI 3; Civil 8; Anthro 8:30; Photo 8; RMC 8:30 | |
| 12 Mar | W | Geol 8; Micro 8 [*CN*]; Pharm 8 | *PCS*: 6 Mar |
| 13 Mar | T | RS 4:30; IEE 8; Math 8; | *N*: Chem 6 Feb; Geol 21 Feb |
| 14 Mar | F | RAS 8; RI 9; Quek 8 | *CN*: Chem 6 Mar; Phys 7 Mar |
| 15 Mar | S | RI 3; SA 9 | *Ath*: RS 6 Mar; Arche 5 Mar; ArcheI 6 Mar; Linn 6 Mar; Zoo 4 Mar; Ent 5 Mar; Chem 6 Mar; Sa 8, 12 Mar; Phys 7 Mar; Short 5 Mar |
| 16 Mar | S | SLS 4 | |
| 17 Mar | M | Med 8:30 | |
| 18 Mar | T | RI 3; Stat 7:45; Civil | |

| | | | |
|---|---|---|---|
| | | 8; Zoo 8:30; Min 8; Path 8:30 | |
| 19 Mar | W | Met 7; Micro 8; SA 8 | *JCS* |
| 20 Mar | T | RS 4:30; IEE 8; Linn 8; Chem 8; Zoo 4 | *N*: RS 6 March; Phys 21 Feb; Linn 6 March; Zoo 4 March |
| 21 Mar | F | Phys 5; Civil 7:30; RI 9 | *CN:* no reports |
| 22 Mar | S | RI 3; Bot 3:45; SA 8 | *Ath*: RS 13 Mar; Geol 12 Mar; Anti 7 Mar; Stat 18 Mar; SA 14, 15, 17, 18, 19 Mar; Math 13 Mar; Huge 12 Mar |
| 23 Mar | S | | |
| 24 Mar | M | Geog 8:30; Med 8:30 | |
| 25 Mar | T | Hort 1, 3 lecture; RI 3; Anthro 8; Civil 8; RMC 8:30 | |
| 26 Mar | W | Geol 8 | |
| 27 Mar | T | Chem 4 (anniversary / election); RS 4:30; IEE 8; | *N*: RS 6 March; Chem 20 Feb; Geol 26 Feb; Ent 5 March; Met 19 March; Math 13 Mar |
| 28 Mar | F | Civil 7:30 (students); RI 9; Quek 8 | *CN*: Phys 21 Mar |
| 29 Mar | S | RI 3; SA 8 | *Ath*: RS 20 Mar; RAS 14 Mar; Geog 24 Mar; Anti 20 Mar; Num 20 Mar; Linn 20 Mar; Zoo 18 Mar; Met 19 Mar; Philol 21 Mar; Civil 18 Mar; Hist 20 Mar; Shaks 14 Mar; Phys 21 Mar; Aris 17 Mar |
| 30 Mar | S | | |
| 31 Mar | M | LI 5; Med 8:30 | |
| 1 Apr | T | Zoo 8:30; Civil 8 [*CN*]; Path 8:30 | |
| 2 Apr | W | Ent 7 | |
| 3 Apr | T | Linn 8; Chem 8; Math 8 | *N*: RS 20 Feb, 27 Mar; Phys 7 Mar; Chem 6 Mar; Geol 12 Mar; Linn 20 Mar |
| 4 Apr | F | | *CN:* no reports |
| 5 Apr | S | | *Ath:* RS 27; Anti 27; Micro 19; Chem 20 |
| 6 Apr | S | | |
| 7 Apr | M | RI 5 (monthly) | |
| 8 Apr | T | Hort 1, lecture 3; Photo 8; RMC 8:30 | |

| | | | |
|---|---|---|---|
| 9 Apr | W | Micro 8 [*CN*]; Pharm 8 | |
| 10 Apr | T | IEE 8 | *N*: RS 27 Mar; Micro 19 Mar; Zoo 18 Mar; Geol 26 Mar |
| 11 Apr | F | RAS 8; Civil 7:30; LonSci 8; Quek 8 | *CN*: Chem 27 Mar (anniversary) *PCS*: 20 Mar, 27 Mar (agm) |
| 12 Apr | S | Bot 3:45 | *Ath*: Geol 26 Mar; Arche 2 Apr; Ent 2 Apr; Zoo 1 Apr; RI 7 Apr; Civil 1 Apr; Math 3 Apr; Aris 31 Mar; Short 2 Apr *JCS* |
| 13 Apr | S | | |
| 14 Apr | M | Eng 7:30; Geog 8:30; Med 8:30 | |
| 15 Apr | T | Civil 8; Zoo 8:30; Photo 8; Path 8:30 | *PCS*: 3 Apr |
| 16 Apr | W | Met 7; Micro 8; Geol 8; | |
| 17 Apr | T | RI 3; RS 4:30; Linn 8; Zoo 4; Chem 8 | *N*: RS 13 Mar, 27 Mar; Phys 21 Mar; Ent 2 Apr; Zoo 1 Apr; Math 3 Apr |
| 18 Apr | F | RI 9; Phys 5 | *CN*: Chem 20 Mar, 27 Mar agm |
| 19 Apr | S | RI 3 | *Ath*: RAS 11 Apr; Chem 3 Apr; Civil 15 Apr; Eng 14 Apr; Shaks 11 Apr; Hell 14 Apr; Aris 14 Apr. |
| 20 Apr | S | | |
| 21 Apr | M | SCI 8; Med 8:30 | |
| 22 Apr | T | Hort 1, 3 lecture; Stat 7:45; Civil 8; Anthro 8:30; RMC 8:30 | |
| 23 Apr | W | | *PCS*: 17 Apr |
| 24 Apr | T | RI 3; RS 4:30; IEE 8 | *N*: RS 17 Apr; Met 16 Apr; Zoo 15 Apr; Linn 3 Apr |
| 25 Apr | F | Civil 7:30 (students); RI 9; LonSci 8; Quek 8 | *CN*: Chem 3 Apr; Phys 18 Apr |
| 26 Apr | S | RI 3; Bot 3:45 | *Ath*: RS 17 Apr; Geol 16 Apr; Anti 17, 23 Apr (anniversary); Arche 17 Apr; Num 17 Apr; Stat 22 Apr; Linn 17 Apr; Zoo 15 Apr; Met 16 Apr; Phil 18 Apr; Hist 17 Apr: Phys 18 Apr. |
| 27 Apr | S | | |

| | | | |
|---|---|---|---|
| 28 Apr | M | Geog 8:30; Med 8:30 | |
| 29 Apr | T | Photo 8; Zoo 4; Civil 8 | |
| 30 Apr | W | SA 8; Micro 8; Geol 8 | |
| 1 May | T | RI 1:30 (annual), 3; RS 4:30; Linn 8; Mech 7:30; Chem 8 | *N*: RS 13 Mar; Linn 17 Apr; Phys 18 Apr; Geol 16 Apr; Chem 20 Mar, 27 Mar (agm) |
| 2 May | F | Phys 5; GeolAssoc 8; Mech 7:30 | *CN*: 17 Apr |
| 3 May | S | RI 3 | *Ath*: RS 24 Apr; Micro 16 Apr; Chem 17 Apr; Aris 28 Apr |
| 4 May | S | | |
| 5 May | M | RI 5 (monthly); Eng 7:30; Med 8:30 (annual); SCI 8 | |
| 6 May | T | Hort [no time], 3 lecture; Civil 8; Zoo 8:30; Path 8:30 | |
| 7 May | W | Ent 7; SA 8 | |
| 8 May | T | RI 3; RS 4:30; IEE 8; Math 8; Chem 8 (extra) | *N*: RS 27 Mar, 24 Apr; Chem 3 Apr, 27 Apr; Micro 16 Apr |
| 9 May | F | RAS 8; RI 9; Bot 4; LonSci 8; Quek 8 | *CN*: RI 1 May, 5 May; *PCS*: 1 May |
| 10 May | S | Bot 3:45 | *Ath*: RS 1 May; Anti 1 May; RSLit 30 May; Geol 30 May; ArcheI 1 May; Linn 1 May; Civil 6 May; RI 1, 5 May; Eng 5 May; Bibl 6 May; Phys 2 May |
| 11 May | S | | |
| 12 May | M | Geog 8:30 | *JCS* |
| 13 May | T | Photo 8; Anthro 8; Civil 8; RMC 8:30 | |
| 14 May | W | SA 8; Geol 8; Micro [*CN*] | |
| 15 May | T | RI 3; RS 4:30; IEE 8; Chem 8 | *N*: RS 1 May; Linn 1 May; Zoo 6 May; Chem 1 May; Math 8 May |
| 16 May | F | Phys 5; RI 5 | *CN*: Chem 1 May; Phys 2 May; |
| 17 May | S | | *Ath*: RS 8 May; Geog 12 May; RAS 9 May; Anti 8 May; Zoo 6 May; Ent 7 May; Math 8 May; Aris 12 May; Short 7 May. |

| | | | |
|---|---|---|---|
| 18 May | S | | |
| 19 May | M | | |
| 20 May | T | Stat 7:45; Civil 8; Zoo 8:30; Min 8; Path 8 | |
| 21 May | W | Met 7; Micro 8; Geol 8 [*CN*]; Pharm 11 (anniversary) | |
| 22 May | T | RI 3; RS 4:30; IEE 8; Zoo 4 | *N*: RS 8 May; Phys 2 May; Geol 30 Apr |
| 23 May | F | LonSci 8; RI 9; Bot 4; Quek 8 | *CN:* no reports |
| 24 May | S | Linn 3 (anniversary) | *Ath*: Geol 14 May; Num 15 May; Stat 20 May; Philol 16 May; Civil 20 May; Hist 15 May; Huge 14 May (annual) |
| 25 May | S | | |
| 26 May | M | | |
| 27 May | T | RI 3; Photo 8; RMC 8:30 | |
| 28 May | W | | |
| 29 May | T | RI 3 | *N*: RS 8 May; Ent 7 May; Met 21 May; Geol 14 May; Zoo 20 May |
| 30 May | F | RI 9; Bot 4 | *CN*: Phys 16 May |
| 31 May | S | Bot 3:45 | *Ath*: RS 22 May; Asiatic 21 May; Anti 22 May; Arche 21 May; Zoo 20 May; Met 21 May; Phys 16 May<br>*PCS*: 15 May |
| 1 Jun | S | | |
| 2 Jun | M | RI 5 (monthly); Eng 7:30; SA 8; SCI 8 | |
| 3 Jun | T | RI 3; Civil 8 (agm); Zoo 8:30 | |
| 4 Jun | W | Ent 7; Geol 8 | |
| 5 Jun | T | RI 3; RS 4 election FRS; Linn 8; Chem 8 | *N*: RS 1 May; Anthro 13 May; Geol 21 May |
| 6 Jun | F | Phys 5; GeolAssoc 8; Bot 4 | *CN*: Chem 15 May |
| 7 Jun | S | | *Ath*: Geol 21 May; Micro 21 May; RI 2 Jun; Eng 2 Jun; Bibl 3 Jun; AntroI 13 May; Aris 2 Jun |
| 8 Jun | S | | |

| 9 Jun | M | | |
|---|---|---|---|
| 10 Jun | T | Hort 1, 3 Lecture; RI 3; Photo 8; Anthro 8; RMC 8:30 | |
| 11 Jun | W | Micro 8 [*CN*] | |
| 12 Jun | T | RI 3; RS 4:30; Math 8 | *N*: RS 5 Jun; Micro 21 May |
| 13 Jun | F | RAS 8; RI 9; Bot 4; Quek 8 | *CN*: Chem 15 May; Phys 16 Jun [misprint for 6]; RI 2 Jun *JCS* |
| 14 Jun | S | Bot 3:45 | *Ath*: RS 5 Jun; Geol 4 Jun; Zoo 3 Jun; Philol 6 Jun: Civil 3 Jun; Short 4 Jun |
| 15 Jun | S | | |
| 16 Jun | M | Geog 2:30 (anniversary) | |
| 17 Jun | T | Stat 7:45; Zoo 8:30 | *PCS*: 5 Jun |
| 18 Jun | W | Met 7; Micro 8; Geol 8 | |
| 19 Jun | T | RS 4:30; Linn 8; Chem 8; Zoo 4 | *N*: RS 12 June; Phys 16 May; Zoo 3 June; Linn 24 May; Ent 4 Jun; Math 12 Jun |
| 20 Jun | F | Phys 5 | *CN:* no reports |
| 21 Jun | S | | *Ath*: RS 12 Jun; Geog 16 Jun; RAS 13 Jun; Stat 17 Jun; Linn 24 May, 5 Jun; Ent 4; Chem 5; Math 12; Phys 6 |
| 22 Jun | S | | |
| 23 Jun | M | | |
| 24 Jun | T | Hort 11, 3 lecture; Stat 5 (annual); Photo 8; Anthro 8 | |
| 25 Jun | W | SA 4 (agm) | |
| 26 Jun | T | RS Club 6:30 (anniversary) | *N*: RS 5 Jun; Linn 5 Jun; Met 18 Jun; Geol 4 Jun |
| 27 Jun | F | SA 9 (conversazione); LonSci 7:30 (conversazione); Quek 8 | *CN*: Chem 5 Jun |
| 28 Jun | S | Bot 3:45 | *Ath*: RS 19 Jun; Arche 18 Jun; Num 19 Jun; Zoo 17 Jun; Antro 10 Jun; Hist 19 Jun; Hell 23 Jun |

| Date | Day | Meetings | Reports |
|---|---|---|---|
| 29 Jun | S | | |
| 30 Jun | M | Geog 8:30 | |
| 1 Jul | T | | |
| 2 Jul | W | Ent 7 | |
| 3 Jul | T | | *N*: RS 12 Jun; Phys 6 Jun; Zoo 17 Jun |
| 4 Jul | F | GeolAssoc 8 | *CN*: Phys 20 Jun |
| 5 Jul | S | | *Ath*: Geog 30 Jun; Geol 18 Jun; Stat 24 Jun; Micro 18 Jun; SA annual 25 Jun; Phys 20 Jun; Short 30 Jun |
| 6 Jul | S | | |
| 7 Jul | M | RI 5 (monthly) | |
| 8 Jul | T | Hort 1, 3 lecture | |
| 9 Jul | W | | *JCS* |
| 10 Jul | T | | *N*: RS 19 Jun; Phys 20 Jun; Anthro 10 Jun; Geol 18 Jun; Micro 18 Jun |
| 11 Jul | F | | *CN*: no reports |
| 12 Jul | S | Bot 3:45 | *Ath*: Arche 3 Jul; Linn 19 Jun; RI 7 Jul |
| 13 Jul | S | | |
| 14 Jul | M | | |
| 15 Jul | T | | |
| 16 Jul | W | | |
| 17 Jul | T | | *N*: Linn 19 Jun; Ent 2 Jul |
| 18 Jul | F | | *CN*: no reports |
| 19 Jul | S | | *Ath*: Ent 2 Jul |
| 20 Jul | S | | |
| 21 Jul | M | | |
| 22 Jul | T | Hort 1; Photo 8 | |
| 23 Jul | W | Hort 1 | |
| 24 Jul | T | | *N*: no London meetings |
| 25 Jul | F | | *CN*: no reports |
| 26 Jul | S | | *Ath*: no reports |
| 27 Jul | S | | |
| 28 Jul | M | | |
| 29 Jul | T | | |
| 30 Jul | W | | |
| 31 Jul | T | | *N*: RS 19 Jun; Anthro 24 Jun |
| 1 Aug | F | | *CN*: no reports |
| 2 Aug | S | | *Ath*: no reports |
| 3 Aug | S | | |

| | | | |
|---|---|---|---|
| 4 Aug | M | | |
| 5 Aug | T | | |
| 6 Aug | W | Ent 7 | |
| 7 Aug | T | | *N:* no London meetings |
| 8 Aug | F | | *CN:* no reports |
| 9 Aug | S | | *Ath:* no reports<br>*JCS* |
| 10 Aug | S | | |
| 11 Aug | M | | |
| 12 Aug | T | Hort 1, 3 lecture | |
| 13 Aug | W | | |
| 14 Aug | T | | *N:* Ent 6 Aug<br>*PCS:* 19 Jun |
| 15 Aug | F | | *CN:* no reports |
| 16 Aug | S | | *Ath:* Ent 6 Aug |
| 17 Aug | S | | |
| 18 Aug | M | | |
| 19 Aug | T | | |
| 20 Aug | W | | |
| 21 Aug | T | | *N:* no London meetings |
| 22 Aug | F | | *CN:* Chem 19 Jun |
| 23 Aug | S | | *Ath:* no reports |
| 24 Aug | S | | |
| 25 Aug | M | | |
| 26 Aug | T | Hort 11, 3 lecture;<br>Photo 8 | |
| 27 Aug | W | | |
| 28 Aug | T | | *N:* no London meetings |
| 29 Aug | F | | *CN:* Chem 19 Jun continued; RI 7 Jul |
| 30 Aug | S | | *Ath:* no reports |
| 31 Aug | S | | |
| 1 Sep | M | | |
| 2 Sep | T | | |
| 3 Sep | W | Ent 7 | |
| 4 Sep | T | | *N:* no London meetings |
| 5 Sep | F | | *CN:* no reports |
| 6 Sep | S | | *Ath:* no reports<br>*JCS* |
| 7 Sep | S | | |
| 8 Sep | M | | |
| 9 Sep | T | Hort 11, 3 lecture | |

| 10 Sep | W | | |
|---|---|---|---|
| 11 Sep | T | | *N*: Ent 3 Sept |
| 12 Sep | F | | *CN*: no reports |
| 13 Sep | S | | *Ath*: Ent 3 Aug |
| 14 Sep | S | | |
| 15 Sep | M | | |
| 16 Sep | T | | |
| 17 Sep | W | | |
| 18 Sep | T | | *N:* no London meetings |
| 19 Sep | F | | *CN*: no reports |
| 20 Sep | S | | *Ath*: no reports |
| 21 Sep | S | | |
| 22 Sep | M | | |
| 23 Sep | T | | |
| 24 Sep | W | | |
| 25 Sep | T | | *N:* no London meetings |
| 26 Sep | F | | *CN*: Chem 19 Jun |
| 27 Sep | S | | *Ath*: no reports |
| 28 Sep | S | | |
| 29 Sep | M | | |
| 30 Sep | T | Photo 8 | |
| 1 Oct | W | Ent 7 | |
| 2 Oct | T | | *N:* no London meetings |
| 3 Oct | F | | *CN*: 19 Jun |
| 4 Oct | S | | *Ath*: no reports |
| 5 Oct | S | | |
| 6 Oct | M | Eng 7:30 | |
| 7 Oct | T | | |
| 8 Oct | W | | |
| 9 Oct | T | | *N:* no London meetings |
| 10 Oct | F | | *CN*: no reports |
| 11 Oct | S | | *Ath*: Ent 1 Oct; Eng 6 Oct *JCS* |
| 12 Oct | S | | |
| 13 Oct | M | | |
| 14 Oct | T | Hort 1, 3 lecture | |
| 15 Oct | W | Micro 8 | |
| 16 Oct | T | | *N*: Ent 1 Oct |
| 17 Oct | F | | *CN*: no reports |
| 18 Oct | S | | *Ath*: no reports |
| 19 Oct | S | | |
| 20 Oct | M | | |

| | | | |
|---|---|---|---|
| 21 Oct | T | | |
| 22 Oct | W | | |
| 23 Oct | T | | *N*: no London meetings |
| 24 Oct | F | | *CN*: no reports |
| 25 Oct | S | | *Ath*: Num 16 Oct; Hell 20 Oct |
| 26 Oct | S | SLS 4 | |
| 27 Oct | M | | |
| 28 Oct | T | Photo 7 [8 in *N*]; Hort 11, 3 lecture | |
| 29 Oct | W | | |
| 30 Oct | T | | *N*: no London meetings |
| 31 Oct | F | | *CN*: no reports |
| 1 Nov | S | | *Ath*: no reports |
| 2 Nov | S | | |
| 3 Nov | M | RI 5 (monthly); Eng 7:30 | |
| 4 Nov | T | Zoo 8:30 | |
| 5 Nov | W | Ent 7 | |
| 6 Nov | T | RA 4; Linn 8; Chem 8 | *N*: no London meetings |
| 7 Nov | F | GeolAssoc 8 (conversazione) | *CN*: no reports |
| 8 Nov | S | Bot 3:45 | *Ath*: Micro 15 Nov; RI 3 Nov; Eng 3 Nov; Bibl 3 Nov; Aris 3 Nov *JCS* |
| 9 Nov | S | SLS 4 | |
| 10 Nov | M | RA 4 | |
| 11 Nov | T | Hort 11, 3 lecture; Civil 8; Photo 8; Geog 8:30; Min 8 (anniversary) | |
| 12 Nov | W | Geol 8 | |
| 13 Nov | T | RA 4; IEE 8; Math 8 | *N*: Micro 15 Oct |
| 14 Nov | F | Phys 5; RAS 8; LonSci 8 | *CN*: no reports |
| 15 Nov | S | | *Ath*: Geog 11 Nov; Arche 6 Nov; Linn 6 Nov; Zoo 4 Nov; Ent 5 Nov; Philol 7 Nov; Civil 11 Nov; Short 4 Nov. |
| 16 Nov | S | SLS 4 | |
| 17 Nov | M | RA 4; LI 5 | |
| 18 Nov | T | Stat 7:45; Civil 8; | *PCS*: 6 Nov |

| | | | |
|---|---|---|---|
| | | Zoo 8:30 | |
| 19 Nov | W | Met 7; Micro 8; SA 8 (opens) | |
| 20 Nov | T | RS 4:30; RA 4; Linn 8; Chem 8 (election); Zoo 4 | *N*: Zoo 4 Nov; Ent 5 Nov; Linn 6 Nov |
| 21 Nov | F | | *CN*: Chem 6 Nov; Phys 14 Nov |
| 22 Nov | S | Bot 3:45 | *Ath*: RAS 14 Nov; Geol 12 Nov; Stat 18 Nov; Math 13 Nov; Phys 14 Nov; Aris 17 Nov; Huge 12 Nov |
| 23 Nov | S | SLS 4 | |
| 24 Nov | M | RA 4; SA 8; Geog 8:30; Med 8:30 | |
| 25 Nov | T | Civil 8; Photo 8; Anthro 8:30; RMC 8:30 | |
| 26 Nov | W | Geol 7:45 [8 *CN*] | *PCS*: 20 Nov |
| 27 Nov | T | RS 4:30; IEE 8 | *N*: Met 19 Nov; Geol 12 Nov; Math 13 Nov; Zoo 18 Nov |
| 28 Nov | F | Phys 5; LonSci 8 | *CN*: no reports |
| 29 Nov | S | | *Ath*: RS 20 Nov; Geog 24 Nov; Arche 19 Nov; Num 20 Nov; Linn 20 Nov; Zoo 18 Nov; Met 19 Nov; Civil 25 Nov; SA 19 Nov, 24, 26 Nov; Shaks 14 Nov; Hist 20 Nov |
| 30 Nov | S | SLS 4 | |
| 1 Dec | M | RI 5; Eng 7:30; SA 8; Micro 8 (conversazione); VI 8; SCI 8; Med 8:30 | |
| 2 Dec | T | Civil 8; Zoo 8:30; Path 8:30 | |
| 3 Dec | W | Ent 7; | |
| 4 Dec | T | Linn 8; Chem 8 | *N*: RS 20 Nov, 27 Nov; Phys 14 Nov; Linn 20 Nov |
| 5 Dec | F | GeolAssoc 8 | *CN*: Chem 20 Nov; RI 1 Dec |
| 6 Dec | S | | *Ath*: RS 27 Nov; Geol 26 Nov; Anti 27 Nov; Civil 2 Dec; RI 1 Nov; Eng 1 Dec; Bibl 2 Dec; Folklore 19 Nov; Aris 1 Dec |
| 7 Dec | S | SLS 4 | |

| | | | |
|---|---|---|---|
| 8 Dec | M | LI 5; SA 8; Geog 8:30; Med 8:30 | |
| 9 Dec | T | Hort 1; Civil 8; Photo 8; Anthro 8:30; RMC 8:30 | |
| 10 Dec | W | SA 8; Geol 8; Pharm 8 | |
| 11 Dec | T | RS 4:30; IEE 8 (agm); Math 8; | *N*: RS 27 Nov; Geol 26 Nov; Zoo 2 Dec |
| 12 Dec | F | Phys 5; RAS 8; LonSci 8 | *CN*: Phys 28 Nov |
| 13 Dec | S | Bot 3:45 | *Ath*: Geog 8 Dec; Arche 3 Dec; Linn 4 Dec; Ent 3 Dec; Philol 5 Dec; Civil 2 Dec; SA 8, 10 Dec; Eng 3 Dec; Phys 28 Dec; Short 2 Dec *PCS*: 4 Dec |
| 14 Dec | S | SLS 4 | |
| 15 Dec | M | SA 8; Med 8:30 | |
| 16 Dec | T | Stat 7:45; Civil 8; Path 8:30 | |
| 17 Dec | W | Met 7; Geol 8; Micro 8 | |
| 18 Dec | T | RS 4:30; Linn 8; Chem 8; Zoo 4 | *N*: no London meetings |
| 19 Dec | F | Quek 8 | *CN*: Chem 4 Dec *JCS* |
| 20 Dec | S | | *Ath*: RS 11 Dec; RAS 12 Dec; Geol 10 Dec; Asiatic 15 Dec; Stat 16 Dec; Math 11 Dec; Anthro 9 Dec; Aris 15 Dec |
| 21 Dec | S | | |
| 22 Dec | M | SA 8 | |
| 23 Dec | T | Photo 8 | |
| 24 Dec | W | RI 3 (juvenile) | |
| 25 Dec | T | | *N*: RS 11 Dec; Phys 28 Nov; Ent 3 Dec; Linn 4 Dec; Anthro 9 Dec; Math 11 Dec |
| 26 Dec | F | | *CN*: Phys 12 Dec |
| 27 Dec | S | RI 3 (juvenile) | *Ath*: RS 18 Dec; Num 18 Dec; Met 17 Dec; Hist 18 Dec; Phys 12 Dec |
| 28 Dec | S | | |
| 29 Dec | M | LI 4 (juvenile) | |

| 30 Dec | T | RI 3 (juvenile) | |
| 31 Dec | W | LI 4 (juvenile) | |

## Notes

1 William Russell, cited in Anonymous [C.E. Groves], 'Annual General Meeting', *Journal of the Chemical Society*, 57 (1890), 428.
2 Mark Turner, 'Periodical Time in the Nineteenth Century', *Media History*, 8 (2002), 191.
3 Bruno Latour, *Science in Action* (Cambridge MA, 1987), p. 132.
4 Isabelle Stengers, *The Invention of Modern Science*, trans. Daniel W. Smith (Minneapolis, 2000), p. 87.
5 Stengers, *Invention*, p. 67.
6 Bruno Latour, *We Have Never Been Modern* (New York, 1993), p. 71.
7 See, for instance, Margaret Beetham, 'Towards a Theory of the Periodical as a Publishing Genre', in *Investigating Victorian Journalism*, eds Laurel Brake, Aled Jones and Lionel Madden (London, 1990), p. 21. W.T. Stead estimated that less than 1% of readers bound their magazines into volumes. W.T. Stead, 'Preface', *Index to the Periodical Literature of the World* (London, 1892), p. 6.
8 The Institution of Electrical Engineers had adopted that name the year before. A useful resource for the history of learned societies around the world is the University of Waterloo's *Scholarly Societies Project* (http://www.scholarly-societies.org/).
9 Frank A.J.L. James, 'Reporting Royal Institution Lectures, 1826–1867', in *Science Serialized: Representations of the Sciences in Nineteenth-Century Periodicals*, eds Geoffrey Cantor and Sally Shuttleworth (Cambridge MA, 2004), pp. 67–79.
10 See Robert Young, 'Natural Theology, Victorian Periodicals, and the Fragmentation of a Common Context', in *Darwin's Metaphor* (Cambridge, 1985), pp. 127–63.
11 See Roy M. MacLeod, 'The Genesis of *Nature*', and 'The Social Framework of *Nature*', in *The 'Creed of Science' in Victorian England* (Aldershot, 2000), pp. 1–28, 1–44 respectively.
12 W.H. Brock, 'The Making of an Editor', *Culture and Science in the Nineteenth-Century Media*, eds Henson and others (Aldershot, 2004), pp. 189–98; 'The *Chemical News*', *Bulletin for the History of Chemistry*, 12 (1992), 31. See also W.H. Brock, *The Fontana History of Chemistry* (London, 1992), p. 458.
13 See 'Societies', *Athenaeum*, 23 May 1891 (1891), 671 and 6 Jun 1891 (1891), 736.
14 See 'Societies', *Athenaeum*, 5 December 1891 (1891), 765–6.
15 See Anonymous, 'Diary of Societies', *Nature*, 43, 20 November 1890 (1890), xxi for an omission of the Royal Society, and Anonymous, 'Diary of Societies', *Nature*, 43, 4 December 1890 (1890), xxxvii and 11 December 1890 (1890), xlv for an omission and then inclusion of the Physical Society. It seems that the delay in listing the Royal Society is because the papers are not fixed eleven days in advance. Sometimes they equivocate, stating 'the following papers will *probably* be read.' See Anonymous, 'Diary of Societies', *Nature*, 41, 20 March 1890 (1890), 480.
16 Sir Frederick Abel, 'Smokeless Explosions', *Nature*, 41, 6 February 1890 (1890), 328–30.

17  'Sir Frederick Abel, C.B., D.C.L., D.Sc., F.R.S., V.P.R.I.', 'Smokeless Explosives', *Chemical News*, 61, 21 March 1890 (1890), 142–4 and 28 March 1890 (1890), 147–50.

18  See 'Professor Thorpe, F.R.S.', 'The Glow of Phosphorous', *Chemical News*, 61, 21 March 1890 (1890), 140–41 and Anonymous, 'The Glow of Phosphorous', 41, *Nature*, 3 April 1890 (1890), 523–4.

19  See Professor Vivian B. Lewes, 'On Gaseous Illuminants', *Chemical News*, 63, 2 January, 9 January, 16 January, 23 January, 6 February 1891 (1891), 3–5, 15–16, 32–3, 40–43, 63–6 and Anonymous, 'Gaseous Illuminants', *Nature*, 43, 8 January, 15 January, 22 January 1891 (1891), 233–5, 257–60, 282–3.

20  Anonymous, 'Miscellaneous', *Chemical News*, 63, 30 January 1891 (1891), 62; Anonymous, 'The Chemical Society's Jubilee', *Nature*, 43, 12 March 1891 (1891), 440–43; Anonymous, 'Proceedings of Societies', *Chemical News*, 63, 20 March 1891 (1891), 137–9.

21  See for instance Anonymous, 'The Jubilee of the Chemical Society' and 'Court Circular', *The Times*, 25 February, 9 and 14; Anonymous, 'The Chemical Society's Jubilee' and untitled leading article, *The Times*, 26 February, 6 and 9.

22  F. Stanley Kipping, PhD., D.Sc. and W.H. Perkin, Jun., PhD., 'Action of Dehydrating Agents on $\alpha\omega$-Diacetylpentane. Synthesis of Methylethylhexamethylene', *Journal of the Chemical Society*, 57 (1890), 13–28; Anonymous, '"Some Crystalline Substances Obtained From the Fruits of Various Species of *Citrus*." By William A. Tilden, D.Sc., F.R.S., and Charles R. Beck.', *Proceedings of the Chemical Society*, 6, 12 March 1890 (1890), 29–34; William A. Tilden, D.Sc., F.R.S., and Charles R. Beck, 'Some Crystalline Substances Obtained From the Fruits of Various Species of Citrus. Part I', *Journal of the Chemical Society*, 57 (1890), 323–7.

23  However the *Pharmaceutical Journal* kept the original, making no secret of its derivation. See Anonymous, '"An Investigation of the Conditions Under Which Hydrogen Peroxide is Formed From Ether." By Professor Wyndham R. Dunstan and T.S. Dymond', *Proceedings of the Chemical Society*, 6, 9 May 1890 (1890), 70; Anonymous, 'Proceedings of Societies in London', *Pharmaceutical Journal and Transactions*, 20, 31 May 1890 (1890), 989; and Anonymous, 'Proceedings of Societies', *Chemical News*, 61, 16 May 1890 (1890), 237.

24  Francis R. Japp, FRS, and G.H. Wadsworth, '*p*-Desylphenol', *Journal of the Chemical Society*, 57 (1890), 968.

25  Anonymous, '"*p*-Desylphenol." By Francis R. Japp, FRS, and G.H. Wadsworth, Associate of the Normal School of Science', *Proceedings of the Chemical Society*, 6, 9 May 1890 (1890), 72.

Conclusions

# Nineteenth-Century Electricity in the Electronic Age

But we submit that physical and natural science – in a word the study of *things* in contradistinction to *words* and *abstractions* – is entitled to eminence as an instrument of intellectual culture. Without it we can never, unless exceptionally gifted by nature, acquire the art of observation.[1]

In his annual 'Address to Students' published in *Chemical News* at the beginning of the academic year in 1890, William Crookes insists that a scientific education can train students in the art of observation as it is concerned with the things themselves rather than their representations. As such, scientific practice is directly opposed to an intellectual culture that locates value in words. 'In our present educational curricula', he writes, 'this art is not merely left untaught, it is crowded out and starved at the very roots because the energies of the student are drawn off in other directions.' Crookes argues that observation is actually a natural faculty that is being neglected by an overemphasis on the linguistic:

A gentleman whose duty it became at one time to administer the somewhat homœopathic doses of science admitted at a public school puts on record the fact that the boys of the lower forms assimilated more readily than the seniors the elementary truths of chemistry and physics. The intellects of the latter had been so modified by a persistent course of verbalism that they could not see any meaning in things.

The younger boys can appreciate science as they are closer to a primitive ideal state. 'In like manner', Crookes continues, 'many working-men, possessing but a very scanty knowledge of the "three r's," were very good observers in botany, entomology, ornithology, & c.' Even 'savages are often better than civilised Europeans or Americans unless the latter have been systematically trained.' There is therefore a moral imperative to address this deficiency. He paraphrases 'an acute contemporary', who 'expressed the fear that the "vice of inobservance," so conspicuous among our upper classes, was being spread to the great mass of the nation in consequence of the exclusively literary character of our present system of education.' Crookes, albeit through the ventriloquism of another, employs the language of sin and disease to criticize a model of civilization that allows natural attributes to atrophy.[2]

Crookes argues instead for a practical, scientific component to education and an abandoning of the current exam-based means of testing. By claiming less civilized young, working-class and 'savage' men have retained the natural art of observation, Crookes suggest that literature and civilization are effeminate while science represents a natural, masculine, faculty. While I certainly do not endorse his politics, Crookes's critique of logocentricism underpins this book. It is only through complementing the interpretive techniques from literary studies with a methodology which does not neglect materiality that we can understand the periodical press. If science, as Latour argues, is a practice that manipulates things, altering their ontological states for specific ends, then publishing too is an analogous process. This book has considered where these processes intersect, and so necessarily draws upon the work of historians of the book, sociologists and historians of science, and literary and cultural critics. As Crookes argues:

> The question how we are to learn is not less important than its companion what we are to learn. The youth who studies chemistry from books, however closely and laboriously, will reap little or no advantage from his labours. If he has done nothing further than read he will still be in the bonds of verbalism, unable to learn from and to interpret phenomena.[3]

Although I certainly do not argue for a rejection of literary learning, I do suggest a greater recognition of the interaction between the social and material realms – or to put it bluntly, material culture – in creating meanings. Books and periodicals are material objects as well as texts; but a methodology that seeks to separate these two aspects – whether by ignoring one or by subsuming one into the other – risks repeating the mistake of the 'youth who studies chemistry from books.' It is only through a sustained engagement that locates both the material and textual as part of wider culture that we can begin to identify the periodical as genre.

By insisting that materiality is never distinct from the cultural practices that create textual meaning, it is possible to conceptualize the plurality of forms of the periodical – whether run, single number, or heterogeneous constitutive elements – while exploring the historical conditions of its production.[4] Although I am hesitant to overemploy Latour's ahistorical metaphor of the network to the late nineteenth century, his work does provide the means to connect material objects (of which texts are a part) to the various spaces and times inscribed within them. Latour recognizes that 'one travels directly from objects to words, from the referent to the sign, but always through a risky intermediary pathway.'[5] By reconnecting the various laboratories, chemicals, scientists, photographs, editors, readers and writers, I have positioned the periodical at the centre of these intermediary pathways and explored the coproduction of both the periodical as object and the various other actors that surround it. Each periodical number connects a unique and contingent configuration of things, people and texts from a variety of different spaces and times, and links them to its own construction in and of the present. It is only by recognizing the contingent deployments of spatialities and temporalities that a '*politics of things*' can be formulated and the rich history of the periodical be understood.[6]

This is increasingly pressing at the time of writing as large tranches of our cultural heritage are undergoing a radical transformation of material form. The things that are deteriorating in archives and on library shelves are being transformed into 'digital surrogates' that both open them up to more users and can be used without deformation. The language of surrogacy still evokes heated debate over preservation and a nostalgia for paper-based forms often rooted in a longing for some sort of 'original.' It also elides the nature of this transformation, whether in terms of the work that must be undertaken to produce it, or the formal properties (such as, for instance, the potential for decay) that are altered as a result. Jerome McGann's comment, quoted in the introduction, that '[u]sing books to study books constrains the analysis to the same conceptual level as the materials to be studied' finds a curious antecedent in Crookes's criticism. Whereas Crookes suggests that 'verbalism' does not equip us for thinking about objects, McGann claims that the limits of the codex predefine the terrain in which we imagine digital editions.[7] In both cases, the relationship between objects is partial: comparisons can be made – it is, after all, entirely legitimate to study objects through texts or model digital resources on books – but only at the dual cost of what is lost and what remains unknown. If we are to understand the nature of digital text, we must be ready to conceptualize the sociological networks that underpin both digital objects and their production. Digitization is a shift in material form that maintains some aspects while altering others: in our eagerness to produce digital forms of extant cultural objects, we risk overlooking the politics and history of this transformation while being seduced by the functionality of their new forms.

Conceiving of objects as sociological networks, which refer to other times and spaces in order to establish their status in the present, provides a mechanism for understanding electronic text. The fundamental difference in material form between the book and the electronic edition is bridged by the replication of at least its text, but often also other aspects of the text's appearance such as typography, layout on the page etc. ... As Kathryn Sutherland notes:

> But it *is* all illusion, and the screen page has, in fact, only the most fragile of existences; it is not one in a series of pages (as the pages of the printed book are) but the only page; and unlike the pages of a book it is not reassuringly available to us during the time in that we are reading some other page.

This 'precarious and illusory immanence of electronic text', in which the actual location of electronic text is elusive, seems to insist on the difference between the reproduction on the screen and the source material.[8] However, as I have shown throughout this book, reproductions suggest continuities as well as discontinuities, and these can exploited to link with what has come before even while marking a difference. Sutherland argues that digital editions of source materials fail to reproduce authenticity:

> Through the computer's mediation, we appear to have access to authentic forms, an authenticity previously denied to us in many cases by the constrictions of the print medium. But this authenticity is a fragile illusion whereby the electronic medium celebrates and eradicates presence simultaneously. Within the museum case of the computer screen the simulacrum of the authentic object may have newly attached search facilities, but its 'presence' is constituted as lost presence.[9]

This, of course, in Benjamin's point about the work of art, but such a reading relies overly on origins.[10] The 'authenticity' of a Shakespeare Folio or Emily Dickinson's fascicles is a moment in the life of these objects when their constitutive parts came together with a human actor and were transformed into something with a different set of properties. Equally, the digital versions of these objects are the product of another moment, in which objects were brought together, filmed, and were organized with supplementary data. The digital objects are versions of the 'authentic', but rather than signal an absence, they signal a presence in another moment of space and time.

An ethnographic approach to objects problematizes reproduction by making source objects contingent on their historical conditions. Rather than employ a rhetoric of reproduction, with good or bad versions of an original, such a methodology insists on re-production in which the extent to which new objects can refer back to previous forms depends on how they are produced and what happens to them afterwards. As I discussed in the introduction, Lefebvre's spatialization of Marxist economics grants historicity to the endless reproductions of capitalism.[11] Even reproductions that are identical to one another have different 'lives' over time that depend on their locations in space. Just as biological reproduction produces necessary mutation, so any form of reproduction will introduce spatial and temporal differences. The elusive materiality of electronic text is thus not qualitatively different from any other object: just as, for instance, a piece in a periodical is a manifestation of a group of actors, human and nonhuman, in a historical moment, and will become the manifestation of another group of actors, at another historical moment, if published again as a book, so a version of a text on the computer screen is produced from its range of actors; actors that include code, the user, his or her machine and the moment in which the text is created. Each act of production has a history that is contingent on its moment, and the final status of whatever is on the page will be decided after they appear. Sutherland notes that we 'have become so used to the book as textual mediator that for the most part we scarcely notice its artefactual state and how it imposes its "machinery" on what we read; we accept a kind of synonymity between text and book.'[12] Just as the book is more than the pages bound together but also stretches to the moment of reading and its material history of production, so the combination of images and text on the screen is both the product of labour in the past, the immediate workings of the technological objects that produced them, and the space and time in which they are read.

The epistemological muddle that results from a variable ontology is precisely what that nineteenth-century reader of objects *par excellence*, Sherlock Holmes, investigates in his cases. Holmes, like William Crookes, also argues for the art of observation against the act of seeing. As I discussed earlier, Holmes claims that the difference between seeing and observation is one of quality; in the *Sign of Four* he explicitly links it to the study of things.[13] This story, published the same year as Crookes's remarks, opens with Holmes discoursing, as is customary, his methods to an incredulous Watson. Glancing at his shoe, Holmes states that Watson visited the Wigmore Street Post Office to despatch a telegram: he knows Watson went to the post office as the mud on his shoe is unique to that space, but he deduces that he sent a telegram as he has eliminated the other factors and 'the one which remains must be the truth.'[14] It is the co-presence of three objects – Watson, his shoe, and the mud – that Holmes observes, allowing him to posit the events that brought them together. Holmes can suggest this narrative because he complements the reading of texts, which is something everybody does in Holmes's middle-class urban milieu, with an appreciation for the history of things. However, what the Holmes stories repeatedly demonstrate is that the line between word and thing (or text and work) is unstable. In the *Sign of Four* Holmes 'reads' a letter:

'The envelope, too, please. Post-mark, London S.W. Date July 7. Hum! Man's thumb-mark on corner – probably postman. Best quality paper. Envelopes at sixpence a packet. Particular man in his stationery. No address.

And then, after considering what it says, reads the handwriting:

'Look at his long letters', he said. 'They hardly rise above the common herd. That *d* might be an *a*, and that *l* an *e*. Men of character always differentiate their long letters, no matter how illegibly they may write. There is vacillation in his *k*'s and self-esteem in his capitals.[15]

Just as the envelope's history is expressed through both its textual and material traces, so Holmes reads the words, treating them like signs while also observing them as objects.

There are similarities between nineteenth-century periodical culture and early twenty-first-century digital culture, and these can be instructive. The study and use of periodicals forces us to confront the categories that are also challenged by hypertextual archives. Periodicals are multiauthored, fragmentary, often combine heterodox content that pertains to different spatial-temporal moments, posit complex hierarchies, encourage 'open' reading styles, and, because they are difficult to republish in paper forms, foreground their materiality. However, there are also fundamental differences, particularly in the way in which they are produced (for instance there is an entirely different economy determining the use of images), the way in which they are laid out and navigated, and the way that their seriality, in the form of updates, is imposed upon on the same space. While I do not want to reduce one publishing genre to another, both exploit the mutability of material form in order to change its temporal and spatial properties. Scientific practice, which as Latour says changes the nature of objects so that they can 'speak' in cultural contexts, provides a model for the study of such transformations that is also a historical precedent. David Greetham maintains that 'the current digitized morph cannot be considered in isolation from its non-digital predecessors, for digitization is only one stage in the evolution and signification of (meta)morphing', and indeed humans have always altered natural objects to render them part of culture.[16] This principle has informed this book throughout: periodicals have been considered as a physical manifestation of a network of interests whose histories can be traced back through transformations rooted in spatial and temporal moments. This enables the composite parts of a periodical text to retain a degree of autonomy, even while recognizing that they are a part of a number, it is a part of a volume, and the volume is part of a run.

This final chapter flirts with the anachronism inherent in my analysis through a discussion of late nineteenth-century electricity. Although electricity has a history that precedes the nineteenth century, its cultural role in the period focuses questions of material form. Taking two titles as examples, I consider how features of their materiality allow electricity to become realized as a cultural object. By applying insights produced in earlier chapters, this analysis acts as both a summary of my arguments so far, while also reflecting on one aspect of the history of the digital age.

## Electricity and the Material Cultures of the Electrical Press

> It would be the lamplit room of the early nineties, and the clock on the mantel would indicate midnight or later.[17]

In its first volume, the *Review of Reviews* maintains an almost obsessive focus on the new technologies that exploited electrical power.[18] W.T. Stead heralds its revolutionary effects:

> We have got to open our eyes to the extent to which Electricity has re-energised the world. What the revival of learning was to the Renaissance, what the discovery of the new world was to the Elizabethan, what the steam engine was to the century of the Revolution, the application of Electricity is to the New Generation. We are standing at the day-dawn of the Electric Age. The thunderbolt of Jove has become the most puissant of the servants of man. It has annihilated time, abolished space, and it will yet unify the world.[19]

With his emphasis on the speed of electricity, Stead anticipates McLuhan in recognizing the potential for it to reconfigure time and space.[20] He also stresses the novelty of electricity, displacing its long history in a celebration of futurity through its antecedents in the present. Stead is describing (and reprinting large portions of) John Macnie's *The Diotha's: or a Far Look Ahead*, which had just been republished to take advantage of the success of Edward Bellamy's futurist utopia *Looking Backwards*. Graeme Gooday has discussed Stead futurism; what is important here is that for Stead electricity can stand metonymically for the modern age, and provide an absolute demarcation at the fundamental levels of the lived experience of space and time between the present and the times that had gone before.[21] In the epigraph above, H.G. Wells does something similar by using lamplight to demarcate a pre-electric nineteenth century from the twentieth. In *Tono-Bungay*, Wells employs the nostalgia implicit within a recognized sense of discontinuity that was both a cultural metaphor and embodied in the various electrical technologies of the late nineteenth / early twentieth century. Although domestic electric lighting was by no means ubiquitous in 1908 (the temporal moment of the narrator), the electric light had become sufficiently familiar that the evocation of gaslight was irrevocably old fashioned.

Electric lighting was a highly visible manifestation of what Stephen Kern and Ronald Schleiffer describe as a 'crisis of abundance' of energy.[22] The rapid proliferation of electric street lighting that followed the amended Electric Lighting Act of 1888 made electricity an inescapable feature of the urban environment. Just as electrically powered transportation systems embodied the flow of electricity above and below ground at street level, so the electric light, allowing the simultaneous illuminations of whole areas, transformed both the way the landscape looked while imposing a new diurnal rhythm. When Edison exported his Pearl Street System from New York to London, setting it up in Holborn under the Electric Light Company in 1882, only the roads from Holborn Circus to Newgate were illuminated; by 1892 nearly all the London Boroughs and most of the major English and Scottish towns and cities had initiated plans to illuminate their thoroughfares.[23] The *Electrical Review*, a 4d weekly, published on a Friday, enthusiastically promoted, supported and policed the socialization of electricity, its pages detailing the wide range of schemes and initiatives intended to take advantage of electrical power. If titles like the *Electrical Review* embody the abundance of forms electricity could take, the Deptford Station, intended to be the largest power station in the world, was a striking manifestation of its material presence.

Electricity, with its rapid movement through conductors or across space through induction, provides a convenient metaphor for the networks which mobilize and stabilize objects. This can only remain a metaphor however: the electrical industry in London remained decentralized and small-scale, and there was no coherent system linking the various electrical technologies. The very public failures of the Deptford Station – firstly to successfully generate electricity in 1890, and secondly to run at full power when it re-opened in 1891 – could only offer a material centre to what was actually a distributed network.[24] The telegraph was still essentially a point-to-point service, with messages being delayed as they were translated from language to language.[25] The telephone, which like the telegraph was appropriated by the General Post Office in Britain, adopted a similar point-to-point organization, with many subscribers only being connected to a telephone on another piece of their own property.[26] The Electric Lighting Acts of 1882 and 1888 had reached a rather awkward compromise between private speculation and public utility.[27] The reluctance of private speculators to finance large, centralized plants combined with the decentralized local government of London, ensured the city was increasingly supplied by a number of small-scale plants using a bewildering variety of systems. In 1890 there were six supply companies, three operating high-tension a.c. systems, and three operating low-tension d.c. systems; by 1913, there were 65 electrical utilities, 70 different stations with an average production of 5285 kw each, 49 different supply systems, 10 different frequencies, 32 different transmission voltages and 24 distribution voltages, and 70 different charging and pricing mechanisms.[28] This range provided a substantial market for the manufacturers of electrical equipment, and a small-scale manufacturing industry of electrical goods, both industrial and commercial, flourished. Between 1890 and 1899, for instance, the number of incandescent lamps grew rapidly: the *Electrician* reports there were 180,000 in 1890; 700,000 in 1893; 1,178,600 in 1895; and 6,869,000 in 1899.[29] This industry alone, which was buttressed by a stipulation in the Electric Lighting Acts that stated power suppliers could not determine products used, supported a bulb and fittings industry which contributed most of the advertisements in the compendious advertising sections of the *Electrical Review*.

Stephen Kern suggests that one of the many consequences of the spread of the electric light was the 'blurring of the division of night and day.'[30] However, as he recognizes, the most profound cultural effects of electricity were realized through its speed.[31] Electricity offered the late nineteenth-century imagination a different way of producing space through its ability to travel quickly. Its speed, well-recognized as the speed of light at 186,000 mph, allowed spaces to be connected instantly. This did not only apply to geographical space: the integration of various electrical technologies linked different orders of space in new configurations. For instance, the *Electrical Review* reported on a new technology called 'Morgan's Automatic Electric Police Signalling System.' Addressing the heightening anxiety in public mind caused by 'the gradual accumulation of undetected crime throughout the country', the system exploits the ability of electricity to bridge the space between the crime scene and the authorities, or the policeman and his superiors. The system involved a network of lampposts fitted with telegraphs and telephones so they would be in constant communication with headquarters. These are designed to supplement conventional lampposts, and would be fitted with a different coloured light in order to summon assistance. London is the 'the very centre of civilization', and possesses 'a protective machinery with which no other city in the world can compare'; yet the 'direst of horrible deeds and the most dissolute of criminal and offences' occur within it. The problem is that the police are human, and 'possessed of but the same capabilities and powers of locomotion as the fugitive.' Unlike the detective, who possesses superior (although still human) abilities, this technology does no more than allow the existing police force to transcend the spatial limits of the human body. As the lampposts would not require the police to leave the scene of the crime to report it or summon help, and any assistance could be despatched immediately after a telegraphic / telephonic conversation or through the light, a safe urban space is produced, subject of course to constant police surveillance.[32]

The rapid transmission and diffusion of electrical technology provided a vocabulary of speediness as well as being newsworthy in its own right. For instance, the *Electrical Review* reported triumphantly that a telegraphic message could travel from San Francisco to Hong Kong in fifteen minutes via New York, Canso, Penzance, Aden, Bombay, Madras, Penang and Singapore.[33] Although they are different technologies, and one did not lead to another, the telephone completed the spatial logic of speed suggested by the telegraph in allowing the co-presence of two voices in a space of their own that was simultaneously in two geographical locations at once. This produced unexpected outcomes: 'The Dangers of Telephones' recounts how when two American telephonists arranged a marriage over the telephone, under the scrutiny of a city official, as a joke, they found to their dismay that the new telephonic space was recognized and, even though they did not have a license, the marriage was binding.[34] This article foregrounds novelty – nobody had been married by telephone before – and so could be considered news. The article that follows, 'The Telephone in the United States', reveals that there are over two million subscribers and 50 telephone companies in America, raising the possibility of many more of these 'modern marriages.'[35] However, as the addressee of the *Electrical Review* is a shrewd reader of technology, it is likely that such spaces could only be permitted to exist in 'other' spaces, whether the foreign space of the United States, or the fantastic realm of fiction.

The potential to confuse the rapidity of electricity, the timeliness of news, and the language used to express these remains however. In February 1890 *Tit-Bits* ran a piece of self-publicity entitled 'Quick Work' which recounted how, on a whim, the *Tit-Bits* management decided to have electric lighting installed. As a busy weekly, they needed the job in record time, and Mr Verity of Covent Garden had the lights installed by 4pm the next day, a feat they describe as 'the quickest piece of work in connection with electric lighting that has ever been accomplished in the Old or New worlds.'[36] This was reprinted verbatim in the *Electrical Review*, thus incorporating that textual object within its material form. However, once there its nature is subject to the interpretation of the readers and, the following week, a parody also entitled 'Quick Work' appears. This substitutes 'the medium for puffs' for *Tit-Bits*, and a gas engineer called Terivy from Cockle Swamp for the electrician.[37] The seriality of the *Electrical Review* allows it to purge the news event of *Tit-Bits's* self-referencing, while also incorporating a slight against the gas trade. However, this only makes sense if the narrative is pursued across both numbers of the *Electrical Review*: without the prior piece, with its links to *Tit-Bits*, the parody becomes a different object altogether.

Just as material components of a periodical can carry embodiments of electricity within them between different textual contexts, so language can also operate as a conductor. The success of electricity as a motive force prompted Lord Bury, the chairman of the Electric Traction Company, to ask readers of *The Times* for suggestions for a monosyllabic verb that could express 'progression by electric power.' Bury (William Coutts Keppel) had written extensively on electricity in the periodical press, and in this letter he establishes a technological precedent for his request, citing the occasion when *The Times* opened its columns for discussion of the terms 'telegram' and 'telephone' and suggesting the nouns used for units be adopted as verbs.[38] The following day (10 April 1890) *The Times* prints 13 responses to Bury's letter, ranging from the sensible ('to spark', 'to ohm', 'to volice', 'to gleam') to the sardonic ('to mote' [as in self-promote], 'to squirm', 'to watt' [to what?], 'to tric' [as in 'tricking home' – the correspondent notes 'that "k" is suggestive and seems necessary']).[39] Further correspondence is printed on the following day (11 April), with a similar mix of suggestions including 'to trize', 'tric-trac', 'to Vril' (a reference to Lytton's *The Coming Race*), 'to chortle' (from Lewis Carroll's 'Jabberwocky'), 'to curr', and 'to biljy' (from the Hindustani for lightning, we are told). The editor ends the column stating that they have only published a selection of the suggestions, and summarizes the others in a list.[40] The next day (12 April), sees yet more letters and another list including the suggestion that 'volt', although fulfilling Bury's criteria, would be unsuitable as a return journey would be a 'revolt.'[41]

The words reveal a curious mix of an antiquarian interest in the history of the language, some passionate arguments in favour of new or adapted words, a reiteration of the connection between electricity and futurity, and a lingering sense that the electrical trade was mercenary and slightly disreputable. Predictably, the discussion was picked up in the *Electrical Review*. The editors first notice the articles and provide a summary on the 11 April 1890, two days after Bury's letter. In the following number they reflect more fully on the suggestions, and reprint a poem 'The Passionate Electrician' from Henley's *Scots Observer*:

> Sweet, shall we volt it? Dearest, shall we ohm
> Our wing'd way across the ocean foam?
> Or were it fairer to electricize
> (Or electrate) our path to happier skies?
> What's in a name when all roads lead to Rome?
> Fairest and rarest under heaven's high dome,
> O shall we squirm, or Watt, or electrate?
> Or, if you feel you'd rather not volize,
> Sweet, shall we volt?
>
> Heart of my heart, no fond or frolic tome
> But the grave *Times*, that moral metronome,
> Bids us coulombs, or spark, or motorize,
> And now I think of it the blue day dies;

'Tis time, 'tis time, that we were moting home –
Sweet, shall we volt.[42]

Their tone is one of wry amusement: they print the whole list of suggestions, but complement them 'with the remark that most of them would, at first sight, appear to have been taken from the "Hunting of the Snark".' The accusation that such discussion is absurd informs their general assumption that Bury's request is superficial. As many of the correspondents of *The Times* point out, the effort to coin a verb is unnecessary as not only is there little difference between the motion caused by steam and electricity, but there are no special verbs to express the older forms of locomotion. The *Electrical Review* thus has little at stake in this debate, and so instead uses the plentiful copy to entertain its readers.

The final report in *The Times* hints at Bury's motives. In the number for the 14 April (there is no edition on the 13 April as it is a Sunday) they once more reprint some of the letters, and produce a list of 'the very numerous further suggestions made by our correspondents.'[43] There is also a leader that expresses its amusement at the interest in Bury's challenge, which they describe as 'the popular puzzle of the hour.' It echoes Stead's association of the 'flu with electricity, noting that 'the interest exhibited by the public in this fascinating amusement is still spreading alarmingly', and announces that it is closing its columns as 'the contributions show by their extravagance or triviality that the subject is nearly exhausted.' However, it is not solely because of the triviality of the discussion that *The Times* brings it to a close. They suggest that 'Lord Bury and his company feel the want of a verb, but the public is hardly conscious of it yet.' Indeed, should Lord Bury adopt any of the words suggested, *The Times* recommends he takes 'the promptest step to compel its ratification by inscribing it in large letters on his electric cars.' For the word to come into existence, *The Times* suggests, it would need to be advertised as there is no extant referent for it to name. In linking Bury's letter with advertising they both hint at his commercial motives while also tacitly acknowledging the role that culture plays in bringing a thing into existence.[44]

Although the *Electrical Review* treated Bury's suggestion as a diversion, the title itself was deeply interested in the relationship between advertising and electricity. As mentioned above, each number contained a large advertising section, usually running to at least 32 pages, and was often complemented by a further advertising supplement of similar size. These advertisements, and the diverse technologies that they represented, testified to the presence of electricity even while the substance itself remained elusive. Electricity, even in the *Electrical Review*, functions as a 'virtual object' – it was manifestly produced, but its existence was only realized through its traces – and so its ontology remains inextricably linked to its representations.[45] Unlike steam or gas, electricity was recognized as invisible, odourless, and often silent; as such, it was only ever directly experienced (as many schoolboys knew) when it flowed through the body. Those responsible for the electrical trade used its uncertain materiality as a reason for their independent expert role:

> With electric currents we are dealing with a subtle influence which can neither be seen, heard, nor offend our sense of smell, and only too frequently is a leak made known by the sudden launching into eternity of an electric lighting company's *employé* or a too venturesome consumer.[46]

Indeed, the *Electrical Review* devotes little of its letterpress to theoretical discussions of electricity, preferring instead to report on its applications. In a rare theoretical article, 'Physical Fields', the editors reprint a piece by A.E. Dolbear from the American journal *Science* that reiterates the Maxwellian theory that electricity is a property of the ether, and is transmitted from one place to another.[47] However, two months later they reproduce correspondence between Dolbear and Nelson W. Perry. Dolbear maintains that electrical force is propagated from one place to another, whereas Perry adopts the opinion that electrification is a property of matter into which a stress is introduced. The rival interpretations are both supported by quotations from well-known authorities including Maxwell, Thomson, and Faraday, but a final model is not put forward.[48] For the electrical engineers who were the implied readers of the *Electrical Review*, electricity is known only through its effects; as these vary according to its embodiments, it was through the more stable objects such as light fittings that they asserted their expertise.[49]

This provides a further motive for their opposition to Cornelius Bennett Harness's Medical Battery Company. This historical episode has been well-discussed elsewhere.[50] To summarize, after acquiring the Pall Mall Electric Association in 1881, Harness built up a substantial business selling electro-medical cures both from his elaborate showrooms and treatment centre at the corner of Rathbone Place and Oxford Street, and also more discretely by post. Takahiro Ueyama points out that, although Harness's own medical qualifications were largely spurious, he was one of many trying to mobilize capital to support electro-medical cures from outside the established medical profession.[51] What made Harness notorious was his highly visible marketing of the electropathic belts. These were conventional supporting garments (with different models for men and women) with galvanic discs of copper and zinc that, when connected to a battery, would apply therapeutic electricity to the body. These were fitted in the luxurious showrooms of the Medical Battery Company, but Harness also sold them through the post. He maintained that even without the battery, perspiration from the body would be sufficient to generate an electrolytic current, and his highly visible claims for their efficacy brought him into conflict with the medical and electrical professions, not to mention some of his disgruntled customers.

As Ueyama states, there were other electro-medical institutions, and Harness was not the only vendor of electropathic belts.[52] What distinguished the Medical Battery Company from its competitors was a highly effective advertising campaign that cost between £30,000 and £75,000 a year.[53] These advertisements, ranging from surreptitious notices tucked in the corners of pages to full-page statements and testimonials proclaiming the efficacy of the belts, appeared in a wide selection of titles including *The Times*, *Graphic*, *Illustrated London News*, *Pearson's Weekly*, *Christian Million* and the *English Mechanic*. Harness was a shrewd manipulator of advertising, and would alter the content of his notices according to the title he was publishing in. For instance Figure 6.1 is an advertisement from the *Illustrated London News* that cites their very own scientific correspondent, Andrew Wilson. Harness was notorious for quoting eminent authorities, usually out of context and without their permission, but would mix their statements with those of respectable middle-class types, and 'ordinary' members of the public.[54] This democratic reach ensured that the widest possible range of customers was addressed, while simultaneously employing a comprehensive repertoire of types to convince the wary of the belt's effectiveness. By breaking up the claims of the belts into individual cases, they were made to seem less miraculous than they would otherwise appear while reassuring those suffering from the more compromising disorders.

The 'Harness Electropathic Swindle', as the *Pall Mall Gazette* called it, has been interpreted variously as an institutional struggle over medical authority, part of a negotiation of the uncertain status of electrical therapeutics, and an emancipatory triumph of consumerism.[55] What I want to emphasize is that it is the variable materiality of electricity that allows it flow through all of these discursive domains, even when it was demonstrated that it did not flow through Harness's belts. As Morus notes, the mobile periodical press is vital in the constitution of this network:

> An expanding mass press anxious for advertising revenue publicized these galvanic gadgets in every middle-class parlour in the land. In a culture where disease was frequently regarded as carrying with it a suggestion at least of moral failure, companies offering a discrete service of consultation and cure by post had their clear attractions.[56]

Lori Loeb's contention that even though scientific testimony condemned the product 'in the courts and in the press', a 'receptive public audience for the scientific findings was only created by the empirical conclusion of customers themselves' seems to underestimate the cultural construction of the healing properties inherent in the belts.[57] While I agree that customers were 'the ultimate arbiters of [Harness's] claims to authority over their bodies', I suggest that, for many customers, their empirical experiences were not simply determined by the belts themselves, but instead were bound up in the hybrid created between the objects, the various representations that were widely circulated through advertisement, pamphlet, and puffing review, and the pleasures of experiencing Harness's luxurious Oxford Street premises. Harness deliberately merged the various strands of his enterprises, using them to mutually support each other. As Loeb herself argues, the luxuriously furnished showrooms provided a stage for the performance of electrical showmanship that distinguished it from other vendors of

**Figure 6.1 Page from *Illustrated London News*, 96, 1 February 1890, p. 159. The advertisement for Harness's belts is the top half of the page, but notice how it disguises the fact that the first column on the left is part of the same advertisement.**

medical goods and services, including the hospitals.[58] This environment – represented as both luxurious space of repose and space of serious scientific research – proved persuasive, and Harness used its influence to encourage customers to fill in blank cheques for more than they might otherwise pay.[59] He also exploited the interest engendered by this space by inviting journalists and then reprinting their articles in his advertisements. For instance, Harness used the textual description of the luxurious interior of his showrooms for an advertisement in *The Times* – an unillustrated newspaper. He then complemented this textual account with a visual representation of the more austere exterior in an advertisement in the *Illustrated London News* (Figure 6.2). Harness thus offers the readers of *The Times* a space in which to imagine the delightful private spaces of the showrooms, while reassuring those of the *ILN* of its respectable external appearance.[60]

The *Electrical Review*'s response was intended to disentangle this hybrid. Although it was a court case in February 1893 that provoked a chain of litigation that led to the issuing of a compulsory winding-up order against Harness in 1894, it was a trial in which one of the editors and proprietors of the *Electrical Review*, T.E. Gatehouse, was a witness that best illustrates this.[61] In May 1892 a bank clerk called Mr Jeffrey went to the Company for a consultation. He was concerned he was 'ruptured' and asked to see somebody qualified; he was actually seen by a Mr Simmonds (a former oriental furniture salesman) who claimed Jeffrey did not have a hernia and sold him a belt for five guineas, accepting an IOU for £2 2s. It was to reclaim this amount that the charge was brought, and Jeffrey's defence, after consulting with some doctors, was that he was ruptured and so was the victim of misrepresentation on the part of Simmonds. Part of the defence was an examination of the electrical properties of the belt, and Gatehouse appeared as an expert witness to demonstrate that only a small electrolytic current was generated, and it did not pass through the body. However, Gatehouse's testimony was over-ruled by the judge who, although finding in favour of Jeffrey, did so on the grounds that Simmonds had been misrepresented as a medical man.[62]

The rhetoric of Harness's advertisements implied that not only did the body help to generate the therapeutic electrical current, but that this would actually re-create nerve force within the body.[63] Gatehouse hoped to break this circuit with his legal testimony, and he inserts an article entitled 'Electropathic Belts' immediately after the account of the proceedings in the *Electrical Review*. This piece states that it 'was quite impossible for this belt to generate any current as worn upon the body, for the external circuit was not completed by the connecting up of zinc and copper poles, nor were any means indicated to the defendant of doing so himself', and then details Gatehouse's experiments on the belts and gives the results.[64] The article attempts to reassert this interpretation of the case, buttressed by electrical expertise, over the that of the judge's, which rests on legal expertise. The author, probably Gatehouse, writes the case is 'of special interest to electricians, because the evidence of an electrical expert was, for the first time, we believe, in the history of the so-called electro-medical appliances, added to other overwhelming evidence

350     THE ILLUSTRATED LONDON NEWS     MARCH 15, 1890

NOVEL.

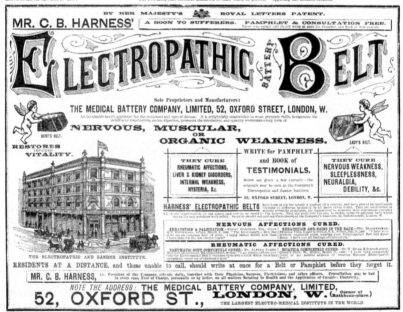

Figure 6.2 Page from the *Illustrated London News*, 96, 15 March 1890, p. 350

testimony as to their worthless nature.'[65] However, in summation the judge had refused to endorse this testimony, saying 'Mr Gatehouse's evidence as to the electrical volume may be right or may be wrong – I do not know; but this (the belt) is the thing put on the man when he was ruptured, and this man was persuaded to buy it on the representation he was not ruptured.'[66] The discourse of the law ignores the object, and the testimony with which Gatehouse attempts to make it 'speak', and instead takes the testimony of Jeffreys' body.

Gatehouse has little authority with medical or legal discourse, but he does have expertise as an electrician and as an editor. 'Electropathic Belts' ridicules the notion of 'a poor debilitated body generating the electricity of alleviation of its own suffering', and claims the 'stepping stone from hallucinations of this kind to the borderland of a profound belief in perpetual motion can be but a narrow one.'[67] By evoking the paradoxer – that amateur, metaphysical 'other' of science and engineering – the *Electrical Review* can reaffirm its status as a representative text for the profession while simultaneously attacking one of its rivals, the *English Mechanic*. As mentioned in Chapter One, the *English Mechanic* permitted paradoxers into its columns as long as its dialogic codes were respected. It also devoted substantial letterpress to electrical matters but, as with its astronomical content, this was predicated on discussion and the title did not seek an authoritative position in the discipline.

This can be seen in the discussion of electropathic belts within the *English Mechanic*. Unlike the *Electrical Review*, which structurally resembles other weeklies (its leaders, for instance, are in the middle, market reports are at the back etc....) and reports on news, the *English Mechanic*'s more open text foregrounds the present but resists the sense of closure inherent in passing. As mentioned in Chapter One, the bulk of its letterpress after the serial articles and leaders are cross-referenced correspondence and queries. This system of numerical cross-referencing resists closure by keeping all discussion in the present: even if an argument is seen to have been resolved, a reference back can revive one half of it and so it begins anew. In June 1892, just before 'Medical Battery Company vs. Jeffrey' reached the courts. 'Electric' asks whether 'any readers [would] assist me with a few hints on the making of an electric body belt for a strong current. What size wire should I use? Also, how many cells would be safe?'[68] On 8 July 1892 W.E. Harper complains his belt no longer works:

> I have been wearing one of these a few weeks […], as a remedy for nervous exhaustion. At first I thought it relieved the aching in the loins; but now it is as bad as ever. Will some reader who is conversant with the subject kindly tell me how long such a belt as I have described will continue to give off electricity, if at all, and can I do anything to improve upon it?[69]

This elicits a response from Selimo Bottone, a prolific author of books on practical electrical matters and the *English Mechanic*'s unofficial arbiter, who writes that beyond 'the relief given by the warmth of the material of which the belts are made, they are absolutely useless.'[70] In the same number, which is published the same week as the 'Medical Battery Company v. Jeffrey' verdict, there is yet another enquiry asking 'any brother-reader of the "E.M." who would kindly inform me how to make an electric belt.'[71] This elicits further responses from S. Robert Bonney, who explains how the belt is made, and Bottone, who ends with the grumble that it 'is absolutely indifferent, theoretically or practically, whether the discs are connected in pairs or not.'[72] Even though these queries and responses are so close to the time of the 22 July *Electrical Review* judgement (and resulting libel allegations – see below) that the correspondents may have been unaware of them, the diverse and continued discussion demonstrates the open-endedness of the seamless present of the *English Mechanic*. The question of the efficacy of the belts is of concern only to Bottone; for the others the principle of exchange that underpins the title precludes any question of ends. On the 5 August 1892 'Jubar' explains to Perry how to make the belt despite suggesting 'faith has a great deal to do with the benefits derived.'[73] In the temporal context of the *English Mechanic*, conclusions are never reached, and so the past is never delimited.

However, it was not with the content of the *English Mechanic* that the *Electrical Review* took issue, but the inappropriate application of their textual politics to advertising. Throughout the Harness affair there are frequent editorial comments regarding the relationship between advertising and the periodical press.[74] On 17 January 1890 the editors specifically mention the *English Mechanic* in an attack on 'advertisements of the Electropathic kind', which they dismiss as 'a tissue of absurdities.' The danger is that, as the '*English Mechanic and World of Science* is read by a class of men ranging from the professor to the merest tyro', the inexperienced may confuse the adverts with science.[75] Not only this, but as I have elaborated throughout previous chapters, the uneasy position of science within intellectual property law brings not only the ownership of ideas into question, but also the materiality of the concepts themselves. The *Electrical Review* recognizes the necessity for scientific authors to advertise the existence of their discoveries, commenting that:

> every paper is of the nature of an advertisement, as the author's object, if not to bring to notice some particular invention which he has devised, is practically to show to the world that he has a knowledge of the subject he is speaking about, and that consequently he is competent to undertake work of a nature similar to that being discussed.[76]

As advertising is a necessary part of scientific practice, it must be employed responsibly: the *English Mechanic*, the editors suggest, carry an inappropriate laxity from their contributed letterpress into the advertising wrapper.

As I mentioned in Chapter One, the structure of the *English Mechanic* increasingly reduces the distance between contribution and advertisement toward the end of each number. 'Queries' is followed by 'Answers to Correspondents', 'Our Exchange Column' and then the final department, 'The Sixpenny Sale

Column', often spans the paginated letterpress and the separately paginated advertising sheets. This confusion between contributions and advertisements is important as it foregrounds both the commercial nature of science publishing and the reliance of scientific objects on their cultural embodiments. Two weeks after their remarks about the *English Mechanic*, the editors of the *Electrical Review* return to the subject of advertising. In 'A Modern Instrument' they write:

> We have not yet arrived at the new journalism, neither have we insured each purchaser against gas explosions, nor offered a guinea for the best electrical tit-bit, nor an annuity to whoever guessed our bank balance; but we think we really ought to give a prize, say a month's free insertion, for the best advertisement connected with lighting and power.[77]

By phrasing this plea for responsible advertising in the language of new journalism, the editors gender the business of journalism as feminine and so, especially in the case of the *English Mechanic*, render the business of selling oneself as prostitution. The *Electrical Review*, however, offers an explicitly masculine role for the electrical engineer. On the same page as their criticism of advertisements in science, they write that for the engineer the 'fairy feminine touch is quite thrown away, it would leave no impression upon the hard fibre and obstinate doggedness of the youth who runs in the way electrical. He might otherwise become a government clerk with a taste for amateur theatricals.' Not only are other pursuits considered effeminate, but pursuing an electrical career actually implies a rejection of the feminine:

> Putting callously aside the hand which would lead him gently from his too odiferous galley pots and noisy bells; unheedful of tears wept over spoilt carpets, suffocating vapours, appalling explosions, and of delicate hints that he might be spending his time better by improving his mind in orthodox fashion or taking his sister out for a walk.[78]

This same masculine stance informs their attitude to the Medical Battery Company:

> It is bad enough that the male sex should submit to be 'examined' by these so-called 'experts,' but to think that gentler, refined, or highly sensitive women should be contaminated by the mere touch of such 'consulting officers,' is utterly abhorrent to the feelings of anybody possessed of a trace of morality or a scrap of manliness.[79]

Not only is treatment by the Medical Battery Company gendered feminine, potentially castrating the masculine electrician, but the implication is that Harness is profiting from the sexual anxieties of customers. Figure 6.3 shows a page from the *English Mechanic* carrying a surreptitious advert for the Medical Battery Company ('The "Very Thing" for Weak Men') that occupies the uneasy space between contributor's items and paid advertising. Using a coded language of 'strong men', 'vitality' and 'vigour of youth', the advert hints at which vital organs

JUNE 17, 1892. ENGLISH MECHANIC AND WORLD OF SCIENCE: No. 1421. 393

brother readers kindly inform me the best method of charging accumulators from a dynamo having 110 volts and 45 ampères, or from a plating dynamo of 6 volts and 90 ampères?—W. M.

[77585.]—**Glacial Period—Saturn's Rings.**—What is the generally-accepted theory of the cause of the Tropical and Glacial periods? What is the present theory as regards the constitution of Saturn's rings? Is it still held that they are minute bodies revolving round Saturn, or are they rings of watery vapour? Is it necessary, by the Nebular Hypothesis, to suppose that the earth had rings like Saturn and belts like Jupiter? What is the theory of the formation of the latter's belts? Are actinic rays necessary to life? Is it possible, with a covering of watery vapour, to shut off the actinic rays from the earth, and what would the result be?—R. W.

[77586.]—**Metal Spinning.**—Can any reader kindly tell me if there is any secret in metal spinning? I want to spin some articles the shape of a basin about 2½in. deep, but I find the brass becomes buckled. I use thin brass, called No. 1.—SPINNER.

## USEFUL AND SCIENTIFIC NOTES.

THE fifteenth conference of the Association for the Reform and Codification of the Law of Nations will be held at Genoa on October 5 and the following days.

IT is claimed that the longest span of telephone wire is across the Ohio river, between Portsmouth, Ohio, and South Portsmouth, Ky. The wires at this point have a span 3,773ft. in length.

THE bold idea of ferrying loaded freight cars across Lake Michigan is soon to be put into practice. A large propeller is under construction at Toledo which will have a capacity of 21 cars, and it is expected to tow a barge carrying 15 cars, making 36 cars, or more than an average freight train. The cost of transferring grain and other freight from cars to steamer and from steamer to cars forms a very heavy item of expenditure which the proposed plan, if successful, will save.

**Fast Trains in the United States.**—The fastest train from Denver to Chicago is now the 9 a.m. on the Burlington, reaching Chicago at 2.15 p.m. the next day. It is also the fastest long run in the West. The distance is 1,028 miles, and the time, allowing for the difference in longitude, is 28¼ hours. Hence the speed from terminal to terminal is 36·4 miles an hour. This is not far behind the speed of the limited trains between New York and Chicago, and is a pretty fast schedule for a run of over 1,000 miles. The fastest New York-Chicago trains are as follows:—New York to Chicago—North Shore Limited via New York Central and Michigan Central, 976 miles in 25 hours. Average speed between terminals, 39 miles an hour. Buffalo to Chicago—North Shore, Limited, via Michigan Central, 536½ miles in 14 1-6th hours. Average speed between terminals, 37·8 miles an hour. New York to Chicago—South Shore, Limited, via New York Central and Lake Shore and Michigan Southern, 964 miles in 24¾ hours. Average speed between terminals, 39 miles an hour. New York to Chicago—Pennsylvania, Limited, via Pennsylvania Railroad, 911 miles in 24½ hours (allowing for the ferry). Average speed between terminals, 37·2 miles an hour. New York to Chicago—Columbian Express via Pennsylvania Railroad, 912 miles in 26¼ hours. Average speed between terminals, 34·7 miles an hour. The South Western, Limited, from New York to St. Louis by the New York Central, &c., runs 1,168 miles in 30¾ hours, or 38 miles an hour between terminals.

**A New Use for Bamboo.**—A new application of the stems of the larger-growing species of bamboo has recently been adopted in China for the manufacture of small trays and ornamental articles for export to Europe. It is known in China as bamboo sheeting, and it is said to be carried on at present only to a limited extent at Wenchow, where, notwithstanding that it is quite a new trade, about ten firms are now engaged in it. The process adopted is as follows:—A length of bamboo is cut off, and then pared with an axe till it is of the thickness required. It is next planed with a spokeshave, and the thin cylinder so obtained is slit up, so that, on being opened out, it forms a sheet. A number of these cylinders, placed one inside the other, are immersed in boiling water for a few minutes, to render them flexible, and they are then unrolled and flattened out, by being subjected to pressure under heavy stones. These sheets are sometimes used for making fretwork and carved screens, fans, &c.; and the small, pale, straw-coloured pin-trays, for toilet tables, which appeared in the London shops last season, are apparently made from this specially prepared bamboo. It seems to adapt itself extremely well for moulding into many forms, and might be made available in this country for various kinds of veneering. The bamboo now appears to be the *Dendrocalamus latiflorus*, and specimens of the sheeting, and articles made from it, may be seen in Museum No. 2 of the Royal Gardens, Kew.

## CHESS.

All communications for this column to be addressed to the CHESS EDITOR, at the Office, 332, Strand.

PROBLEM No. 1310.—BY F. H. GUEST.

*Black.*

*White.* [2 + 5

**White to play and mate in three moves.**

(*Solutions must be posted before June 24.*)

SOLUTION of Problem No. 1307. By Walter Gleave. Key-move, 1 R-B 8. Twelve variations.

CORRECT solutions from E. W. Barnett, C. S. Bright, H. N. Fellows (very pretty), A. G. Fellows, L. Beeman, T. Guest (very nice problem), F. H. Guest, H. P. Hosken, W. T. Hurley (a grand variety of mates), J. Kistruck, J. Hood, W. Mackenzie, W. Pilkington (ingenious), W. L. Smith, E. C. M., J. P. Dawbarn, W. R. Taylor, jun., S. A. Stewart (very good; took me a long time to solve it), A. Waterhouse (mates are very neat), G. Armitage, C. J. B., Miss M. Berkley, R. W. Houghton (very good), L. Morris.

TO CORRESPONDENTS.

C. S. BRIGHT (Genoa).—We have acknowledged all the solutions received. Glad you are still sending in.

T. GUEST.—No trace of missing problem.

E. C. M.—Solving problems from the diagram is the best way, and it improves your powers of analysis.

G. A. MACBETH.—Regret you are not competing, as we prefer regular solvers.

THE Pike's Peak telephone line is said to be eclipsed in altitude by a line that crosses the Andes, on the Trans-Andean railroad, at an elevation of about 16,500ft. above sea level.

A FRENCHMAN has succeeded, it is said, in producing an excellent driving belt by parchmenting the leather instead of tanning it. The belts have greater durability and do not stretch.

AN ingenious method is followed in some German steelworks to secure rails of exactly the same length. During the process of cutting it often happens that even with the same gauge one rail will be longer than the others, owing to the different heat at which they enter the saws. Those which were the hottest when cut are the shortest when cold, having contracted more than the others after cutting. In the German mills the workmen look at the heated rail through a dark glass, so tinted that when the metal has cooled to a certain temperature the rails cannot be seen at all. A dark blue or orange yellow glass will make a red-hot rail invisible. It may be considered a fact that any two rails looked at through the same pair of glasses will disappear at the same temperature. If every rail is allowed to cool until it is just invisible through a certain pair of glasses all will be of the same temperature, and their lengths will be the same.

**Fishing for Sponges.**—The British consul, in his report on the trade of Tripoli, remarks that the sponge fishery on that coast is entirely in the hands of Greeks, and is carried on by means of numerous small craft, employing about 700 men amongst them. The fishing takes place in the summer months only, and is effected by machine boats provided with proper diving apparatus, or by trawlers and harpoon boats. Last season there were twenty-one diving machines in use. These, as the divers have time to select and cut them, naturally secure the best sponges, but the trawl nets and harpoon boats, which can only fish in comparatively shallow waters, to a greater or less extent damage the sponges by tearing them from the bottom. The best sponges are found to the westward of Tripoli, the quality becoming inferior towards the east. The diving is dangerous owing to the presence of sharks and other accidents to be met with, such as remaining too long under the water or diving beyond the proper limits, which often exhausts the divers and proves fatal to them.

## ANSWERS TO CORRESPONDENTS.

*** *All communications should be addressed to the* EDITOR *of the* ENGLISH MECHANIC, *332, Strand, W.C.*

HINTS TO CORRESPONDENTS.

1. Write on one side of the paper only, and put drawings for illustrations on separate pieces of paper. 2. Put titles to queries, and when answering queries, put the numbers as well as the titles of the queries to which the replies refer. 3. No charge is made for inserting letters, queries, or replies. 4. Letters or queries asking for addresses of manufacturers or correspondents, or where tools or other articles can be purchased, or replies giving such information, cannot be inserted except as advertisements. 5. No question asking for educational or scientific information is answered through the post. 6. Letters sent to correspondents, under cover to the Editor, are not forwarded, and the names of correspondents are not given to inquirers.

*** Attention is especially drawn to hint No. 4. The space devoted to letters, queries, and replies is meant for the general good, and it is not fair to occupy it with questions such as are indicated above, which are only of individual interest, and which, if not advertisements in themselves, lead to replies which are. The "Sixpenny Sale Column" offers a cheap means of obtaining such information, and we trust our readers will avail themselves of it.

The following are the initials, &c., of letters to hand up to Wednesday evening, June 15, and unacknowledged elsewhere:—

DELLZUPH.—W. A. Ryan.—A. E. K.—Harry.—W. D. L.—Menka-ra.—W. A. L. M.—Enfant Malaide.—T. S.—E. P. Alexander and Son.—Notts.—A. Captlatzl.—Bootle.—H. Fry.—G. J. B.—A. Gadd.—A Fellow of the Royal Astronomical Society.—C. Roberts.—J. H.—Rev. C. M. C. Bone.—R. Woolridge.

L. H., Northampton. (Thanks; much appreciated. You will see we have deleted part of your letter. We cannot import the theological argument.)—A. VINCENT. (That may have been; but it is so no longer. People say to us sometimes: "Are you not making the ENGLISH MECHANIC too scientific—too much above the heads of the people?" Our answer is that the people themselves have made the ENGLISH MECHANIC what it is; and that whereas twenty years ago we had to wade through oceans of rubbish in the way of correspondence, it is now altogether different. Our regret is, nowadays, that so much really useful stuff has to be sacrificed for want of space. Now, this remarkable rise in the level of the intelligence of the workman is becoming as marked in political as in other matters, and the results presently will be manifest.)—T. JACOBS. (No room; there is a very good "Gardening" column in the *Weekly Times and Echo* every week.)—T. E. PHILLIPS. (You can easily ascertain by search at the Patent Office whether the patent is still in force, or whether it was abandoned.)—AN AGNOSTIC. (If once we begin the theological argument, we shall have no end of it. Mr. Davis's statement, which we quite admit was a dogmatic one, must be taken and left for what it is worth.)—PLUMBER. (Better write the Secretary of the Sanitary Institute. We suppose that body issues notices of its examinations and copies of past questions.)—SIX MONTHS' SUFFERER. (See back vols., or consult Dr. Allinson through the medical column of the *Weekly Times and Echo*.)

**The "Very Thing" for Weak Men.**—Mr. Harness' new combined appliance for men consists of an Electropathic Body Belt, with suspender attached. It generates invigorating electric currents, and imperceptibly conveys them direct from the spinal cord to the vital organs. By its aid strong men maintain the full vigour of youth, and the debilitated are speedily restored to health. (This fact we can prove beyond dispute.) As a safe, convenient, and certain cure for varicocele, nervous exhaustion, and the many distressing symptoms of impaired vitality, this remarkable invention has no equal. All men, therefore, are invited to call, if possible, and see it scientifically tested at the Electropathic Institute, 52, Oxford-street, London, W. Private consultations are free, either personally or by letter. If unable to call, write for Mr. Harness' new pamphlet on "Varicocele and Kindred Ailments."

IN steel bridges the greatest stress allowed by the Board of Trade is not more than 6½ tons per square inch.

AN important improvement in the fitting of derrick cranes, which will save much risk and danger to the public, has been patented by Messrs. E. Lea and W. H. Thompson, of 147, Queen Victoria-street, and Peterborough, and has been publicly tried before a number of scientific gentlemen on the premises of the Royal College of Music (now being constructed on the Albert Hall Estate), South Kensington. The appliance is very simple, and is confined to the head of the jib, the chain-pulley of which has a ratchet-wheel attached on each side of it, into which a pair of pawls or detents become engaged immediately the jib-chain breaks or fails, and thereby the jib and its load are immediately arrested. The action of the detents to catch into the ratchet-teeth is by means of a strong spring, which is attached to the end of jib-chain. A trial was made on both a small model crane, and also on one lifting three tons. Immediately the jib-chain was let go or cut, the ratchet was brought into action, and the heavy block of stone suspended at the end of the hoisting-chain is instantly stopped in its descent, and with it, of course, the jib. The brake or catch acts equally the same with a heavy load or with a light load—in fact, the heavier the load suspended is, the quicker the arrest.

**Figure 6.3 Page from *English Mechanic*, 55, 17 June 1892, p. 393. The advetisement for Harness's belts is below 'Answers to Correspondents.'**

might be affected by 'nervous exhaustion' and remedied by an electropathic belt 'with suspender attached.'[80] Not only were the Medical Battery Company claiming authority as experts, but this advert, targeting the male readership of the *English Mechanic*, called into question the masculinity and sexual prowess of the electrical engineer.

By attacking the belts, false advertising, and those competitors that tolerated the Medical Battery Company for the possible advertising revenue, the *Electrical Review* attempted to remove Harness's belts from the centre of their electrical network. As the counter-constructions of the efficacy of the belts began to circulate, their stability as cultural objects began to fragment. This is not to argue that consumers naively believe in advertisement, but instead that the advertisements, along with the pleasurable spaces, hope of cure, and all the other nebulous aspects of the belt, could only be experienced as long as the links in the network were reasonably stable. The focus of the *Electrical Review* on advertising reveals the central role that such representations play in stabilizing electricity as a concept. Their piece discussing responsible advertising, 'A Modern Instrument', is immediately followed by a report that the electric chair has been successfully tested on a steer. Such combinations reveal the necessarily different use of objects in the advertising wrapper and the 'authored' letterpress. Each number of the *Electrical Review* carried advertisements for technological objects ranging from industrial plant fittings to more trivial items such as the General Electric Company's 'Domestic Novelties.'[81] As advertisements, these are unequivocal recommendations that maintain the efficacy of the objects they describe. The contents of each number, however, present a much more varied version of the success of these objects. Much of the weekly letterpress is filled with accounts of electrical fires, deaths, bankruptcies and injuries. There was political capital to be gained by publicizing the failure of electricity (and its rival industries) as it not only highlighted the need for expert supervision, but in commenting on the disasters also enacted supervision textually. These two spaces, the paginated letterpress and the advertising wrapper, both argue that electricity, if not directed through the appropriate objects, can be dangerous. However, the objects within each play different roles: within the letterpress the reports of electrical disasters enact the imposition of expert supervision over electrical practice; in the advertisements, however, supervision is displaced by endorsement.

Periodicals, of course, are also objects, and the *Electrical Review* directed its gaze to the *English Mechanic* in order to enforce a division between the objects that can conduct electricity in the adverts, and discussion of objects that might conduct electricity in letterpress. As the *English Mechanic* blurs this division it foregrounds the role of commodities – whether represented in its pages, or the submitted contributions themselves – in structuring the periodical as a commodity in its own right. The *Electrical Review*, presenting themselves as arbiters of the electrical trade, suppress this relationship with the market, instead offering their advertising pages as a gallery of electrical objects. The double nature of the periodical as commodity and vehicle for commodities is vital here: rather than present these as items to be shopped for, and so subject to a femininized gaze, they are instead offered as objects which can be judged by the expert masculine eye of the electrical engineer; by keeping them at the margins of the text, the editors can deny the role of content in creating the periodical as commodity, and so keep the grubby business of selling oneself outside the 'real' portions of the text.

## Conclusions: 'Movable Types'

Mary Howarth's short story 'The Telegram', published in the *Pall Mall Magazine* in 1896, narrates how objects can disrupt spatial and temporal domains. The story is unusual as it is accompanied by a series of photographs which, interspersed with the letterpress, illustrate the narrative. It begins with two friends by a cosy fireside: Horace Keith, whose father owns the (fictional) radical daily *The Meteor*; and Laurence Morris, a painter who is about to depart on a commission to paint a portrait of the Prime Minister. The portrait has been delayed due to the ill health of the Prime Minister, and Keith asks Morris to telegram him immediately should the Prime Minister die so *The Meteor* can run the exclusive. Keith's father, the owner of the paper, is the Prime Minister's estranged half brother and, by coincidence, is also in Brighton having just finished a rather spiteful obituary of him before leaving London. Horace Keith receives the telegram from his artist friend Morris saying the Prime Minister is dead and so runs the obituary by his father in a special edition. However, the telegram has been mistranscribed, and the Prime Minister and Keith's father are at that moment resolving their differences in Brighton. Laurence Morris, having finished his portrait, returns to London and quickly realizes the error. When the news of the Prime Minister's 'death' reaches Brighton, and Horace Keith's father realizes that his spiteful obituary has been published, he feels he has betrayed his reconciled half-brother and rushes back to the Prime Minister's hotel. Luckily, the Prime Minister did die shortly after Keith's father had departed, and so remained oblivious to the debacle.[82]

Howarth's story illustrates the new temporal and spatial configurations created by late nineteenth-century socialization of information technology. The telegraph offered the potential for the instant transmission of linguistic information: whereas before Brighton would always be a few hours train journey from London, the telegraph enabled Brighton time and London time almost to coexist. However, as the story indicates, the points of translation, where words on paper become electronic signals and then words on paper once more, was not a completely reliable process. In the newspaper office Barton, the 'working secretary', warns against using telegrams without getting them repeated. For Barton (and indeed Keith's father), the chain that links the telegram and its source is not stable, but for Horace Keith, a mercurial representative of the next generation, 'all the laws of sequence are against its being inaccurate.'[83] It is the relationships between these objects – the Prime Minister, the telegram, the obituary, and the newspaper – that allow London and Brighton to exist in the same temporal moment and as part of the same region of space. It is the failure of this network of things that produces the curious situation where the Prime Minister is dead in London but alive in Brighton. This spatial-temporal disjunction, violating the laws of sequential linear time and the principle that human beings are confined to a single space, does not last for long: as the story unfolds, and news, carried in other objects and by other people, begins to reach Brighton, the Prime Minister actually does die, bringing the two moments together once more.

It is not the obituary that fractures space-time, but the circulation of the obituary as part of the *Meteor* and then reproduced elsewhere. Throughout this book I have considered periodicals as composite objects that bring together components from a variety of times and spaces, and then distribute them anew. Chapter One explored how the status of these components is contested as they are reproduced: just as Barton insists that the telegram does not map onto the Prime Minister's body; so the astronomers reading *Knowledge* maintained that Ranyard's reproductions did not have the same relationship to space and time that their negatives did. Chapter Two considered the role that photographs played in testifying to the contemporaneous existence of other realms of space. The photographs that illustrate 'The Telegraph' also signal another dimension: exploiting the conceit that the camera was brought into the same space as the object it photographs, these images provide a further space, representing the fictional space-time of the narrative as occurring simultaneously with the moment of reading.

Chapters Three, Four, and Five shifted the emphasis to time. As Bergson and Bakhtin argue, time can be realized spatially, and Chapter Three considers how objects are deployed to indicate the existence of the contemporary. Although a range of times and spaces are represented in periodicals, often coded to correspond to their perceived readers, the dominant temporality is the present. News operates through making what is distant (in terms of space), present (in terms of time). Just as the value of the *Meteor* in 'The Telegram' is predicated on how 'present' it can be, so Chapter Three considers how news (and indeed obituaries) mark texts in ways that link them with wider cultural events. News especially is marked by the forms that connect it to the distant (but contemporary) events that it narrates: as such, it is marked by the processes that allow these events to be present on the page. This raises significant problems in terms of authorship, as human intervention into these technologies risks the fiction of unmediated access to events.

Chapter Four focused on scientific discovery, but might also apply to any situation in which new things enter culture. As Latour argues, discovery involves a complex process in which a new thing is allocated a moment of discovery while simultaneously granted a constant (but hidden) presence throughout all time. This creates two histories after the moment of discovery, one which stretches back prior to this moment, and the other that follows the discovered thing as it circulates through culture. This latter history establishes the former by reproducing the object, allowing it to populate other cultural spaces and encourage the recognition of its past. In 'The Telegram', of course, it is the proliferation of reports of the Prime Minister's death that create a space in which this event has happened; but when a social consensus about their authenticity is reached, this now false history is forgotten.

Chapter Five analyzed the interaction between textual representations of temporality, the appearance of the objects that carried them, and the events that they describe. The calendars of 1890 and 1891 constrain the dynamic of discovery into a complex set of interlocking rhythms. News is predicated on its deviation from the norm, but its production is limited by the temporal rhythms of the objects that allow it to move through space. Only really exceptional events are granted a special material form such as a supplementary edition, the remainder are limited to largely predetermined temporal structures and textual spaces. By tracing the papers across different domains, it is possible to see how these environments shape the things they contain. Periodicity also plays a part in the 'The Telegram': as a daily, there is not enough time between the appearance of the most current number – the one that is in the present – and the death of the Prime Minister, so the piece must be written in advance; it is the disparity between the moment of writing, when the two half-brothers are estranged, and the moment of publication, when their relations are restored, that is exposed when both are made to share the same present.

The discussion of the electrical press in this chapter brings together much of the above. By restricting the presence of Harness's belts to their paginated letterpress, the *Electrical Review* places them in a space where their status as electrical objects can be contested from within the text. The dialogic structure of the *English Mechanic* complements my reading of the *Strand* by offering a space in which exclusive discourses can mark the same object. The discussion in *The Times* about new words to describe electrical motion parallels the controlled processes of nomination so essential for chemical practice. Both are about property: nomination in chemistry seeks to define a discrete object and grant it a degree of cultural autonomy while retaining its links to an 'author'; while Bury's request for help aspires to create a word that would distinguish the motive power with which he is associated from that of his rivals. Finally, both the *English Mechanic* and the *Electrical Review* use the Harness affair to associate themselves with the present. However, in each title it is different: whereas the *Electrical Review*, in its weekly representation of the electrical profession, categorically judged the belts continuously as part of its performance of the present, the *English Mechanic* tolerated rival constructions of the efficacy of the belts, allowing the hybrid to escape any finalizing judgements. Although both are weeklies, only the *Electrical Review* engages with the Harness affair as news. However, their periodicity works against them: 'Tibbits vs. Alabaster and Others', the case in which Tibbits sued the *Electrical Review* for their alleged libellous review of his pamphlet, lasted from Wednesday the 15 to Friday the 17 February 1893; The *Electrical Review*, as I have mentioned above, was published on a Friday and so they could only cover half of the case in their weekly 'Legal' department. In the number for the 17

February they only print the day and a half of the trial; and readers were forced to either read elsewhere or to wait for the following week for the remainder of the law report and the all-important outcome. This temporality, imposed upon the trial by the rhythm of the publishing process, means that only half of it is represented as in the present.

It is electricity's reconfiguration of space and time that links the above to my wider discussion of electronic publication. The apparent speed in which content is delivered to monitors, elides materiality in the rhetoric of the virtual and obscures the transformations that produce it. Just as there is a network of interests surrounding periodical texts, astronomical photographs, chemical compounds, or electropathic belts, so there are a network of interests surrounding digitization, writing, code, storage, processing, display and interpretation. The considerable labour required to transform dusty volumes into electronic images reveals the cultural practices that underlie this process. I argue that it is important we not only recognize this work, but also its role in shaping the materiality of its products. Materiality is not the property of a natural realm divorced from culture, nor is it prior to it; rather, it is a complex interaction between the two that is determined by spatial and temporal conditions. For instance, the Royal Society of Chemistry digitized their periodical holdings in 2004 in two batches, the first containing all its titles from 1841 to 1996, the second adding content up until 2004. Consequently, readers no longer have to locate the bound volumes, probably within library archives, to access Kipping and Perkin's 'Action of Dehydrating Agents on $\alpha\omega$-Diacetylpentane. Synthesis of Methylethylhexamethylene', discussed above in Chapter Four. However, the necessity of electronic display predicates the co-presence of reader and monitor, and access restrictions limit these spaces to those IP addresses with a subscription or a computer actually within the Society's network. The Society has reproduced facsimiles of the *Journal*'s pages, and housed these within an impressive database that offers access to surrogates that appear to substitute for the hard copy elsewhere. The framing of these facsimiles within browser windows creates a new space through which they are accessed. Equally, the user interface transforms navigation through the archive: as it incorporates free text searching and the interrogation of metadata fields, this archive substitutes the existing system of tables of contents and abstracts with more sophisticated ways to order the material. The level of violence that can be done to the linear sequence of pages in numbers, numbers in volumes, and volumes on a shelf, demonstrates the radical extent to which this material has changed.

In producing electronic editions we choose to retain certain elements of material form at the expense of others. Isabelle Stengers' notion of the event, in which interested actors are brought together and retrospectively judge its significance from the terrain that it has produced, also applies to electronic publication. Digital versions of historical objects produce new audiences in whose hands the fate of these things will lie. In choosing which elements are preserved in digital form, we should remember that these references shape the terrain from which they will be judged. Kipping and Perkin carefully wrote the laboratory into their account of $\Delta^1$-orthomethyltetrahydrobenzene methyl ketone as, even though it was limited to a specific time and space, it would shape the subsequent life of the chemical. Also, the institutional mechanisms through which they published their paper ensured a certain type of reader who would recognize their ownership of the phenomena described within. The audiences for digital editions are unlikely to be who we imagine them to be, and so all we can do is design these objects with properties that will allow them to flourish. However, we need to recognize that what we digitize is itself the product of a transformation, amalgamating other objects into a new whole. Our digital transformations are the latest in the history of these things and, if it is history we want to recognize, it is important we remember – and incorporate – what it was that determined prior decisions about their status.

The ontological does apply in the digital domain (indeed, it is part of the language of computer science), and digital versions of historical objects can preserve the relationships through which their materiality is and was negotiated. Despite a much heralded 'material turn' in cultural studies, and a rigorous examination of material aspects of print culture, a lingering reluctance to deal with the things that shape our societies remains in historical, cultural and literary studies.[84] Ideas, words and texts do not exist in a disembodied virtual state – even in the digital age – and it is only by acknowledging the presence of the people, objects and technologies that mobilize them that the full array of social actors can be revealed. I prefaced this book with Carlyle's comment that '[h]e who first shortened the labour of Copyists by device of *Movable Types*' created a 'whole new democratic world.' Perhaps a recognition of the existence of 'movable types' is not enough: I propose a thorough examination of how and why these types can move.

### Notes

1 Anonymous [William Crookes], 'Address to Students', *Chemical News*, 62, 19 September 1890 (1890), 139.
2 Anonymous [William Crookes], 'Address to Students', 139.
3 Anonymous [William Crookes], 'Address to Students', 139.
4 Margaret Beetham, 'Towards a Theory of the Periodical as a Publishing Genre', in *Investigating Victorian Journalism*, eds Laurel Brake, Aled Jones and Lionel Madden (London, 1990), p. 23.
5 Bruno Latour, *Pandora's Hope* (Cambridge MA, 1999), p. 40.
6 Latour, *Pandora's Hope*, p. 28. Emphasis is Latour's.
7 Jerome McGann, *Radiant Textuality* (New York, 2001), pp. 55–6, 80.
8 Kathryn Sutherland, 'Introduction', in *Electronic Text*, ed Kathryn Sutherland (Oxford, 1997), p. 12.
9 Sutherland, 'Introduction', pp. 13–14.
10 Walter Benjamin, 'The Work of Art in the Age of Mechanical Reproduction', *Illuminations*, ed. and trans. Hannah Arendt (Frankfurt, 1969), pp. 220–37.

11 Henri Lefebvre, *The Production of Space*, trans. Donald Nicholson-Smith (1991; Oxford, 2001), pp. 341–2.

12 Sutherland, 'Introduction', p. 12

13 Arthur Conan Doyle, 'Adventures of Sherlock Holmes: I. A Scandal in Bohemia', *Strand Magazine*, 2, July 1891 (1891), 61–75.

14 Arthur Conan Doyle, *The Sign of Four* (1890; London 2001), p. 9.

15 Doyle, *Sign of Four*, pp. 15, 17.

16 David Greetham, 'Coda: Is It Morphin Time?', in *Electronic Text*, p. 201.

17 H.G. Wells, *Tono-Bungay* (1908; London, 1994), p. 136

18 The Sciper index lists 20 articles on electricity in the first year of the *Review of Reviews* (1890). *Science in the Nineteenth-Century Periodical: An Electronic Index*, v. 1.0, hriOnline, http://www.sciper.org [accessed, 31 March 2006].

19 W.T. Stead, 'Looking Forward: A Romance of the Electric Age', *Review of Reviews*, 1, March 1890 (1890), 230.

20 Marshall McLuhan, *Understanding Media: The Extensions of Man* (1964; Cambridge MA, 1994), pp. 151–2.

21 Graeme Gooday, 'Profit and Prophecy: Electricity in the Late-Victorian Periodical', in Cantor and others, *Science in the Nineteenth-Century Periodical* (Cambridge, 2004), pp. 238–54.

22 Stephen Kern, *The Culture of Space and Time, 1880–1918* (London, 1983), p. 9 and Ronald Schleiffer, *Modernism and Time: The Logic of Abundance in Literature, Science, and Culture, 1880–1930* (Cambridge, 2000), pp. 131–2.

23 C. Mackenzie Jarvis, 'The Generation of Electricity', in *A History of Technology: 5 The Late Nineteenth Century c1850–1900*, eds Charles Singer and others, 7 vols (Oxford, 1950), pp. 177–207, especially 195–6. See also Thomas P. Hughes, *Networks of Power: Electrification in Western Society 1880–1930* (Baltimore, 1983), pp. 53–65, 227–60.

24 Hughes, *Networks of Power*, pp. 238–47.

25 Roger Luckhurst, *The Invention of Telepathy*, (Oxford, 2002), pp. 141–3.

26 Brian Winston, *Media Technology and Society: A History From the Telegraph to the Internet* (London, 1998), pp. 250–55.

27 Hughes, *Networks of Power*, pp. 60–65.

28 Anonymous, 'English Authorities on High-Tension Underground Circuits', *Electrical Review*, 26, 18 April 1890 (1890), 441–4; Hughes, *Networks of Power*, p. 227.

29 Figures from the *Electrician*, 5 January 1894, 246, 3 January 1896, 319 and 5 January 1900, 370. Cited in Carolyn Marvin, *When Old Technologies Were New: Thinking About Electric Communication in the Late Nineteenth Century* (Oxford, 1988), p. 164. Hughes cites a survey carried out for the Frankfort am Maine Exhibition in 1891 which claims London had 473,000 lamps, more than Berlin (75,000) and Paris (67,000): Hughes, *Networks of Power*, p. 247.

30 Kern, *Culture of Time and Space*, p. 29.

31 For a romp through the way the speed of electricity affected transport, growth, industrial production, and newspaper English see Kern, *Culture of Time and Space*, pp. 114–15.

32 Ernest de Vere Hill, 'Morgan's Automatic Electric Police Signalling System', *Electrical Review*, 26, 7 March 1890 (1890), 259–64.

33 Anonymous, untitled note, *Electrical Review*, 26, 31 January 1890 (1890), 123.

34 Anonymous, 'The Dangers of Telephones', *Electrical Review*, 26, 14 March 1890 (1890), 292.

35 Anonymous, 'The Telephone in the United States', *Electrical Review*, 26, 14 March 1890 (1890), 292.

36 Anonymous, 'Quick Work', *Tit-Bits*, 17, 1 February 1890 (1890), 263; Anonymous, 'Quick Work', *Electrical Review*, 26, 7 February 1890 (1890), 153.

37 'R.T.T.', 'Quick Work', *Electrical Review*, 26, 14 February 1890 (1890), 191.

38 Lord Bury, 'Wanted, a Word', *The Times*, 9 April 1890, 7. For William Coutts Keppel and the periodical press see Gooday, 'Prophet and prophecy', pp. 240–5.

39 W.H. Noble and others, 'A Verb for Electricity', *The Times*, 10 April 1890, 7.

40 E.C. Robinson and others, 'A Verb for Electric Progression', *The Times*, 11 April 1890, 5.

41 J.B. Harbord and others, 'A Verb for Electric Progression', *The Times*, 12 April 1890, 8.

42 Anonymous, 'Nomenclature', *Electrical Review*, 26, 18 April 1890 (1890), 423.

43 Albert Kaye Rollit, 'A Verb for Electric Progression', *The Times*, 14 April 1890, 6.

44 Anonymous, 'London, Monday, 14 April, 1890', *The Times*, 14 April 1890, 9.

45 John Law, 'Organizing Accountabilities: Ontology and the Mode of Accounting', in *Accountability: Power, Ethos and the Technologies of Accounting*, ed. Rolland Munro and Jan Mouritsen (London, 1996), p. 298.

46 Anonymous, 'Argumentum ad. Hominem', *Electrical Review*, 26, 10 January 1890 (1890), 26.

47 A.E. Dolbear, 'On Physical Fields', *Electrical Review*, 26, 31 January 1890 (1890), 115–16.

48 Anonymous, 'Physical Fields', *Electrical Review*, 26, 11 April 1890 (1890), 413–17. In an earlier article the editors chastize a 'Mr Schoolbred' for criticizing the language of flow and current, endorsing instead transmission of instability between molecules. They write 'We cannot say that Mr Schoolbred's definition is incorrect; we only remind his that it is not yet generally recognized.' Anonymous, 'The Vagaries of Electricians', *Electrical Review*, 26, 7 February 1890 (1890), 142.

49 The cultural network through which electricity flowed was therefore not congruent with the transmission networks of electrical power. It is important to reiterate the historical contingency of the network, as to imply its transcendence imposes an anachronistic concept from late twentieth-century systems analysis onto the past, creating a teleological reading of the history of technology that sees it as an aberrant, imperfect ancestor.

50 See Iwan Morus, 'Batteries, Bodies and Belts: Making Careers in Victorian Medical Electricity', in *Electric Bodies: Episodes in the History of Medical Electricity*, eds Paola Bertucci and Giuliano Pancaldi (Bolgona, 2001), pp. 209–38; Lori Loeb, 'Consumerism and Commercial Electrotherapy: The Medical Battery Company in Nineteenth Century London', *Journal of Victorian Culture*, 4 (1999), 252–75; Takahiro Ueyama, 'Capital, Profession and Medical Technology: the Electro-Therapeutic Institutes and the Royal College of Physicians 1888–1922', *Medical History*, 42 (1997), 150–81.

51 Ueyama, 'Capital, Profession and Medical Technology', 172.

52 Two of his staff formed a rival company in 1887. Ueyama, 'Capital, Profession and Medical Technology', 172. For other electropathic belts see the advertisements for 'Dr Pierce's Magnetic Electric Truss', *Illustrated London News*, 96, 26 April 1890 (1890), 541 and 'Pulvermacher's Galvanic Establishment', *The Times*, 25 December 1885, 2.

53 The variation is because Harness characteristically used these figures as advertising in their own right. See Lori Loeb, 'Consumerism and Commercial Electrotherapy',

252–75; Anonymous, 'The Charges Against Mr Harness', *The Times*, 16 November 1893, 10; Anonymous, 'Advertisements', *The Times*, 25 May 1891, 12, respectively.

54 For instance the advertisement in *The Times*, 6 October 1890, 12 combines 'A Barrister's Opinion' with 'A Clergyman's Opinion' and 'A Lieutenant's Opinion.' It also offers the contrast between 'Interesting to Cricketers', indicating the belt's utility for sportsmen, and 'Important for Weak Men', which promises restoration of vitality for those who '"sow their wild oats" to such a lamentable extent.'

55 See Ueyama, 'Capital, Profession and Medical Technology'; Morus, 'Batteries, Bodies and Belts'; Loeb, 'Consumerism and Commercial Electrotherapy.'

56 Morus, 'Batteries, Bodies and Belts', p. 229.

57 Loeb, 'Consumerism and Commercial Electrotherapy', 269.

58 Loeb, 'Consumerism and Commercial Electrotherapy', 258.

59 See for instance the details of Leeson v. General Medical Council: Anonymous, 'News', *The Times*, 14 December 1889, 11. A reporter from *Pearson's Weekly*, quoted in an advertisement printed in *The Times*, rhapsodizes on the scientific research that goes on in the showrooms while also detailing their private, comfortable nature. See Anonymous, 'Advertisements', 12

60 See Anonymous, 'Advertisements', 12, and Anonymous, 'Mr C.B. Harness's Electropathic Belts', *Illustrated London News*, 96, 15 March 1890 (1890), 350.

61 For details of the three libel cases that eventually ruined Harness see 'Tibbits vs Alabaster and Others' in 'Law Reports', *The Times*, 16 and 17 February 1893, 13 and 14 respectively. Further details emerged when Alabaster sued Harness for the funds won in 'Tibbits vs Alabaster' in 1894: see Anonymous, 'Law Reports', *The Times*, 16 February 1894, 13. See also Ueyama, 'Capital, Profession and Medical Technology', 169–74.

62 Anonymous, 'Legal: The Medical Battery Company v. Jeffrey', *Electrical Review*, 22 July 1892, 99–101.

63 See for instance Anonymous, untitled advertisement, *Illustrated London News*, 96, 19 April 1890 (1890), 512.

64 Anonymous, 'Electropathic Belts', *Electrical Review*, 31, 22 July 1892 (1892), 101.

65 Anonymous, 'Legal: The Medical Battery Company v. Jeffrey', 101.

66 Anonymous, 'Legal: The Medical Battery Company v. Jeffrey', 101.

67 Anonymous, 'Electropathic Belts', 102.

68 'Electric', 'Electric Body Belt', *English Mechanic*, 55, 24 June 1892 (1892), 417.

69 W.E. Harper, 'Electric Belts', *English Mechanic*, 55, 8 July 1892 (1892), 464.

70 S. Bottone, 'Electric Belts', *English Mechanic*, 55, 15 July 1892 (1892), 485.

71 D. Perry, 'Electric Belt', *English Mechanic*, 55, 15 July 1892 (1892), 488.

72 S. Robert Bonney, 'Electric Belt', *English Mechanic*, 55, 22 July 1892 (1892), 510, and S. Bottone, 'Electric Belt', *English Mechanic*, 55, 22 July 1892 (1892), 510.

73 'Jubar', 'Electric Body Belt', 5 August 1892 (1892), 557.

74 For instance Anonymous, 'The Press and Electro-Medical Remedies', *Electrical Review*, 32, 17 March 1893 (1893), 301–2 and Anonymous, 'Electricity and the Medical Profession', *Electrical Review*, 31, 23 September 1892 (1892), 365–67.

75 Anonymous, untitled, *Electrical Review*, 26, 17 January 1890, (1890), 55–6.

76 Anonymous, 'Scientific Societies' Advertisements', *Electrical Review*, 26, 3 January 1890 (1890), 1.

77 Anonymous, 'A Note on a Modern Instrument', *Electrical Review*, 26, 31 January (1890), 121.

78 Anonymous, 'Electrical Engineers', *Electrical Review*, 26, 3 January 1890 (1890), 1.

79 Anonymous, 'Electropathic Belts', 102.
80 Anonymous, untitled, *English Mechanic*, 55, 17 June 1892 (1892), 393. This advertisement was one of several that ran through *The Times* and the *English Mechanic* in 1892.
81 See the wrapper to *Electrical Review*, 26, 3 January 1890, i–xx.
82 Mary Howarth, 'The Telegram', *Pall Mall Magazine*, 6, July 1895 (1895), 355–64.
83 Howarth, 'The Telegram', 357.
84 See the Introduction. At the British Society for the History of Science Annual Conference, Liverpool Hope University College 25–27 June 2004, a special panel chaired by Peter Morris, Senior Curator of Chemistry at the Science Museum in London, entitled 'Using Objects in the History of Science and Technology' explored why historians did not use museum collections as a historical resource.

# Bibliography

Entries are listed alphabetically by surname and then by date.

Abel, C.B., D.C.L., D.Sc., F.R.S., V.P.R.I., Sir Frederick, 'Smokeless Explosives', *Chemical News*, 61, 21 March 1890 (1890), 142–4.

———, 'Smokeless Explosives', *Chemical News*, 61, 28 March 1890 (1890), 147–50.

Abel, Sir Frederick, 'Smokeless Explosions', *Nature*, 41, 6 February 1890 (1890), 328–30.

Alberti, Samuel J.M.M., 'Amateurs and Professionals in One County: Biology and Natural History in Late Nineteenth Century Yorkshire', *Journal of the History of Biology*, 34 (2001), 115–47.

Allen, Grant, 'Character Sketch: Professor Tyndall', *Review of Reviews*, 9, January 1894 (1894), 21–6.

'An Analytical Chemist', 'Simple Exercises in Technical Analysis', *English Mechanic*, 47, 20 April 1888 (1888), 159–60.

Anderson, Benedict, *Imagined Communities: Reflections on the Origin and Spread of Nationalism* (1983; London: Verso, 1991).

Anonymous, 'Prize Competition', *Great Thoughts*, 1, 5 January 1884 (1884), 1.

Anonymous, 'Pulvermacher's Galvanic Establishment', *The Times*, 25 December 1885, 2.

Anonymous, untitled advertisement, *Companion to the Observatory* (1889), unpaginated.

Anonymous, 'News', *The Times*, 14 December 1889, 11.

Anonymous, 'Electrical Engineers', *Electrical Review*, 26, 3 January 1890 (1890), 1.

Anonymous, 'Scientific Societies' Advertisements', *Electrical Review*, 26, 3 January 1890 (1890), 1.

Anonymous, 'Metropolitan and Provincial News', *British and Colonial Druggist*, 17, 4 January 1890 (1890), 5–10.

Anonymous, 'Threshold of Manhood', *Great Thoughts*, 13, 4 January 1890 (1890), 6–7.

Anonymous, 'Gaseous Illuminants', *Nature*, 43, 8 January 1890 (1890), 233–5.

Anonymous, 'Argumentum ad. Hominem', *Electrical Review*, 26, 10 January 1890 (1890), 26.

Anonymous, 'Provincial Reports', *Chemist and Druggist*, 36, 11 January 1890 (1890), 30–33.

Anonymous, 'Gaseous Illuminants', *Nature*, 43, 15 January 1890 (1890), 257–60.

Anonymous, untitled, *Electrical Review*, 26, 17 January 1890, (1890), 55–6.

Anonymous, 'Edinburgh Chemists' Assistants' and Apprentices Association', *Chemist and Druggist*, 36, 18 January 1890 (1890), 70–72.

Anonymous, 'Blank and the Epidemic', *Chemist and Druggist*, 36, 18 January 1890 (1890), 78.

Anonymous, 'Gaseous Illuminants', *Nature*, 43, 22 January 1890 (1890), 282–3.

Anonymous, 'A Note on a Modern Instrument', *Electrical Review*, 26, 31 January (1890), 121.

Anonymous, untitled note, *Electrical Review*, 26, 31 January 1890 (1890), 123.

Anonymous, 'Report of the Council to the Seventieth Annual General Meeting of the Society', *Monthly Notices of the Royal Astronomical Society*, 50, February 1890 (1890), 141–264.

Anonymous, 'Quick Work', *Tit-Bits*, 17, 1 February 1890 (1890), 263.

Anonymous, 'The Vagaries of Electricians', *Electrical Review*, 26, 7 February 1890 (1890), 142.

Anonymous, 'Quick Work', *Electrical Review*, 26, 7 February 1890 (1890), 153.

Anonymous, 'The Jubilee of the Chemical Society', *The Times*, 25 February 1890, 9.

Anonymous, 'Court Circular', *The Times*, 25 February 1890, 14

Anonymous, 'The Chemical Society's Jubilee' *The Times*, 26 February 1890, 6.

Anonymous, untitled leading article, *The Times*, 26 February 1890, 9.

Anonymous, 'What is a Patent Medicine?', *Pharmaceutical Journal*, 1 March 1890 (1890), 714–15.

Anonymous, '"Some Crystalline Substances Obtained From the Fruits of Various Species of *Citrus*", by William A. Tilden, D.Sc., F.R.S., and Charles R. Beck', *Proceedings of the Chemical Society*, 6, 12 March 1890 (1890), 29–34.

Anonymous, 'The Dangers of Telephones', *Electrical Review*, 26, 14 March 1890 (1890), 292.

Anonymous, 'The Telephone in the United States', *Electrical Review*, 26, 14 March 1890 (1890), 292.

Anonymous, 'Diary of Societies', *Nature*, 41, 20 March 1890 (1890), 480.

Anonymous, 'The Glow of Phosphorous', *Nature*, 41, 3 April 1890 (1890), 523–4.

Anonymous, 'Physical Fields', *Electrical Review*, 26, 11 April 1890 (1890), 413–17.

Anonymous, 'London, Monday, 14 April, 1890', *The Times*, 14 April 1890, 9.

Anonymous, 'Nomenclature', *Electrical Review*, 26, 18 April 1890 (1890), 423.

Anonymous, 'English Authorities on High-Tension Underground Circuits', *Electrical Review*, 26, 18 April 1890 (1890), 441–4.

Anonymous, untitled advertisement, *Illustrated London News*, 96, 19 April 1890 (1890), 512.

Anonymous, 'Dr Pierce's Magnetic Electric Truss', *Illustrated London News*, 96, 26 April 1890 (1890), 541.

Anonymous, '"An Investigation of the conditions under which hydrogen peroxide is formed from ether." By Professor Wyndham R. Dunstan and T.S. Dymond', *Proceedings of the Chemical Society*, 6, 9 May 1890 (1890), 70–71.

Anonymous, 'Proceedings of Societies', *Chemical News*, 61, 16 May 1890 (1890), 237–79.

Anonymous, 'Societies', *Athenaeum*, 23 May 1891 (1891), 671.

Anonymous, 'Proceedings of Societies in London', *Pharmaceutical Journal and Transactions*, 20, 31 May 1890 (1890), 989–94.

Anonymous, 'Publications', *The Observatory*, 13, July 1890 (1890), 252–5.

Anonymous 'British Association for the Advancement of Science', *Nature*, 42, 28 August 1890 (1890), xxxviii.

Anonymous, 'The British Association, Leeds, Tuesday Evening', *Nature*, 42, 4 September 1890 (1890), 454–6.

Anonymous, 'Sir Frederick Abel, C.B., FRS', *Illustrated London News*, 97, 6 September 1890 (1890), 292.

Anonymous, 'The British Association', *Illustrated London News*, 97, 6 September 1890 (1890), 302.

Anonymous, 'The British Association, Wednesday Morning', *Nature*, 42, 11 September 1890 (1890), 463–85.

Anonymous, 'Chemistry at the British Association', *Nature*, 42, 25 September 1890 (1890), 530–31.

Anonymous, 'Officers and Council,', *Journal of the British Astronomical Association*, 1, October 1890 (1890), 8–9.

Anonymous, 'Report of the Meeting of the Association Held November 26, 1890', *Journal of the British Astronomical Association*, 1, November 1890 (1890), 49–58.

Anonymous, 'Diary of Societies', *Nature*, 43, 20 November 1890 (1890), xxi.

Anonymous, 'E. Dent & Co.', *The Observatory*, 13, December 1890 (1890), unpaginated.

Anonymous, 'Diary of Societies', *Nature*, 43, 4 December 1890 (1890), xxxvii.

Anonymous. 'Diary of Societies', *Nature*, 43, 11 December 1890 (1890), xlv.

Anonymous, 'Portraits of Celebrities at Different Times of their Lives', *Strand*, 1, January 1891 (1891), 41–8.

Anonymous, 'Miscellaneous', *Chemical News*, 63, 30 January 1891 (1891), 62.

Anonymous, 'Portraits of Celebrities at Different Times of their Lives', *Strand*, 1, February 1891 (1891), 154–61.

Anonymous, 'Report of the Meeting of the Association Held March 25, 1891', *JBAA*, 1, March 1891, (1891), 295–7.

Anonymous, 'The Chemical Society's Jubilee', *Nature*, 43, 12 March 1891 (1891), 440–43.

Anonymous, 'Proceedings of Societies', *Chemical News*, 63, 20 March 1891 (1891), 137–9.

Anonymous, 'Societies', *Athenaeum*, 6 Jun 1891 (1891), 736.

Anonymous, 'Advertisements', *The Times*, 25 May 1891, 12.

Anonymous, 'Portraits of Celebrities at Different Times of their Lives', *Strand*, 2, September 1891 (1891), 274–80.

Anonymous, 'Dollond's', *Journal of the British Astronomical Association*, 2, October 1891 (1891), unpaginated.

Anonymous, 'Portraits of Celebrities', *Strand*, 2, December 1891 (1891), 600–607.

Anonymous, 'Societies', *Athenaeum*, 5 December 1891 (1891), 765–6.

Anonymous, untitled, *English Mechanic*, 55, 17 June 1892 (1892), 393.

Anonymous, untitled editorial note, *Strand*, 4, July 1892 (1892), 82.

Anonymous, 'Legal: The Medical Battery Company v. Jeffrey', *Electrical Review*, 22 July 1892 (1892), 99–101.

Anonymous, 'Electropathic Belts', *Electrical Review*, 31, 22 July 1892 (1892), 101–2.

Anonymous, 'Electricity and the Medical Profession', *Electrical Review*, 31, 23 September 1892 (1892), 365–7.

Anonymous, 'Autumn Revelations', *Great Thoughts* 13, 15 October 1892 (1892), 42.

Anonymous, 'Tennysoniana', *Great Thoughts*, 13, 22 October 1892 (1892), 71.

Anonymous, 'Counsels for Young Men', *Great Thoughts*, 18, 12 November 1892 (1892), 106.

Anonymous, 'Portraits of Celebrities', *Strand*, 4, December 1892 (1892), 589–93.

Anonymous, 'A Description of the Offices of the *Strand Magazine*', 4, December 1892 (1892), 594–606.

Anonymous, 'The Press and Electro-Medical Remedies', *Electrical* Review, 32, 17 March 1893 (1893), 301–2.

Anonymous, 'Meeting of the British Association at Nottingham', *Illustrated London News*, 103, 9 September 1893 (1893), 323–4.

Anonymous, 'The British Association at Nottingham: Professor Burdon Sanderson Delivering the Inaugural Address', *Illustrated London News*, 103, 23 September 1893 (1893), 371.

Anonymous, 'The British Association at Nottingham: Professor Burdon Sanderson Delivering the Inaugural Address', *Illustrated London News*, 103, 23 September 1893 (1893), 387.

Anonymous, 'The Charges Against Mr Harness', *The Times*, 16 November 1893, 10.

Anonymous, 'Professor Tyndall', *Great Thoughts*, 20, 30 December 1893 (1893), 270–73.

Anonymous, *Minutes of the Publication Committee 27 January 1887–21st December 1893*, unpublished minute book, Royal Society of Chemistry (1893).

Anonymous, *Chemical Society: Minutes of Council Meetings 19 April 1883–27 March 1893*, unpublished minute book, Royal Chemical Society (1893).

Anonymous, 'Counsels for Young Men', *Great Thoughts*, 20, 27 January 1894 (1894), 359.

Anonymous, 'Law Reports', *The Times*, 16 February 1894, 13.

Anonymous, 'Advertisements', *The Times*, 23 March 1895, 2.

Anonymous, 'Tour the Waterloo Directory of English Newspapers and Periodicals, 1800–1900', *Waterloo Directory of Victorian Periodicals: 1800–1900*, ed. John S. North, www.victorianperiodicals.com [accessed 31 March 2006].

Anonymous [H.E. Armstrong], *The Jubilee Chemical Society of London 1891: Record of the Proceedings Together with an Account of the History and Development of the Society 1841–1891* (London, 1896).

Anonymous [A.A. Common and H.H. Turner], untitled editorial note, *The Observatory*, 13, August 1890 (1890), 279.

Anonymous [William Crookes], 'Sealed Papers', *Chemical News*, 61, 14 March 1890 (1890), 123.

Anonymous [William Crookes], 'Address to Students', *Chemical News*, 62, 19 September 1890 (1890), 139–40.

Anonymous [Arthur Conan Doyle], 'The Voice of Science', *Strand*, 1, March 1891 (1891), 312–17.

Anonymous [Robert P. Downes], '£50 Cash Prizes', *Great Thoughts*, 20, 14 October 1893 (1893), unpaginated.

Anonymous [C.E. Groves], 'Annual General Meeting', *Journal of the Chemical Society*, 55 (1889), 251–85.

Anonymous [C.E. Groves], 'Annual General Meeting', *Journal of the Chemical Society*, 57 (1890), 426–57.

Anonymous [C.E. Groves], 'Instructions to Abstractors, giving the Nomenclature and System of Notation Adopted in the Abstracts', *Journal of the Chemical Society*, 58 (1890), i–lxii.

Anonymous [E.W. Maunder], 'Rules of the British Astronomical Association', *Journal of the British Astronomcial Association*, 1, October 1890 (1890), 9–14.

Anonymous [A.C. Ranyard], 'The Great Nebula in Andromeda', *Knowledge*, 12, March 1889 (1889), 108.

Anonymous [W.T. Stead], 'History of Periodicals', *Index to the Periodicals of the World* (London, 1892), 6–8.

Anonymous [John Richard Vernon], 'Clevedon and A.H.H', *Great Thoughts*, 18, 12 November 1892 (1892), 106–7.

Anonymous [A.C. Wootton], 'The Pharmacopœia Addendum', *Chemist and Druggist*, 36, 25 January 1890 (1890), 117.

Armstrong, Isobel, *Victorian Poetry: Poetry, Politics and Poetics* (London: Routledge, 1993).

Arnold, Matthew, *Culture and Anarchy* (Cambridge: Cambridge University Press, 1970).

A.W.R [Alexander Wood Renton] and T.A.I. [Thomas Allan Ingram], 'Patents', *Encyclopaedia Britannica*, 20, 11th ed. (Cambridge, 1911), pp. 903–11.

Bakhtin, M.M., / P.N. Medvedev, *The Formal Method in Literary Scholarship*, trans. Albert J. Wherle (1978; Baltimore: John Hopkins University Press, 1991).

———, 'Forms of time and of the chronotope in the novel: Notes towards a Historical Poetics', in *The Dialogic Imagination*, ed. Michael Holquist, trans.

Michael Holquist and Caryl Emerson (1981; Austin: University of Texas Press, 1996), pp. 84–258.

———, 'Discourse in the Novel', in *The Dialogic Imagination*, ed. Michael Holquist, trans. Michael Holquist and Caryl Emerson (1981; Austin: University of Texas Press 1996), pp. 259–422.

Barnard, E.E., 'On the Comparison of the Photographs of the Milky Way in α=17H 56M. δ=-28° in *Knowledge* for July 1890, and March 1891', *Knowledge*, 14, May 1891 (1891), 93.

Barthes, Roland, 'From Work to Text', *Image, Music, Text*, ed. and trans. Stephen Heath (1961; London: Fontana, 1977), pp. 155–64.

Bastian, H.C., 'Spontaneous Generation: A Reply to Professor Tyndall', *Nineteenth Century*, 3, February 1878 (1878), 261–77.

Becker, Barbara J., 'Priority, Persuasion, and the Virtue of Perseverance: William Huggins's Efforts to Photograph the Solar Corona Without an Eclipse', *Journal for the History of Astronomy*, 31 (2000), 223–43.

Beetham, Margaret, 'Open and Closed: the Periodical as a Publishing Genre', *Victorian Periodicals Review*, 22 (1989), 96–100.

———, 'Towards a Theory of the Periodical as a Publishing Genre', in *Investigating Victorian Journalism*, eds Laurel Brake, Aled Jones and Lionel Madden (London: Macmillan, 1990), pp. 19–32.

Benjamin, Walter, 'The Work of Art in the Age of Mechanical Reproduction', *Illuminations*, ed. and trans. Hannah Arendt (Frankfurt: Suhrkamp Verlag, 1969), pp. 220–37.

Bennett, Tony, 'Media, "Reality", Signification', in *Culture, Society and the Media*, eds Michael Gurevitch and others (1982; London: Routledge, 1988), pp. 287–308.

Berger, John, *Ways of Seeing* (London: Penguin, 1972).

Bergson, Henri, *Time and Free Will*, trans. F.L. Pogson (1910; London: Allen and Unwin, 1971).

Berman, Morris, '"Hegemony" and the Amateur Tradition in British Science', *Journal of Social History*, 8 (1975), 30–50.

Berridge, Virginia, and Griffith Edwards, *Opium and the People: Opiate Use in Nineteenth Century England* (London: Allen Lane, 1981).

Bertucci, Paola, and Giuliano Pancaldi (eds), *Electric Bodies: Episodes in the History of Medical Electricity* (Bolgona: Università di Bologna, 2001).

Bonney, S. Robert, 'Electric Belt', *English Mechanic*, 55, 22 July 1892 (1892), 510.

Bottone, S., 'Electric Belts', *English Mechanic*, 55, 15 July 1892 (1892), 485.

———, 'Electric Belt', *English Mechanic*, 55, 22 July 1892 (1892), 510.

Boys, C.V., 'Quartz Fibres', *Nature*, 42, 16 October 1890 (1890), 604–8.

Brake, Laurel, Aled Jones and Lionel Madden (eds), *Investigating Victorian Journalism* (London: Macmillan, 1990).

———, *Subjugated Knowledges: Journalism, Gender and Literature* (London: Palgrave, 1994).

————, Bill Bell and David Finkelstein (eds), *Nineteenth-Century Media and the Construction of Identities* (London: Palgrave, 2000).

Brock, W.H., 'The Development of Commercial Science Journals in Victorian Britain', in *Development of Science Publishing in Europe*, ed. A.J. Meadows (Amsterdam, 1980), 95–122.

————, 'The *Chemical News*', *Bulletin for the History of Chemistry*, 12 (1992), 30–35.

————, *The Fontana History of Chemistry* (London: Fontana, 1992).

————, 'The Making of an Editor', *Culture and Science in the Nineteenth-Century Media*, eds Henson and others (Aldershot: Ashgate, 2004), pp. 189–98.

Brock, W.H., and A.J. Meadows, *The Lamp of Learning* (1984; London: Taylor and Francis, 1998).

Brodie, Frederick, untitled correspondence, *The Observatory*, 13, August 1890 (1890), 279.

Broks, Peter, *Media Science before the Great War* (London: Macmillan, 1996).

Brown, E., 'An Amateur Astronomers' Association', *English Mechanic*, 51, 25 July 1890 (1890), 463.

————, 'Solar Section', *JBAA*, 1, November 1890 (1890), 58–60.

Bud, R.F., and G.K. Roberts, *Science versus Practice: Chemistry in Victorian Britain* (Manchester: Manchester University Press, 1984).

Bury, Lord, [William Coutts Keppel], 'Wanted, a Word', *The Times*, 9 April 1890, 7.

Cahn, R.S., and O.C. Dermer, *Introduction to Chemical Nomenclature*, 5th ed (1959; London and Boston: Butterworths, 1979).

Caillon, Roger, 'The Detective Novel as Game', in *The Poetics of Murder: Detective Fiction and Literary Theory*, eds Glenn W. Most and William W. Stowe (San Diego: Harcourt, Bruce, Javonavich, 1983), pp. 1–12.

Callon, Michel, and John Law, 'On interests and their transformation: Enrolment and counter-enrolment', *Social Studies of Science*, 12 (1982), 615–26.

Calver, G., 'The Telescope', *English Mechanic*, 51, 1 August 1890 (1890), 488.

Cantor, Geoffrey, and Sally Shuttleworth, 'Introduction', *Science Serialized: Representations of the Sciences in Nineteenth-Century Periodicals*, eds Geoffrey Cantor and Sally Shuttleworth (Cambridge MA: MIT Press 2004), pp. 1–15.

———— (eds), *Science Serialized: Representations of the Sciences in Nineteenth-Century Periodicals* (Cambridge MA: MIT Press, 2004).

Cantor, Geoffrey, and others, 'Introduction', in *Culture and Science in the Nineteenth-Century Media*, ed. Louise Henson and others (Aldershot, 2004), pp. xvii–xxv.

Cantor, Geoffrey, and others, *Science in the Nineteenth Century Periodical* (Cambridge: Cambridge University Press, 2004).

Cantor, Geoffrey, and others, *Science in the Nineteenth-Century Periodical: An Electronic Index*, v. 1.0, hriOnline, http://www.sciper.org [accessed, 31 March 2006].

Cardwell, D.S.L., *The Organization of Science in England* (1957; London: Heinemann, 1972).

Carlyle, Thomas, *Sartor Resartus*, ed. Kerry McSweeney and Peter Sabor (1833; Oxford: Oxford University Press, 1987).

Carr-Saunders, A.M., and P.A. Wilson, *The Professions* (Oxford: Clarendon, 1933).

Cetina, Karin Knorr, 'The Couch, the Cathedral, and the Laboratory', in *Science as Practice and Culture*, ed. Andrew Pickering (Chicago: University of Chicago Press, 1992), pp. 113–36.

Chapman, Allan, *The Victorian Amateur Astronomer* (Chichester: Praxis, 1998).

Churnside, R.C., and J.H. Hamence, *The Practising Chemists: A History of the Society for Analytical Chemistry 1874–1974* (London: Society for Analytical Chemists, 1974).

Clapham, T.R., untitled correspondence, *The Observatory*, 13, August 1890, (1890), 279.

Clapperton, Jane Hume, *Margaret Dunmore, or A Socialist Home* (1888; London: Swan Sonnenschein, 1892).

Clerke, Agnes. M., *The System of the Stars* (London: Longmans, Green and Co., 1890).

Clodd, Edward, and Capt Noble, 'In Memoriam: Richard Anthony Proctor', *Knowledge*, 11, November 1888 (1888), 265.

Collins, Wilkie, *Heart and Science: a Story of the Present Time* (1883; Peterborough Ontario: Broadview, 1996).

Cooter, Roger, and Steven Pumfrey, 'Separate Spheres and Public Places: Reflections on the History of Science Popularization and Science in Popular Culture', *History of Science*, 32 (1994), 237–67.

Creese, Mary R.S., 'British Women of the Nineteenth and Early Twentieth Centuries Who Contributed to Research in the Chemical Sciences', *British Journal for the History of Science*, 24 (1991), 275–305.

———, 'Elizabeth Brown, solar astronomer', *Journal of the British Astronomical Association*, 108 (1998), 193–7.

———, *Ladies in the Laboratory: American and British Women in Science, 1800–1900* (London: Scarecrow Press, 1998).

Crosland, Maurice P., *Historical Studies in the History of Chemistry* (London: Heinemann, 1962).

Daston, Lorraine, 'The Coming into Being of Scientific Objects', in *Biographies of Scientific Objects*, ed. Lorraine Daston (Chicago: Chicago University Press, 2000), pp. 1–14.

Desmond, Adrian, 'Artisan Resistance and Evolution in Britain, 1819–1848', *Osiris*, 3 (1987), 375–404.

'Dick Donovan' [J.E. Preston Muddock], 'The Tuft of Red Hair', *The Man-Hunter: Stories from the Notebook of a Detective* (London, 1888), pp. 77–94.

———, 'A Romance from a Detective's Casebook: The Jewelled Skull', *Strand*, 4, July 1892 (1892), 70–82.

Dolbear, A.E., 'On Physical Fields', *Electrical Review*, 26, 31 January 1890 (1890), 115–16.

Downes LLD., Robert P., 'Preface to Volume XVIII', *Great Thoughts*, 18 (1893), unpaginated.

Downes, Robert P., *Pillars of Our Faith: A Study in Christian Evidence* (London: A.W. Hall, 1893).

Doyle, Arthur Conan, 'A Physiologist's Wife', *Blackwood's Edinburgh Magazine*, 148, September 1890 (1890), 339–51.

———, 'Adventures of Sherlock Holmes: I. A Scandal in Bohemia', *Strand Magazine*, 2, July 1891 (1891), 61–75.

———, 'Adventures of Sherlock Holmes: III. A Case of Identity', *Strand*, 2, September 1891 (1891), 248–59.

———, 'Adventures of Sherlock Holmes: II. The Red-Headed League', *Strand*, 2, August 1891 (1891), 190–204.

———, 'Adventures of Sherlock Holmes: IV. The Boscombe Valley Mystery', *Strand*, 2, October 1891 (1891), 401–16.

———, 'Adventures of Sherlock Holmes: VII. The Adventure of the Blue Carbuncle,' *Strand*, 3, January 1892 (1892), 73–85.

———, 'Adventures of Sherlock Holmes: VIII. The Adventure of the Speckled Band', *Strand*, 3, February 1892 (1892), 142–57.

———, 'The Adventures of Sherlock Holmes: IX. The Engineer's Thumb', *Strand*, 3, March 1892 (1892), 276–88.

———, 'Adventures of Sherlock Holmes: XII The Adventure of the Copper Beeches', *Strand*, 3, June 1892 (1892), 613–28.

———, 'Adventures of Sherlock Holmes: XIII. The Adventure of Silver Blaze', *Strand*, 4, December 1892 (1892), 645–60.

———, 'Adventures of Sherlock Holmes: XV. The Adventure of the Yellow Face', *Strand*, 5, February 1893 (1893), 162–72.

———, 'Adventures of Sherlock Holmes: XX. The Adventure of the Crooked Man', *Strand*, 6, July 1893 (1893), 22–32.

———, 'Adventures of Sherlock Holmes: XXIV. The Final Problem', *Strand*, 6, December 1893 (1893), 559–70.

———, *The Sign of Four* (1890; London: Penguin, 2001).

Duke, P.F., 'Planetary and Star Matters', *English Mechanic*, 49, 22 March 1889 (1889), 91.

———, 'British Astronomical Association', *The Observatory*, 12, December 1890 (1890), 391.

'The Editor' [Robert P. Downes], 'Preface to Vol. XX', *Great Thoughts from Master Minds*, 20 (1894), unpaginated.

'Eds' [A.A. Common and H.H. Turner], 'Correspondence', *The Observatory*, 13, August 1890 (1890), 276.

'Electric', 'Electric Body Belt', *English Mechanic*, 55, 24 June 1892 (1892), 417.

'E.L.G.', 'Flat Earth v. Round Earth', *English Mechanic*, 47, 4 May 1888 (1888), 216.

Elger, T.G.E., 'Selenographical Notes', *The Observatory*, 13, December 1890 (1890), 387–8.

Elvins, A., 'Planetary Influence on Weather', *English Mechanic*, 51, 8 August 1890 (1890), 512.

Ericson, Richard, Patricia Baranek and Janet Chan, *Visualizing Deviance: a Study of News Organization* (Toronto: University of Toronto Press, 1987).

'F.C.A.', 'Practical Electric Bell Fitting', *English Mechanic*, 47, 20 April 1888 (1888), 159–60.

Fido, Martin, *The World of Sherlock Holmes* (London: Carlton, 1998).

Fitzgerald, William G., 'Some Wonders of the Microscope', *Strand*, 12, August 1896 (1896), 210–16.

'Flauto', 'Piccolo', *English Mechanic*, 47, 2 March 1888 (1888), 20.

Foucault, Michel, 'What is an Author?', *Screen*, 20 (1970), 13–29.

———, *The Order of Things* (London: Tavistock, 1970).

———, *The Archaeology of Knowledge* (1972; London: Tavistock, 2001).

Francis, S. Trevor, 'Tennyson', *Great Thoughts*, 22 October 1892 (1892), 71–2.

Franks, W.S., 'Coloured Star Section', *Journal of the British Astronomical Association*, 1, November 1890 (1890), 68–72.

———, 'Coloured Star Section', *Journal of the British Astronomical Association*, 1, December 1890, (1890), 122–5.

———, 'The Determination of Star Colours', *Journal of the British Astronomical Association*, 1, March 1891 (1891), 301–2.

'FRAS', 'American Criticism on the Lick Observatory – Books Worth Reading – Velocity of the Earth in her Orbit – Ordnance Datum – other Planetoids – Telescope – Adjusting Eyepiece', *English Mechanic*, 47, 20 April 1888 (1888), 167.

———, 'Stellar spectra: the Henry Draper Memorial – Erratum – Alioth and other Circumpolar Stars and the *Nautical Almanac* – Whether "Forecasts" are Worth Making? – Alcoholism – Eclipses – Aneroid Barometers – Rifle-Ball and Gravity – "Si Momentum Requiris" – Dr Terby and "FRAS" – Second Revolution (?) of the Earth – Pendulum – Achromatic Object-Glass', *English Mechanic*, 51, 13 June 1890 (1890), 334–5.

———, 'Errata – Saturn – Electricity and Photography: the Duration of a Lightning Flash – Planetary Influence on Weather – Huggins – Rain-Gauge – Deviation of the Magnetic Needle – The Liverpool Astronomical Society – Grant's "History of Physical Astronomy" – Astro-Meteorology – "Fellows" of Societies – Moonrise from Snowdon – Camera Lucida', *English Mechanic*, 51, 22 August 1890 (1890), 551–2.

Fraser, Hilary, Judith Johnstone, and Stephanie Green, *Gender and the Victorian Periodical* (Cambridge: Cambridge University Press, 2003).

Frow, John, 'Intertextuality and Ontology', in *Intertextuality: Theories and Practices*, eds Michael Worton and Judith Still (Manchester, 1990), pp. 45–55.

'F.S.S.', 'Flat Earth v. Round Earth' *English Mechanic*, 47, 11 May 1888 (1888), 234.

Garnett LLD., Richard, 'The Late Professor Tyndall', *Illustrated London News*, 103, 16 December 1893 (1893), 759–60.

Gay, Hannah, 'Invisible Resource: William Crookes and his Circle of Support, 1871–81', *British Journal for the History of Science*, 29 (1996), 311–36.

Gooday, Graeme, 'Profit and Prophecy: Electricity in the Late-Victorian Periodical', in Cantor and others, *Science in the Nineteenth-Century Periodical* (Cambridge, 2004), 238–54.

Green, Richard Lancelyn, 'Explanatory Notes', in Arthur Conan Doyle, *The Adventures of Sherlock Holmes*, ed. Richard Lancelyn Green (Oxford: Oxford University Press, 1993), pp. 297–389.

Greetham, David, 'Coda: Is It Morphin Time?', in *Electronic Text*, ed. Kathryn Sutherland (Oxford: Clarendon, 1997), pp. 199–226.

Habermas, Jürgen, *The Structural Transformation of the Public Sphere*, trans. Thomas Burger with the assistance of Frederick Lawrence (London: Polity Press, 1989).

Hammond, J.R., *Herbert George Wells: An Annotated Bibliography of His Works* (New York: Garland, 1977).

Hammond, P.W., and Harold Egan, *Weighed in the Balance: a history of the Laboratory of the Government Chemist* (London: HMSO, 1992).

Hampden, John, 'The Southern Heavens and the Flat Earth', *English Mechanic*, 47, 27 April 1888 (1888), 190.

———, 'Gradients', *English Mechanic*, 47, 4 May 1888 (1888), 217.

———, 'Flat Earth', *English Mechanic*, 47, 11 May 1888 (1888), 235.

Hampden, John, and George Peacock FRGS, *Is the World Flat or Round?* (Gloucester: John Bellowes, 1871).

Haraway, Donna, 'Modest_Witness@Second_Millennium', in *The Haraway Reader* (New York: Routledge, 2004), pp. 223–50.

Harbord, J.B., and others, 'A Verb for Electric Progression', *The Times*, 12 April 1890, 8.

Harper, W.E., 'Electric Belts', *English Mechanic*, 55, 8 July 1892 (1892), 464.

Henson, Louise, and others (eds), *Culture and Science in the Nineteenth-Century Media* (Aldershot: Ashgate, 2004).

Holden, Edward S., 'On Some Features of the Arrangement of Stars in Space', *Monthly Notices of the Royal Astronomical Society*, 50, December 1889 (1889), 61–4.

Hopkins, B.J., 'The Determination of Star Colours', *Journal of the British Astronomical Association*, 1, March 1891 (1891), 304.

Houghton, Walter E., ed., *Wellesley Index to Victorian Periodicals, 1824–1900*, 5 vols (Toronto: University of Toronto Press, 1966–1979).

How, Harry, 'A Day with Dr Conan Doyle', *Strand*, 4, August 1892 (1892), 182–8.

Howarth, Mary, 'The Telegram', *Pall Mall Magazine*, 6, July 1895 (1895), 355–64.

Hughes, Thomas P., *Networks of Power: Electrification in Western Society 1880–1930* (Baltimore: John Hopkins Press, 1983).

Huxley FRS, T.H., *The Crayfish: An Introduction to Zoology* (London: Kegan Paul, 1880).

Jackson, Kate, *George Newnes and the New Journalism in Britain, 1880–1910* (Aldershot: Ashgate, 2001).

James, Frank A.J.L., 'Reporting Royal Institution Lectures, 1826–1867', *Science Serialized: Representations of the Sciences in Nineteenth-Century Periodicals*, eds Geoffrey Cantor and Sally Shuttleworth (Cambridge MA: MIT Press, 2004), pp. 67–79.

Jann, Rosemary, *The Adventures of Sherlock Holmes: Detecting Social Order* (New York: Twayne Publishers, 1995).

Japp, FRS, Francis R., and G.H. Wadsworth, '*p*-Desylphenol', *Journal of the Chemical Society*, 57 (1890), 965–73.

Jarvis, C. Mackenzie, 'The Generation of Electricity', in *A History of Technology: 5 The Late Nineteenth Century c1850–1900*, eds Charles Singer and others, 7 vols (Oxford, 1950), pp. 177–207.

Jeffries, Richard, 'The Sunshine of an Autumn Afternoon', *Great Thoughts* 13, 15 October 1892 (1892), 32.

'J.F.', 'Chimpanzees and Dwarfs in Central Africa', *Nature*, 42, 24 July 1890 (1890), 296.

'Jubar', 'Electric Body Belt', *English Mechanic*, 55, 5 August 1892 (1892), 557.

Kern, Stephen, *The Culture of Time and Space, 1880–1918* (Cambridge MA: Harvard University Press, 1983).

———, *The Culture of Time and Space, 1880–1918* (1983; Cambridge MA: Harvard University Press, 2003).

King, Andrew, *The* London Journal*, 1845–1883: Periodicals, Production and Gender* (Aldershot: Ashgate, 2004).

Kipping, PhD., D.Sc., F. Stanley, and W.H. Perkin, Jun., PhD., 'Action of Dehydrating Agents on αω-Diacetylpentane. Synthesis of Methylethylhexamethylene', *Journal of the Chemical Society*, 57 (1890), 13–28.

Klein, Ursula, 'Paper Tools in Experimental Cultures', *Studies in History and Philosophy of Science Part A*, 32 (2001), 265–352.

Kristeva, Julia, 'Word, Dialogue and Novel', *The Kristeva Reader*, ed. Toril Moi (New York: Columbia University Press, 1986), pp. 35–61.

———, 'Woman's Time', in *The Kristeva Reader*, ed. Toril Moi (New York: Columbia University Press, 1986), pp. 187–213.

Lancashire, Julie Ann, 'An Historical Study of the Popularization of Science in General Science Periodicals in Britain 1890–1939' (Unpublished PhD. thesis, University of Kent at Canterbury 1988).

Lankford, John, 'Amateurs versus Professionals: The Controversy over Telescope Size in Late Victorian Science', *Isis*, 72, (1981), 11–28.

Latour, Bruno, *Science in Action* (Cambridge MA: Harvard University Press, 1987).

————, 'Drawing Things Together', in *Representation in Scientific Practice*, eds Michael Lynch and Steve Woolgar (London: MIT Press, 1990), pp. 18–60.

————, *We Have Never Been Modern* (New York: Harvester Wheatsheaf, 1993).

————, *Pandora's Hope* (Cambridge MA: Harvard University Press, 1999).

————, *Reassembling the Social* (Oxford: Oxford University Press, 2005).

Law, John, 'Actor Network Resource: An Annotated Bibliography', Version 2.3, http://www.lancs.ac.uk/fass/centres/css/ant/antres.htm [accessed 31 March 2006].

Leary, Patrick, 'Googling the Victorians', *Journal of Victorian Culture*, 10 (2005), 72–86.

Lefebvre, Henri, *The Production of Space*, trans. Donald Nicholson-Smith (1991; Oxford: Blackwell, 2001).

Levi, Primo, 'The Language of Chemists (I),' in *Other People's Trades*, trans. Raymond Rosenthal (1989; London, Abacus 1999), pp. 100–105.

————, *Other People's Trades*, trans. Raymond Rosenthal (1989; London, Abacus 1999).

Lewes, Professor Vivian B., 'On Gaseous Illuminants', *Chemical News*, 63, 2 January 1890 (1890), 3–5.

————, 'On Gaseous Illuminants', *Chemical News*, 63, 9 January 1890 (1890), 15–16.

————, 'On Gaseous Illuminants', *Chemical News*, 63, 16 January 1890 (1890), 32–3.

————, 'On Gaseous Illuminants', *Chemical News*, 63, 23 January 1890 (1890), 40–43.

————, 'On Gaseous Illuminants', *Chemical News*, 63, 6 February 1890 (1890), 63–6.

Lightman, Bernard, '*Knowledge* Confronts *Nature*: Richard Proctor and Popular Science Periodicals', in *Culture and Science in the Nineteenth Century Media*, eds Louise Henson and others (London, 2004), pp. 199–221.

Loeb, Lori, 'Consumerism and Commercial Electrotherapy: the Medical Battery Company in Nineteenth Century London', *Journal of Victorian Culture*, 4 (1999), 252–75.

Loewenstein, Joseph, *The Author's Due: Printing and the Prehistory of Copyright* (Chicago: University of Chicago Press, 2002).

Loon, Joost van, '"A Contagious Living Fluid:" Objectification and Assemblage in the History of Virology', *Culture, Theory and Society*, 19 (2002), 107–24.

Low, Sidney, 'Newspaper Copyright', *National Review*, 19, July 1892 (1892), 648–66.

Lowe, Philip, 'The British Association and the Provincial Public', in *The Parliament of Science*, eds Roy MacLeod and Peter Collins (Northwood, 1981), pp. 118–44.

Lubbock, Sir John, 'Beauty in Nature: I. Introduction', *Strand*, 3, February 1892 (1892), 158–67.

Luckhurst, Roger, *The Invention of Telepathy, 1870–1901* (Oxford: Oxford University Press, 2002).

Lynch, Michael and Steve Woolgar, 'Introduction: Sociological Orientation to Representational Practice in Science', in *Representation in Scientific Practice*, eds Michael Lynch and Steve Woolgar (London: MIT Press, 1990), pp. 1–17.

——— (eds), *Representation in Scientific Practice* (London: MIT Press, 1990).

McDonald, Peter D., *British Literary Culture and Publishing Practice, 1880–1914* (Cambridge: Cambridge University Press, 1997).

McGann, Jerome, *Radiant Textuality; Literature after the World Wide Web* (New York: Palgrave, 2001).

———, 'Culture and Technology: the Way We Live Now, What Is to Be Done?', *Interdisciplinary Science Reviews*, 30 (2005), 179–89.

McKenzie, D.F., 'Foreword', in *Bibliography and the Sociology of Texts* (Cambridge: Cambridge University Press, 1999), pp. 1–6.

McKenzie, D.F., *Bibliography and the Sociology of Texts* (Cambridge: Cambridge University Press, 1999).

MacLeod, Roy M., 'Resources of Science in Victorian England', in *Science and Society 1600–1900*, ed. P. Mathias (Cambridge: Cambridge University Press, 1972), pp. 111–66.

———, 'The Genesis of *Nature*', in *The 'Creed of Science' in Victorian England* (Aldershot: Ashgate, 2000), pp. 1–28

———, 'The Social Framework of *Nature*', in *The 'Creed of Science' in Victorian England* (Aldershot: Ashgate, 2000), pp. 1–44

———, 'Education: Science and Technical', in *The 'Creed of Science' in Victorian England* (Aldershot: Ashgate, 2000), pp. 196–225.

MacLeod, Roy and Peter Collins (eds), *The Parliament of Science* (Northwood: Science Reviews, 1981).

McLuhan, Marshall, *Understanding Media: the Extensions of Man* (1964; Cambridge MA: MIT Press, 1994).

Mansford, Charles J., 'Shafts from an Eastern Quiver: I. The Diamond of Shomar's Queen', *Strand*, 4, July 1892 (1892), 21–8.

———, 'Shafts from an Eastern Quiver: IV. Darak, the Scorn of the Afghans,' *Strand*, 4, October 1892 (1892), 407–14

Manzer, Bruce M., *The Abstract Journal 1790–1900* (Metuchen NJ and London: Scarecrow Press, 1957).

Marvin, Carolyn, *When Old Technologies Were New: Thinking About Electric Communication in the Late Nineteenth Century* (Oxford: Oxford University Press, 1988).

Marx, Karl, *Capital: An Abridged Edition*, ed. David McLellan (Oxford: Oxford University Press, 1999).

Mathias, P., (ed), *Science and Society 1600–1900* (Cambridge: Cambridge University Press, 1972).

May, Thomas, 'Flat Earth v. Round Earth', *English Mechanic*, 47, 4 May 1888 (1888), 216–17.

Meade, L.T., and Clifford Halifax, M.D., 'The Adventures of a Man of Science: I. The Snake's Eye', *Strand*, 12, July 1896 (1896), 57–68.

———, 'The Adventures of a Man of Science: V. At the Steps of the Altar', *Strand*, 12, November 1896 (1896), 529–41.

Meadows, A.J., *Science and Controversy: A Biography of Sir Norman Lockyer* (London, 1972).

———, 'Access to the Results of Scientific Research: Developments in Victorian Britain', in *Development of Science Publishing in Europe*, ed. A.J. Meadows (Amsterdam: Elsevier Science Publishers, 1980), pp. 43–62.

———, ed., *Development of Science Publishing in Europe* (Amsterdam: Elsevier Science Publishers, 1980).

Miller, David Philip, 'Method and the "Micropolitics" of Science: the Early Years of the Geological and Astronomical Societies of London', in *The Politics and Rhetoric of Scientific Method* (Dordrecht: D. Reidel, 1986), pp. 227–57.

Miller, F. Fenwick, *Harriet Martineau* (London: W.H. Allen, 1888).

———, 'The Ladies Column', *ILN*, 96, 1 February 1890 (1890), 154.

Moi, Toril, ed., *The Kristeva Reader* (New York: Columbia University Press 1986).

Monck, W.H.S., 'An Amateur Astronomers' Association', *English Mechanic*, 51, 18 July 1890 (1890), 445–56.

Moore, Tom Sidney, and James Charles Philip, *The Chemical Society 1841–1941: A Historical Review* (London: Chemical Society, 1947).

Morrell, Jack, 'Professionalization', in *Companion to the History of Modern Science*, eds Robert C. Olby et al. (London: Routledge, 1990), pp. 980–89.

———, 'W.H. Perkin, Jr., at Manchester and Oxford: from Irwell to Isis', *Osiris*, 8 (1993), 104–26.

Morus, Iwan, 'Batteries, Bodies and Belts: Making Careers in Victorian Medical Electricity', in *Electric Bodies: Episodes in the history of medical electricity*, eds Paola Bertucci and Giuliano Pancaldi (Bolgona: Università di Bologna, 2001), pp. 209–38.

Morveau, Louis Bernard Guyton de, and others, *Method of Chymical Nomenclature*, trans. James St. John, (London: Johnson's Head, 1788).

Most, Glenn W., and William W. Stowe (eds), *The Poetics of Murder: Detective Fiction and Literary Theory* (San Diego: Harcourt, Bruce, Javonavich, 1983).

Murphy, Patricia, *Time is of the Essence: Temporality, Gender, and the New Woman* (New York: State University of New York Press, 2001).

Mussell, James and Suzanne Paylor, '"Mapping the Mighty Maze": the *Nineteenth-Century Serials Edition*', *19: Interdisciplinary Studies in the Long Nineteenth Century*, 1 (2005), www.19.bbk.ac.uk [accessed 31 March 2006].

Noble, W.H., and others, 'A Verb for Electricity', *The Times*, 10 April 1890, 7.

Norman, D., 'The Development of Astronomical Photography', *Osiris*, 5 (1938), 560–94.

North, John S., ed., *Waterloo Directory of English Newspapers and Periodicals, 1800–1900*, second series, 20 vols (Waterloo Ontario: North Waterloo Academic Press, 2003).

Northcroft, George J.H., 'Robert Percival Downes, LLD.: Father and First Editor of *Great Thoughts*', *Great Thoughts*, 81, May 1924 (1924), 85.

Olby, Robert C., and others (eds), *Companion to the History of Modern Science* (London: Routledge, 1990).

Onslow, Barbara, *Women of the Press in Nineteenth-Century Britain* (London: Macmillan, 2000).

Osterbrock, Donald E., 'The Rise and Fall of Edward S. Holden (1)', *Journal for the History of Astronomy*, 15 (1984), 81–127.

Ousby, Ian, *Bloodhouds of Heaven: the Detective in English Fiction from Godwin to Doyle* (Cambridge MA: Harvard University Press, 1976).

Pang, Alex Soojung-Kim, 'Victorian Observing Practices, Printing Technology, and Representation of the Solar Corona (I): the 1860s and 1870s', *Journal of the History of Astronomy*, 25, (1994), 249–74.

———, 'Victorian Observing Practices, Printing Technology, and Representation of the Solar Corona (II): The Age of Photomechanical Reproduction', *Journal for the History of Astronomy*, 26 (1994), 63–75.

Payn, James, 'Our Note Book', *Illustrated London News*, 96, 18 January 1890 (1890), 66.

———, 'Our Note Book', *Illustrated London News*, 96, 25 January 1890 (1890), 98.

———, 'Our Note Book', *Illustrated London News*, 96, 17 May 1890 (1890), 610.

Pearson, Karl, *The Grammar of Science* (London: Walter Scott, 1892).

Pels, Dick, Kevin Hetherington and Frédéric Vandenberghe, 'The Status of the Object: Performativity, Mediations and Techniques', *Theory, Culture and Society*, 19 (2002), 69–89.

Perkin, Jun., PhD, FRS, W.H., 'Contributions from the Laboratories of the Heriot Watt College, Edinburgh: On Berberine. Part II', *Journal of the Chemical Society*, 57 (1890), 992–1106.

Perry, D., 'Electric Belt', *English Mechanic*, 55, 15 July 1892 (1892), 488.

Pickering MA, Spencer Umfreville, 'The Nature of Solutions, as Elucidated by a Study of the Density, Electric Conductivity, Heat Capacity, Heat of Dissolution, and Heat of Sulphuric Acid Solution', *Journal of the Chemical Society*, 57 (1890), 64–184.

———, 'The Present Position of the Hydrate Theory of Solutions', *Nature*, 42, 23 October 1890 (1890), 626–31.

———, 'Discussion on the Theory of Solutions', *Chemical News*, 63, 26 Mar 1891 (1891), 147–51.

———, 'Discussion on the Theory of Solutions', *Chemical News*, 63, 2 April 1891 (1891), 157–9.

———, 'Discussion on the Theory of Solutions', *Chemical News*, 63, 9 April 1891 (1891), 169–71.

Plunkett, John, 'Celebrity and Community: The Poetics of the Carte-de-visite', *Journal of Victorian Culture*, 8 (2003), 57–79.

———, *Queen Victoria: First Media Monarch* (Oxford: Oxford University Press, 2003).

Poe, Edgar Allan, 'The Murders in the Rue Morgue', *Great Short Works of Edgar Allan Poe*, ed. G.R. Thompson (1841; New York, 1970), pp. 272–312.

Poole, William Frederick, ed., *Poole's Index to Periodical Literature*, 2 vols (London, 1882).

Porter, B.Sc., Alfred W., 'The New Photography', *Strand*, 12, July 1896 (1896), 107–17.

Poulton, E.B., 'Mimicry', *Nature*, 42, 2 October 1890 (1890), 557–8.

Pound, Reginald, *The Strand Magazine 1891–1950* (London: Heinemann, 1966).

Pykett, Lyn, 'Reading the Periodical Press: Text and Context,' in *Investigating Victorian Journalism*, eds Brake, Jones and Madden (London: Macmillan, 1990), pp. 3–18.

———, 'The Material Turn in Victorian Studies', *Literature Compass*, 1 (2003–2004), available from http://www.blackwell-compass.com/subject/literature/ [accessed 31 March 2006].

Ranyard, A.C., 'To Our Readers', *Knowledge*, 12, November 1888 (1888), 1.

———, 'Automatic Recording Instruments of the Lick Observatory', *Knowledge*, 12, January 1889 (1889), 58.

———, 'The Great Nebula in Andromeda', 12, February 1889 (1889), 75–6.

———, 'The Great Nebular in Orion', *Knowledge*, 12, May 1889 (1889), 145–6.

———, 'The Collotype Process and Photo-engraving', *Knowledge*, 13, February 1890 (1890), 71–2.

———, 'On the Distribution of the Stars in the Milky Way', *Knowledge*, 13, July 1890 (1890), 174–5.

———, 'The Milky Way in the Southern Hemisphere', *Knowledge*, 14, March 1891 (1891), 50–51.

———, untitled editorial note, *Knowledge*, 14, September 1891 (1891), 173.

Read, Donald, *The Power of News: The History of Reuters* (Oxford: Oxford University Press, 1999).

Reed, David, *The Popular Magazine in Britain and the United States, 1880–1960* (London: British Library, 1997).

Rigg, James, 'October', *Great Thoughts* 13, 15 October 1892 (1892), 24.

Robertson-Smith, J.W., 'Some Newspaper Men', in *Sell's Dictionary of the World's Press* (London: Sell's Advertising Agency, 1888), 118–27.

Robinson, E.C., and others, 'A Verb for Electric Progression', *The Times*, 11 April 1890, 5.

Rollit, Albert Kaye, 'A Verb for Electric Progression', *The Times*, 14 April 1890, 6.

'R.T.T.', 'Quick Work', *Electrical Review*, 26, 14 February 1890 (1890), 191.

Rothermal, Holly, 'Images of the Sun: Warren De La Rue, George Biddell Airy and Celestial Photography', *British Journal for the History of Science*, 26 (1993), 137–69

Russell, H.C., 'On the Comparison of Photographs of the Milky Way', *Knowledge*, 14, September 1891 (1891), 172–3.

'R.W.J.', 'The Late Lunar Eclipse', *English Mechanic*, 47, 4 May 1888 (1888), 216.

Schaaf, Larry J., *Out of the Shadows: Herschel, Talbot, and the Invention of Photography* (London: Yale University Press, 1992).

Schaffer, Simon, 'Astronomers Mark Time: Discipline and the Personal Equation', *Science in Context*, 2 (1988), 115–45.

Schleiffer, Ronald, *Modernism and Time: The Logic of Abundance in Literature, Science, and Culture, 1880–1930* (Cambridge: Cambridge University Press, 2000).

Schuster, John A., and Richard R. Yeo (eds), *The Politics and Rhetoric of Scientific Method* (Dordrecht: D. Reidel, 1986).

Secord, Anne, 'Science in the Pub: Artisan Botanists in Early Nineteenth-Century Lancashire', *History of Science*, 32 (1994), 269–15

Secord, James, *Victorian Sensation:The Extraordinary Publication, Reception, and Secret Authorship of* Vestiges of the Natural History of Creation (Chicago: University of Chicago Press, 2000).

Shattock, Joanne, and Michael Wolff, 'Introduction', in *Victorian Periodical Press: Samplings and Soundings*, eds Joanne Shattock and Michael Wolff (Leicester: Leicester University Press, 1982), pp. xiii–xix.

——— (eds), *Victorian Periodical Press: Samplings and Soundings* (Leicester: Leicester University Press, 1982).

Sheets-Pyenson, Susan, 'Popular Science Periodicals in Paris and London: The Emergence of a Low Scientific Culture, 1820–1875', *Annals of Science*, 42 (1985), 549–72.

Sherman, Stuart, *Telling Time: Clocks, Diaries and English Diurnal Form, 1660–1785* (Chicago: University of Chicago Press, 1996).

'Sigma' [John T. Sprague], 'The Southern Heavens and a Flat Earth – The Moon's Heat – Dying By Effort of Will,' *English Mechanic*, 47, 20 April 1888 (1888), 168.

Simon, Jonathon, 'Authority and Authorship in the *Method of Chemical Nomenclature*', *Ambix*, 49 (2002), 206–26.

Slater, J.W., 'Scientific Terminology', *Chemical News*, 61, 9 May 1890 (1890), 228.

Smith, Crosbie, 'Nowhere But in a Great Town: William Thomson's Spiral of Classroom Credibility', in *Making Space for Science: Territorial Themes in the Shaping of Knowledge*, eds Crosbie Smith and John Agar (Basingstoke: Macmillan, 1998), pp. 118–46.

Smith, Crosbie, and John Agar (eds), *Making Space for Science: Territorial Themes in the Shaping of Knowledge* (Basingstoke: Macmillan, 1998).

Spearman, Edmund R., 'Mistaken Identity and Police Anthropometry', *Fortnightly Review*, 46, March 1889 (1889), 361–76.

Stead, W.T., 'Programme', *Review of Reviews*, 1 (1890), 14.

———, 'The Progress of the World', *Review of Reviews*, 1, February 1890 (1890), 87–95

———, 'Looking Forward: A Romance of the Electric Age', *Review of Reviews*, 1, March 1890 (1890), 230–41.

———, 'Preface', *Index to the Periodical Literature of the World* (London, 1892), p. vii.

———, 'Preface', *Index to the Periodical Literature of the World* (London, 1893), pp. 5–6.

———, 'Preface', *Index to the Periodicals of 1894* (London, 1895), pp. iii–iv.

Stengers, Isabelle, *The Invention of Modern Science*, trans. Daniel W. Smith (Minneapolis: University of Minneapolis Press, 2000).

Strick, J.E., *Sparks of Life: Darwinism and the Victorian Debates Over Spontaneous Generation* (Cambridge MA: Harvard University Press, 2000).

Sutherland, Kathryn, 'Introduction', in *Electronic Text*, ed Kathryn Sutherland (Oxford: Clarendon, 1997), pp. 1–18.

——— (ed), *Electronic Text* (Oxford: Clarendon 1997).

'Tempus', 'Weather Forecast', *English Mechanic*, 51, 30 May 1890 (1890), 294–5.

Thomas, Ronald R., *Detective Fiction and the Rise of Forensic Science* (Cambridge: Cambridge University Press, 1999).

Thompson, E.P., 'Time, Work-Discipline, and Industrial Capitalism', *Past and Present*, 38 (1967), 56–97.

Thorpe, Jocelyn Field, 'Section II', *The Life and Work of Professor William Henry Perkin MA, ScD, LLD, PhD, FRS*, by A.J. Greenaway, J.F. Thorpe, and R. Robinson (London, 1932), 38–74.

Thorpe, F.R.S., Professor, 'The Glow of Phosphorous', *Chemical News*, 61, 21 March 1890 (1890), 140–1.

Tilden D.Sc., F.R.S., William A, and Charles R. Beck, 'Some Crystalline Substances Obtained From the Fruits of Various Species of Citrus. Part I', *Journal of the Chemical Society*, 57 (1890), 323–7.

Topham, Jonathan .R, 'Beyond the "Common Context": The Production and Reading of the *Bridgewater Treatises*', *Isis*, 89 (1998), 233–62.

———, 'Introduction: *BJHS* Special Section: Book History and the Sciences', *British Journal for the History of Science*, 33 (2000), 155–8.

Totheroh, W.W., 'Manly Boys', *Great Thoughts*, 13, 8 February 1890 (1890), unpaginated.

Turner, H.H., 'Paradoxers', *The Observatory*, 13, November 1890 (1890), 341–4.

Turner, Mark, *Trollope and the Magazines: Gendered Issues in Mid-Victorian Britain* (Basingstoke: Palgrave, 2000).

———, 'Periodical Time in the Nineteenth Century', *Media History*, 8 (2002), 183–96.

Tyndall, John, 'Spontaneous Generation', *Nineteenth Century*, 3, January 1878 (1878), 1–21

Ueyama, Takahiro, 'Capital, Profession and Medical Technology: the Electro-Therapeutic Institutes and the Royal College of Physicians 1888–1922', *Medical History*, 42 (1997), 150–81.

Vere Hill, Ernest de, 'Morgan's Automatic Electric Police Signalling System', *Electrical Review*, 26, 7 March 1890 (1890), 259–64.

Walkowitz, Judith, *City of Dreadful Delight: Narratives of Sexual Danger in Late-Victorian London* (London: Virago, 1992).

Wallace, Alfred Russel, *My life, a Record of Events and Opinions*, 2 (New York: Dodd Mead, 1905).

Watson, Katherine D., 'The Chemist as Expert: The Consulting Career of Sir William Ramsay', *Ambix*, 42 (1995), 143–59.

'W.C.' [William Crookes], 'M. Lecoq de Boisbaudron on the Rare Earths', *Chemical News*, 61, 7 March 1890 (1890), 111.

Wells, H.G., *Textbook of Biology* (London: University Correspondence College Press, 1892).

——, 'Popularising Science', *Nature*, 50, 26 July 1894 (1894), 300–1.

——, *Tono-Bungay* (1908; London: Everyman, 1994).

Wells, H.G., with R.A. Gregory, *Honours Physiography* (London: Joseph Hughes, 1893).

Willis, Chris, '"Out flew the web and floated wide": An Overview of Uses of the Internet for Victorian Research', *Journal of Victorian Culture*, 7 (2002), 297–310.

Wilson, Andrew, 'Science Jottings – Our Monthly Look Round', *Illustrated London News*, 96, 1 February 1890 (1890), 146.

——, 'Science Jottings – Our Monthly Look Around', *Illustrated London News*, 96, 1 March 1890 (1890), 267.

——, 'Science Jottings – A Display of Energy', *Illustrated London News*, 96, 26 April 1890 (1890), 530.

——, 'Science Jottings – A Corner of Kent', *Illustrated London News*, 96, 17 May, (1890), 626.

——, 'Science Jottings – The Way of Growth', *Illustrated London News*, 96, 24 May, (1890), 662.

——, 'Science Jottings – Our Monthly Look Around', *Illustrated London News*, 97, 6 September 1890 (1890), 310.

——, 'Science Jottings', *Illustrated London News*, 103, 23 December 1893 (1893), 806.

Winston, Brian, *Media Technology and Society: A History From the Telegraph to the Internet* (London: Routledge, 1998).

Wittgenstein, Ludwig, *Tractatus Logico-Philosophicus* (London: Routledge, 1997).

Witz, Anne, 'Patriarchy and the Professions: The Gendered Politics of Occupational Closure', *Sociology*, 24 (1990), 675–90.

Wootton, A.C., *Chronicles of Pharmacy*, 2 vols (London: Macmillan, 1910).

'W.T.S' [W.T. Stead], 'Introduction', *Index to the Periodical Literature of the World* (London, 1894), pp. vii–viii.

'W.T.S' [W.T. Stead], 'Introduction', *Index to the Periodical Literature of the World* (London, 1895), pp. v–vii.

Yeo, Richard, 'Scientific Method and the Image of Science 1831–1891', in *The Parliament of Science*, ed. Roy Macleod and Peter Collins (London: Science Reviews, 1981), pp. 65–88.

Yeo, Richard R., 'Scientific Method and the Rhetoric of Science in Britain, 1830–1917', in *The Politics and Rhetoric of Scientific Method*, eds John A. Schuster and Richard R. Yeo (Dordrecht: D. Reidel, 1986), pp. 259–97.

Young, Robert, 'Natural Theology, Victorian Periodicals, and the Fragmentation of a Common Context', in *Darwin's Metaphor* (Cambridge: Cambridge University Press, 1985), pp. 127–63.

Žižek, Slavoj, *Looking Awry: An Introduction to Jacques Lacan through Popular Culture* (Cambridge MA: MIT Press, 1991).

# Index

For Product Safety Concerns and Information please contact our EU
representative GPSR@taylorandfrancis.com
Taylor & Francis Verlag GmbH, Kaufingerstraße 24, 80331 München, Germany

www.ingramcontent.com/pod-product-compliance
Ingram Content Group UK Ltd.
Pitfield, Milton Keynes, MK11 3LW, UK
UKHW021441080625
459435UK00011B/333

* 9 7 8 0 3 6 7 8 8 7 9 5 7 *